Spirit and Power

Spirit and Power

The Growth and Global Impact of Pentecostalism

EDITED BY
DONALD E. MILLER
KIMON H. SARGEANT
RICHARD FLORY

OXFORD
UNIVERSITY PRESS

OXFORD

UNIVERSITY PRESS

Oxford University Press is a department of the University of Oxford.
It furthers the University's objective of excellence in research, scholarship,
and education by publishing worldwide.

Oxford   New York
Auckland   Cape Town   Dar es Salaam   Hong Kong   Karachi
Kuala Lumpur   Madrid   Melbourne   Mexico City   Nairobi
New Delhi   Shanghai   Taipei   Toronto

With offices in
Argentina   Austria   Brazil   Chile   Czech Republic   France   Greece
Guatemala   Hungary   Italy   Japan   Poland   Portugal   Singapore
South Korea   Switzerland   Thailand   Turkey   Ukraine   Vietnam

Oxford is a registered trademark of Oxford University Press
in the UK and certain other countries.

Published in the United States of America by
Oxford University Press
198 Madison Avenue, New York, NY 10016

Library of Congress Cataloging-in-Publication Data
Spirit and power : the growth and global impact of pentecostalism / edited by Donald E. Miller,
Kimon H. Sargeant, and Richard Flory.
pages cm
Includes index.
ISBN 978–0–19–992059–4 (pbk. : alk. paper)—ISBN 978–0–19–992057–0 (alk. paper)—
ISBN 978–0–19–992058–7 (ebook)   1. Pentecostalism.   I. Miller, Donald E. (Donald Earl), 1946–
editor of compilation.
BR1644.M57 2013
270.8'3–dc23
2012047870

1 3 5 7 9 8 6 4 2
Printed in the United States of America
on acid-free paper

CONTENTS

CONTRIBUTORS

Afe Adogame is Associate Professor in Religious Studies and World Christianity at the University of Edinburgh, UK. His current research interests include religion in the new African Diaspora; African Pentecostalism; indigenous African religions; religious transnationalism; and religion, migration, and globalization. He has authored Celestial Church of Christ: The Politics of Cultural Identity in a West African Prophetic-Charismatic Movement (1999). He has co-edited Religion in the Context of African Migration (2005) and Christianity in Africa and the Africa Diaspora: The Appropriation of a Scattered Heritage (2008). His most recent book publications are the co-edited (with J. Spickard) Religion Crossing Boundaries: Transnational Religious and Social Dynamics in Africa and the New African Diaspora (2010) and the edited Who Is Afraid of the Holy Ghost? Pentecostalism and Globalization in Africa and Beyond (2011).

Estrelda Alexander is President of William Seymour College. Her most recent work is Black Fire: 100 Years of African American Pentecostalism (2011) and a companion Black Fire Reader (2012). Other monographs include Limited Liberty: The Ministry and Legacy of Four Pentecostal Women Pioneers (2008) and The Women of Azusa Street (2006). She has also co-edited two volumes: Women in the Pentecostal Movement (2009) and Afro-Pentecostalism: Black Pentecostal and Charismatic Christianity in History and Culture (2011). Dr. Alexander has contributed numerous articles to academic journals and edited volumes related primarily to gender and race within contemporary Pentecostalism. She is currently editing the Dictionary of Pan-African Pentecostalism. She is a past president of the Society for Pentecostal Studies.

Allan H. Anderson was a Pentecostal and Baptist minister, principal of Tshwane Theological College, and part-time researcher at the University of South Africa before joining Selly Oak Colleges as director of the Centre for New Religious Movements in 1995, becoming an honorary lecturer and then (1999) lecturer at the University of Birmingham. He is the author of four books on South African Pentecostalism, one on African independent churches, and two books on global Pentecostalism that have received international acclaim. He is also author of many articles, and he has jointly edited two collections on Pentecostalism. He is a founder and member of the European Research Network on Global Pentecostalism. Anderson is currently working on a history and theology of Pentecostalism in the global South. He has written seven monographs on African Christianity and global Pentecostalism, the latest being Spreading Fires: The Missionary Nature of Early Pentecostalism (2007), An Introduction to Pentecostalism: Global Charismatic Christianity (2004), African Reformation: African Initiated Christianity in the Twentieth Century (2001), and Zion and Pentecost: The Spirituality and Experience of Pentecostal and Zionist/Apostolic Churches in South Africa (2000). He has edited (with Walter J. Hollenweger) and written three chapters of a volume entitled Pentecostals After a Century: Global Perspectives on a Movement in Transition (1999). With Edmond Tang, he has edited a volume on Asian Pentecostalism entitled Asian and Pentecostal: The Charismatic Face of Asian Christianity (2005). He is currently working on Global Pentecostal and Charismatic Christianity.

Katherine Attanasi holds a PhD from Vanderbilt University and is Visiting Assistant Professor of Paideia at Luther College in Decorah, Iowa. Her research constructs ethical methodologies and focuses on global feminisms and global Christianity. Recent publications include "Biblical Ethics, HIV, and South African Pentecostal Women: Constructing an A-B-C-D Prevention Strategy," Journal of the Society of Christian Ethics 33 (2013); co-edited with Amos Yong, Pentecostalism and Prosperity: The Socio-economics of the Global Charismatic Movement, Christianities of the World 1 (2012); co-authored with Brooke Ackerly, "Global Feminisms: Theory and Ethics for Studying Gendered Injustice," New Political Science (2009); and "Getting in Step with the Spirit: Applying Pentecostal Commitments to HIV/AIDS in South Africa," Political Theology (2008).

R. Andrew Chesnut is Bishop F. Walter Sullivan Chair in Catholic Studies and Professor of Religious Studies at Virginia Commonwealth University. Professor Chesnut's early work, Born Again in Brazil: The Pentecostal Boom and the Pathogens of Poverty (1997), traces the meteoric rise of Pentecostalism among the popular classes in Brazil. His second book, Competitive Spirits: Latin America's New Religious Economy (2003) focuses on the three groups that have prospered most in the region's pluralist landscape, Pentecostalism, the Catholic Charismatic Renewal, and African diasporic religions. His most recent work, Devoted to Death: Santa Muerte, the Skeleton Saint (2012) is the first academic book in English on the mushrooming cult of Saint Death. His current research focuses on folk saints in Latin America.

Richard Flory (Ph.D., University of Chicago) is Associate Research Professor of Sociology and director of research in the Center for Religion and Civic Culture at the University of Southern California. He is the author of Growing Up in America: The Power of Race in the Lives of Teens, with Brad Christerson and Korie Edwards (2010), Finding Faith: The Spiritual Quest of the Post-Boomer Generation, with Donald E. Miller (2008), and GenX Religion, with Donald E. Miller (2000). He is currently writing two books on Pentecostalism in Los Angeles, and is co-director of the Religion, Politics and Culture in Southern California working group at the University of Southern California. Flory's research has been supported by grants from the Louisville Institute, the Pew Charitable Trusts, the Lilly Endowment, the Haynes Foundation, and the John Templeton Foundation.

Paul Freston is CIGI Chair in Religion and Politics in Global Context at the Balsillie School of International Affairs and Wilfrid Laurier University, Waterloo, Ontario, Canada, and professor colaborador at the Universidade Federal de São Carlos, Brazil. He is Distinguished Senior Fellow at Baylor University's Institute for Studies of Religion (ISR). His publications include Evangelicals and Politics in Africa, Asia and Latin America (2001), and Evangelical Christianity and Democracy in Latin America (2008).

Henri Gooren is Associate Professor of Anthropology at Oakland University in Rochester, Michigan. He is the author of Rich among the Poor: Church, Firm, and Household among Small-Scale Entrepreneurs in Guatemala City (1999) and most recently Religious Conversion and Disaffiliation: Tracing Patterns of Change in Faith Practices (2010). He conducted fieldwork research on the Pentecostalization of religion and society in Paraguay and Chile in 2010–12, sponsored by the John Templeton Foundation and administered by the University of Southern California in the Pentecostal and Charismatic Research Initiative. He is currently working on a monograph elaborating his Pentecostalization concept. Personal webpage: http://www.oakland.edu/socan/faculty/gooren.

John C. Green is a Distinguished Professor of Political Science at the University of Akron. He is also a Senior Fellow with the Pew Forum on Religion & Public Life, and is best known for his work on religion and politics. He is co-author of The Bully Pulpit: The Politics of Protestant Clergy, Religion and the Culture

Wars: Dispatches From the Front, and The Diminishing Divide: Religion's Changing Role in American Politics.

Todd M. Johnson is Associate Professor of Global Christianity and Director of the Center for the Study of Global Christianity at Gordon-Conwell Theological Seminary. Johnson is visiting Research Fellow at Boston University's Institute for Culture, Religion and World Affairs, leading a research project on international religious demography. He is co-editor of the Atlas of Global Christianity and co-author of the World Christian Encyclopedia (2nd ed.) and World Christian Trends. He is editor of the World Christian Database and co-editor of the World Religion Database.

William K. Kay. After undergraduate studies at Trinity College, Oxford, William Kay worked part time with the University of Reading where he took an M.Edd and a Ph.D. in comparative education and psychology. Shortly after this he registered at the University of Nottingham and completed a PhD in theology. In 2009 the University of Nottingham conferred a DD on him on the basis of his published works. He was Senior Lecturer in the Department for Education and Professional Studies at King's College, London; and Director of the Centre for Pentecostal and Charismatic Studies, Bangor University; Professor of Theology at Glyndŵr University and Professor of Pentecostal Studies at the University of Chester. He is an ordained minister with British Assemblies of God. He has edited (with Anne Dyer) Pentecostal and Charismatic Studies: a reader (2004), written Pentecostals in Britain (2000), Apostolic Networks in Britain (2007), Pentecostalism (core text) (2009) and Pentecostalism: a very short introduction (2011) as well as numerous articles.

Matthew T. Lee is Professor and Chair of Sociology at the University of Akron. He is co-author of "The Heart of Religion: Spiritual Empowerment, Benevolence, and the Experience of God's Love" and co-editor of "The Science and Theology of Godly Love" as well as "Godly Love: Impediments and Possibilities."

Juan Francisco Martínez is Associate Provost for Diversity and International Programs, Director of the Hispanic Center, and Associate Professor of Hispanic Studies and Pastoral Leadership in the School of Theology at Fuller Theological Seminary in Pasadena, California. Most recently Martínez has published the books Los Protestantes: An Introduction to Latino Protestantism in the United States (2011), Churches, Cultures and Leadership: A Practical Theology of Ethnicities and Congregations (with Mark Lau Branson, 2011), Los Evangélicos: Portraits of Latino Protestantism in the United States (co-edited with Lindy Scott, 2009), Walk with the People: Latino Ministry in the United States/Caminando entre el pueblo: Ministerio latino en los Estados

Unidos (2008), and Vivir y servir en el exilio: Lecturas teológicas de la experiencia latina en los Estados Unidos (co-edited with Jorge Maldonado, 2008). Additonally, he was a regional editor for the Global Dictionary of Theology (2008). He is currently involved in a research project on Latino Pentecostalism in Los Angeles through the Center for Religion and Civic Culture of the University of Southern California.

Danny McCain is a Professor of Biblical Theology in the Department of Religion and Philosophy of the University of Jos, Nigeria, where he has worked since 1991. Between 2010 and 2012 he served at the project director of a Nigeria-wide study of Pentecostalism, coordinated by the Center for Religion and Civic Culture of the University of Southern California and funded by the John Templeton Foundation. He is the director of the Nigeria Centre for Pentecostal and Charismatic Studies, based in the University of Jos and the editor-in-chief of the African Journal of Pentecostal and Charismatic Studies. He is currently conducting research and writing a book about the changes taking place within the Pentecostal and Charismatic movements in Nigeria. He is also directing an archival project to collect audio and video recordings of the Pentecostal leaders who were most influential in the rapid expansion of Nigerian Pentecostalism in the 1970's. McCain is also the founder and international director-at-large of International Institute for Christian Studies (IICS), a USA-based organization that helps to recruit and place Christian academics in public universities around the world.

Donald E. Miller is Firestone Professor of Religion and executive director of the Center for Religion and Civic Culture at the University of Southern California. He received the Ph.D. degree in Religion (Social Ethics) from USC in 1975. He is the author, co-author, or editor of nine books, including Finding Faith: The Spiritual Quest of the Post-Boomer Generation, with Richard Flory (2008), Global Pentecostalism: The New Face of Christian Social Engagement, with Ted Yamamori (2007), Armenia: Portraits of Survival and Hope (2003), GenX Religion, with Richard Flory (2000), Reinventing American Protestantism (1997), Survivors: An Oral History of the Armenian Genocide (1993), Homeless Families: The Struggle for Dignity (1993), Writing and Research in Religious Studies (1992), and The Case for Liberal Christianity (1981). Professor Miller oversees a Templeton Foundation research initiative, the Pentecostal and Charismatic Research Initiative, and is involved in several research projects, including one in Rwanda dealing with the experience of survivors of the 1994 genocide. He is a sociologist of religion with interest in global religious trends, new patterns of religious practice, and innovative organizational responses to cultural change. In addition, he has done extensive research on genocide, including oral history projects on the Armenian genocide that occurred in 1915 and the Rwandan genocide in 1994. He has received major grants from the John Templeton Foundation, Pew Charitable Trusts, the Lilly Endowment, Inc., The James Irvine Foundation, the John Randolph and Dora Haynes Foundation, the California Endowment, California Council for the Humanities, the Tides Foundation, the David and Lucile Packard Foundation, and Fieldstead & Company.

Margaret M. Poloma (Ph.D., Case Western Reserve University, 1970) has written extensively about religious experience in contemporary American society, including pioneering studies of prayer, Pentecostalism, contemporary revivals and divine healing. Much of this work has focused on diverse pentecostal spiritualities (i.e., denominational Pentecostal, charismatic, Third Wave, neo-pentecostal, etc.), as reported in Charismatic Movement; The Assemblies of God at the Crossroad; Main Street Mystics; Blood and Fire (with Ralph W. Hood); and The Assemblies of God (with John C. Green). Her pioneering research on prayer (see, e.g., Varieties of Prayer with George H. Gallup Jr.) has served as a bridge between Pentecostal spirituality and common spiritual experiences of American Christians through data collected in two national surveys (1989 and 2009). Through the use of both qualitative and quantitative measures to explore the experiential dimension of religion, Poloma was able to mine research nuggets that suggested religious experience does indeed impact human behavior. Most recently she has collaborated with some twenty other colleagues in the John Templeton Foundation–sponsored Flame of Love Project (www.godlyloveproject.org) to develop a model of "Godly Love" that demonstrates the dynamic process in which experiences of the divine contribute to a better understanding human benevolence. Major findings from this research are found in Matthew T. Lee, Margaret M. Poloma, and Stephen G. Post, The Heart of Religion (2013).

Cecil M. Robeck, who has worked at Fuller Seminary since 1974, is Professor of Church History and Ecumenics and Director of the David J. DuPlessis Center for Christian Spirituality. His recent historical research centers on the Azusa Street Mission and Revival and its African American pastor William Seymour. An ordained minister with the Assemblies of God, Robeck has also worked on ecumenical dialogue for nearly 30 years with the World Council of Churches, the Vatican, the World Alliance of Reformed Churches, and other groups. Robeck is author of The Azusa Street Mission and Revival: The Birth of the Global Pentecostal Movement (2006). He is the editor of Witness to Pentecost: The Life of Frank Bartleman (1985) and Charismatic Experiences in History (1985), and co-editor of The Azusa Street Revival and Its Legacy (2006) and The Suffering Body: Responding to the Persecution of Christians (2006). For nine years, he was editor of Pneuma: The Journal of the Society for

Pentecostal Studies. He is also part of the Azusa Street Memorial Committee and has lectured locally on the early Pentecostal sites in Los Angeles at UCLA, USC, Vanguard University, and the Japanese American National Museum.

Kimon H. Sargeant is Vice President, Human Sciences at the John Templeton Foundation, and is responsible for developing new research initiatives that apply the tools of sociology, psychology, and other disciplines to moral and spiritual concepts such as generosity, purpose, gratitude, and forgiveness. Prior to joining the Foundation, he served as a program officer at The Pew Charitable Trusts, where he was responsible for a $20 million portfolio in the area of religion and public life. Sargeant received his B.A. in history from Yale University and his doctorate in sociology from the University of Virginia. He is the author of Seeker Churches: Promoting Traditional Religion in a Nontraditional Way (2000).

Timothy H. Wadkins is Professor of Religious Studies and Theology and directs the Institute for the Global Study of Religion at Canisius College through the auspices of the Peter Canisius Distinguished Teaching Professorship. Professor Wadkins has published extensively in Post Reformation theological and cultural history in Europe and Britain, and most recently he authored an analysis of the Pentecostal groundswell in El Salvador, which was published in the World Council of Churches' International Review of Mission (2008). He is currently working on a monograph entitled The Preferential Option for the Spirit: Pentecostals and Culture in Modern El Salvador.

Robert D. Woodberry is Associate Professor, Department of Political Science, National University of Singapore. His research looks at the long-term impact of missionaries and religious groups on economic development and political democracy in postcolonial societies. Recent publications include "The Missionary Roots of Liberal Democracy" American Political Science Review (2012); the concluding chapter of the book Introducing World Christianity (2012); "Religion and Educational Ideals in Contemporary Taiwan," Journal for the Scientific Study of Religion (2011); "Religion and the Spread of Human Capital and Political Institutions" in The Oxford Handbook of the Economics of Religion (2011); and "Christian Missions and Education in Former African Colonies," Journal of African Economies (2010). Other articles appear in the American Sociological Review, Social Forces, the Annual Review of Sociology, and elsewhere.

Spirit and Power

Introduction

Pentecostalism as a Global Phenomenon

DONALD E. MILLER

Several years ago I was in São Paulo, Brazil, during the annual March for Jesus. Over a million people from hundreds of Pentecostal and charismatic churches lined one of the city's central boulevards. Every hundred yards or so a semi-truck draped with hip antidrug signs pulled a double-tiered trailer, and on the top tier a rock band sang the latest hit praise songs, blasting their music through huge amplified speakers. Lining the route for several miles were "born-again" Christians wearing "Jesus" headbands and sporting T-shirts proclaiming their faith. Some people danced; others walked arm-in-arm. Fathers carried children on their shoulders, and the crowd included thousands of teenagers and young adults. The parade culminated in a park where tens of thousands of people congregated for a live concert. This march is the Christian alternative to Carnival or Mardi Gras. People were high on Jesus, seemingly not needing any additional stimulant.

On other occasions I have visited numerous Pentecostal and charismatic churches and gatherings in São Paulo and other cities in Brazil. While these gatherings differ in size, they have many of the same characteristics. They often meet in converted theaters or malls. Unlike Catholic churches, these churches lack such European architectural influences as stained glass, bell towers, religious images, and pipe organs. Rather than choirs, Pentecostal churches have "bands" with singers situated at separate microphones, each inviting the Holy Spirit into their midst, often with arms outstretched. The music has a contemporary beat to it, although it is modulated to reflect various moods of worship, from praise to interior reflection. The words to choruses and songs are projected onto a wall so that all can see and sing along. There are no hymnbooks or prayer books. Pastors sometimes dress in suits, but the worship leaders, as well as the audience, wear street clothes. Typically there is a testimony by someone whose life has been radically altered after they "gave their heart" to Jesus. The sermon is always based on a biblical text, but also includes personal examples from the life of the preacher. The worship service always starts on an upbeat note with music that gets people on their feet, often with hands in the air. And it ends on a joyous note with people leaving the church to conquer the world for Christ.

In São Paulo, I once spent an evening at a "deliverance" service of the Universal Church of the Kingdom of God, which occupies a complete city block. The ushers were going up and down the aisles, grabbing "demon-possessed" people by the hair. I kept slumping deeper in my chair, hoping that none of my "demons" were evident! On the stage, a woman shouted profanities as her son looked on. In the course of about fifteen minutes she went through a complete transformation as the pastor prayed for her, commanding the demons to depart. The same dramatic change was happening to dozens of people who had been gathered by the ushers at the front of the auditorium. Eventually the audience quieted. The battle over Satan had been won. In place of a multitude of demonic spirits, the unitary Spirit of God was reigning.

When I returned on Sunday to this same church, I expected more fireworks. Instead, Bishop Macedo gave an extremely low-key biblical message. It seems that exorcisms are reserved for one day each week. I also encountered another surprise. Browsing through the church's elaborate bookstore after the service, I saw numerous videos about their social ministries to people who are poor, drug addicted, and in need of food and shelter. The senior pastor of a very large Assemblies of God church told me that they cannot begin to compete with the Universal Church in terms of service to the community, although he was a little cynical about their good works, saying that this is a way to buy legitimacy with the government. I was also struck by the very prominent menorah on the altar. The connection to Israel was reinforced several years later when I visited their church in Rio de Janiero. In addition to an office complex and concert-size auditorium, the church had an enormous exhibit room with a replica of what the city of Jerusalem looked like in the first century, complete with city streets, lighting, and temple structures.

In Rio de Janiero, I also took a tram to the top of the Santa Marta *favela* where Michael Jackson shot part of his "They Don't Care About Us" video. On a small concrete platform stood a bronze statue of Jackson, looking across a wide expanse to a hilltop that holds the famous "Christ the Redeemer" statue of Jesus with outstretched arms. On the other side of the wall is a Pentecostal church that holds no more than 50 people. There I interviewed a community organizer who spent years dealing drugs in this community, protecting his turf with a gun, before he met Jesus. He now works with young people to show them that there is an alternative to gang violence. Small churches such as this one are common in Brazil and around the world. The pastor is typically bi-vocational, supporting himself with a secular job while he ministers to his small flock. I toured one slum area in Rio de Janiero that had a storefront Pentecostal church on almost every block, leading me to wonder how they can all survive, but also suggesting the possibility that supply may drive demand, rather than the reverse.

While the Catholic Church in Brazil has lost many of its nominal members to Pentecostal churches, some Catholic priests are embracing a style of worship that resembles Pentecostalism—perhaps to compete more effectively with this upstart religion. Father Marcelo Rossi, who is sometimes referred to as the "singing priest," particularly impressed me. I attended Sunday worship at a makeshift church building that was bereft of the usual images of the Virgin Mary and instead resembled many of the Pentecostal churches I have attended, with folding chairs in place of pews. Several thousand people had their hands in the air, swaying to the songs led by Father Marcelo. At the end of the service, people danced their way out of the church, and I watched with great interest as a mother and daughter whirled into each other's arms at the end of a song. The only thing that seemed "Catholic" about this service was the way in which the Eucharist was celebrated. Otherwise, the ambience, even the songs, was very Pentecostal. One scholar I interviewed said that Marxist-inspired Liberation Theology was prominent among Catholics in the 1970s and '80s, but the poor opted for Pentecostalism.

Pentecostalism is not simply about raised hands and warm embraces. Pentecostals have also become a voting block in Brazil. The Universal Church has promoted specific candidates who are members of their church, as have the Assemblies of God and other Pentecostal denominations. As their numbers increased, so did their political participation, as well as the temptation for political and financial corruption. However, Pentecostals are developing a reputation in Brazil and around the world for effectively addressing social issues within their community. For example, in Rio de Janeiro, government officials have called on a local Pentecostal pastor to break up prison riots. On a regular basis this pastor and other Pentecostal clergy hold worship services in the prisons. In some prisons the wardens have created self-governing wards for born-again Christians, who are almost inevitably Pentecostal.

One of my more memorable experiences in Rio de Janeiro was visiting a Pentecostal-sponsored residential facility for people who had recently gotten out of prison. In interviews, men were transparent about their crimes, including homicide, and women made no effort to cover up their former drug use or prostitution. The atmosphere is pervaded by a spirit of honesty, love, and pursuit of a fresh beginning. Men and women live separately, but they collaborate in cooking, washing, and other maintenance activities. When not doing domestic chores, they study the Bible and worship together, hoping to reenter society as transformed individuals.

These brief accounts of Pentecostalism in Brazil offer a small window into several decades of my research studying Pentecostalism, first in the United States and then in more than 20 countries in Asia, Africa, Latin America, and the former Soviet Union. I have also had the privilege of overseeing a large research initiative on global Pentecostalism, which has allowed me to travel to places where one might not expect to see Pentecostal churches, such as Indonesia and Russia. In the rest of this chapter I will reference some of these experiences of observing Pentecostal and charismatic churches, as well as interviewing their leaders, but first it is necessary to give some background on where Pentecostalism started and how it fits into the larger movement of global Christianity.

Origins of Pentecostalism

The roots of Pentecostalism are described in the New Testament book of the Acts of the Apostles, chapter 2. Fifty days after Jesus's reported resurrection, the Holy Spirit descended on his disciples and followers, enabling them to "speak in tongues" (to speak in languages they did not know, a practice termed "glosslalia" by scholars) and empowering them to heal those who were sick, as well as prophesy and appropriate other "gifts" of the Spirit. Pentecost (50 days after Jesus's resurrection) is often referred to as the birth of the Christian church, which spread throughout Asia Minor and then around the world. Christianity became established as a national religion under Constantine and was organized into a hierarchical structure in subsequent centuries. Increasingly the priestly class controlled access to the sacred and mediated its presence to the general population through ritual. On occasion there were spontaneous eruptions of the Spirit by the people, and even mystics who sought oneness with God that defied institutional mediation, but in general the ecstatic element evident at Pentecost was sequestered and managed by institutions.

There are various theories about when these first-century practices of Jesus's disciples were revived, but one explanation dates the recurrence of speaking in tongues to 1901, when students at Bethel Bible School in Topeka, Kansas, were moved by the Spirit under the tutelage of Charles F. Parham. A few years later, Parham took his message regarding Spirit baptism to Houston, Texas, where William J. Seymour, a black Holiness preacher, became convinced that the Holy Spirit was still in the business of working supernatural miracles. Seymour then began preaching the same message to a small gathering of people in 1906 in Los Angeles, igniting what became known as the Azusa Street revival, attended by thousands of people and named after the street where an interracial gathering began to replicate the acts of the first-century apostles: speaking in tongues, healing the infirm, and prophesying. From Azusa Street, hundreds of missionaries took the Pentecostal message around the world. They created churches, renewal movements, and denominations that have grown, fractured, disappeared, split off, expanded, and taken root in the four corners of the globe in an impressive but dynamic and unpredictable pattern led by the spiritual entrepreneurs who often are at the heart of Pentecostal growth.

In the 1960s and 1970s, another movement of the Pentecostal spirit emerged in a number of Roman Catholic and mainline Protestant churches under the banner of the "charismatic renewal." Once again, people spoke in tongues, many claimed supernatural healing, and a more intimate form of worship emerged that emphasized prayer and meditation. Within Catholicism, this emphasis on the Holy Spirit became known as the Charismatic Renewal Movement. It typically exists as an element within a local church, and worship and prayer are often led by laypersons in meetings during the weekday or sometimes after the regular mass. While the Charismatic Renewal Movement is officially sanctioned by the Vatican, on occasion a local bishop may rein it in, especially if lay people are assuming roles and authority reserved for the priestly class.

Among Protestants, the Charismatic Renewal Movement has sometimes led to divisions within a congregation, with elements of a membership rejecting what they perceived to be irrational exuberance—especially when people claimed healing powers and were "slain" in the Spirit and spoke in tongues. On the other hand, a number of Protestant churches have been influenced by the renewal movement and have embraced a milder version of Pentecostalism, acknowledging the possibility of supernatural healing and affirming a theology that gives more prominence to the role of the Holy Spirit in worship, including collective periods—typically short and controlled—when members pray in tongues. There is also a recognition within these congregations that some individuals have specialized gifts of the Spirit, such as prophecy—not in the sense of foretelling the future, but rather in speaking authoritatively in the voice of God regarding what the church or individuals are called to do.

In research studies such as the Pew Forum surveys referenced in the appendix, these various Catholic and Protestant manifestations of Pentecostalism and charismatic Christianity have been combined into a broad category of "renewalists." This category includes members of Pentecostal denominations as well as Christians of all traditions who believe that supernatural acts, such as healing, prophecy, and other manifestations of the Spirit, are not confined to the first century but are to be practiced today by Christians. In general, renewalists tend to reject formalized worship in favor of more spontaneous and less ritualized expressions that invite an intimate experience of the Holy Spirit. Prayer, both personal and public, may involve people speaking in tongues, although few Pentecostals today believe that they are actually speaking a foreign language. Instead, speaking in tongues is viewed as speaking a "prayer language" that allows communion with God in ways that transcend normal discourse.

Contextualizing Pentecostalism

Where do the world's half billion renewalists fit within the larger context of global religion? How do they compare to other Christian groups? Do they have a unique role within global Christianity? To answer these questions we need to start with a broad portrait of the world's major religious groups.

The world's population is slightly over seven billion people, with about 2.2 billion identifying as Christians, 1.6 billion as Muslims, and one billion as Hindus. Buddhists are a much smaller percentage of the world's population, with fewer than 500 million adherents. There are numerous religious groups, including Jews, who number less than 20 million worldwide, as well as Sikhs, Jains, Zoroastrians, and others. Agnostics and atheists are growing in number, both in countries that have suppressed religion, such as China and Russia, but also in some Western European countries where weekly attendance at worship services is extremely low (between 2 and 10 percent), at least when compared to the United States where it is about 40 percent. Approximately 1.1 billion people around the world have no religious affiliation.

Within every religion there are subgroups, or what are sometimes called denominations, that reflect theological, historical, and cultural differences. For example, within Christianity there are three major groups: Catholics (which account for about half of all Christians), Protestants (with hundreds of different denominations), and Orthodox (including Greek, Russian, Armenian, Serbian, and other national religions). Renewalists can be found in all three of these major classifications, although there are relatively few in the Orthodox branch of Christianity.

This book focuses on a specific element within Protestant Christianity that includes Pentecostal denominations, such as the Assemblies of God, Foursquare Gospel, and the Church of God in Christ, which all have American origins, plus hundreds of indigenous Pentecostal denominations in Africa, Asia, and Latin America. As stated previously, charismatic Catholics, and especially those who are part of the Catholic Charismatic Renewal Movement, are included in our discussion, as well as numerous Christians in Protestant denominations that share many of the characteristics of Pentecostals and "renewed" Catholics. An increasing number of Christians, however, have little use for these sorts of categorizations and dismiss the importance of denominational labels altogether. They view themselves simply as Christians who practice the teachings of Jesus and follow the example of the disciples in the early Christian church.

In terms of theology, Pentecostal and charismatic Christians of all stripes tend to be "evangelical." They affirm the literal virgin birth of Jesus and his physical resurrection. They believe that God divinely inspired the Bible. They believe that salvation requires that one accept Jesus as one's personal savior. Some Pentecostals also believe that there are additional stages in the Christian experience beyond being "born again," such as "sanctification" (an elevated holiness), as well as an experience of the "baptism of the Holy Spirit" when one speaks in tongues. However, recent survey research has demonstrated that many Pentecostals and charismatic Christians seldom speak in tongues; for them, supernatural healing is more common than glossolalia. In actual practice, the line between Pentecostals and Christians who identify themselves as "evangelicals" is blurring, since many evangelicals have "Pentecostalized" their worship, and most Pentecostals affirm the beliefs of evangelicals, except for those of "dispensational" evangelicals who believe that the supernatural acts of the Holy Spirit are limited to the first century.

One label that does *not* fit Pentecostal and charismatic Christians is "fundamentalist," which refers to a specific movement in the United States that began in the 1920s and continues today entrapped in various legalistic practices that place a premium on proper "beliefs" (the "fundamentals" of the Christian faith), deemphasizing religious experience. In contrast, there is a freedom within Pentecostal and charismatic worship that does not exist within fundamentalist churches, which tend to be dogmatic and rationalistic. Pentecostals and charismatic Christians believe that God continues to speak today to Christians. While the Bible is an important point of reference, for Pentecostals and charismatic Christians the Holy Spirit is an active presence in the lives of believers, speaking to them in very personal and even mystical ways.

While fundamentalists may use modern technology, there is a substantial difference between their style of worship and Pentecostals'. Pentecostals and charismatic Christians typically utilize contemporary technology, such as electric guitars, amplified basses, and high-tech sound systems in their worship. Their worship is more free-form than fundamentalists' and includes a constantly evolving set of freshly written choruses and songs. Furthermore, they are often culturally savvy, embracing contemporary styles and modes of dress, as well as reading the latest books on leadership. Nevertheless, Pentecostals and charismatic Christians are morally conservative, even ascetic in their lifestyle, prohibiting alcohol, gambling, and extramarital sex. This does not preclude a joyous, even ecstatic, worship experience, which is mirrored in an optimistic view of life's possibilities, including financial well-being for those that embrace the "prosperity gospel." At the same time, Pentecostals and charismatic Christians have a dualistic worldview that distinguishes between the sacred and profane, the church and the world, and good versus evil.

Religious Renewal Movements

Sociologically, Pentecostalism and charismatic Christianity can be viewed as renewal movements that are reinventing the external forms of religion to enable individuals to experience the sacred or God in less mediated ways. Rituals that have become encrusted with centuries of tradition are simplified. The role of the priestly class is challenged; individuals can approach God directly without going through licensed clergy. In turn, the Holy Spirit may speak directly to believers, unmediated by a priest or pastor, with religious experience valued over tradition. Yet renewal movements such as Pentecostalism are actually very important to the survival of ancient religious traditions. All social organizations undergo a process that sociologists refer to as routinization, whereby institutions become increasingly bureaucratized and ordered, often infused with procedures that pander to individuals who want to protect their positions of privilege and power. What religious renewal movements do is strip away these layers of bureaucracy and attempt to recapture the original animating spirit of the religion, legitimating the validity of direct religious experience. Interpretation of what one experiences in these encounters of the holy, sacred, or divine need not be explained exclusively by the priestly class; individuals can directly access the source materials of the tradition, such as the Bible, and read it for themselves, seeking to interpret the meaning of their own experience. This process, of course, can lead to chaos and "heresy," as defined by the official interpreters of the sacred texts. But it also often serves as a source of creativity and innovation, renewing rituals that were previously done by rote and providing access to the sacred in ways that have been choked off by the official managers of the tradition.

In time, of course, renewal movements themselves become stultified and wooden, which is why many of the older Pentecostal traditions are growing at a slower rate than what are sometimes referred to as "neo-Pentecostal" churches, which often are led by individuals that grew alienated from the structures that had evolved in the more historic Pentecostal denominations. It is also not surprising that bishops and clergy within Catholic and Orthodox churches may feel threatened by renewal movements within their congregations. Lay people are increasingly supplanting the clergy as they attempt to enact changes to the liturgy and established procedures that permit more direct access to the sacred.

The Growth of Pentecostalism

Given the somewhat amorphous character of Pentecostal and charismatic Christianity, it is difficult to know how many people fit this classification, but most estimates put the number of renewalists at more than 500 million, or about a quarter of the total Christian population. It is widely regarded as the fastest growing element of Christianity and as a consequence it is reshaping the demography of Christianity, with the majority of Christians now living in the Southern Hemisphere rather than in Europe or North America. For example, in 1910, 80 percent of Christians were Europeans or North Americans; today, this number is less than 40 percent. Simultaneously, there has also been an explosion in the number of denominations, many of them emerging out of the global south.

Although statistics are difficult to assess because of the somewhat nebulous character of the renewalist movement, it appears that Latin America has the largest number of Pentecostal and charismatic Christians, followed by Africa and then Asia. North America lags far behind these three regions of the world. In terms of percentage of country populations that are Pentecostal or charismatic, Pew Forum surveys (see appendix) found that in Kenya and Guatemala, over half of the population fit their classification for being renewalists, and in Brazil, South Africa, and the Philippines, over one-third were renewalists. Contradicting stereotypes about Pentecostals, the Pew Forum surveys in 10 different countries did not find that renewalists were disproportionately from lower socioeconomic sectors of society compared to other religionists. The Pew Forum surveys also found that renewalists often hold progressive political views on social welfare issues, although they are conservative on issues related to sexuality. In addition, the Pew Forum surveys did not find renewalists disproportionately female, although many other studies of Pentecostalism say that women outnumber men by two to one, at least in church attendance.

Pentecostalism is also having a significant impact on politics. For example, countries in Latin America that were almost exclusively Catholic now have significant numbers of Pentecostals: in 1940, only 1 percent of Latin America was Protestant; today, it is about 12 percent Protestant, and about 75 percent of all Protestants are Pentecostals. As a result, it is very common to see Pentecostals running for public office, and sometimes a particular denomination or set of churches in Latin America actively promotes a specific candidate. There is some indication that the growth of Pentecostalism is actually contributing to democratic governance in some countries, challenging the monopoly of state-sponsored religions, and thereby providing voters with a broader range of choice.

The same demographic transformation is also occurring in Africa and Asia. Pentecostal and charismatic Christian churches, many of which have no connection to North American missionary activity, are fueling the growth of Christianity. For example, the Redeemed Christian Church of God (RCCG), which started in Nigeria, is now in 60 countries in Africa, the United States, Europe, and parts of Asia and the Middle East. In Nigeria alone it has 2,000 congregations. The RCCG holds an annual convention attended by several million people: the largest meeting of Christians in the world. Throughout Africa there are indigenous churches and denominations, some of which are extremely large and are continually planting "daughter" churches, both in their own country and throughout the world. In fact, the criteria for success in a number of these Pentecostal and charismatic movements is not the size of one's own church, but how many new congregations one has started.

In modernized, affluent countries such as Singapore, some Pentecostal churches have grown so large that they are meeting in stadiums and convention centers. In South Korea, the Yoido Full Gospel Church has a half million members and has tens of thousands of people meeting for worship each weekend in multiple services. In China there has been an explosion of "house" churches, many of them charismatic and operating under the radar of official religion. In the Philippines there is a huge charismatic movement, El Shaddai, associated with the Catholic Church, as well as a number of booming Pentecostal churches, such as the Jesus is Lord movement. In Moscow, a Word of Life church has 3,000 attending weekly, and in Yerevan, Armenia, a branch of the same Pentecostal denomination has over 10,000 members, despite the fact that Orthodox Christianity dominates as the state religion in both Russia and Armenia.

The Role of Religious Experience

At the heart of vital Pentecostal and charismatic churches is religious experience, rather than formal liturgy, creedal statements, or abstract theological doctrines. In China, the Philippines, and other parts of Asia, almost every conversion testimony I heard involved an account of supernatural healing. In fact, in India I heard several accounts of people being raised from the dead. In Kenya I interviewed a pastor who said he had observed a demon-possessed individual levitating off the floor.

In Hong Kong I encountered a particularly memorable expression of glossolalia at St. Stephen's Society. St. Stephen's Society is a program for drug addicts started several decades ago by Jackie Pullinger, who came to Hong Kong as a youthful missionary from the United Kingdom. Heroin addicts typically seek out St. Stephen's after they have been arrested multiple times by the police and have heard through word of mouth that there is a place where they can come to kick their habit—painlessly. The first meeting I attended included 70 or 80 men. After a long period of melodic singing and some encouraging words of scripture about the potential to change one's life, former addicts, now born-again Christians, started praying for drug-addicted individuals by placing an arm on their shoulder and quietly asking the Holy Spirit to fill them. On the spot, some of these individuals started speaking in tongues, apparently not knowing what they were saying or what was occurring. Jackie Pullinger told me after the meeting that these men would later begin to understand that the Holy Spirit has entered their life, which is the first step in their recovery when they join one of St. Stephen's yearlong residential programs. Feeling skeptical of the claim that it was possible to experience painless withdrawal from heroin, I visited several of the Society's residential treatment facilities and heard testimony after testimony of individuals who had been addicted for years, including women who had prostituted themselves to pay for drugs, and were now off heroin after relatively painless withdrawal.

A more typical experience of glossolalia, however, is first becoming a convert and then receiving the "gift" of speaking in tongues, as in the case of a young woman I interviewed in Warsaw, Poland. She had been addicted to drugs as a teenager and was working as a prostitute to support her addiction when several Christians persisted in greeting her at the street corner where she conducted her business. At first she resisted their invitation to join them, but she finally succumbed. She told me that in this group she experienced unconditional love for the first time in her life. After several months of living with these Christians in their drug rehab center, she was asked if she wanted to receive the Holy Spirit. She agreed and was prayed for, with hands laid on her by a group of Christians. At first nothing happened, and then she had a surprising experience in which she began to praise God in an unknown but very melodic language. This "in-filling" of the Holy Spirit became a very important part of her prayer and worship life as she continued to pursue sobriety.

Glossolalia is not the only dramatic form of Pentecostal practice. My first experience of Pentecostalism was at a Vineyard Fellowship healing conference in Southern California. At the end of the service, dozens of people came forward for prayer. Lay ministers put their hands on these individuals and many of them started trembling and falling to the floor in a trance-like state. At another Vineyard healing meeting, I witnessed the phenomenon of "holy laughter," in which John Wimber, the founder of the movement, quietly said, "The Holy Spirit wants to refresh and bless you," and people throughout the meeting started laughing so hard that some actually fell out of their chairs. These phenomena were then experienced by people in Canada at the Airport Vineyard in what became known as the Toronto Blessing.

The experience of being "slain in the Spirit" and falling to the floor is quite common in Pentecostal churches, so much so that many churches have members specially designated to catch those who are falling. I recall videotaping an all-night prayer meeting in Santiago, Chile. After asking permission to film, I situated myself in a side aisle with my camera and tripod. Midway through the service, one of the pastors requested that I come up on the podium so that I could have a better view, which I did. With a youth choir singing in the background accompanied by drums and guitarists, people were falling under the power of the Holy Spirit below me as the pastor touched their heads, one by one. In the enthusiasm of the moment, I was knocked off the podium with my camera. Something similar happened in Alexandria, South Africa, when a large man knocked me off my feet as he went down under the power of the Spirit.

In the hundred years or so since Pentecostalism was launched in its contemporary form, a broad spectrum of religious experience has developed. Significant numbers of Pentecostals and charismatic Christians say that they have *never* personally spoken in tongues. In some large megachurches, glossolalia is carefully orchestrated and confined to a few minutes of praising God in tongues during Sunday morning services. Exorcism and healing are also sometimes confined to special services, perhaps in part so that these more exotic phenomena do not alienate potential converts. Some of the more extreme expressions of the supernatural are limited to animistic cultures where spirit possession is common and access to medical intervention is difficult. What almost all Pentecostals have in common, however, is a confidence that God through the Spirit is active, powerful, and moving in the world today. Pentecostalism is a movement that celebrates the immanence or nearness of the Divine, in contrast to the transcendent and distant notions of the Divine in more ritualistic Christian traditions.

Myths about Pentecostalism

Outside observers of Pentecostal worship often think that it is irrational, in keeping with Karl Marx's description of religion as the "opiate" of the masses. There is some degree of truth to this characterization, but it is not the whole story. Pentecostalism was originally marketed to the lower classes of society, where it found considerable reception. There was an appeal to the idea that the trials and tribulations of this world are not the only reality; that soon Christ would return and that converts would live out eternity in heaven, where individuals are evaluated by their virtue rather than their earthly possessions.

There is little doubt that ecstatic worship may serve as a cathartic release from the challenges of everyday life. But there is an element of the Pentecostal experience that defies the Marxist analysis of religion: namely, that many people feel empowered by Pentecostal worship and their experience of the gifts of the Spirit. Rather than feeling like they are "nobody," they leave worship believing that they have value because they were made in God's image. They also have hope regarding the future. Preachers tend to be visionary in their message, pointing believers to future possibilities, both for themselves and for the congregation. Sometimes preachers even offer advice on how to prosper financially. Rather than a "drug" that pacifies believers, religion is a force driving them to reach beyond their present circumstances. While this may be "false consciousness" in the Marxist sense, my own observation is that the comfort offered by Pentecostalism often functions to empower people, rather than simply serving as a narcotic that dulls the pain of life.

Pentecostalism increasingly is finding a market among upwardly mobile people, including many middle-class individuals. I have interviewed hundreds of pastors and lay leaders of Pentecostal churches who are educated, sophisticated people. For them, speaking in tongues is a *non-rational* form of communing with the Spirit of God, but not an *irrational* experience. Communion with God—or whatever terms one uses, such as the Divine, the Holy, the Sacred, et cetera—may defy normal speech patterns. In the course of my research, I have not found most Pentecostals to be hostile to modern medicine, even though they believe in supernatural healing. There are cases in which clergy have promised healing from AIDS and other incurable diseases, but I have interviewed numerous Pentecostals who are critical of these practices. There are Pentecostal churches that advocate "health and wealth," enticing members to give to the church so that they in turn will be financially rewarded. But again, there are many Pentecostals who are very critical of these "prosperity gospel" churches. Pentecostal and charismatic Christianity is a mixed bag; there is undoubtedly some corruption and manipulation, but there may also be life-affirming practices that give people hope, that inspire them to heroic acts of altruism, and that make this world a better place.

Finally, a common stereotype of Pentecostals is that they are so "heavenly minded" that they are no "earthly good." Even in the early days of Pentecostalism, this stereotype needs qualification. Converts cared for each other in times of need and often extended this concern to their nonbelieving neighbors. More recently, many Pentecostal churches have created "cutting-edge" social ministries. In a recent book based on travel in twenty countries, my coauthor and I documented the following eight types of social outreach ministries in Pentecostal and charismatically oriented churches (Miller and Yamamori, 2007):

1. *mercy ministries*, providing food, clothing, and shelter;
2. *emergency services*, responding to floods, famine, and earthquakes;
3. *education*, providing day care, schools, and tuition assistance;
4. *counseling services*, helping with addiction, divorce, depression;
5. *medical assistance*, establishing health clinics, dental clinics, psychological services;
6. *economic development*, providing microenterprise loans, job training, affordable housing;
7. the *arts*, training in music, dance, drama; and
8. *policy change*, opposing corruption, monitoring elections, advocating a living wage.

The extensiveness of these social services typically depends on the size of the congregation and its financial capacity. Sometimes these social services are arranged in partnership with international agencies, such as World Vision, Compassion International, or Food for the Hungry. The programs usually reflect the social needs in the immediate community: in one city, AIDS; in another, family violence or agricultural development, and so on. Unlike Liberation Theology, very few Pentecostal churches address social problems at a political or structural level. Instead, they tend to address individual human needs. In addition, they often create model programs related to education, health care, and even economic development projects that serve as a model to the larger community.

Maggie Gobran (known by locals as Mama Maggie), the founder of Stephen's Children in Egypt, is a good example of someone who combines heroic social ministry with her charismatically oriented Coptic Christian faith. She has created an extensive network of nursery schools in the slums of Cairo that serve thousands of children whose parents support themselves by sorting garbage, separating metal, paper, and plastic for resale. Maggie was born into a wealthy family in Cairo and married a professor at one of Egypt's best universities. Years ago, as part of her charity work as a member of Cairo's upper class, she ventured into the poor districts of the city once or twice a year, and on one of these occasions she came across a woman, wrapped in a blanket, who was supporting her family as a street vendor. Maggie approached the woman and engaged her in conversation. When the woman left to tend her other children, her daughter remained to carry on the family business, and Maggie, taking pity on the child, offered to buy her a new pair of shoes. The girl replied, however, that she would rather her mother have the shoes, since she had nothing to protect her feet from the cold. Maggie said that as she looked at the girl, she saw the eyes of Jesus staring back at her. In that instant she realized that not only could this girl be her own daughter but, except for the accident of birth, she could be this woman. In the epiphany of that moment her identity as a Christian was transformed; she understood that the way to touch Jesus was by ministering to the poor.

Mama Maggie is exceptional, but she is not an exception in Pentecostal circles. Thousands of churches and countless Pentecostals demonstrate love and concern for their neighbors. One example is an Assemblies of God church I spend considerable time documenting in Johannesburg, South Africa. At that time, the church was all white. Its leadership realized that they were living in isolation from the black population, and that if the church closed its doors, only a small proportion of the community would miss it. In response, they developed a model program for training women in the townships to develop their own businesses of providing quality daycare for the children of working mothers. Modeled after Montessori instruction, it adopted methods that were both affordable and appropriate to the children living in the black townships. The church developed a mixed-race nursery school on its own property that served as a training program for aspiring women entrepreneurs. In Nairobi, Kenya, I visited a church-sponsored medical clinic that was providing nearly free services by utilizing generic medications and emphasizing old-fashioned methods of diagnosis that did not rely on advanced technology. When I visited the clinic, a medical student from Harvard University was observing how the church was operating the clinic at such low cost with a view toward implementing its strategies elsewhere.

The Importance of Music

Based on my global travels, I believe it is difficult to overestimate the importance of culturally current worship music. As I spent most of my adult life in the Episcopal (Anglican) Church, it was something of a shock to my worship sensitivities when I started researching Pentecostal and charismatic churches some thirty years ago. For example, it was difficult to find an organ or choir in these churches. Instead, there were bands, worship leaders, and singers. Guitars, drums, and very sophisticated amps and speakers seemed to predominate, even in poor communities. New converts who had previously been entertaining in clubs and pop venues brought their music into the church, changing only the lyrics, not the beat or sound. This style of worship plays a very important role in connecting with a younger generation of potential converts who otherwise might question the relevance of religion to their lives.

There is something very "hip" about many Pentecostal churches. They exude a feeling of joy and life; they do not rely on eighteenth-century hymns or creeds that were written hundreds of years ago.

It is not only megachurches that exemplify this spirit. I was invited to attend an all-night prayer meeting of youth in Caracas, Venezuela, held in a home on a hillside where recent rains had washed away several houses and hosted by a woman whose son had been killed in a drug deal. In his memory, she had built a room onto her house where kids his age could meet to worship and hang out as an alternative to gang engagement. After making my way through a maze of houses, I entered this home to see teens dancing to gospel tunes that were being beaten out on an overturned crate. The words to the songs, which included enacting references to casting out Satan, were framed by a short biblical teaching that one of the teens delivered from notes that she had carefully written. This experience of worship was quite different from the professionally orchestrated music I have heard in large Pentecostal churches, where there is a considerable pool of musical talent from which to draw, but I'm not certain that it was any less effective in communicating a message of God's love and the importance of keeping oneself pure for his service.

One of the most important elements of Pentecostalism is its ability to adapt to local contexts, embracing culturally appropriate music and worship styles. In a small village church in India I listened to worship music that was distinctly non-Western and accompanied by a single drum. In a church in Alexandria, South Africa, there was no instrumentation at all—just the human voice. In contrast, the worship music I witnessed in some of the large megachurches in Singapore, Hong Kong, Brazil, and elsewhere was utterly contemporary, and was led by bands that could have performed in secular venues. Whatever the style of music, the goal is to enable the worshipper to experience God directly. Worship music works at a subliminal level on the emotions; it has the potential to lower one's defenses and transport one to another level of human consciousness, enabling the worshipper to move into interior spaces that are normally guarded during everyday life. Many worship leaders recognize, however, that people respond differently to different genres of music. Worship leaders are also sensitive to the musical inclinations of different age groups. For example, a musician in Nairobi, Kenya, told me that he has different worship bands for different services, depending on the age cohort. Even if the same songs are played at various Sunday services, the tempo is altered for different audiences.

Most services begin with upbeat songs that get people on their feet, clapping, dancing, and raising their hands in praise. The music then tones down as the sermon approaches, putting people into a receptive mood to listen to the preacher. If there is an "invitation" to accept Christ at the end of the sermon, the music is soft and wooing. If there is a period when demons are exorcised, the music is discordant and then transitions to something that is peaceful and worshipful. Inevitably, the worship service ends on a joyous note as people enter the profane world, seeking to share the good news of their faith.

Why Is Pentecostalism Growing?

The simplest explanation for the growth of Pentecostalism is that it is outperforming the competition. Increasingly in the modern world—including the developing world—religion is not simply an inherited birthright. Individuals have a choice of religion, or of whether they will be religious at all. More hierarchical and mediated forms of religion have a difficult time competing with churches that have vibrant music, a compassionate community of caring people, visionary preaching, affirmation of one's dignity as a child of God, and life-changing encounters with the sacred.

It has been observed that women are often the first members of a family to join a Pentecostal church. If the family has migrated from the tight-knit community of a rural area to the anomie of a city, they may seek a replacement for the extended family that they left behind. In the local Pentecostal church, including small storefronts, they experience a warmth and community that is not otherwise available to them. They see the church as a safe place for their children—a community with strong moral values—in contrast to what they experience around them in urban society. Eventually a woman may persuade her husband to attend as well. Over time he may become less abusive, spend less of the family income on alcohol, gambling, and womanizing, and become a better father to their children. In addition, he (and his wife) may gain status within the church that is not otherwise available to him in society, as an usher, leader of a Bible study, head of a church committee, and so on.

There is also something about the ascetic and strict moral code of Pentecostalism, when teamed with ecstatic worship, that motivates people to market their religion to others. They believe they have found the truth; they can point to the transformation in their own lives; and they have found a community where they can celebrate the good things of life with like-minded people. There is also a spirit of joy and hope within many of these churches, which is a precious commodity in many societies, especially when people are confronted with problems or are struggling financially for survival.

Additionally, many Pentecostal churches are remarkably flexible and entrepreneurial compared to non-evangelical churches. Starting a new program or even a new church does not require approval by a dozen committees. The principle of the "priesthood of all believers" releases the ministry to the people. There may be a charismatic figure at the helm of the church who will say "no" to a member's perceived leading of the Spirit, but in the fastest growing churches there is a tendency to embrace creative and visionary leadership by the laity.

The personal charisma of pastors, as well as creative leadership skills, appear to be more important than sophisticated theological training in attracting new members to the church. Many of the pastors of the large churches were former businessmen who experienced a radical change in their life after conversion. They studied the Bible intensively, but did not go to seminary. Instead, many of them started out leading a home cell group in their church. In this setting they honed their knowledge of the Bible and their ability to communicate effectively and demonstrated their natural leadership skills. From there they were led by the Spirit to start a church, or else were commissioned by the congregation to plant a daughter church, and in a relatively short time the new congregation blossomed.

I remember sitting with a group of young pastors in Manila who were part of the Jesus is Lord movement. As they went around the circle introducing themselves, I asked each one to say how many members were in their church. The numbers were staggering: 2,000, 3,000 and more, and these pastors were in their late twenties and early thirties. None of them had attended a three-year seminary, as is the custom in many Protestant denominations. Instead, they were creatively addressing the needs of their people. In listening to them I was reminded of what a Pentecostal church leader told me in Kenya: "The shepherd must smell like the sheep." In his view, the problem with theologically sophisticated and highly educated clergy is that fellow pastors become their peer group and they tend to lose connection with the needs and mentality of their flock.

The zeal of many of the pastors and lay leaders of these Pentecostal churches is quite astounding. Not only are they visionary and creative, but they are also fearless. If the Holy Spirit tells them to do something, they pursue it regardless of the odds. The amazing thing is that many of their dreams and visions are realized. In fact, one of the more interesting developments in the last decade or so is a "reverse missionary movement" in which churches from the global south are planting churches in the "heathen" Western countries of Europe and the United States. Brazil, Korea, and Nigeria are the most prolific "sending" countries, and their most common initial toehold is among immigrants who have departed to Western countries from their own shores, but in time they have begun to expand beyond their own national group. Religious zeal is a difficult thing to measure, but Pentecostals and charismatic church leaders seem to have it in spades.

The Spirit Factor

A strict market analysis does not adequately explain the exponential growth of Pentecostalism, although it offers a helpful perspective. Religion is not the equivalent of toothpaste. If individuals do not have authentic encounters of a self-transcending nature—with a source that they perceive to be outside of themselves—then marketing will have short-term results. Entertainment or flashy programming is also not enough to sustain long-term commitment. The uniqueness of Pentecostalism is its ability to facilitate experiences of the sacred that are more powerful and more profound than those available in the marketplace of religious alternatives.

This does not mean that Pentecostal religion is wholly free of corrupt institutional practices and that it never panders to inflated egos or fosters immature religious dependence. Religion is always a mixture of the human and divine, and Pentecostalism is no exception. All institutions are human constructions, including religion. However, simply reducing the animation that occurs in ecstatic worship to what the French sociologist, Émile Durkheim, called collective effervescence—a somewhat primitive celebration of the values and beliefs that bind a community together—seems to me to be highly reductive, or at least a bit arrogant.

Whether the Holy Spirit has an ontological reality is certainly not solved through logical thought processes. It is a matter of faith, and Pentecostals would say that it is a matter of experience. What Pentecostal churches provide is a laboratory in which individuals can pursue a divine encounter. It is a place where the "big" existential questions of life—"What is my purpose?" "Why do I exist?"—can be addressed. More practically, and perhaps experientially, human beings have profound needs for community (to counter the threat of isolation and loneliness), for renewal (when discouraged and guilt-ridden), and for joy and ecstasy (which rational thought processes seldom produce). Religions that respond to all of these complex elements of human life and meaning have the potential to prosper.

Karl Marx, Max Weber, and Émile Durkheim thought that religion would surely disappear by the twenty-first century, or at least that its role in human society would diminish. The opposite seems to be the case. Religious practice may be declining in many European countries, but this is not true in the United States or many developing countries in Africa, Latin America, and Asia. Furthermore, secularization theories suggest that religion, if it survived, would reside primarily in the private sphere of life. Instead, we are witnessing a very public role for religion, both in the United States and globally. In the following chapters, the evolution and social role of one religious movement is documented in some detail. The significance of Pentecostalism is its transformative effect on Christianity, the largest religious tradition in the world.

PENTECOSTAL ORIGINS: FROM AZUSA STREET TO GLOBAL NETWORKS

Although it has long been argued that the Los Angeles–based Azusa Street revival in 1906 was the origin of the global Pentecostal movement (indeed, there is even a city sponsored cultural marker identifying Azusa Street as the "cradle" of the worldwide Pentecostal movement), more recently there have been persuasive arguments that similar revivals were taking place simultaneously in different parts of the world. In this first section of the book, we have arguments on both sides of the issue.

First, Allan Anderson argues that Pentecostalism was from the beginning a "polynucleated" movement with a primary missionary impulse. That is, that it was centered not in one place—Azusa Street—but was emerging simultaneously at several different places around the globe, and at its core was the desire to spread its message through missionary activity. Anderson contends that (1) the Azusa Street revival in the United States and the Mukti revival in India were part of a wider series of revivals and had *equal* significance in the early promotion of Pentecostal beliefs and values throughout the world; (2) existing missionary networks, especially that of the Christian and Missionary Alliance, which predated Azusa Street, were fundamental in spreading Pentecostalism internationally; (3) Pentecostal media, in particular periodicals that were sent to missionaries in the "field," were not only significant in spreading Pentecostalism internationally but were the foundation of the meta-culture that arose in global Pentecostalism in its earliest forms; and (4) the various centers and events in early Pentecostalism were part of a series of formative stages in the emergence of a new missionary movement that took several years to develop a distinctive identity.

However, Cecil M. Robeck, Jr., presents a slightly different perspective than Anderson, focusing on the central role of Azusa Street, and provides a very useful metaphor for understanding the primary importance of the Azusa Street Mission and all of its activities in setting off an explosion of Pentecostal activity around the globe. Robeck asks the reader to picture a perfect break in a game of billiards, to give the idea that the people who were active in Azusa Street went out from Los Angeles and they "hit" others, and the influence of Azusa was spread around the world. Nearly all of them, Robeck shows, are traceable to the Azusa Street Mission in Los Angeles as the initial billiard shot—or perhaps cue ball—that reverberated around the world. Robeck details the contributions of the Azusa Street Mission to the global reach of Pentecostalism, such as the rapid and global spread of Pentecostal missionary efforts that, as early as 1910, had been established across the United States and into Canada, Mexico, Europe, the Caribbean, Africa, India, China, the Middle East, and elsewhere. For Robeck, in contrast to Anderson, the Azusa Street Mission was the central and unsurpassed source of global Pentecostalism and mission from that time period.

Regardless of the outcome of the debate over how primary Azusa Street should be considered when thinking about the global Pentecostal movement, each chapter presents remarkably similar insights into how the early Pentecostal leaders and missionaries organized themselves into a global movement. For example, each chapter emphasizes the importance of Pentecostal media in the form of newsletters and other periodicals, which not only served to spread Pentecostal ideas and beliefs, but also functioned to help establish relationships between Pentecostal missionaries in the field and between missionaries and their supporters at home. Thus ideas and relationships were fundamentally spread and established through networks—whether preexisting or emergent—which allowed the movement to spread much more quickly and to be more nimble than it could have been if it had been governed by formal organizational structures. This emphasis on networks continues to this day, and despite the fact that many Pentecostal denominations have been established, networks both within and across those more formal structures function in much the same way that Anderson and Robeck argue was the case in Pentecostalism's emergent phase.

Finally, these two chapters raise important questions about Pentecostalism 100 years after its emergence as a modern religious movement. Several of the themes that Anderson and Robeck emphasize, including Pentecostal media and networks, but also others like the development of personal empowerment and agency that are instigated by religious experience, anticipate themes found in other chapters in this volume. One trait of Pentecostalism that both Anderson and Robeck highlight is the emphasis within Pentecostalism that

Jesus would return any day, which served as a primary motivator for their missionary impulse in their effort to "save" as many people as they could before Jesus returned. However, the emphasis on the imminent return of Jesus (at least in so literal a way that it was expressed at the turn of the twentieth century), does not seem to have the same hold for Pentecostals now, their emphasis being on fulfillment in the here and now, whether spiritual or material. Thus, if the belief that Jesus could return at any time no longer holds the same importance for Pentecostals, has anything replaced this belief as a motivator for their actions in the world? Are there other motivations that have been developed within Pentecostalism that can explain the growth and spread of Pentecostalism around the world?

1

The Emergence of a Multidimensional Global Missionary Movement

Trends, Patterns, and Expressions

ALLAN H. ANDERSON

Early Development of a Pentecostal Meta-Culture

By 1916, only ten years after the beginning of the Los Angeles Azusa Street revival, western Pentecostal missionaries were found in at least forty-two nations outside North America and Europe.[1] This was indeed a remarkable achievement, especially in view of the lack of central organization and coordination, the naiveté of most of these missionaries, and the physical difficulties and opposition they encountered. This chapter looks at the polynucleated origins and the development of a global network in early Pentecostalism and how this contributed to the formation of a multidimensional global movement. Pentecostal denominations were still in the process of formation, and in most countries they did not exist as organizations with centralized structures. Most of these early missionaries were novices who had never ventured outside their own, often-narrow cultural setting. Those who left America in the wake of the Azusa Street revival did so with the conviction that they could speak the languages of the nations to which they had been called. European Pentecostals from the Pentecostal Missionary Union, being rather more phlegmatic and having the experience of their leader Cecil Polhill, formerly of the China Inland Mission, to guide them, went out to China, India, and central Africa expecting to need to learn these languages. Many of the early missionaries lacked financial means (including funds to take furloughs in their homelands); they were subject to impoverished living conditions, and many died from tropical diseases. Some of their stories are indeed tragic.

It is possible, however, to understand the present global proliferation of Pentecostalism from these rather chaotic beginnings and to discern the essential characteristics that made it ultimately the most successful Christian missionary movement of the twentieth century. Pentecostalism has always been a movement with a global orientation and inherent migrating tendencies that, coupled with its strong individualism, made it fundamentally a multidimensional missionary movement. Very soon its ambassadors were indigenous people who went out to their own people in ever-increasing numbers. Networks were formed, crisscrossing nations and organizations. These networks were essential in the globalizing process and were aided and abetted by rapid advances in technology, transportation, and communications. As the twentieth century progressed Pentecostalism became increasingly globalized, and the power and influence of the former colonizing nations and their representatives diminished.

Charismata or "spiritual gifts" and ecstatic or "enthusiastic" forms of Christianity have been found in all ages, albeit sometimes at the margins of the established church, and they have often been a characteristic of the church's missionary advance, from the early church to the pioneer Catholic missionaries of the Middle Ages. Protestantism as a whole did not favor such enthusiasm, however, and it often suppressed any expressions of Christianity that would seek to revive spiritual gifts. The histories of the Anabaptist, Quaker, and Irvingite movements are cases in point. It took new revival movements in the nineteenth century (especially of the Methodist and Holiness type) and movements among other radical Protestants who espoused similar ideas, to stimulate a restoration of spiritual gifts to accompany a missionary thrust believed to be at the end of time. The many and various revival movements at the start of the twentieth century had the effect of creating a greater air of expectancy for worldwide Pentecostal revival before the imminent return of Christ. The signs that this revival had come would be similar to the earlier revivals: an intense desire to pray, emotional confessions of sins, manifestations of the coming of the Spirit, successful and accelerated evangelism and world mission, and especially spiritual gifts to confirm that the power of the Spirit had indeed come.

Key to understanding the globalization process in early Pentecostalism was the role of the periodicals. There were at least three features of this process. First, the early periodicals were sent all over the world and provided the mass media for the spread of Pentecostal ideas. Second, they also formed the social structures that were necessary during this time of creative chaos, when the only form of missionary organization was often linked to the support engendered by these periodicals. International travel was an increasing feature of the early missionaries and their networks and conferences were the means by which their message spread. One cannot read these different early periodicals without noticing how frequently a relatively small number of the same Pentecostal missionaries are referred to in all the periodicals. Division and schism were to come later; but the periodicals promoted a unity of purpose and vision that has since been lost.

Third, this internationalism, this global meta-culture of Pentecostalism, was evident in these years through the influence of both the periodicals and the missionary networks. In the beginning, the missionary networks like those of A. B. Simpson's Christian and Missionary Alliance (CMA) were essential for the spread of Pentecostal ideas. The CMA was open to Pentecostal beliefs at least until estrangement occurred over the new Pentecostal dogmatism over tongues in 1915, when longtime CMA missionary in China, William W. Simpson, resigned.[2] Azusa Street missionaries Alfred G. and Lillian Garr arrived in Calcutta in December 1906 and immediately began sharing their Pentecostal teaching with experienced missionaries.[3] Those who received Spirit baptism Pentecostal style began to spread it within their missionary networks and ultimately to their indigenous leaders. The periodicals were distributed free of charge to the missionaries and played their part in standardizing a Pentecostal meta-culture. At the same time, Pentecostal missionaries like William Burton in the Congo saw the globalization that occurred by which native peoples were adopting western ways as "a marvelous, an unparalleled opportunity for presenting the realities of Christ" to replace the now discarded old beliefs in witchcraft, fetishes, and charms.[4] André Droogers has outlined three broad but common features of transnational Pentecostalism that help us understand the ideology that makes Pentecostals feel part of a global community or meta-culture. These features are: (1) the central emphasis on the experience of the Spirit, accompanied by ecstatic manifestations like speaking in tongues; (2) the "born again" or conversion experience that accompanies acceptance into a Pentecostal community; and (3) the dualistic worldview that distinguishes between the "world" and the "church," between the "devil" and the "divine," between "sickness" and "health."[5] These three common features of a Pentecostal meta-culture have been with the movement from its start and can be traced throughout its history.

Multidimensional Global Pentecostalism

From its beginnings, Pentecostalism throughout the world is both transnational and migratory, or "missionary," in its fundamental nature. Its earliest propagators at the start of the twentieth century were individuals driven by an ideology that sent them from North America and Western Europe to Eastern Europe, Asia, Africa, Latin America, and various islands of the world within a remarkably short period of time. A particular ideology of migration and transnationalism has been a common feature of all types of Pentecostalism. In these migratory processes the various movements remain stubbornly consistent, for they see the "world" as a hostile place to move into and "possess" for Christ. Transnationalism and migration do not affect the essential character of Pentecostalism, even though its adherents have to steer a precarious course between contradictory forms of identity resulting from the migratory experience. Pentecostalism developed its own characteristics and identities in different parts of the world during the twentieth century without losing its transnational connections and international networks. The widespread use of the mass media, the setting up of new networks that often incorporate the word "international" in their title, frequent conferences with international speakers that reinforce transnationalism, and the growth of churches that provide total environments for members and international connections are all features of this multidimensional Pentecostalism, which promotes this Charismatic global meta-culture constantly.[6]

Early Pentecostal missionaries were obsessed with a crusading mentality that saw their task of bringing "light" to "darkness," who frequently referred in their newsletters to the "objects" of their mission as "the heathen," and who were often slow to recognize national leadership when it arose with creative alternatives to western forms of Pentecostalism.[7] Missionary paternalism, even if it was "benevolent" paternalism, was widely practiced, perhaps universally so. In country after country, white Pentecostals abandoned their egalitarian roots and followed the example of other expatriate missionaries in this regard. They kept tight control of churches and their national founders, and especially of the finances they raised in Western Europe and North America. Most wrote home believing that they were mainly (if not solely) responsible for the progress of the Pentecostal work in the countries to which they had gone. These actions were often prompted by an unconscious imperialist attitude on the part of white missionaries who were convinced of the innate superiority of their own European and Euro-American civilization. The truth was often that the national churches grew in spite of (and not because of) these missionaries, who were actually denying their converts gifts of leadership. But the Holy Spirit was anointing ordinary people to "spread the fire" to their friends, relatives, neighbors, and even to other communities, peoples, and nations. These early missionaries were certainly no angels on assignment. Sometimes western Pentecostal missionaries were patronizing and impolite about the people they were "serving" and on a few occasions their racism was blatant. It is probably not so remarkable that some of these racist comments were published in Pentecostal periodicals without disclaimer. In spite of these weaknesses and failures, the exploits of western missionaries were certainly impressive, and it cannot be assumed that all of them were bigoted racists. Their sacrificial efforts and (in most cases) their selfless dedication were admirable, and many laid down their lives through the ravages of tropical disease and, in some cases, through martyrdom. They were often very successful in adapting to extremely difficult circumstances; and many showed a servant heart and genuine love for the people they worked with. They achieved much against what was sometimes overwhelming odds. The so-called "native workers" also had qualities of dedication, courage in the face of stiff opposition, and selfless love for the people they were serving and reaching out to. But we cannot ignore the clear evidence that some of the missionaries supposedly responsible for the spread of the Pentecostal gospel throughout the world were by no means exemplary.

Although Pentecostals have been around for only a century, today they are among the most significant role players in Christian missions, with perhaps three-quarters of them in the Majority World. The Pentecostal jump from the first to the last decade of the twentieth century has been an enormous one, and it is important to understand the historical process involved. According to the statistics of Johnson, Barrett, and Crossing, in 2011 64% of the world's Christians (1,396 million) were in Asia, Africa, Latin America, and Oceania, while those of the two northern continents (including Russia) constituted only 36%. When this is compared to 1900, when 82% of the world Christian population was found in Europe and North America, we have dramatic evidence of how rapidly the western share of world Christianity has decreased during the twentieth century. According to these statisticians, if present trends continue, 69% of the world's Christians will live in the South by 2025.[8] In the Pew Forum's *Spirit and Power* study, conducted in 2006, it was discovered that in all the countries surveyed, Pentecostalism constituted a very significant percentage of Christianity. In six of the countries Pentecostals and Charismatics were over 60% of all Protestants. In Brazil, Guatemala, Kenya, South Africa, and the Philippines, they constituted over a third of the total population—in Guatemala and Kenya it was over half.[9]

But it is not only in terms of overall numbers that there have been fundamental changes. Christianity is growing most often in Charismatic forms, and many of these are independent of both western "mainline" Protestant and "classical Pentecostal" denominations and missions. What Andrew Walls describes as the "southward swing of the Christian center of gravity" is possibly more evident in Pentecostalism than in other forms of Christianity.[10] In 2000 Barrett and company estimated a total of 523 million, or 28% of all Christians, to be Pentecostal and Charismatic. This number is divided into four groups: (1) 18 million "peripheral quasi-Pentecostals," 3% of the total; (2) 66 million "denominational Pentecostals," 12%; (3) 176 million "Charismatics" (including 105 million Catholics), 32%; and (4) the largest group of 295 million

"Neocharismatics (Independents, Postdenominationalists)," a massive 53% of the total.[11] Of course these figures are controversial,[12] but nevertheless they give an indication that something highly significant is taking place in the global complexity of Christianity as a whole and of multidimensional Pentecostalism in particular.

The terms "Pentecostals" and "Pentecostalism" signify this multidimensional variety of movements where the emphasis is on receiving the Spirit and practicing spiritual gifts, especially prophesying, healing, and speaking in tongues. This includes what eventually became Pentecostal denominations, Charismatic renewal groups in the older churches, and a wide range of independent churches—over half the numbers in Barrett's statistics. However we interpret these figures or the categories, we need to acknowledge the multidimensional diversity in Pentecostalism. This has amounted to a twentieth-century reformation of Christianity that has precipitated a resurgent interest in pneumatology and spirituality. Whereas older Protestant churches have bemoaned their ever-decreasing membership and possible demise in the West in the early twenty-first century, a most dramatic church growth continues to take place in Pentecostal and independent Charismatic churches, especially outside the western world. During the 1990s, it was estimated that the Majority World mission movement had grown at seventeen times the rate of western missions.[13] Countries like South Korea, Nigeria, Brazil, and India have become major Christian missionary-sending nations, many of whose missionaries are Pentecostal. Half the world's Christians today live in developing, poor countries, where forms of Christianity are very different from those of western Christianity. These Christians have been profoundly affected by several factors, including the desire to have a more contextual and culturally relevant form of Christianity, the rise of nationalism, a reaction to what are perceived as "colonial" and foreign forms of Christianity, and the burgeoning Charismatic renewal. These factors play a major role in the formation of independent churches throughout the world.

Multiple Origins of Global Pentecostalism

With regard to the origins of global Pentecostalism, the following are what I regard as four important central assumptions. These are that: (1) the Azusa Street revival in the USA (1906–9) and the Mukti revival in India (1905–7) were equally part of a wider series of revivals at the beginning of the twentieth century that had significance in the early promotion of Pentecostal beliefs and values throughout the world; (2) the existing missionary networks, especially that of the CMA, were fundamental in spreading Pentecostalism internationally; (3) the Pentecostal periodicals that were posted to missionaries in the "field" were not only significant in spreading Pentecostalism internationally but were the foundation of the meta-culture that arose in global Pentecostalism in its earliest forms; and (4) the various centers and events in early Pentecostalism were part of a series of formative stages in the emergence of a new missionary movement that took several years to take on any distinctive identity.

The Azusa Street revival was undoubtedly the most significant of the early twentieth century revival centers in America that were formative in the process of creating a distinct Pentecostal identity. Azusa Street was also the main cause for the rapid internationalizing of American Pentecostalism.[14] But there were other similar movements at this time and even earlier,[15] the most noteworthy of which was the Mukti ("Salvation") revival in India (1905–7) under the famous Brahmin Christian woman Pandita Ramabai at her Mukti Mission near Pune. This revival lasted for a year and a half and resulted in 1,100 baptisms at Ramabai's school, confessions of sins and repentances, prolonged prayer meetings, and the witnessing of some seven hundred of these young women in teams into the surrounding areas, about a hundred going out daily and sometimes for as long as a month at a time. Ramabai formed what she called a "Bible school" of two hundred young women to pray in groups called "Praying Bands" and to be trained in witnessing to their faith. The Praying Bands spread the revival wherever they went and some remarkable healings were reported.[16]

This revival, in which these women also spoke in tongues before they had any knowledge of such occurrences at Azusa Street and elsewhere, had at least four far-reaching consequences. First, it is clear that Frank Bartleman, William Seymour (the African American leader of the Azusa Street revival), and other writers in the revival's periodical *The Apostolic Faith* saw the Indian revival as a precedent to the one in which they were involved—a sort of prototype, earlier Pentecostal revival that they thought had become "full-grown" in Los Angeles.[17] It is more likely, however, that Mukti and Azusa Street were simultaneous rather than sequential events in a general period of revival in the evangelical world accompanying the beginning of the century.

Second, women played a more prominent role in the Indian revival than in the American one—although by this I do not want to minimize the very significant role of women leaders in both the Azusa Street revival and in the early American missionary movement that issued from it.[18] But the fact that Ramabai was an Indian woman who resisted both patriarchal oppression in India and western domination in Christianity and was attracted to what a biographer calls "the gender-egalitarian impulse of Christianity," was even more significant.[19] Or as her assistant Minnie Abrams put it, Ramabai was "demonstrating to her countrymen that women have powers and capabilities which they have not permitted them to cultivate."[20] The Mukti revival was pre-eminently a revival among women and led by women, motivating and empowering those who had really been marginalized and cast out by society. This was another case of Pentecostalism's early social activism, empowering the marginalized and oppressed for service and bestowing dignity on women. In this the Mukti revival and Ramabai herself were pioneers within global Christianity and without precedent. This was to result in an unparalleled missionary outreach of Indian Christians into surrounding areas and further abroad. As one periodical observed, Ramabai's "Praying Bands" of young women were going "in every direction to scatter the fire that has filled their own souls" and the result was that "many parts of India are hearing of the true and living God."[21] A relatively untold story is that of how these women were an essential part of the early spread of Pentecostalism in North India.[22]

The third consequence was that both Ramabai in her ministry and the revival she led demonstrate an openness to other Christians, an ecumenicity and inclusiveness that stand in stark contrast to the rigid exclusivism of most subsequent Pentecostal movements. This was undoubtedly one result of the pluralistic context of India and Ramabai's indebtedness to her own cultural and religious training in Brahmin philosophy and national consciousness, despite her later Christian fundamentalism. The fourth consequence was its impact on Latin American Pentecostalism. Minnie Abrams, who worked under Ramabai and gave the first reports of the revival in Mukti, sent her friend and former Bible school classmate, May Louise Hoover in Valparaiso, Chile, a report of the revival contained in a booklet she wrote in 1906 titled *The Baptism of the Holy Ghost and Fire*. In its second edition later that year, the booklet included a discussion of the restoration of speaking in tongues (the first written Pentecostal theology of Spirit baptism), and thirty thousand copies were circulated widely. As a result of Abrams's booklet and her subsequent correspondence with the Hoovers, the Methodist churches in Valparaiso and Santiago were stirred to expect and pray for a similar revival, which began in 1909. Willis H. Hoover, who with his wife May Louise was a Methodist Episcopal missionary, became leader of the new Chilean Methodist Pentecostal Church that resulted out of those expelled from the Methodist church because of their Pentecostal experience. Chilean Pentecostalism has its roots in the Mukti revival and was specifically a Methodist revival that did not promote a doctrine of "initial evidence." An alternative to the "initial evidence" form of Pentecostalism was developing globally and Mukti was its earliest expression.[23] Mukti operated as a center for Pentecostalism, not only in India, for it was visited by scores of early Pentecostal traveling preachers and missionaries. The Mukti revival can legitimately be regarded with Azusa Street as one of the most important early formative centers of Pentecostalism.[24] Pentecostalism has always had revival centers for international pilgrimage—the Azusa Street Apostolic Faith and the Mukti Mission were the most prominent of the earliest ones, but there were several others both in North America and beyond.

The various revival movements in Mukti, Los Angeles, Valparaiso, and elsewhere were all part of a series of events that resulted in the emergence of global Pentecostalism. Missionaries from these various revival movements went out into faith missions and independent missions, some joining Holiness and radical evangelical organizations like the CMA, and then they became Pentecostal. The coming of the Spirit was linked to a belief that the last days had arrived and that the "full gospel" would be preached to all nations before the coming of the Lord. Considerations of religious pluralism, colonialism, and cultural sensitivity were not on the agenda of those who rushed out to the nations with this revivalist message believing that they had been enabled to speak those languages they needed for the task. The stage was set for the coming of a new Pentecost to spread across the world in the twentieth century. The means by which these Pentecostal fires would spread was a global network of these same faith missionaries and so-called "native workers" whose devotion to Christ and enthusiastic zeal were unrivalled by most of their contemporaries. The Pentecostalism emerging was essentially a missionary migratory movement of unprecedented vigor.

Pentecostalism and Independent Churches

Another very important aspect of early Pentecostal origins was the impact upon independent churches, especially in Africa, India, and China. The evidence in these regions that Pentecostalism converged with and strongly influenced the phenomenon of independency is incontrovertible. China was the largest of the early fields for Pentecostal missions. It has been estimated that there could have been as many as 150 expatriate Pentecostal missionaries there by 1915, and the emergence of the Assemblies of God in 1914 and the affiliation of the majority of these missionaries with them meant that by 1920 they were by far the largest Pentecostal body in China.[25] But even more significant was the fact that by that time there were already strong nationalist forces forming churches totally independent of western missions and developing a Pentecostal spirituality that was distinctively Chinese. These Chinese churches already formed the majority of Pentecostals by the time the expatriate missionaries were forced to leave China in 1949. Questions concerning how these churches differ from western-founded Pentecostal institutions and the extent of conscious or unconscious adaptation to the Chinese context require much more research. Pentecostalism, in its emphasis on the supernatural was in sync with Chinese folk religion, its offer of spiritual power to everyone regardless of status or achievements, and its deep suspicion of hierarchical and rationalistic Christianity, encouraged the development of new, anti-western independent churches. Resentment against western interference in Chinese affairs and patriotism increased during the 1920s, which was when most of these churches began. Pentecostal missionaries were unwittingly drawn into this process. W. W. Simpson was in contact with Chinese independent churches in Manchuria and made pleas for more missionaries to come to China to work with them, and other Pentecostal missionaries frequently interacted with Chinese independent churches in this period. Their policy of creating self-supporting Chinese churches assisted in developing independency. A missionary writing from Taiyuan in Shanxi wrote of a strong Pentecostal church he visited that was started in 1914 and was run completely by Chinese leaders with four full-time workers.[26] As Deng Zhaoming has pointed out, independent Chinese Pentecostalism had both foreign and domestic influences in its formation. Pentecostal missionaries from the West brought their teachings of divine healing (although not a new idea for some Chinese Christians) and speaking in tongues. At the same time there was a strong anti-western and nationalistic feeling in China at the beginning of the twentieth century, causing many newly emerging Chinese Christian groups to distance themselves from western missionaries.[27] The two largest Chinese Pentecostal denominations to arise during this period were the True Jesus Church and the Jesus Family, both of which came under these two influences. They are still active in China today: the True Jesus Church (being Oneness and Seventh-Day) is the largest Protestant denomination in China, and the Jesus Family set up separate living and self-supporting communities after the model of an Assemblies of God mission in Taiyuan, Shandong, under the American missionaries converted to Pentecostalism in China, the Anglins.[28]

In South India, several Indian preachers associated with American Pentecostal missionary Robert F. Cook were instrumental in starting independent Pentecostal churches there. K. E. Abraham joined Cook in 1923, was ordained by Ramankutty Paul of the Ceylon Pentecostal Mission in 1930, and he founded the Indian Pentecostal Church of God in 1934, now (with the Assemblies of God) one of the two largest Pentecostal denominations in India.[29] The Ceylon Pentecostal Mission (now The Pentecostal Mission) is a unique church that encourages celibacy for its pastors and community living for its members.[30] De Alwis was an early convert in Sri Lanka, receiving Spirit baptism in 1912, preparing for the coming of American missionary W. D. Grier to Colombo in 1913 and becoming his main coworker, taking charge of his work in Peradeniya in 1915.[31] Some have suggested that Pentecostalism in Sri Lanka began with the Danish actress Anna Lewini and former British soldier in India Walter Clifford, who arrived in Colombo in 1919 and 1923 respectively. From their work evolved the Assemblies of God and the Pentecostal Mission of de Alwis and Paul founded in 1921. It is also suggested that the de Alwis family became Pentecostals as a result of Clifford's healing services, whereas de Alwis had already been a Pentecostal for at least ten years prior to these meetings.[32] This is an early example of the many places where a careful reconstruction of Pentecostal history is necessary.[33]

The pressures of religious change occurring in colonial Africa at the end of the nineteenth century resulted in many movements of resistance. The "Ethiopian" independent churches in southern Africa and the "African" churches in West Africa were not as much movements of religious reform and innovation as were the later "prophet-healing" churches, but were primarily movements of political protest, expressions of resistance against European hegemony in the church. Although they rejected the political dominance of white-led churches, they framed their protest in familiar Protestant categories and therefore did not seriously contest its social, religious, and cultural components.[34] They were the first to overtly challenge social structures of inequality and oppression in the church and to give a religious ideology for the dignity and self-reliance of the black person—thus foreshadowing the African nationalist movements and forming a religious justification for them. These secessions were often the result of tension between an increasingly self-aware African Christian community and a multiplying number of zealous European missionaries with colonial expansionist sympathies. The secessions that began in South Africa and Nigeria were to set a pattern for the next century. Secession was not a peculiarly African phenomenon, as Africans were simply continuing what had become commonplace in European Protestantism. By the end of the nineteenth century there were already hundreds of new denominations, "faith missions," and other mission societies springing up in the West, from where missionaries were sent to Africa. These multiplied denominations and societies were reproduced there, and it is hardly surprising that it was considered quite a natural thing for secessions to occur—urged on by the mission policies and colonial politics of the time that were highly prejudicial to Africans.[35] The Freedom Charter that marked the creation of the African National Congress in South Africa in 1912 had several prominent Ethiopian church leaders as signatories. These churches were also seeking to make Christianity more African and therefore more appealing and relevant for ordinary people.

The entrance of Pentecostalism into the African melting pot of a multitude of new denominations and mission agencies had the effect of stimulating more radically transforming forms of independent churches. The "African" and

"Ethiopian" churches were overshadowed in the early twentieth century by new, rapidly growing "prophet-healing" or "churches of the Spirit"—so named because of their emphasis on the power of the Spirit in healing, prophesying, and speaking in tongues. Along the West African coast, churches associated with the Liberian prophet William Wade Harris and the Nigerian Garrick Sokari Braide emerged. They were later followed by churches known by the Yoruba term "Aladura" ("owners of prayer") from the 1920s onward in southwestern Nigeria, where the emphasis was on prayer for healing. The revival movements that began in West Africa in the 1910s and 1920s had few, if any, connections with Pentecostalism in the North, and there is evidence that spiritual gifts including speaking in tongues were being practiced in this region long before western Pentecostal missionaries arrived. It was the African leaders of revival and healing movements in Ghana and Nigeria that first invited British Pentecostal missionaries there in the 1930s.[36]

The existence of large and strong independent churches in southern Africa today has much to do with early Pentecostal missions. There are indications that Pentecostal missionaries tapped into a new phenomenon that was particularly strong in South Africa. One of them, American Pentecostal Jacob Lehman, wrote of a whole tribal community in the northwest of the country that had, with their chief, seceded from "a certain missionary society" because of the highhandedness and exploitation of the missionaries. The reference is obscure, but he may have meant the event in 1885, when Tswana chief Kgantlapane helped found a church seceding from the London Missionary Society in Taung, Botswana, called the Native Independent Congregational Church. Near Middelburg, Transvaal, Lehman and his fellow missionaries held services to welcome a group of secessionists into the Pentecostal fold and John G. Lake, the Canadian evangelist who first brought North American Pentecostalism to South Africa, visited an "Ethiopian" church conference that was seeking affiliation with his Apostolic Faith Mission (AFM). Lake wrote of a "native missionary," Paul Mabiletsa, who told Lake about a paralyzed woman healed through prayer in the Germiston district. Mabiletsa founded the Apostolic Church in Zion in 1920, to become one of the larger Zionist churches whose leadership remained in the Mabiletsa family throughout the twentieth century. Lake himself reported that twenty-four "native Catholic churches" and "five large Ethiopian churches" had decided to affiliate with the AFM in 1910 and that the "African Catholic Church" with seventy-eight preachers joined in January 1911. Again in 1911 the "Ethiopian Church" affiliated with Modred Powell, a British missionary, to become the Apostolic Faith Church of South Africa. Clearly, many of the early Pentecostal "converts" in South Africa were already members of Christian churches, especially African independent ones.[37] But the flow went both ways—by 1915 there were several secessions from the Pentecostals, especially from the AFM. Azusa Street missionary Henry Turney complained of African women who had "risen up refusing to acknowledge any authority in the church" and who were now "trying to establish a church of their own, with a native as leader."[38] There is little doubt that many of the secessions which occurred early in western Pentecostal mission efforts in Africa, China, India, and elsewhere were at least partly the result of cultural and social insensitivities on the part of the missionaries, and in some cases there was racism, ethnocentrism, and ethical failure. It is true that missionaries may not have been sensitized to these issues in the ways that we are today and equally true that we now have the hindsight of history—although neither sensitization nor hindsight seems to have changed contemporary human prejudice.

It is important to note the role of Pentecostalism and expatriate Pentecostal missionaries in the early years of African, Indian, and Chinese independency and the links with some of its most significant leaders. This was a form of Pentecostalism that differed considerably from western forms and even from region to region. The Zion Christian Church is the largest denomination in South Africa, and independent "Zionist" and "Apostolic" churches together form the largest grouping of Christians in that country today. Although many of the independent churches may no longer be described as "Pentecostal" without further qualification, the most characteristic features of their theology and praxis is overwhelmingly Pentecostal and, in the case of southern Africa, also influenced by the Zionist movement of John Alexander Dowie, a controversial healer at Zion City, Chicago, at the beginning of the twentieth century. Healing, prophesying, speaking in tongues, baptism by immersion (usually threefold), and even the rejection of medicine and the eating of pork are some of these features that remain among these African churches. Whatever their motivation might have been, Pentecostal missions were unwitting catalysts for a much larger movement of the Spirit that was to dominate African Christianity for the rest of the twentieth century. Although these Zionist and Apostolic churches have gradually increased the distance between themselves and "classical" Pentecostalism in liturgy and practice, their growth and proliferation are further evidence of the rapidly "spreading fires" of the Spirit in Africa and deserve to be accounted for in any historical research on Pentecostalism.

There are several aspects of Pentecostal origins that require further research. Historians speak of the need to formulate a new history written in deliberate reaction to traditional history and its paradigms, a history concerned with the whole of human activity, "history from below" rather than "history from above," history taken from the perspective of the poor and powerless rather than from that of the rich and powerful. So in the writing of

Pentecostal history there needs to be "affirmative action" to redress the balance, where the contribution of national workers, pastors, and evangelists is emphasized rather than that of foreign missionaries. Scholars, especially outside the western world, must plumb the depths of oral histories and written archives to illuminate that which has been concealed or unknown for so long. Consequently, the work of western missionaries who came from countries of power and wrote newsletters for their own specific purposes is put into correct perspective. We cannot ignore the failings of these missionaries and give exaggerated importance to those whose role was often catalytic rather than central. Asia, Africa, and Latin America have their own Christian heroes who should be more visible in the writing of Pentecostal histories. Information on western missionaries to Africa, Asia, the Pacific, the Caribbean, and Latin America is disproportionate to their role and contribution, mainly through the scarcity of written information on national leaders. A serious and extensive revision of global Pentecostal history needs to be done in which the enormous contributions of these pioneers is properly recognized, so that some classical Pentecostals in particular shed their assumption that Pentecostalism is a made-in-the-USA product that has been exported to the rest of the world. The revising of the history of Pentecostalism in the twenty-first century should be undertaken, not by emphasizing the missionary "heroes" of the powerful and wealthy nations of the world, but by giving a voice to the people living in the world's most marginalized parts. We can listen to the "margins" by allowing the hitherto voiceless and often nameless ones to speak, if that is ever really possible. We can recognize the contribution of those unsung Pentecostal laborers of the past who have been overlooked in the histories and hagiographies. Assumptions at the World Missionary Conference in Edinburgh in 1910 were that Christianity would not flourish without white missionary control.[39] Providentially, early Pentecostalism gave the lie to that assumption and probably became the main contributor to the reshaping of Christianity itself from a predominantly western to a predominantly non-western phenomenon during the twentieth century.

The skew in Pentecostal historiography is partly because of the exoticization and marginalization of "the other" that has been prevalent in all western literature, creating Orientalism and colonialist or androcentric stereotypes. These stereotypes were usually unconsciously transferred onto the "subjects" of the missionary enterprise to create a distorted representation of them. The marginalization of women and national workers is also because most of the main sources used in the writing of these histories (early Pentecostal periodicals, reports of missionaries, and missionary letters) were originally written for home consumption and fundraising. If national workers were mentioned at all, it was usually as anonymous "native workers" or, at best, they were mentioned by a single name that does not clearly reveal their identity today. Their memory is now extremely difficult or impossible to retrieve. This is not only a problem in Pentecostal mission history, as Brian Stanley has pointed out, because at the beginning of the twentieth century the missionary movement as a whole was overwhelmingly "indigenous" in the areas of its greatest expansion, even though there was scant acknowledgment of this.[40] Yet because of its emphasis on the empowering ability of the Spirit to equip ordinary believers for missionary service without requiring prior academic qualifications, Pentecostalism was probably more dependent on "national workers" than any other missions were at the time.

The Missionary Nature of Pentecostalism

Pentecostalism has always been a global missionary movement in foundation and essence. It emerged with a firm conviction that the Spirit had been poured out in "signs and wonders" in order for the nations of the world to be reached for Christ before the end of the age. Its missionaries proclaimed a "full gospel" that included individual salvation, physical healing, personal holiness, baptism with the Spirit, and a life on the edge lived in expectation of the imminent return of Christ. For this message, its pioneers were prepared to lay down their lives and many of them did exactly that. These very human vessels of this "full gospel" cannot be emulated in many respects—especially when it came to attitudes to other religions and cultures and matters of race—but we should not throw out the baby with the bathwater. The selfless dedication and sacrifices in the face of immense difficulties of these courageous women and men can only be greatly admired. Without them we would be the poorer, and the composition of global Christianity today would certainly look very different and possibly even be in a state of permanent decline. We cannot fully understand the contemporary multidimensional plurality of global Pentecostalism without revisiting again their historical roots.

The extent to which globalization and migration have affected the shape of this very significant religious sector is something that requires a much more careful analysis than this chapter offers, but is surely an important task for future research. The shapes of the new Pentecostalisms that have emerged as a result of the globalization process, how they differ from the older networks of denominational Pentecostalism, and specifically what the features of this global shift of center to the South means for Pentecostalism have yet to be precisely analyzed. Another area for further investigation is the extent to which Pentecostalism has permeated and affected the beliefs, values, and practices of other Christians, seen especially in the popular Christianity that dominates public events like weddings and funerals. Only when these investigations have taken place will we be better able to understand those external forces that forge the religious identities of people in our contemporary societies and the increasingly important role of Pentecostalisms in this pluralistic world.

This chapter has pointed to some of the polynucleated origins, global orientations, inherent migrating tendencies, and the development of a global network in early Pentecostalism—diffuse yet united in focus and determination to expand throughout the world. The concept of a global meta-culture outlined here must not detract from the fact that contemporary Pentecostalism is multidimensional. The seeds of proliferation and variety were sown at this early stage, contributing to the formation of the contemporary multidimensional global movement that is still a religious force of extreme significance in the twenty-first century.

NOTES

1. Allan H. Anderson, *Spreading Fires: The Missionary Nature of Early Pentecostalism* (London: SCM & Maryknoll, NY: Orbis, 2007), 288.
2. Paul L. King, *Genuine Gold: The Cautiously Charismatic Story of the Early Christian and Missionary Alliance* (Tulsa, OK: Word and Spirit Press, 2006), 151–60; Anderson, *Spreading Fires*, 130–33.
3. Anderson, *Spreading Fires*, 89–90.
4. Max Wood Moorhead (ed.), *Missionary Pioneering in Congo Forests: A Narrative of the Labours of William F. Burton and his Companions in the Native Villages of Luba-land* (Preston, UK: R. Seed & Sons, 1922), 81–82.
5. André Droogers, "Globalisation and Pentecostal Success," in André Corten & Ruth Marshall-Fratani (eds.), *Between Babel and Pentecost: Transnational Pentecostalism in Africa and Latin America* (Bloomington: Indiana University Press, 2001), 44–46.
6. Simon Coleman, *The Globalisation of Charismatic Christianity: Spreading the Gospel of Prosperity* (Cambridge: Cambridge University Press, 2000), 65–71.
7. *Confidence* 1:2 (May 1908), 19; 2:5 (May 1909), 110.
8. Todd M. Johnson, David B. Barrett, & Peter F. Crossing, "Christianity 2011: Martyrs and the Resurgence of Religion," *International Bulletin of Missionary Research* 35:1 (2011), 29.
9. Pew Forum on Religion and Public Life, *Spirit and Power: A 10-Country Survey of Pentecostals* (Washington, D.C: Pew Research Center, 2006), http://pewforum.org/surveys/pentecostal/, accessed 3 August 2007.
10. Andrew F. Walls, "Of Ivory Towers and Ashrams: Some Reflections on Theological Scholarship in Africa," *Journal of African Christian Thought* 3:1 (June 2000), 1.
11. David B. Barrett, Todd M. Johnson, & Peter F. Crossing, "Missiometrics 2006: Goals, Resources, Doctrines of the 350 Christian World Communions," *International Bulletin of Missionary Research* 30:1 (2006), 28; Stanley M. Burgess (ed.), *New International Dictionary of Pentecostal and Charismatic Movements* (Grand Rapids, MI: Zondervan, 2002), 286–87.
12. Allan H. Anderson, "Varieties, Taxonomies, and Definitions," in Allan Anderson and others, *Studying Global Pentecostalism: Theories and Methods* (Berkeley: University of California Press, 2010), 13–14.
13. Michael Jaffarian, "Are There More Non-western Missionaries than Western Missionaries?," *International Bulletin of Missionary Research* 28:3 (July 2004), 132.
14. Cecil M. Robeck, Jr., *The Azusa Street Mission and Revival: The Birth of the Global Pentecostal Movement* (Nashville, TN: Nelson, 2006).

15. Allan H. Anderson, *To the Ends of the Earth: Pentecostalism and the Transformation of World Christianity* (New York: Oxford University Press, 2013), 11–36.
16. *Word & Work* 28:4 (Apr 1906), 16; *Trust* 9:8 (Oct 1910), 12–13.
17. Frank Bartleman, *Azusa Street* (S. Plainfield, NJ: Bridge Publishing, [1925] 1980), 19, 90.
18. Estrelda Alexander, *The Women of Azusa* Street (Cleveland, TN: Pilgrim Press, 2006); Robeck, *Azusa Street Mission*.
19. Meera Kosambi (ed. & trans.), *Pandita Ramabai through Her Own Words: Selected Works* (New Delhi: Oxford University Press, 2000), 18.
20. *Triumphs of Faith* 31:1 (Jan 1911), 5.
21. *Word & Work* 28:5 (May 1906), 145.
22. Anderson, *Spreading Fires*, 98–101.
23. *Pentecost* 2:11–12 (Nov-Dec 1910), 9; *Latter Rain Evangel* 3:7 (Apr 1911), 19; *Bridegroom's Messenger* 126 (1 Feb 1913), 1.
24. A full account of the Mukti revival can be found in Anderson, *Spreading Fires*, 77–89; cf. Gary B. McGee, "'Latter Rain' Falling in the East: Early-Twentieth-Century Pentecostalism in India and the Debate over Speaking in Tongues," *Church History* 68:3 (1999), 651, 656–57, 664.
25. *Trust* 19:3 (May 1920), 11.
26. *Triumphs of Faith* 35:2 (Feb 1915), 47; *Word & Work* 37:3 (Mar 1915), 92–93; *Christian Evangel* 73 (9 Jan 1915), 4; 77 (13 Feb 1915), 1; *Weekly Evangel* 202 (11 Aug 1917), 12; 204 (25 Aug 1917), 12.
27. Deng Zhaoming, "Indigenous Chinese Pentecostal Denominations," in Allan Anderson & Edmond Tang (eds.), *Asian and Pentecostal: The Charismatic Face of Christianity in Asia* (Oxford: Regnum, 2011), 371.
28. Deng, "Indigenous Chinese," 372–93; Anderson, *Spreading Fires*, 136, 137; *Triumphs of Faith* 37:6 (June 1917), 127; *Latter Rain Evangel* 11:3 (Dec 1917), 16.
29. *Confidence* 6:1 (Jan 1913), 20; *Word & Work* 36:6 (June 1914), 187; 36:10 (Oct 1914), 316; 36:11 (Nov 1914), 349–50; 42:1 (Jan 1920), 14, 20; 42:6 (June 1920), 13; *Christian Evangel* 56 (29 Aug 1914), 4; *Word & Witness* 12:5 (May 1915), 6.
30. *Word & Witness* 9:1 (Jan 1913), 2; 9:11 (Nov 1913), 4; 9:12 (Dec 1913), 1; 10:4 (Apr 1914), 4; 12:5 (May 1915), 7; *Bridegroom's Messenger* 144 (15 Nov 1913), 1; *Christian Evangel* 70 (12 Dec 1914), 4; *Weekly Evangel* 91 (22 May 1915), 4.
31. *Weekly Evangel* 145 (24 June 1916), 11; 186 (21 Apr 1917), 12.
32. *Word and Witness* 9:1 (Jan 1913), 2; 9:11 (Nov 1913), 4; 9:12 (Dec 1913), 1; 10:4 (Apr 1914), 4; 12:5 (May 1915), 7; *Bridegroom's Messenger* 144 (15 Nov 1913), 1; *Christian Evangel* 70 (12 Dec 1914), 4; *Weekly Evangel* 91 (22 May 1915), 4; G. P. V. Somaratna, *Origins of the Pentecostal Mission in Sri Lanka* (Marihana-Nugegoda: Margaya Fellowship of Sri Lanka, 1996), 12–23, 27–32, 41, 45–47.
33. Michael Bergunder, *The South Indian Pentecostal Movement in the Twentieth Century* (Grand Rapids, MI: Eerdmans, 2008).
34. Jean Comaroff, *Body of Power, Spirit of Resistance: The Culture and History of a South African People* (Chicago: University of Chicago Press, 1985), 176.
35. Adrian Hastings, *The Church in Africa 1450–1950* (Oxford: Clarendon, 1994), 499.
36. Anderson, *To the Ends*, chapter 7.
37. *Bridegroom's Messenger* 52 (15 Dec 1909), 4; *Upper Room* 1:10 (May 1910), 6; 2:2 (Sept–Oct 1910), 3; 2:4 (Jan 1911), 6, 8; 2:5 (May 1911), 6; *Confidence* 4:12 (Dec 1911), 284; Allan H. Anderson, *African Reformation: African Initiated Christianity in the 20th Century* (Trenton, NJ & Asmara, Eritrea: Africa World Press, 2001), 97.
38. *Weekly Evangel* 124 (22 Jan 1916), 13.
39. Brian Stanley, "Twentieth Century World Christianity: A Perspective from the History of Missions," in Donald M. Lewis (ed.), *Christianity Reborn: The Global Expansion of Evangelicalism in the Twentieth Century* (Grand Rapids, MI: Eerdmans, 2004), 77.
40. Stanley, "Twentieth Century World Christianity," 71–72.

2

Launching a Global Movement: The Role of Azusa Street in Pentecostalism's Growth and Expansion

CECIL M. ROBECK, JR.

Setting the Stage

Holy Roller religion! That is what outsiders called the worship that took place within the walls of the Azusa Street Mission, the worship that spread like wildfire to the communities that surrounded Los Angeles as worshippers from the Mission clambered aboard local streetcars, turning them into makeshift pulpits while they rode to their next preaching point. The term "Holy Roller religion" conjured up visions of freewheeling ecstasy, unbridled emotionalism, seething spirituality, fanatical abandonment, high-voltage antics, and for many more reserved worshippers, general pandemonium. The sweat-drenched passion of the "Holy Rollers" was easily visualized, quickly given over to stereotype and ridicule, and often dismissed just as quickly because it was thought to hold nothing more than cheap, vulgar, primitive entertainment value for the run-of-the-mill observer.

Holy Roller religion! The pejorative names given to the people of the Azusa Street Mission by the press seemed endless, and "Holy Roller" was just one of them. During its first year the Mission endured stifling heat, the stench of rancid sweat, and a plague of flies. Noise levels were often deafening, keeping neighbors awake for blocks around. Yet a racial assortment of people such as Los Angeles had not seen before flocked to the Mission by the hundreds. Those who came to worship, stayed to sing, pray, weep, testify, preach, prophesy, heal, speak or sing in tongues, shout, jump, dance, fall or roll on the floor, and experience trance-like states. "Holy Rollers!" That's what they were.

Others came only for the show. As a reporter described it after one evening visit,

> All classes of people gathered in the temple last night.
>
> There were big Negroes looking for a fight, there were little fairies dressed in dainty chiffon who stood on the benches and looked on with questioning wonder in their baby-blue eyes.
>
> There were cappers from North Alameda Street, and sedate dames from West Adams Street.
>
> There were all ages, sexes, colors, nationalities and previous conditions of servitude.
>
> The rambling old barn was filled and the rafters were so low that it was necessary to stick one's nose under the benches to get a breath of air.
>
> It was evident that nine out of every ten persons present were there for the purpose of new thrills. This was a new kind of show in which the admission was free—they don't even pass the hat at the Holy Rollers' meeting—and they wanted to see every act to the drop of the curtain.
>
> They stood on benches to do it. When a bench wasn't handy they stood on each other's feet.
>
> No choir led this gathering in song. Someone happened to want to sing a song and started it. Every one followed. If one didn't want to sing the song then on the program he sang some other one. It was all the same.
>
> No one in particular led in prayer. They all prayed. They all made different prayers and the confusion of tongues had the tower of Babel backed off the boards.[1]

Like most reporters and many visitors, from the perspective of insiders he missed the point. The phenomena were present in abundance, but such things were not what insiders viewed as the primary goal of their worship. These phenomena were little more than means to an end. They were there to meet God. They were intent upon encountering the Spirit of God. And they did so in order to gain what they viewed as "divine power" that they believed was necessary for them to be successful in the tasks of end-time evangelistic and missionary work.

Summing Up the First Decade

We believe that God's design in raising up the Apostolic Faith Church in America was to evangelize over these lands. As a proof hereof we have seen since 1906 that time of an extraordinary work of God extending throughout all the United States and Territories, and throughout the whole world.[2]

With these words, Pastor William J. Seymour summed up the first decade of existence for the Apostolic Faith Mission at 312 Azusa Street in Los Angeles, California.[3] It was not some hollow boast. By all accounts, its first years of existence had been extremely difficult. The Mission had been publicly criticized by the Los Angeles Church Federation as well as leaders of many of Los Angeles's congregations. It had been ridiculed regularly by the press. It had been threatened repeatedly with closure by law enforcement and other government officials. Some of its key figures had been arrested. Still, the number of evangelists and missionaries that went out from the Mission during this period was staggering!

As a result of the Mission's work, the number of congregations throughout North America and around the world that identified with the Pentecostal message had burgeoned during this first decade. Several existing Wesleyan-Holiness denominations, among them the Churches of God in Christ, the Free Will Baptists, the Church of God (Cleveland, TN), the Fire Baptized Holiness Church, and the Pentecostal Holiness Church, had all become Pentecostal denominations. New Pentecostal denominations such as the General Council of the Assemblies of God, the Pentecostal Assemblies of the World, and the Iglesia Apostólica de la Fe en Christo Jesús had also been formed. These and other organizations would soon provide a more or less cohesive institutional foundation to a movement very much in the making. Missionary agencies, such as the Pentecostal Missionary Union (1909), had come into existence on both sides of the Atlantic, assuring greater funding and collaboration among workers who, together with the thousands of others that would follow them, would come to influence what the Pew Foundation's survey of Pentecostals, *Spirit and Power*, has today called "renewalists," as many as 600,000,000 people worldwide in less than a century.[4]

While these basic facts are clear, and largely undisputed, considerable debate over the origins of the Pentecostal Movement is currently taking place in the field of Pentecostal historiography. The dust from these discussions has not yet settled. At least one scholar has argued that the movement began in Topeka, Kansas, in 1901 under the ministry of a white pastor, Charles Fox Parham.[5] Others have contended that there is no "Father" of the movement. One would either have to go back to the first Pentecost to find him,[6] or one could explain the origins of the movement as the result of spontaneous but connected interventions by God in the form of a network of regional revivals,[7] or one could cite a growing number of sources and stories emerging from different locations around the world that have previously been overlooked by historians.[8]

Other scholars have suggested that the Azusa Street Mission, with its African American pastor, is the real birthplace of the global Pentecostal Movement.[9] A couple of others have suggested that while the Azusa Street Mission may have had some role in the birth and spread of Pentecostalism, it has received far too much credit for what it actually accomplished. While the Azusa Street Mission has provided the most widely accepted "myth" for the movement's origins, the emergence of Pentecostalism elsewhere came into being independently.[10]

Regardless of where this debate finally ends, the superlative contribution that the Azusa Street Mission made to the growth and expansion of the earliest manifestations of the Pentecostal Movement cannot be ignored. It is premature to call for the dismissal of Azusa Street as having played a central, if not the preeminent role in the birth, growth, and spread of global Pentecostalism until we have a complete, accurate, and credibly documented telling of its story. That has not yet taken place.[11]

The location of the Azusa Street Mission in 1906 Los Angeles with the Port of San Pedro at the growing edge of the "Pacific Rim" gave it boundless opportunity for northward and westward expansion. And the recent arrival of several transcontinental railroad lines into Los Angeles provided the city with easy access to the east and beyond.[12].

One could liken what happened at the Mission to the perfect break in a billiard game. By December 1906, just eight months after the outbreak of the Azusa Street revival on April 9, "evangelists" who had been "baptized in the Holy Spirit" at the Azusa Street Mission had scattered in every direction like so many billiard balls. Wherever they went, they spoke to other people—in essence, tapping another ball—thereby passing along the word and often the experience to which they bore witness, and setting still others into motion. They went up and down the west coast of the United States. Pentecostal missions were soon established in San Diego, Riverside, San Bernardino, Santa Barbara, San Jose, Santa Rosa, Oakland, and San Francisco, California. They could be found in Salem, Eugene, and Portland, Oregon, and in Spokane and Seattle, Washington. And all of this came as a direct result of workers who went from the Azusa Street Mission beginning in August 1906.

By December 1906, workers had established missions or aided in the sometimes painful transformation of existing Holiness missions and congregations into this newly emerging Pentecostal Movement in a variety of cities across the United States, cities like Colorado Springs and Denver, Colorado; Alliance, Akron, Columbus, and Cleveland, Ohio; even New York City. They had also ventured into northern Mexico and southern Canada. By early 1907, they or those they had influenced had established Pentecostal missions and churches throughout the United States, in places like Dunn, North Carolina; Memphis and Chattanooga, Tennessee; Danville and Norfolk, Virginia; Chicago,

Illinois; Indianapolis, Indiana; Minneapolis, Minnesota; and in a number of smaller towns around these larger urban centers.

Beyond the Pacific or Atlantic shores, these evangelists, a growing group of missionaries, and those that they had influenced were also establishing missions and churches. By early 1907 the Mission had emissaries throughout Scandinavia, Britain, Germany, the Netherlands, Switzerland, Syria, Palestine, Lebanon, Liberia, Angola, India, China, Hong Kong, Macau, Malaysia, and Japan. By 1908 the movement had spread throughout the Caribbean. It had also established congregations in South Africa, Estonia, Latvia, Lithuania, Poland, Ukraine, Belarus, and Russia. By 1910, Pentecostal churches had also arrived in Argentina, Brazil, and Chile, and in every instance, it is possible to demonstrate that there was a substantial link with the Azusa Street Mission.

For too long, the stories of the Azusa Street Mission and its revival have reflected the denominational, cultural, racial, and ethnic biases of its historians. More recently, they have reflected biases that have constructed the current norms of political correctness in certain guilds. Even the historian of *California's Spiritual Frontiers* during this period, who wrote an otherwise excellent book, consciously ignored the impact of this revival, claiming that the Azusa Street Mission had "little long-term impact on its region."[13] It has taken an entire century to come anywhere close to telling the story of "Azusa Street" in a way that begins to take seriously the larger social, political, and ecclesial contexts out of which it emerged.[14]

From his perspective, Pastor Seymour viewed *the single purpose* of the Mission, in fact, of the entire "Apostolic Faith" people, as evangelization—the evangelization of the entire world. During that decade (1906–1915), Seymour had witnessed the teachings of the "Apostolic Faith," including the call to personal repentance and faith, the pursuit of personal and corporate holiness, and the quest for and acceptance of power for ministry through the baptism in the Holy Spirit, become the basic message of hundreds of pastors, evangelists, missionaries, and congregations across North America, Europe, Africa, Asia, and Latin America.

During this same decade, the Azusa Street Mission probably commissioned and sent more missionaries abroad than any other single congregation in the Pentecostal Movement. Using the Mission's more or less regular publication, *The Apostolic Faith*, Seymour attempted to fill the needs of evangelists and especially of foreign missionaries as they sailed around the world.[15] The initial funding of the missionaries may have been sufficient only to purchase one-way tickets to their respective fields of ministry, but Seymour kept their needs before the newspaper's readers and he used *The Apostolic Faith* to raise funds for them and to broker ongoing communication between the missionaries, their supporters, and the Mission.

Thus, the transformation of several Wesleyan-Holiness denominations into Pentecostal ones, the development of new Pentecostal denominations, the emergence of scores of new, and often independent, congregations across North America, and the extraordinary recruitment and sending of new Pentecostal missionaries sent by the this single congregation during its first decade of existence, all bear witness to the substantial role that the Azusa Street Mission played in the formation of the movement. The fact that this story has been told so poorly, ignored, or treated as a relatively meaningless blip on the work of mainstream historians is curious to say the least. While the Azusa Street Mission may not in the end be viewed as providing the primary genesis for the worldwide Pentecostal Movement, its contribution remains unsurpassed during the first decade, and that fact needs to be acknowledged.

Establishing a Base of Believers

Several factors contributed to Azusa Street's unparalleled role in the establishment of global Pentecostalism. The first of these was the establishment of a congregational base. Pastor Seymour believed that everyone who came to the Azusa Street Mission had a reason for doing so. His job was to help people find answers to their spiritual quests by pointing them to God. He accomplished this primarily through a program that contained three simple steps. From the beginning, these steps were published in tract form and distributed freely to those who attended the Mission. Beginning with the initial issue of the Mission's newspaper, *The Apostolic Faith*, Seymour published these three steps in what amounted to the Mission's statement of faith for the newspaper's subscribers.[16]

The first step was what Seymour called justification. Sometimes described as the "first work of grace," it amounted to a moment when the seeker knelt before God in repentance, the seeker's sins were forgiven, and conversion took place. To show how important this act was, Seymour had arranged the congregation in a circle, with the pulpit and the altar, where all seekers initially knelt, at the very center of the sanctuary. While we do not have a specific count of all those who were converted at the Mission, the number was substantial, probably in the thousands. Pastor Seymour baptized at least 223 new converts in the waves of the Pacific between April and October 1906.[17] Over 100 more were baptized during the following summer in the Arroyo Seco Creek that runs between nearby Pasadena and downtown Los Angeles.[18] There is also evidence to suggest that other baptismal services took place during that same year and that as many as 400 to 500 new converts could be cited in the Mission's first year of existence.

From the perspective of the Azusa Street Mission, conversion brought about a kind of personal transformation that ultimately led to a second step called sanctification. But conversion itself was understood as a transformative event. New converts were expected to make past wrongs right if it was in their power to do so, that is, to admit past sins and make restitution. As the first number of the Mission's newspaper reported,

> The preaching of old time restitution is owned of the Lord. People have been paying up old debts, making wrongs right, getting hard feelings out of the way, etc. One who was saved from drink, confessed to crimes and offered himself to pay the penalty of the law. People living in adultery or where one party had a living husband or wife have separated, and God is wonderfully pouring out His Spirit on this line of things.[19]

This "second work of grace," called sanctification, drew upon John Wesley's teaching on Christian Perfection. It was said to make the believer holy, a position defended on the basis of such passages as John 17:15, 17; 1 Thessalonians 5:23; and Hebrews 12:14. Seymour believed that it was accomplished when the Holy Spirit cleansed the heart of the believer and removed the very root of sin. Evidence that a person had undergone this cleansing varied from the shedding of tears to shouting, but the most commonly accepted evidence was said to be the manifestation of "divine love" in the ongoing life of that individual. Many claimed not only to have been converted at the Mission, but also to have been sanctified. Others who had been previously converted also found their sanctification at the Mission. Still others from various Wesleyan-Holiness congregations came to the Mission during the revival because of this emphasis on "holiness." Thus, the numbers who went through the second stage of spiritual development as outlined by Seymour were larger than those who went through the initial process of conversion.

The findings of *Spirit and Power* on how "renewalists," especially Pentecostals, approach both moral and social issues today bear out the impact of the teaching on sanctification that has long been associated with these groups. Codes of conduct and definitions of "worldliness" are frequently found among Pentecostals even today. The emphasis that Pentecostals have placed on personal holiness among people who have often been redeemed from the dregs of society has tended to put special significance on the sanctity of sex and marriage.[20]

While the first step, justification or conversion, was shared by most Christians around the world, the second step, sanctification, was largely limited to those who followed the teachings of the Methodist Church and members of churches and associations of the Wesleyan-Holiness tradition or through the Keswick Movement, popular in evangelical Anglicanism and parts of the Holiness Movement in England and the United States.[21] But it was the third step in the Christian walk that was unique to the ministry of William J. Seymour and the Azusa Street Mission in 1906 Los Angeles.

Seymour contended that it was important for believers to have a life-transforming encounter with God in which they were baptized in the Holy Spirit. It was not considered a third work of grace, but rather, as "a gift of power upon the sanctified life."[22] That gift of power enabled recipients to enter fully into what might be described as the "apostolic life," a life that allowed them to do many of the things that the earliest apostles did, such as heal the sick, perform miracles, exorcise demons, and speak in languages that they had not learned. It also meant that recipients were mandated to take the message of salvation, holiness, and Pentecost wherever the Holy Spirit led them. Seymour understood and taught that the evidence that one had such an encounter was their ability to speak in other tongues, though their lives had to be tempered by "divine love" for it to be fully recognized.[23]

Seymour worked hard to lead hundreds, if not thousands, of people through this threefold sequence of spiritual development, a sequence that he firmly believed had been established in scripture. By taking this position, Seymour convinced ordinary people that they need not pursue ordinary means to participate in ministry, for it was God who had commissioned them to share their experience with others and lead them into their own encounter with God.

The number of people who visited the Mission each week during this important revival is difficult to ascertain, but there is sufficient evidence to suggest that while most services ran between 500 and 700 people, as many as 1,500 people were served by the Mission each week, making it the largest congregation in Los Angeles to be led by an African American.[24] In addition to this exploding base of new converts, there were two other factors at work that helped to spread the revival from Los Angeles.

Spreading of the Revival through the Press

The role of the Azusa Street Mission was enhanced by the coverage its meetings received in both the secular and religious press, even when it represented the worst of religious bias and yellow journalism. It attracted the attention of the people of Los Angeles and around the world. The Mission quickly learned that the press was a free form of advertising.[25] One man wrote to the Mission that it was the cartoons that had appeared in newspapers he read that had initially drawn him to the meetings. He went on to testify that he attended and "got a touch of heaven" in his soul.[26] Going by the written testimonies that have been preserved in the Mission's newspaper, he was typical of many who attended. The fact that a newspaper described the antics of the worshippers in well-crafted word pictures or in equally picturesque drawings was enough to draw a good crowd in the day of yellow journalism and without competition from radio or television.

From the first known and subtly titled article that introduced the Azusa Street Mission, "Weird Babel of Tongues," with subtitles that warned, "New Sect of Fanatics Is Breaking Loose," or gossiped, "Wild Scene Last Night on Azusa Street," and "Gurgle of Wordless Talk by a Sister," the die was cast.[27] Other equally titillating titles would follow. "Rolling and Diving Fanatics 'Confess'," clamored the *Times* three months later.[28] "'Holy Kickers' Baffle Police," it barked. "Hold High Carnival in Azusa Street until Midnight." "Authorities Put Stop to High Kicking Feats of Women but Have Not Been Able to Break Up Meetings." "Frenzied Woman Embraces Man on Street." These were the alluring subtitles designed to sell newspapers, the kind of headlines that grab the "inquiring minds" of tabloid readers even today.[29]

Similarly, the allegation made by the *Los Angeles Herald* that "it was evident that nine out of every ten persons present were there for the purpose of new thrills," was also sufficient to draw a crowd of thrill seekers.[30] If everyone was going to this free show, they might as well go, too. Many came to see for themselves what was being reported. As the writer quoted above put it, "they wanted to see every act to the drop of the curtain. They stood on benches to do it. When a bench wasn't handy they stood on each other's feet."[31]

In light of these facts, beginning in September 1906 William Seymour and a secretary with previous editorial experience in the Holiness Movement, Clara Lum, developed a more or less regular newspaper of their own, *The Apostolic Faith*. They began with the publication of 5,000 copies of the first issue, but by mid-1908 they were sending 50,000 copies to far-flung regions of the world.[32] They used *The Apostolic Faith* to spread the story of the revival, and through its pages a network of believers was brought into conversation with the Mission and with one another. People from across America and around the world began to write to the Mission, asking for prayer, sharing their testimonies, and documenting the spread of the revival from city to city and from nation to nation.

Among the hundreds who wrote in to *The Apostolic Faith* was a pastor from Cristiana (Oslo), Norway, the Reverend Thomas Ball Barratt. Barratt was a Methodist minister who had come to the United States while on a fundraising tour. His desire was to build a new center for social outreach among the marginalized of Norwegian society. He took a room at the Alliance House in New York City, operated by the Christian and Missionary Alliance, one of the existing networks of churches among which the Azusa Street revival had some success. It was there that he came across a copy of the first issue of *The Apostolic Faith*, published by the Azusa Street Mission in September 1906. After reading the story of what was taking place in Los Angeles, he wrote to the Mission inquiring about how he might receive the baptism in the Holy Spirit they were describing. Over several weeks Barratt corresponded with at least three members of the Azusa Street staff, and they encouraged him and advised him on what to do.[33]

In November 1906, Mrs. Lucy Leatherman, who had recently been baptized in the Spirit at the Azusa Street Mission, arrived in New York City. She, too, had ties to the Christian and Missionary Alliance, having attended the Alliance College in Nyack, New York. She was planning to go as a missionary to Jerusalem, but before she went, she would spend about six weeks coordinating the arrival of a number of Azusa Street missionaries from Los Angeles. Leaving Los Angeles at different times, and traveling across the country by different routes, they would gather in New York City in early December and then sail together to Liverpool England before going their separate ways.

When Barratt heard that Mrs. Leatherman had arrived from the Azusa Street Mission and that she had received the "Baptism of the Holy Ghost, and the gift of Tongues," Barratt quickly sought her out. She referred him to a friend, Maude Williams, who had just arrived from Zion, Illinois, with her Pentecostal testimony and had opened meetings in the city. Barratt did as instructed and attended one of Miss Williams's meetings. On Thursday, November 15, Barratt and Leatherman finally met, and with the aid of an unnamed Norwegian man, she laid hands on Pastor Barratt. Within a short time, Barratt was speaking "in a foreign language."[34] Now baptized in the Spirit, Barratt worshipped daily with the 13 newly arriving missionaries fresh from Azusa Street, several of whom were African Americans. Barratt joined them as they worshipped together in a small mission in the city in which three additional African Americans were recruited to join their venture.[35] On December 8, 1906, all of them, including Pastor Barratt, sailed on the *S.S. Campania* to Liverpool, England. Barratt returned to Norway, and in early 1907 he began to hold Pentecostal meetings in Cristiana. In short, the cue ball hit in Los Angeles had struck its next major subject in New York, Pastor Barratt. He would become the first significant propagator of the revival in Europe.

In early 1907, Barratt held well-advertised Pentecostal meetings in Christiana. Among those who attended, received the baptism in the Holy Spirit, and became Pentecostal leaders were Lewi Pethrus, who would lead the movement in Sweden for the next half century;[36] Alexander A. Boddy, the Anglican priest who would serve as the senior Pentecostal leader in England for the next decade;[37] and the Lutheran Pietist, Jonathan Paul, who would lead the movement in Germany.[38] In 1911, Barratt visited Finland, part of the

Russian Empire at that time and a territory then occupied by Russian troops. He preached in Kuopio, Viborg, Helsingfors (now Helsinki), Gamarfors, and Abo (now Turku). He went on to St. Petersburg, Russia, where in the course of three meetings he spoke to Russian, Swedish, Finnish, and Estonian Christians.[39] In a sense, the Barratt ball tapped these other Europeans, passing along the dynamism and legacy that he had received from the Azusa Street Mission.

While the impact of the Azusa Street revival was felt by Barratt first in the form of the Mission's press, it took on a human face with the arrival of Mrs. Leatherman. Barratt continued that human face by taking the message to Europe. Other Pentecostals, like Boddy and Paul on the Continent, had different experiences ranging from welcome to ridicule. Germans sought to distance themselves from the phenomena in Los Angeles because of the persecution they faced in the German press regarding the press's criticism of the Azusa Street revival. On the other hand, the English, Scandinavians, and ultimately the Dutch, through the work of the former Salvation Army officer, Gerrit Roelof Polman,[40] embraced the Azusa revival, developing ties with the Mission, especially through a series of Whitsuntide Conventions led by Father Alexander Boddy at his Anglican parish in Sunderland, England.[41]

Spreading of the Revival with the Aid of Seasoned Workers

The role of the Azusa Street Mission was further enhanced when those who were already active in Christian ministry made their pilgrimage to the Mission and experienced baptism in the Holy Spirit. Equipped and empowered through this experience, they often returned to their churches, which they subsequently led into the movement. Others left their previous places of ministry in order to establish new Pentecostal works.

In the list of over 500 names of Azusa Street participants that I have collected, roughly 200 of these people lived in Los Angeles or within a reasonable commuting distance from the Mission and may be counted as regular members of the Mission. Approximately 45% were African American, 45% were Anglo Americans, and 10% fell into other categories, the majority of which were Mexicans or Mexican American. Nearly all of the remaining 300 names are of Anglo Americans from outside the area who attended services, mainly because of reading about the revival in newspapers or hearing by word of mouth from others who had visited the Mission. Of the 500 names, nearly 30% were evangelists, pastors, missionaries, or were involved as a full-time Christian worker in some other form of ministry. In 1925, Frank Bartleman, a former Holiness preacher and mission worker who became the leading participant-observer of the Azusa Street meetings summarized it this way:

> It seemed that every one had to go to "Azusa." Missionaries were gathered there from Africa, India, and the islands of the sea. Preachers and workers had crossed the continent, and come from distant islands, with an irresistible drawing to Los Angeles. "Gather my saints together, etc."—Ps. 50:1–7. They had come up for "Pentecost," though they little realized it. It was God's call.[42]

While this may seem surprising on the surface, Christian workers who are in search of something more in their own spiritual walks often look to those places where it seems that something new or important is taking place. In fact, with all the news that swirled around what the Azusa Street Mission did or did not stand for, it was almost incumbent upon any credible pastor, especially within the Wesleyan-Holiness Movement, to have attended the Mission or read broadly enough to have formed an opinion about it.

In 1906 Los Angeles, this was exactly what happened. Even the Los Angeles Church Federation sent its president, Edward Ryland, pastor of Trinity Methodist Church, South, to investigate and report back to the Federation. His report was sympathetic to the missionary zeal of the Mission's participants, but he raised questions about other of the Mission's claims.[43] Ironically, his report provoked the Federation to take actions modeled on those of the Mission in order to counter the Mission's successes. The Federation churches soon held street meetings, added prayer and evangelistic services, and began a citywide campaign to enlist new members.[44] There were a number of local pastors and church leaders, however, who were not members of the Federation, who went to the Azusa Street Mission, joined in the worship services, were baptized in the Spirit, and cast their lot with the newly organizing Apostolic Faith Movement. Among those who came from elsewhere in Los Angeles and from nearby communities were Ansel H. Post, who was holding tent meetings in nearby Pasadena under the auspices of the Household of God; Pastor Owen Adams of Monrovia's Holiness Tabernacle; William Pendleton, pastor of the Los Angeles Holiness Church; church planter Frank Bartleman, who quickly founded the Eighth and Maple Assembly; independent evangelist Glenn Cook, who was holding tent meetings on the corner of Seventh and Spring; Edward McCauley, a controversial street preacher in Long Beach; Alfred G. Garr, pastor of the Burning Bush; Pastor F. E. Hill of the Second Church of the Nazarene; Elmer K. Fisher, pastor of the Upper Room Mission; Pastor Thomas Atteberry of the People's Church; George B. Studd of the Peniel Mission; and Abundio and

Rosa de Lopez, who led God's Detective Mission for Mexican workers on the Southern Pacific Railroad.[45] Dr. Finis Yoakum and his Pisgah Home Movement in nearby Highland Park joined hands with those at the Azusa Street Mission as well.[46]

The one exception was Pastor Joseph Smale of First New Testament Church. After a visit to Wales in 1905, Smale, who at that time was pastor of First Baptist Church, announced that a revival was coming to Los Angeles. He had tried to ready his people for this revival, but a number of leaders in the congregation pressed him to end this line of preaching. Instead, he resigned. The next week, over 300 of his former parishioners asked him to start another congregation. When members of his new congregation, First New Testament Church, began speaking in tongues, prophesying, performing exorcisms, and laying hands on people for healing, Smale supported their efforts and in so doing, he cautiously accepted the Azusa Street revival as well. While he supported the revival for nearly six months, he ultimately withdrew that support when problems related to the revival emerged within his congregation.[47] Still, within 18 months, there were at least 10 Pentecostal congregations in Los Angeles, with others in the surrounding suburbs, and some of them, such as the Upper Room Mission, had begun to send out missionaries as well.

From the beginning, workers took the message proclaimed at the Azusa Street Mission and preached it wherever they could, on street corners, in storefronts, and to existing congregations. By the end of its first year, literally scores of evangelists and ordinary people were on the road with the message. One of the largest groups of people commissioned by the Mission to take its message on the road was a group that went up the coast of California into Oregon. Led by Mrs. Florence Louise Crawford, it included nine individuals who founded congregations in California and Oregon, but also did so in China, Sweden, and the Middle East.[48]

Azusa Street's Missionaries

Missionaries bore the heat of the day as the revival spread around the world, further enhancing the role of the Mission.[49] Between April 1906 and the end of the year, the Azusa Street Mission commissioned 19 first-time missionaries. They went to India, Sweden, Palestine, Angola, and Liberia.[50] Five of the ten missionaries who went to Liberia were African Americans. Maria Gardiner, another African American, went to India to serve as the nanny for the daughter of Azusa Street missionaries Alfred and Lillian Garr. The following year the Mission sent out 12 more first-time missionaries, 10 of whom were also African Americans. All of them went to Liberia.[51]

Thomas and Helen Junk, who had left the Azusa Street Mission with the evangelistic party led by Florence Crawford in August 1906, helped to establish a Pentecostal congregation in the Seattle area before moving on at the end of 1907 to their field of ministry in Northern China.[52] Meanwhile, Lucy Leatherman, having finished helping Azusa Street's first group of missionaries to Africa, was finally free to pursue her own missionary interests in the Middle East.[53] Miss Lillian Keyes and Miss Edith Gumbrell, members of First New Testament Church who had received their baptism in the Spirit at Azusa Street, left Los Angeles for Northern China as first-time missionaries.[54]

Nine more first-time missionaries, including Thomas and Charlotte Hezmalhalch, and John G. and Jenny Lake, and their three sons, sailed for South Africa in 1907.[55] Hezmalhalch had served as the secretary of the Verdugo Land Improvement Association in Glendale and served as pastor of the Holiness Church in Pasadena. Lake was a former Methodist minister who, following the healing of his wife under the ministry of John Alexander Dowie in Zion, Illinois, had served as an elder in Dowie's Catholic Apostolic Church. They were joined in May 1908 by Henry A. and Anna E. Turney.[56]

Mae Field Mayo had worked for several years among the Chinese in the San Joaquin Valley of central California with the Peniel Mission. In the summer of 1906 under the outreach ministry of Azusa Street in nearby Monrovia, California,[57] she was baptized in the Spirit. Later, she began foreign missionary service in Nanking and then in Kiang-Pu Hsien, China.[58] Thus, in less than three years, the Mission commissioned and sent out at least 45 first-time missionaries, a third of whom were African Americans.

Meanwhile, Martin L. Ryan, a pastor in Salem, Oregon, visited the Mission in August 1906 and was baptized in the Spirit. After asking the Azusa Street Mission repeatedly to send workers who could help lead his Salem congregation into "Pentecost," they arrived and a controversial revival began in Salem. By the following year, Ryan had recruited 13 workers to accompany him, and they set out for Japan. Poorly organized and woefully under-funded, Ryan's work was more or less doomed to failure from the beginning. While Ryan and his followers remained abroad for only four years, they were able to establish a permanent Pentecostal presence in Japan.[59]

A dozen or more veteran missionaries also spread the message of Pentecost after being baptized in the Spirit at Azusa Street. In the spring of 1906, Samuel and Ardella Mead, who had spent 20 years as self-supporting Methodist missionaries in Angola, visited the Mission. They were soon baptized in the Spirit there, where they subsequently attempted to ascertain the various manifestations of "tongues" that people spoke, for possible use in missionary service.[60] By September 1906, they had cast their lots with other "Apostolic

Faith" missionaries and announced that they would return for another stint in Angola, this time as Pentecostals.[61]

George and Mary Berg, who had served as missionaries in India with a Holiness organization between 1901 and 1905, returned to India in 1908 after they were baptized in the Spirit at Azusa Street. They worked for a number of years as Apostolic Faith missionaries.[62]

After hearing reports of the revival taking place at the Azusa Street Mission, other missionaries visited the Mission while on furlough. There they were baptized in the Spirit, left their previous missionary organizations, and became independent "Apostolic Faith" missionaries. Among them were the Presbyterian missionary Antoinette Moomau, working in Su-chou-fu; the independent Norwegian missionary Bernt Berntsen, working in Chêng-ting-fu; and Hector and Sigrid McLean, working with the China Inland Mission.

Antoinette Moomau left the Presbyterian Church and began an Apostolic Faith work in Shanghai that she led until her death in 1937.[63] On his return to China by way of Seattle, Bernt Berntsen recruited 11 additional short-term missionaries to join him in him in proclaiming the "Apostolic Faith." When he arrived in China, he led his wife, Magna, and their two sons into the baptism in the Spirit. They established an independent "Apostolic Faith" ministry in Chêng-ting-fu (now Zhengding) west of Peking (now Beijing).[64] Hector and Sigrid McLean aided Antoinette Moomau for a short time and helped the Pentecostal Missionary Union to launch new missionaries in northern China before moving on to their own pioneering work in Yun-nan Province. There they established and led a number of "Apostolic Faith" churches until their retirement in 1927.[65]

Establishing a Network of Networks

Not every "Apostolic Faith" missionary enterprise in the opening decade of Pentecostal missions came into being as a direct result of the Azusa Street Mission, but the role that the Azusa Street Mission played in the growing network of revivals is clear. Other revivals were taking place around the world, most notably in India with the famous work of Pandita Ramabai, but there are also reports in which people who knew little or nothing of Azusa Street were speaking in tongues. What all of this activity suggests is a large part of the web-like set of relationships formed a complex network of individuals and churches that in many cases can be traced back to an initial contact with the Azusa Street Mission. A couple of illustrations should help me make the point.

William H. Durham, a seasoned Chicago evangelist and pastor, traveled to Los Angeles to visit the Azusa Street revival where, in February 1907, he was baptized in the Holy Spirit.[66] He returned to Chicago reinvigorated by the experience, and he led his and several other congregations in the area into the Pentecostal Movement. Among his members was a recent Irish immigrant, Mr. Robert Semple. Semple showed great promise and went on the road as an evangelist into Ontario, Canada, where he met and subsequently married Aimee Kennedy. Later, Durham ordained the Semples, and they continued to minister with Durham in the upper Midwest and Canada. In 1910, the Semples went to Hong Kong as missionaries. Shortly after their arrival, Robert Semple contracted and died of malaria, leaving Aimee with an unknown future.[67] Later, she became the flamboyant evangelist Aimee Semple McPherson who founded of the International Church of the Foursquare Gospel.

William Durham also played an important role among churches founded and led by Italian, Swedish, and Iranian immigrants. Durham led them into a Pentecostal experience and then ordained them for service in a variety of locations. Two Swedish Baptist immigrants, Gunnar Vingren and Daniel Berg, came into the movement in just this way, and in November 1910, they arrived in Pará, Brazil. There they began what would become the Assemblies of God in Brazil.[68]

Similarly, a number of recent immigrants from Tuscany began to attend Durham's meetings. They were baptized in the Spirit and two of them, Luigi Francescon and Peter Ottolini, formed an Italian Pentecostal denomination in the United States, the Assemblea Cristiana. In October 1909 Luigi Francescon, Giácomo Lombardi, and Lucía Menna founded the first Pentecostal denomination in Argentina, La Iglesia Asamblea Cristiana. The following year, 1910, Francesecon founded the Congregação Cristã in Brazil.[69] Both of them are vital Pentecostal denominations today.

Similarly, in 1908 Andrew Urshan, a recent immigrant from Iran, was led into the Pentecostal Movement through Durham's preaching. Just before the onset of World War I, Urshan traveled to Iran, where he established several small Pentecostal congregations. When the war broke out, he traveled with other refugees from Tehran through the Caucuses Mountains and ultimately found his way north to St. Petersburg, Russia. Along the way he preached and established a number of congregations.[70] He would later become the president of the United Pentecostal Church in the United States.

It is difficult to imagine that these immigrant missionaries from Sweden, Italy, and Iran would have entered the movement and then gone on to Brazil, Argentina, Iran, and Russia had Durham not provided them with a link from the Azusa Street Mission. If we return to the illustration of the billiard table, the cue ball of the Azusa Street Mission hit William Durham who, in turn, had a profound impact on these immigrant missionaries and their work in

Latin America, the Middle East, and Russia. And through Aimee Semple McPherson, who founded the International Church of the Foursquare Gospel, Durham's impact, and hence that of Azusa Street, may be found in many other places around the world.

Before very long, new Pentecostal denominations, new missionary-sending agencies, and new periodicals were paving the way for the expansion of the Apostolic Faith Movement. One such periodical was published in Indianapolis by J. Roswell Flower, future general secretary of the Assemblies of God. News from Indianapolis and the Azusa Street revival dominated its earliest pages. From September 1908, Flower listed the names of "Apostolic Faith" missionaries, pointing to their need for continuing prayer and financial support. All except one of them had been baptized in the Spirit at the Azusa Street Mission.[71] Other names were added to the list, many of them from "Azusa Street," as they were recognized by this growing network of churches in Los Angeles, Indianapolis, and beyond.[72]

In the first two years of its existence, then, scores of people took the message of salvation, holiness, and power from the Azusa Street Mission across the United States and around the world. It is difficult to imagine any other Pentecostal source from that period having played such a significant role in the expansion of the Pentecostal Movement worldwide as that of Pastor William J. Seymour and the Apostolic Faith Mission at 312 Azusa Street in Los Angeles, California.

NOTES

1. "How Holy Roller Gets Religion," *Los Angeles Herald* (September 10, 1906), 7.
2. W. J. Seymour, *The Doctrines and Discipline of the Azusa Street Apostolic Faith Mission of Los Angeles, Cal. 1915 with Scripture Readings* (Los Angeles, CA: privately published, 1915), 12.
3. The first book-length biographies on Seymour to appear in print are Rufus G. W. Sanders, *William Joseph Seymour: Black Father of the 20th Century Pentecostal/Charismatic Movement* (Sandusky, OH: Alexandria Publications 2001), and Craig Borlase, *William Seymour: A Biography* (Lake Mary, FL: Charisma House, 2006). Neither is written by a trained historian.
4. David B. Barrett, Todd M. Johnson, and Peter F. Crossing, "Global Table A. 50 Shared Goals: Status of Global Mission, AD 1900 to AD 2025," *International Bulletin of Missionary Research* 30:1 (2006), 28. Citing the *World Christian Database*, the Pew Forum on Religion & Public Life's *Spirit and Power: A 10-Country Survey of Pentecostals*, (Washington, D.C: Pew Research Center, October 2006), p. 1, speaks of 25% of the world's Christians as belonging to the Pentecostal and the closely related charismatic movements. For a copy of this survey see http://pewforum.org/surveys/pentecostal/. I am aware of the limitations that such estimates pose. For a helpful critique in this regard, see Allan Anderson, *An Introduction to Pentecostalism: Global Charismatic Christianity* (Cambridge: Cambridge University Press, 2004), 10–14.
5. James R. Goff, Jr., *Fields White Unto Harvest: Charles F. Parham and the Missionary Origins of Pentecostalism* (Fayetteville: University of Arkansas Press, 1988), 3–16.
6. Carl Brumback, *Suddenly … From Heaven: A History of the Assemblies of God* (Springfield, MO: Gospel Publishing House, 1961), 48.

7. Gary B. McGee, "The Story of Minnie F. Abrams: Another Context, Another Founder," in James R. Goff, Jr. and Grant A. Wacker, eds., *Portraits of a Generation: Early Pentecostal Leaders* (Fayetteville, AR: University of Arkansas Press, 2002), 100–104; Michael Bergunder, *The South Indian Pentecostal Movement in the Twentieth Century* (Grand Rapids, MI: Eerdmans, 2007), 1–14.

8. Anderson, *Introduction to Pentecostalism*, 166–183.

9. Leonard Lovett, "Black Origins of the Pentecostal Movement," in Vinson Synan, Ed. *Aspects of Pentecostal-Charismatic Origins* (Plainfield, NJ: Logos International, 1975), 123–141; Douglas J. Nelson, "For Such a Time as This: The Story of Bishop William J. Seymour and the Azusa Street Revival, A Search for Pentecostal/Charismatic Roots," Ph.D. diss. (Birmingham, UK: Faculty of Arts, Department of Theology, University of Birmingham, 1981); Iain MacRobert, *The Black Roots and White Racism of Early Pentecostalism in the U.S.A.* (London: Macmillan, 1988); Robert R. Owens, *Speak to the Rock: The Azusa Street Revival: Its Roots and Its Message* (Lanham, MD: University Press of America, 1998); Walter J. Hollenweger, *Pentecostalism: Origins and Developments Worldwide* (Peabody, MA: Hendrickson Publishers, 1997), 18–24.

10. Edith Blumhofer, "For Pentecostals, A Move toward Racial Reconciliation," *Christian Century* 111:14 (April 27, 1994), 445; Edith Blumhofer, "Azusa Street Revival," *Christian Century* 123:5 (March 7, 2006), 22; Joe Creech, "Visions of Glory: The Place of the Azusa Street Revival in Pentecostal History," *Church History* 65:3 (September 1996), 405–424.

11. Anthea Butler, "Constructing Different Memories: Recasting the Azusa Street Revival," in Harold D. Hunter and Cecil M. Robeck, Jr., eds., *The Azusa Street Revival and Its Legacy* (Cleveland, TN: Pathway Press, 2006), 193–201.

12. "Three Great Transcontinental Railroads Center Here," *Evening News* [Los Angeles, CA] (October 24, 1906), IV:4.

13. Sandra Sizer Frankiel, *California's Spiritual Frontiers: Religious Alternatives in Anglo-Protestantism, 1850–1910* (Berkeley: University of California Press, 1988), 117.

14. Frank Bartleman, *My Story: "The Latter Rain"* (Columbia, SC: John M. Pike, 1909). Since 1925, Pentecostals have cited Frank Bartleman, *How Pentecost Came to Los Angeles: As It Was in the Beginning* (Los Angeles, CA: F. Bartleman, 1925) as the primary eyewitness of the Azusa Street Mission and revival. Leonard Lovett, "Perspective on the Black Origins of the Contemporary Pentecostal Movement," *Journal of the Interdenominational Theological Center* 1:1 (Fall 1973), 36–49 and "Black Origins of the Pentecostal Movement," 123–141, first pointed to the substantial African American contribution to Pentecostalism based upon the Azusa Street Mission, and in 1981, Douglas J. Nelson completed a dissertation on the subject, "For Such a Time as This." See also Douglas J. Nelson, "The Black Face of Church Renewal: The Meaning of a Charismatic Explosion, 1901–1985," in Paul Elbert, ed. *Faces of Renewal: Studies in Honor of Stanley M. Horton* (Peabody, MA: Hendrickson, 1988), 172–191. More recently, Owens, *Speak to the Rock*, Larry Martin, *The Life and Ministry of William J. Seymour and a History of the Azusa Street Revival* The Complete Azusa Street Library CASL 1 (Joplin, MO: Christian Life Books, 1999), and Cecil M. Robeck, Jr., *The Azusa Street Mission and Revival: The Birth of the Global Pentecostal Movement* (Nashville, TN: Nelson Reference and Electronic, 2006) have attempted to fill gaps in our knowledge.

15. See, for example, the Untitled Item, *The Apostolic Faith* [Los Angeles, CA] 1.4 (December 1906), 3.4; "Latest Report from Our Missionaries to Africa," *The Apostolic Faith* [Los Angeles, CA] 1.5 (January 1907), 3.1; Untitled Item, *The Apostolic Faith* [Los Angeles, CA] 1.12 (January 1908), 2.1; "Chinese Pentecostal Paper," *The Apostolic Faith* [Los Angeles, CA] 1.13 (May 1908), 2.1; "Cheng Ting Fu, Chih-li, North China," *The Apostolic Faith* [Los Angeles, CA] 1.13 (May 1908), 4.3. [For citations from *The Apostolic Faith*, the first numbers given are volume and issue numbers; the final numbers are page and column numbers].

16. "The Apostolic Faith Movement," *The Apostolic Faith* [Los Angeles, CA] 1.1 (September 1906), 2.1.

17. "Holy Jumpers on Way to Terminal," *Daily Telegram* [Long Beach, CA] (July 24, 1906), 1; "Holy Kickers Baptized 138," *Daily Telegram* [Long Beach, CA] (July 25, 1906), 1;

Untitled Item, *The Apostolic Faith* [Los Angeles, CA] 1.1 (September 1906), 4.3; "Buried with Him in Baptism," *The Apostolic Faith* [Los Angeles, CA] 1.2 (October 1906), 4.4.

18. "Everywhere Preaching the Word," *The Apostolic Faith* [Los Angeles, CA] 1.10 (September 1907), 1.1; "Loud Prayers Stir Protest," *Los Angeles Daily Times* (July 18, 1907), II.13 makes it clear that baptism was by immersion.

19. *The Apostolic Faith* [Los Angeles, CA] 1.1 (September 1906), 3.4.

20. See especially, Pew Forum, *Spirit and Power*, 34–40.

21. Donald W. Dayton, *Theological Roots of Pentecostalism* (Peabody, MA: Hendrickson Publishers, [1987] 1991).

22. "The Apostolic Faith Movement," *The Apostolic Faith* [Los Angeles, CA] 1.1 (September 1906), 2.1.

23. Cecil M. Robeck, Jr. "William J. Seymour and the 'Bible Evidence'," in Gary B. McGee, Ed., *Initial Evidence: Historical and Biblical Perspectives on the Pentecostal Doctrine of Spirit Baptism* (Peabody, Mass.: Hendrickson Publishers, 1991), 72–95.

24. Arthur Osterberg, "I Was There," *Full Gospel Business Men's Fellowship International: Voice* (May 1966), 18. Cf. Cecil M. Robeck, Jr., "The Azusa Street Mission and the Historic Black Churches: Two worlds in Conflict in Los Angeles' African American Community," in Amos Yong and Estrelda Alexander, eds., *Afro-Pentecostalism: Black Pentecostal and Charismatic Christianity in History and Culture* (New York: New York University Press, 2011), 21–41.

25. Untitled Item, *The Apostolic Faith* [Los Angeles, CA] 1.1 (September 1906), 1.3.

26. Untitled Item, *The Apostolic Faith* [Los Angeles, CA] 1.3 (November 1906), 1.2.

27. "Weird Babel of Tongues," *Los Angeles Daily Times* (April 18, 1906), 2.1.

28. "Rolling and Diving Fanatics 'Confess'," *Los Angeles Daily Times* (June 23, 1906), 1.7.

29. "'Holy Kickers' Baffle Police," *Los Angeles Daily Times* (July 12, 1906), 1:13.

30. "How Holy Roller Gets Religion," *Los Angeles Herald* (September 10, 1906), 7.

31. "How Holy Roller Gets Religion," 7.

32. Glenn A. Cook, "The Azusa Street Meeting," (Los Angeles, CA: Glenn A. Cook, no date), 2. This is a pamphlet.

33. Thomas Ball Barratt, *When the Fire Fell and an Outline of My Life* (Oslo, Norway: Alfons Hansen & Sønner, 1927), 108–109, 123–124; David Bundy, "Spiritual Advice to a Seeker: Letters to T.B. Barratt from Azusa Street, 1906," *Pneuma: The Journal of the Society for Pentecostal Studies* 14:2 (Fall 1992), 159–170.

34. T. B. Barratt, "The Seal of My Pentecost," *Living Truths* 6:12 (December 1906), 736–738. "Baptized in New York," *The Apostolic Faith* [Los Angeles, CA] 1.4 (December 1906), 3.2; Barratt, *When the Fire Fell*, 128–131.

35. The three first-time missionaries recruited in New York City included Mr. and Mrs. F. M. Cook (Liberia), December 1906 and Mrs. Lee (Liberia), December 1906.

36. For a recent, fascinating, and bestselling biographical novel, loosely based upon the life of Lewi Pethrus and his sometime colleague Sven Lidman, see Per Olov Enquist, *Lewi's Journey* (New York, NY: Overlook Duckworth, 2005).

37. On Alexander Boddy, see Peter Lavin, *Alexander Boddy, Pastor and Prophet: Vicar of All Saints Sunderland, 1886–1922* (Monkwearmouth, Sunderland, UK: Wearside Historic Churches Group, 1986) and Gavin Wakefield, *Alexander Boddy: Pentecostal Anglican Pioneer* Carlisle, England: Paternoster Press, 2006.

38. On Jonathan Paul, see Ernst Geise, *Jonathan Paul, Ein Knect Jesu Christi: Leben und Werk* (Altdorf, Germany: Missionsbuchhandlung und Verlag, 1965).

39. "Pastor Barratt in Finland," *Confidence* 4:10 (October, 1911), 234.

40. On Gerrit Polman, see Cornelis van der Laan, *Sectarian against His Will: Gerrit Roelof Polman and the Birth of Pentecostalism in the Netherlands*, Studies in Evangelicalism (Metuchen, NJ: Scarecrow, 1991).

41. Cornelis van der Laan, "What Good Can Come from Los Angeles: Changing Perceptions of the North American Pentecostal Origins in Early Western European Pentecostal Periodicals," in Harold D. Hunter and Cecil M. Robeck, Jr. eds., *The Azusa Street Revival and Its Legacy* (Cleveland, TN: Pathway Press, 2006), 141–159.

42. Bartleman, *How Pentecost Came to Los Angeles*, 54.

43. "Churches Aroused to Action," *Los Angeles Express* (July 18, 1906), 12; "Young Girl Given Gift of Tongues," *Los Angeles Express* (July 20, 1906), 1.
44. "Praying Bands for Churches," *Los Angeles Express* (July 25, 1906), 6. "Praying Bands for Churches," 6; "Evangelists to Work in Summer," *Los Angeles Herald* (July 25, 1906), 4; cf. "Church Federation of Los Angeles and Its Plans for Great Evangelistic Campaign," *Los Angeles Express* (December 7, 1907), 9.
45. "Get Into the Cornfield," *The Apostolic Faith* [Los Angeles, CA] 1.2 (October 1906), 1.3; "Vernon Mission," *The Apostolic Faith* [Los Angeles, CA] 1.3 (November 1906), 1.4.
46. Even a cursory reading of the community's periodical *Pisgah*, said to be "devoted to the material welfare, bodily healing, moral uplift and spiritual life of the stricken in body, victim of drink, outcast, cripple, hungry, friendless and whosoever is in need of the waters of life" is sufficient to demonstrate the common cause shared by Dr. Yoakum and the Azusa Street Mission. This periodical was first published in January 1909 and continued on a more or less occasional basis through the September–October–November 1922 issue.
47. "Trouble in Congregation," *Los Angeles Herald* (September 21, 1906), 8; "Sift [sic.] Of Tongues Splits Flock?" *Los Angeles Herald* (September 23, 1906), 4.
48. Robeck, *Azusa Street Mission and Revival*, 214.
49. For a look at the early Pentecostal missionary movement, including many from the Azusa Street Mission, see Allan Anderson, *Spreading Fires: The Missionary Nature of Early Pentecostalism* (London: SCM Press, 2007).
50. Among the first time missionaries were Andrew Johnson (Sweden), November 1906; Louise M. Condit (Palestine–Jews), November 1906; Lucy Farrow (Liberia), December 1906; Julia W. and Willis Hutchins (Liberia), December 1906; Leila McKinney (Liberia), December 1906; George Batman and Daisy Batman (Liberia), December 1906 and their three children, Bessie, Robert, and an Infant Batman (Liberia), December 1906; Robert and Myrtle K. Schideler (Angola), December 1906; Alfred G. and Lillian Garr; their nanny, Maria Gardiner; and their daughter, Elizabeth Garr (India, Sri Lanka, Macao, Hong Kong), July 1906; and Eric Hollingsworth and Mrs. Hollingsworth (Sweden), December 1906.
51. Among the first time missionaries sent out were William Henry Cummings and Emma Cummings and their children, Frank, Bessie, John, Mattie, and Marjorie Cummings (Liberia), May 1907; Edward and Molly McCauley (Liberia), October 1907, Rosa Harmon (Liberia), November 1907; and Lucy Leatherman (Middle East), 1908.
52. "Holy Roller Jailed in Seattle," *Eastside News* [Portland, OR] (November 26, 1906), 4.
53. In August 1907, Leatherman wrote to M. L. Ryan, telling him that she expected to sail to Jerusalem in September 1907; Cf. "Jerusalem the Goal," *The Apostolic Light*, No. 183 (August 28, 1907), 1.5. She was in Jerusalem before September 1908, and that she left Jerusalem on October 8, 1908 for what is now Lebanon, Syria, and the upper Galilee. Cf. "Letter from Jerusalem," *Word and Work* 30:11 (November 1908), 346–347; "A Missionary Trip through Syria and Palestine," *The Pentecost* 1.4 (December 1908), 5.
54. Wm. Bernard, "Liverpool," *Confidence: A Pentecostal Paper for Great Britain*, no. 8 (November 15, 1908), 13.
55. "Missionaries for Africa," *The Pentecost* 1.1 (August 1908), 2–3, 6–7.
56. "Honolulu," *The Apostolic Faith* [Los Angeles, CA] 1.11 (October–January 1908), 1.1; "Missionaries to Johannesburg, South Africa," *The Apostolic Faith* [Los Angeles, CA] 1.13 (May 1908), 4.1; Hannah A. James, "South Africa: Pretoria," *Confidence* 2:12 (December 1910), 292–293 notes that she had traveled with the Turneys from England, which they had left 18 months earlier. See also Peter Watt, *From Africa's Soil: The Story of the Assemblies of God in Southern Africa* (Cape Town, SA: Struik Christian Books, 1992), 20.
57. The Peniel Mission work among the Chinese in Bakersfield, CA, had been started by Dr. Cullis. Mae Mayo worked there from 1902. Cf. "Peniel Missions," *Peniel Herald* 8:6 (June 1902), 3.
58. "Elderly Missionary Dies," *The Pentecostal Evangel* #2306 (July 20, 1958), 13.
59. Paul Tsuchido Shew, "History of Early Pentecostal Movement in Japan: The Roots and Development of the Pre-War Pentecostal (1907–1945)," PhD diss., Pasadena, CA: Fuller Theological Seminary, School of Theology, 2003.

60. "A Message Concerning His Coming," *The Apostolic Faith* [Los Angeles, CA] 1.4 (December 1906), 3.3; "Bro. G. W. Batman's Testimony," *The Apostolic Faith* [Los Angeles, CA] 1.4 (December 1906), 4.1.

61. S. J. Mead, "From a Missionary to Africa," *The Apostolic Faith* [Los Angeles, CA] 1.1 (September 1906), 3.1; "From Los Angeles to Home and Foreign Fields," *The Apostolic Faith* [Los Angeles, CA] 1.4 (December 1906), 4.1; "Latest Report from our Missionaries to Africa," *The Apostolic Faith* [Los Angeles, CA] 1.5 (January 1907), 1.1; F. Bartleman, "Letter from Los Angeles," *Triumphs of Faith* 26:12 (December 1906), 249.

62. George E. Berg, "Greetings from India," *The Latter Rain Evangel* 1:11 (August 1909), 10; George E. Berg, "Echoes from the Jungles of India," *The Latter Rain Evangel* 2:7 (April 1910), 14–15; "Among the Jungle Tribes," *The Latter Rain Evangel* 2:11 (August 1910), 12–13; George E. Berg, "Another Letter from South India," *The Latter Rain Evangel* 3:3 (December 1910), 10; George E. Berg, "The Signs Following in India," *The Latter Rain Evangel* 3:5 (February 1911), 15–16.

63. See Robeck, *Azusa Street Mission and Revival*, 262–264.

64. Bernt Berntsen visited the Azusa Mission in September 1907. On Bernsten, see Untitled Item, *The Apostolic Faith* [Los Angeles, CA] 1.10 (September 1907), 1.3; B. Berntsen, "Came from China to America for Pentecost," *The Apostolic Faith* [Los Angeles, CA] 1.12 (January 1908), 3.4; "Cheng Ting Fu, Chih-li, North China," *The Apostolic Faith* [Los Angeles, CA] 2.13 [sic.] (May 1908), 4.3; B. Berntsen, "Letter from China," *Word and Work* 30.7 (July 1908), 218–219; "Letter from Bro. Berntsen," *The Bridegroom's Messenger* 2.26 (November 15, 1908), 4.4–5; B. Berntsen, "From China," *The Bridegroom's Messenger* 2:27 (December 1, 1908), 4.4; B. Berntsen, "One Year's Work in China, the Year's Report," *The Bridegroom's Messenger* 2.34 (March 15, 1909), 4.3.

65. Sigrid McLean, *Over Twenty Years in China* (Minneapolis, MN: Sigrid McLean, 1927).

66. W. H. Durham, "A Chicago Evangelist's Pentecost," *The Apostolic Faith* [Los Angeles, CA] 1.6 (February–March 1907), 4.2. Durham also gives his testimony in "Personal Testimony of Pastor Durham," *Pentecostal Testimony* 1.1 (March 1910), 5–7. Without the title page, it is impossible to date this latter series of pages precisely, but by analyzing the internal evidence of this fragment, Wayne Warner, Director of the Flower Heritage Center (now retired) has chosen to designate it in this way.

67. Edith L. Blumhofer, *Aimee Semple McPherson: Everybody's Sister* (Grand Rapids, MI: William B. Eerdmans Publishing Company, 1993).

68. Edith L. Blumhofer, "William H. Durham: Years of Creativity, Years of Dissent," in James R. Goff, Jr. and Grant Wacker, eds., *Portraits of a Generation: Early Pentecostal Leaders* (Fayetteville: University of Arkansas Press, 2002), 132, n 47; Joseph Colletti, "Ethnic Pentecostalism in Chicago: 1890–1950," Ph.D. diss. (Birmingham, England: University of Birmingham, 1990), 168–246; Ivar Vingren, *Det började I Pará: Svensk Pingstmission I Brasilien*, ed. Gunilla Nyberg, Jan-Åke Alvarsson, and Jan-Endy Johannesson (Ekerö, Sweden: MissionsInstitutet-PMU, 1994), 27–28.

69. Colletti, "Ethnic Pentecostalism in Chicago," 128–167; Key Yuasa, "Louis Francescon: A Theological Biography 1866–1964," Th.D. diss. (Genève, Switzerland: Faculté Autonome de Théologie Protestante de L'Université de Genève, 2001), 118–126 describes how Francescon was led into the "Apostolic Faith" by William Durham. Chapter 7 tells how Franciscon established the Congregação Cristã no Brasil.

70. On Urshan and his ministry, see Andrew D. Urshan, "Pentecost among the Persians in Chicago," *The Bridegroom's Messenger* 3.69 (September 1, 1910), 3; Andrew D. Urshan, *The Story of My Life* (St. Louis, MO: Gospel Publishing House, 1918); Andrew D. Urshan, *The Life Story of Andrew Bar David Urshan: An Autobiography of the Author's First Forty Years* (Portland, OR: Apostolic Book Publishers, 1967, rpt. 1982).

71. "Apostolic Faith Directory," *The Pentecost* 1.2 (September 1908), 8.

72. "Apostolic Faith Directory," 8.

WHY IS PENTECOSTALISM GROWING?

While it is clear that the global Pentecostal movement has grown phenomenally since its emergence in 1906 and in fact shows no signs of abating, the question remains, what explains its rapid and global growth? In the previous section, Anderson and Robeck suggested that Pentecostalism has been a missionary movement from its origins, intent on spreading its message throughout the world, but this characteristic does not really explain why it has seen successful growth in some countries and regions and not in others. Further, the emphasis on missionary activity alone fails to account for the demographic shift in Pentecostalism from the West to the global South. That is, how can both growth and non-growth (or at least a leveling off of growth rates, if not a decline as among large Pentecostal denominations in the U.S.) be explained from a social scientific perspective? What are the social and cultural conditions that allow for a thriving Pentecostal movement(s) in some places, but not in others?

R. Andrew Chesnut approaches this problem using the metaphor of an unregulated "free-market economy of faith" that has developed across Latin America, in which different forms of Pentecostal and charismatic Christianity have created the social space for Latin Americans to choose *not* to be Catholic. People are making this "rational choice" based on several different but related factors that Pentecostalism provides but that Catholicism does not. In this, Chesnut gives us some memorable images with which to think about Pentecostalism; he focuses on the appeal of Pentecostalism's *products,* such as faith healing and recovery and health over the long term; *marketing* (or evangelization) that exploits personal networks as a key pathway to spread the Pentecostal message; *sales representatives,* which includes all Pentecostal believers, who also have the added feature of sharing social class, geographic region, similar educational levels, and other social ties with those being converted; and the *organizational structure* of Pentecostalism, that through its differentiation and specialization—which means there is an organizational home for all consumer tastes—can outperform the more bureaucratic and authoritarian Catholic Church. Thus for Chesnut, Latin American Pentecostalism has been able to capitalize on the inefficiencies and gaps in the Catholic product line and has offered a religious product better suited to the needs of the Latin American people.

Henri Gooren takes a somewhat broader, although complementary, approach to explain why Pentecostalism has failed to grow in Paraguay at anywhere near the rates of growth it has enjoyed in other parts of Latin America. Gooren's perspective does not turn on the master narrative of a rational religious consumer making choices in a free religious market; rather, he argues that broader social, political, and cultural factors influence the growth (and lack of growth) of Pentecostal churches. Thus Gooren emphasizes both internal and external *religious factors* like the appeal of a particular religious doctrine or responses from the Catholic hierarchy to non-Catholic church growth, as well as internal and external *nonreligious factors*, such as the appeal of church organizations (for Pentecostals this would be, as Chesnut suggests, less hierarchical, more relational) and the urbanization process, which uproots people and is assumed to make them more susceptible to the new religious opportunities.

Taken together, these chapters highlight the ability of Pentecostalism to exploit certain organizational advantages it enjoys over less nimble religious organizations. At the same time, we see that in order for Pentecostalism to be able to capitalize on its built-in advantages, certain social, political, economic, and religious factors need to be in place for it to take root and flourish. Thus Pentecostalism may flourish in a free religious marketplace; but can it flourish to the same degree when there is a more restricted religious marketplace? Does less religious freedom, whether through state prohibitions or religious monopoly, inhibit Pentecostalism from realizing its full market share in any given society?

3

Spirited Competition

Pentecostal Success in Latin America's New Religious Marketplace

R. ANDREW CHESNUT

As the premier non-Catholic religion of Latin America, Pentecostalism has been the primary religious architect and developer of the region's new free market of faith. If the region's popular consumers are now free to choose to consume the religious goods that best satisfy their spiritual and material desires, it is largely due to the unparalleled growth of Pentecostal churches over the past half-century. This charismatic branch of Protestantism single-handedly created religious and social space where Latin Americans from the popular classes are free not to be Catholic. Given Catholicism's historical role as one the constituent elements of Latin American national identities, Pentecostalism's construction of an alternative religious identity for those dissatisfied with their inherited faith is no minor achievement. For more than four centuries, to be Colombian or Mexican, for example, was to be Catholic. The tiny minorities who began to convert to historic Protestant denominations, such as Methodism and Presbyterianism, in the latter half of the nineteenth century risked social ostracism and sometimes even violence at the hands of Catholics who viewed Protestant converts as traitorous to the One True Faith, if not the nation itself. Not surprisingly, Protestant converts during this period tended to be those Latin American men and women who had the least religious, social, political, and financial capital to lose in abandoning their native religion. Rarely did members of the privileged classes shed their Catholic identities.

That not more than one percent of Latin Americans identified themselves as Protestant as late as 1940 is evidence of the failure of historic Protestantism and the numerous faith missions to attract a critical mass of converts. Since Pentecostal churches currently account for approximately 75 percent of all Latin American Protestants after almost a century of evangelization,[1] the obvious conclusion is that Pentecostalism's predecessors did not offer attractive religious goods and services to popular religious consumers. If the social cost of renouncing Catholicism had been the only factor impeding conversion to Protestantism, the historic churches and faith missions would be thriving at present, now that there is much less social stigma attached to shedding one's Catholic identity. However, the only historic churches able to compete effectively with the Pentecostals are those that have embraced spirit-filled worship and Pentecostalized. In Brazil these schismatic churches generally maintain their denominational title but distinguish themselves from their non-charismatic brethren by adding the term "renewed" (*renovada*) to their name. So great is the Pentecostalization of Latin American Protestantism that only 22 percent of Brazilian and Chilean Protestants are not Pentecostal or "renewed." The figure drops to only 15 percent for Guatemala.[2]

The main objective of this study is to explore the reasons for Pentecostalism's unparalleled success in the region's free-market economy of faith. The roughly seventy-five million Latin American Pentecostals represent the same number of adherents as their chief competitors, the Catholic Charismatic Renewal.[3] Through examination of the elements that determine the success or failure of any religious organization competing in an unregulated religious economy, Pentecostalism's recipe for success will become clear. Analyses of the Pentecostal product, marketing, its sales representatives, organizational structure, and consumers will illuminate the determining factors in this ecstatic religion's commanding position in the free religious market.[4]

Maria Hernandez, an Archetypical Consumer

Since it is the tastes and preferences of religious consumers that largely determine the fate of any given religious enterprise in a competitive economy, consideration of the large class of popular religious consumers who have purchased the Pentecostal product is imperative. In other words, who are these millions of Hondurans, Paraguayans, Bolivians, and Guatemalans, among others, who have converted to Pentecostalism since it first sunk roots in Latin American soil in the initial decades of the twentieth century? Sufficient research on Ibero-American Pentecostalism has been conducted over the past decade to allow for a fairly accurate socioeconomic profile of believers.

The archetypical Latin American Pentecostal is Maria Hernandez, a poor, married woman of color in her thirties or forties living on the urban periphery. She works as a domestic servant in the home of a privileged compatriot and was a nominal Catholic before converting to the Assembly of God during a time of personal crisis related to her experience of material deprivation. Of course charismatic Protestantism is so widespread and differentiated now that there are hundreds of thousands of believers who possess none of these constituent elements of the Pentecostal archetype. For example, many of the members of the Neo-Pentecostal denominations in Guatemala such as El Shaddai and El Verbo are upper-middle-class, professional men. Nonetheless, Maria Hernandez personifies the most common socioeconomic traits found among the vast population of believers.

Most salient among the socioeconomic characteristics of Latin American *crentes* (or believers as they are often called in Brazil) are poverty, a nominal Catholic background, and gender. Historically, the great majority of Pentecostal converts have been poor non-practicing Catholics. Numerous studies, including my own in Brazil, have shown that not only are Latin American Pentecostals poor, but also that they tend to have lower incomes and less education than the general population. The largest study ever conducted of Latin American Protestantism, the 1996 ISER (Instituto Superior da Religião) survey of the Protestant population of Rio de Janeiro found *crentes* to be considerably more likely to live in poverty and have less schooling than the *carioca*[5] population at large (ISER 12).[6] Although Pentecostalism has ascended the region's socioeconomic pyramid, particularly since the 1980s, it continues to be predominantly a religion of the popular classes.

In addition to social class, most Latin American Pentecostals share a common former religious identity. The majority of *creyentes* had been nominal or cultural Catholics before converting (Miguez in Smith, ISER, Chesnut 1997). Most would have been baptized in the Catholic Church and perhaps had even taken first communion, but their contact with the institutional church was minimal. However, their weak or nonexistent ties to the *ecclesia* in no way meant that their worldview had become secularized or disenchanted. In times of both need and celebration, nominal Catholics, like their practicing coreligionists, would send prayers of supplication or thanksgiving to the Virgin or one of the myriad saints. Thus, due to their estrangement from the church and perennial shortage of clergy, no priest or pastoral agent is likely be present at the time of their poverty-related crisis, which so often leads afflicted individuals to the doors of a Pentecostal temple. It is among this vast field of nominal Catholics, who compose the majority of the Ibero-American population, that Pentecostal evangelists have reaped such bountiful harvests of converts.

While the third salient characteristic of the Pentecostal consumer market, the great female majority among believers, is not peculiar to the faith, it merits discussion due to the religion's status as the most widely practiced faith among women of the popular classes. Pentecostalism holds extraordinary appeal among impoverished Latin American women. Hence, product development and marketing strategies naturally must take into account the fact that women believers outnumber men by a ratio of two to one. In one of Brazil's largest and fastest growing Pentecostal denominations, the Universal Church of the Kingdom of God (UCKG), the ratio climbs to four to one (ISER 53). Male believers, of course, continue to monopolize the pastorate and high-ranking church offices, but Pentecostalism is largely sustained and spread by sisters in the faith.

Practical Products

The above profile of Pentecostal consumers allows for a better understanding of the religious products that believers are purchasing and consuming in *crente* churches and in their daily lives. Defining religious products as the doctrine and worship services of faith-based organizations, this section of the paper considers the spiritual goods and services that have resulted in Pentecostalism's unmatched success in the free market of faith. Thus, the task at hand is not to identify every single Pentecostal product but to examine those whose popularity among consumers has led to pneumacentric Protestantism's dramatic expansion in Latin America since the 1950s.

The utilitarian nature of Pentecostalism and popular religion in general means that the spiritual products offered to consumers of the divine must prove useful in their daily lives. Products that do not relate to believers' quotidian existence will find few purchasers in the popular religious marketplace. This does not mean that popular consumers are only religious instrumentalists who evaluate spiritual products solely on the basis of their capacity to provide relief from the afflictions of everyday poverty. However, since the relation between religion and society is dialectical, spiritual products that hold little relevance to the social reality of impoverished believers will collect dust on the lower shelves of the market. If Pentecostalism is thriving in the Latin American marketplace, it is largely due to the utility of its products in consumers' everyday lives.

Since most Latin American religious consumers are much better acquainted with Catholic products, rival spiritual firms, in order to compete, must offer goods that are simultaneously familiar and novel. That is, the non-Catholic product must provide sufficient continuity with Catholic doctrine or worship to maintain the potential consumer's comfort level. Yet, at the same time the product must offer novelty that piques consumer interest enough to draw them away from the Catholic product. Pentecostalism possesses exactly this type of product in its doctrine and practice of faith healing. More than any other of its line of products, it is the Pentecostal belief that Jesus and the Holy Spirit have the power to cure believers of their spiritual, somatic, and psychological ills that impels more Latin Americans to affiliate with *crente* churches. All

Catholics, whether practicing or nominal, are familiar, if not experienced, with the healing powers of the saints and Virgin. In fact, it is their status as powerful agents of divine healing that has won such world renown for Virgins such as Guadalupe, Fatima, and Medugorje.

Pentecostal faith healing thus is really not a new product per se but a greatly improved one. With the great exception of the Catholic Charismatic Renewal, divine healing has existed on the fringes of the contemporary Ibero-American Catholic Church. The curing of all types of ailments through promises and petitions to the Virgin and saints has customarily taken place beyond the pale of the institutional church, and if any human mediators were involved at all, they were more likely to be *curanderas* (folk healers) than priests. In striking contrast, Pentecostal preachers from the earliest days made *cura divina* a centerpiece of both doctrine and practice. Indeed, it was an act of faith healing in 1911 that led to the birth of the Western Hemisphere's largest Pentecostal denomination, the Brazilian Assembly of God (Chesnut 1997, 27). Whereas Catholic Masses offered little liturgical space for the healing of believers' quotidian afflictions, Pentecostal worship services and revivals in which Jesus or the Holy Spirit would fail to operate through the congregation to cure worshipers of their illnesses are almost unimaginable. Of such importance is faith healing to the mission of the Brazilian Universal Church of the Kingdom of God that two days of its weekly schedule of services are devoted to it. Hence, Latin American Pentecostalism took what had been a marginal product in institutional Catholicism and turned it into the sine qua non of its own religious production.

If the product of faith healing, more than any other, induces religious consumers to join the Pentecostal enterprise, it is another good that facilitates the recovery and maintenance of believers' health over the long term. The doctrine of conversion in which joining a Pentecostal church is conceptualized as part of a process of spiritual rebirth allows the believer to be born again into a healthy new environment where the demons of poverty can be neutralized. Conceived of as a "positive transformation of the nature and value of a person," religious conversion appeals most to those individuals and groups who have been stigmatized or negatively evaluated by society (Stark and Bainbridge 197). A conversionist religion, then, which offers the possibility of a new life far removed from the afflictions of the old, would be understandably popular among those millions of Latin Americans seeking to turn away from family conflict, alcoholism, and illness.

The doctrine and experience of conversion provides the type of rupture with secular society that many afflicted men and women are looking for. In accepting Jesus and receiving baptism by the Holy Spirit, neophytes are called upon to abandon their worldly life for a holy one. What this implies on a practical level is a reorientation from the mundane pleasures and perils of the street to the godliness of church and family life. The theological dualism and asceticism of this conversionist religion present the street, on one hand, and church and home, on the other, as polarities on a continuum of good and evil. The street is the Devil's playground with its crime, prostitution, gambling, and substance abuse. In stark contrast, God is manifest in the fraternal worship of the church and harmonious family life. Converts thus learn to demonize the street and its devilish temptations and thereby renounce the very patterns of comportment that might have led them to convert to Pentecostalism in the first place.

Of such importance is this element of conversion that two-thirds of my male informants in Brazil mentioned the repudiation of "vice" as the most important change in their life since conversion. And not surprisingly, they cited worldly temptations as their second greatest problem after financial hardship (Chesnut 1997, 112). Since the streets of Latin America, especially on the urban margins, are still largely a male domain, it follows that the rupture of conversion to Pentecostalism is greater for men. In short, the product of conversion allows believers to reclaim and maintain their health through their rebirth into a salutary new environment, largely devoid of the demons of the street.

If believers find themselves assailed by such demons, their religion offers them a specific brand of faith healing to exorcise them. Exorcism, usually referred to as liberation, *libertação* in Portuguese, has been practiced by Pentecostal preachers since the early days, but over the past two decades, Neo-Pentecostal churches have brought it from the fringes of religious practice to center stage. Indeed, in its weekly calendar of worship, the Universal Church devotes Fridays to *cultos de libertação* (exorcism services). Far removed from the Assembly of God preachers who used to prefer to keep the demons at bay, Universal pastors actually invoke the evil spirits, inviting them to "manifest themselves" in tormented worshipers. In scenes often reminiscent of the *Exorcist* or the staged wrestling matches that are so popular in Latin America, pastors demonstrate their superior spiritual power by forcefully "tying up" (*amarrando*) the demons, thus releasing their human victims from their malevolent grip.

Pentecostalism's final salient product, ecstatic power, is one that it shares with its main religious rivals but possesses in greater measure than African diasporan faiths and Charismatic Catholicism. Just as the dialectic between illness and faith healing attracts millions of converts, a similar one between socioeconomic impotence and spiritual power appeals to many impoverished Latin Americans. With direct access to the Holy Spirit through Baptism in the Spirit and charismata, such as glossolalia and prophecy, economically impotent Pentecostals experience intense spiritual power. Filled with the power of the Holy Spirit, poor believers are fortified to do battle with the demons of deprivation, which can make life on the urban and rural margins seem hellish at times. The often-ecstatic nature of Pentecostalism's spiritual power, in which believers enter a dissociated state of consciousness, allows them to temporarily transcend their difficult earthly station and experience the rapture of communion with the Holy Spirit. Since Pentecostalism prohibits popular mundane sources of ecstasy, such as psychotropic drugs and casual sex, worship services and prayer groups are the main loci in which believers can experience the sensation of being transported from their social place (ekstasis) to an extraordinary space of supernatural rapture.

A Faith in Marketing

As any business student knows, it is not sufficient for a firm simply to possess an appealing product. In modern consumer societies where prospective customers are presented with a dizzying array of goods and services, businesses must aggressively market their product, attempting to pierce the cacophony of omnipresent advertising and deliver their message to consumers. So important is marketing, particularly in affluent consumer societies such as the United States, that the way in which a particular product is packaged and advertised often has greater bearing on its sales than the actual qualities of the product itself.

Admittedly, the science of marketing is not as developed in religious economies as commercial ones, but without a successful strategy of evangelization that offers doctrine and worship directly to prospective believers, spiritual firms operating in a free market of faith will find it hard to compete with their rivals who actively and creatively evangelize. And in the religious economies of present day Ibero-America no religion has evangelized as successfully as Pentecostalism. If pneumacentric Protestantism has been able to convert millions of nominal Catholics and claim at least three-quarters of the region's total Protestant population in less than a century, it is in no small measure due to Pentecostal marketing of the faith. This section, then, considers the ways in which the Assemblies of God, Foursquare Gospel Church, and other Pentecostal denominations have successfully delivered their religious products to spiritual consumers through advertising and packaging. In the Evangelical idiom, what follows is examination of the methods of evangelization that have won myriad souls for Jesus.

Like their Pentecostal brethren in the United States, Latin American *crentes* are the most skilled marketers in the region's new religious economy. They have utilized diverse media to deliver the simple but potent message to prospective converts that affiliation with Pentecostalism will imbue them with sufficient supernatural strength to vanquish the demons of poverty. It is the dynamic and controversial Universal Church of the Kingdom of God that has captured the essence of Pentecostal advertising in its evangelistic slogan, "stop suffering." The pithy phrase *pare de sofrer*, typically printed in bright red letters, calls out to the afflicted poor of Brazil from the church walls, pamphlets, and newspapers of this innovative denomination. A combination of low- and high-tech media invite religious consumers, mainly nominal Catholics, to relieve their suffering by embracing Jesus and the Holy Spirit specifically within the walls of the particular church that is advertising its product.

One of the most effective means of marketing the Pentecostal product is the oldest method of *creyente* evangelization in Latin America, home visits. The founders of the Assembly of God in Brazil, Swedish-American immigrants Gunnar Vingren and Daniel Berg, proselytized in early twentieth-century Belem through visits to victims of a yellow fever epidemic and other maladies (Chesnut 1997). Since then, hundreds of thousands of Pentecostal pastors and lay persons have knocked on flimsy doors throughout Latin America's urban periphery and countryside to spread the good news of healing to those suffering from poverty-related afflictions. In the Assemblies of God, laywomen evangelists, called *visitadoras* (visitors) proselytize not only door to door but also in hospitals filled with those who are especially predisposed to accept a dose of divine healing. Until the Charismatic Renewal developed its own home-visit campaign in the 1980s targeting nominal Catholics, Pentecostals and Neo-Christians, such as Mormons and Jehovah's Witnesses, were the only groups who brought their products directly to Latin American spiritual consumers in their own homes.

Indeed it is within the household that Pentecostalism recruits most of its converts. However, it is not the visit of a church evangelist that most often results in affiliation with a Pentecostal denomination but intimate contact with believers in the family. Almost half of my ninety Pentecostal informants in Belem had first come into contact with the faith through family members (Chesnut 1997, 76). In Guatemala, Pedrone-Colombani found a similar pattern with friends and colleagues also figuring as agents of conversion (174). In the intimacy of the home, nonbelieving family members can observe the benefits that affiliation with the faith has brought to kin who have purchased the Pentecostal product. It is one thing to hear the conversion testimonial of a stranger and quite another to actually witness firsthand the positive changes experienced by a family member as a result of her adherence to the faith. Despite the considerable investment in high-tech marketing, it is low-tech advertising in which family members, coworkers and friends tout the advantages of charismatic Protestantism among each other that has been the most efficient media for attracting new religious consumers.

For those Ibero-Americans who do not come into contact with Pentecostalism through low-tech marketing, evangelists have made it hard to avoid exposure to their product through its advertisement in the mass media of radio, television, and even the internet. Despite the rapid growth of Pentecostal televangelism in the region since the early 1980s, it is the oldest form of electronic media, radio, that continues to account for the bulk of *crente* broadcasting. Whereas even Pentecostal-owned television stations, such as the UCKG's Rede Record, transmit mostly commercial programs, many radio stations broadcast nothing but Pentecostal preaching, music, and conversion testimonials twenty-four hours a day.

Radio's advantage over television as a marketing tool for the Pentecostal product is twofold. First and foremost it is significantly cheaper than television. Only the largest denominations, such as the Assemblies of God, UCKG, and Foursquare Gospel Church can afford the high costs associated with proprietorship of a station or production of programs. In contrast, some smaller churches that could never dream of appearing on television possess the funds to purchase small amounts of air time, particularly on the AM band of the close to one thousand stations in Latin America that carry Protestant programming (Moreno in Sigmund 51). Second, while TV antennae have become a permanent fixture on the skyline of the urban periphery, radio is still more ubiquitous among the Latin American popular classes. A 1993 survey on mass media revealed radio to be the most frequently accessed medium in greater Sao Paulo, especially among the lowest income groups (Mariano 68 n. 38). In short, Pentecostal marketers reach a larger audience and deliver their product more cost effectively on radio.

Following in the footsteps of their North American brethren who dominate religious broadcasting in the United States, a few large Pentecostal denominations enjoy a commanding position in the transmission of spiritual programs. With the exception of the pioneering but short-lived programs of the nationalistic Brazil for Christ denomination in the 1960s and the Universal Church in the early 1980s, Latin American owned and produced Pentecostal television did not take root until the late 1980s. Since the early part of the decade, U.S. televangelists, such as Assembly of God members Jimmy Swaggart and Jim Bakker, had dominated Protestant broadcasting in Latin America. Given the superior resources of the North American televangelists, it was only natural that they serve as the trailblazers in Latin American Pentecostal television.

However, by the end of the decade a few major *crente* churches, particularly in Brazil, such as the Assemblies of God, Foursquare Gospel, UCKG, and International Church of the Grace of God (Igreja Internacional da Graca de Deus) were producing their own programs, and in the case of the UCKG, purchasing its own station. In November of 1989, the Universal Church made Latin American history in buying the Rede Record television and radio stations for U.S. $45 million. With Record owned by the UCKG and Rede Globo, Latin America's largest broadcasting corporation, by the staunch Catholic impresario, Roberto Marinho, the battle for Christian market share has erupted on to the small screens of Brazil. Both networks have aired *novelas* (evening soap operas) satirizing and even demonizing each other. And Padre Marcelo, the dashing young superstar of the Catholic Charismatic Renewal, has appeared on numerous occasions in the late 1990s on Rede Globo's variety and talk shows.

Ever seeking a novel way to sell their product, large Latin American Pentecostal churches have joined the revolution in information technology and have developed websites on the internet.[7] The UCKG website even has its own chatroom in which members and the curious can discuss matters of faith in "real time." The small but increasing minority of Latin American believers who have internet access can take pride in the fact that their denominations have embraced the latest mass medium as a novel way to market their religious product to those in need of healing.

The Pentecostal product sold in the mass media is most appealing when sold in the packages of testimonials, music, and exorcism. Whether on television, on radio, or at rallies in soccer stadiums, the conversion narrative of a Pentecostal convert is often a powerfully emotive account of how Jesus or the Holy Spirit restored the believer's health or saved her from one of the demons of deprivation. Listeners and viewers experiencing their own crisis hear and see how someone from the same or similar social class dramatically turned his life around through acceptance of Jesus and affiliation with the church broadcasting the program. Such advertising is ubiquitous among even nonreligious commercial firms, of course: for example, dramatic before-and-after photos, along with testimony, of consumers who supposedly used a particular diet product invite obese North Americans to remake themselves as slim and fit men and women.

Pentecostal sales representatives also package their product in the emotional form of music. Romantic ballads, pop songs, and regional rhythms all set to evangelical lyrics blare from Pentecostal radio and television stations, in addition to worship services. The most musical of all the major branches of Christianity, Pentecostalism rouses its believers and attracts new converts through its melodic electric guitars, drums, tambourines, and synthesizers. Whether it is background mood music or moving hymns, melodic rhythms constitute such an integral part of *crente* worship services that in Brazil they are sung and played during at least two-thirds of the typically two-hour-long service. Likewise, songs of praise occupy significant time on Pentecostal radio and television programs. The decision to purchase the Pentecostal product, or convert, is usually a highly emotional one made in the midst of personal crisis, and sacred music playing on an Evangelical radio program can put the afflicted individual in the right state of mind that allows her to surrender herself to Jesus.

Fully cognizant of the fact that most Latin Americans convert to Pentecostalism through its premier product of faith healing, Pentecostal pastors advertise and package the doctrine and practice of *cura divina* in a manner that directly addresses the poverty-related afflictions of the popular classes. As a brand of faith healing, exorcism not only delivers believers from the demons of quotidian poverty but also serves as a useful marketing tool in the battle with African diasporan religions for the souls of religious consumers in the Caribbean and Brazil. In Trinidad, Brazil, Haiti, and Cuba, among other Caribbean nations, the demons that Pentecostal pastors triumphantly exorcise from possessed worships are no ordinary evil spirits. Rather, the demonic agents are the *exus*, or liminal trickster spirits of Umbanda, Candomblé, Voodoo, and Santeria. Considered amoral spiritual entities by the mothers and fathers of the saints who preside over diasporan *terreiros* (houses of worship), the *exus*, such as Seven Skulls (Sete Caveiras in Brazil), possess no such ambiguity among Pentecostals. For *creyentes*, they are nothing less than tangible manifestations of pure evil that sow only misery and destruction in believers' lives. In driving Seven Skulls back to his lair at the cemetery through exorcism, Pentecostal pastors demonstrate to religious consumers the superior spiritual power of their faith. The *exus* simply cannot resist the omnipotence of the Pentecostal Holy Spirit and time and again are "tied up" and expelled to their stations at the crossroads and cemeteries of Brazil and the Caribbean.

It would be difficult to find a more literal demonization of a religious rival than the case at hand. In the late 1980s the Universal Church initiated a small-scale holy war against Umbanda and Candombléin which zealous members actually invaded and desecrated *terreiros* and assaulted mothers and fathers of the saints. The overarching Pentecostal strategy, then, is to portray its dynamic diasporan competitors as satanic cults that offer nothing but greater misery to religious consumers. At the beginning of this century, Pentecostal products have outsold those of their African diasporan competitors. In conclusion, Latin American Pentecostals have proved themselves to be the region's most skillful marketers of the faith by effectively employing every form of media available to them to offer their product to religious consumers. From the low-tech method of home visits to the high-tech internet, *creyente* marketers have packaged and sold their product in Latin America's new religious marketplace with unrivaled acumen.

Army of Amateurs

The successful marketing of a product depends in large part on the skill and zeal of a firm's sales representatives. Without a motivated corps of salespersons who believe in the goods and services they are selling, even the most appealing product, whether spiritual or temporal, will often prove a difficult sell. And it is here again that Pentecostalism has developed a great advantage over its Protestant rivals, and has also proven competitive superiority over other religious competitors. *Creyente* sales specialists are not well educated like their Catholic and mainline Protestant rivals but have proven themselves to be superior vendors of religious goods and services for several reasons.

Perhaps of greatest importance is that each believer, whether clergy or laity, is a potential sales representative for his or her church. Contrariwise, it is only with the development of the Charismatic Renewal in the 1980s that the Latin American Catholic Church started to send lay missionaries door to door to evangelize nominal Catholics. Until then what little proselytizing took place was carried out by priests. Conversely, for most of the nearly a century that Pentecostalism has been operating in the region, it is zealous lay evangelists who have done most of the knocking on the doors of Latin American homes. And when not making home visits, lay members sell the Pentecostal product very successfully to their family members, coworkers, and friends. Indeed, as has previously been mentioned, the majority of converts first come into contact with the faith along such interpersonal networks. Thus it is probably the case that these amateur sales representatives, the laity, have sold more Pentecostal products than the professionals, the pastorate. Leaving aside the fact that Pentecostal pastors outnumber Catholic priests in the region, charismatic Protestantism enjoys the enormous competitive advantage of possessing millions of amateur sales persons who are eager to sell the same product that improved their lives to sisters and brothers, daughters and sons, and friends and colleagues.

If it were not enough to be able to rely on a force of dedicated amateurs to do most of the selling, Pentecostalism also excels at marketing because of the entrepreneurial skills and evangelical zeal of its professional sales representatives, the pastorate. Besides outnumbering their mainline Protestant and Catholic cohorts, *creyente* pastors enjoy several distinct advantages over their religious rivals. First, as ironic as it may seem, Pentecostal pastors are more likely to share the common elements of nationality and social class with prospective converts than Catholic clergy do with theirs. Surprisingly, in a region that is putatively the most Catholic in the world, in most countries the majority of the priests are foreign. Leading the region is the most Pentecostal nation, Guatemala, where in the early 1980s, an astounding 87 percent of the clergy were foreign born, especially in Spain. Bolivia, Mexico, Honduras, and Venezuela follow as nations in which more than two-thirds of the priests were foreigners. And non–Latin American clergy also constituted the majority in Chile, Paraguay, and Peru. Indeed only in Uruguay, Ecuador, and top-ranking Colombia did national priests significantly outnumber their foreign confreres (Barrett 1982). In diametrical opposition, the great majority of the Pentecostal pastorate in every Latin American country is native born. Other factors being equal, religious consumers are more likely to purchase products sold by compatriots who speak their same language fluently and share their same national culture. Paradoxically, a religion that less than a century ago was brought to the region by foreign missionaries is now more authentically Latin American, at least in terms of its clergy, than the faith that has had half a millennium to sink its roots from Argentina to Mexico.

Compatriotism, however, is not the only competitive advantage possessed by professional Pentecostal sales representatives. That *crente* pastors normally belong to the same socioeconomic class as those they seek to convert also makes for easier sale of Pentecostal products. Not only does nationality distance the majority of Catholic clergy from prospective practitioners, but so do their educational levels. Years of seminary training place priests among the educational elite of Latin America. Even if they came from humble origins, they have acquired considerable sacred and secular knowledge through higher education and no longer speak the language of the unlettered *pueblo*. Hence, the gap between the highly educated foreign priest and the potential parishioner with no more than an elementary school education makes for a harder sell of the Catholic product.

In contradistinction, the professional Pentecostal salesman is not only a fellow Mexican, for example, but also an individual who had to quit school in the sixth grade to work to help support his family. He makes his sales pitch in the same colorful and often ungrammatical Spanish spoken by his prospective consumers, who will recognize him as both a *paisano* (compatriot) and a *carnal* (a term employed by the Mexican popular classes that roughly translates into the U.S. slang of "blood" or "brother"). Marketed in the popular idiom of the Latin American *pueblo*, the Pentecostal product proves a much easier sell than religious goods and services offered in sophisticated and often foreign-accented Spanish and Portuguese.

The final major competitive advantage enjoyed by the professional Pentecostal sales force derives from the organizational structure of many *crente* churches. In almost all of the storefront churches in which one or two houses of worship constitute the extent of the "denomination," and even in many large churches, the local pastor's salary depends on the tithes and offerings of members. The more pesos or bolivars collected at worship services, the greater the pastoral remuneration. The logic of the organization thus motivates the professional sales representatives to sell their dynamic product to an ever-greater number of religious consumers who can augment the Pentecostal vendor's salary and prestige through their donations. Those pastors who recruit a critical mass of congregants can earn enough to be able to quit their day jobs as bus drivers, popcorn vendors, security guards, and other low-ranking positions in the service sector. The cold logic of the free religious market means that those pastors who are not able to attract a critical mass of members will either continue to work in the "world" or might even be forced to suspend their pastoral vocation and close the church.

Among the major Pentecostal denominations of the region, most of which are relatively bureaucratized, the UCKG stands out as an extreme in its emphasis on collecting tithes and offerings from believers. That typically a full hour of two-hour UCKG worship services is devoted to preaching, soliciting, and collecting the tithe should come as little surprise in a denomination in which pastoral promotions are largely dependent on a preacher's ability to multiply his talents for attracting tithes from members. Those with a gift for collecting "ten percent for Jesus" and who have demonstrated unswerving fealty to chief bishop, Edir Macedo, become likely candidates for promotion to the highest church office of bishop. Even in churches such as Latin America's oldest Assembly of God in Belem, where local pastors receive only reimbursement for travel expenses and nothing more, professional advancement hinges to a great extent on the ability to develop a sizeable congregation and collect tithes from it (Chesnut 1997).

Whereas the professional Pentecostal sales representative is a religious entrepreneur, his Catholic cohort, as scholar and former Maryknoll missionary, Phillip Berryman, points out, is more of a bureaucrat (185–186). Pentecostal competition has led to a novel emphasis on tithing in parishes throughout the region, but in no way is clerical advancement dependent upon a priest's skill at fundraising. Although with increasing levels of competition, this may change in the not too distant future. Thus, in nine decades of selling their Pentecostal product in Ibero-America, *creyente* churches have outsold the competition by reliance on a huge army of amateur vendors, the laity, and dedicated professionals, the pastorate, who outnumber their Protestant and Catholic counterparts and share the common elements of nationality and class with potential consumers whose contributions to church coffers largely determine their pastoral fate.

Organizational Charisma

The final contributing factor to Pentecostalism's unmatched success in Latin America's new religious economy is its organizational structure, or polity in the ecclesiastical idiom. In accord with the logic of the commercial economy, the ways in which religious firms organize their operations have a direct bearing on their fate in the free market of faith. In the popular religious marketplace where consumers and producers are strapped for resources, those spiritual organizations that have structured their operations in efficient, cost-effective ways will enjoy obvious advantages over their competitors. On a larger plane, Pentecostalism as a whole benefits from its unrivaled differentiation. That is, the hundreds, if not thousands, of distinct Pentecostal denominations that crowd the popular marketplace allow for a high degree of specialization and niche marketing that targets specific sets of consumers. Believers, for example, looking for a liberal dose of exorcism in worship services will find the Universal Church of particular interest. Hence, this final section will consider how Pentecostal polities have contributed to making charismatic Protestantism the most dynamic producer of religious goods and services in Latin America.

The great differentiation of Pentecostalism obviates discussion of a uniform polity found in all denominations and churches. Rather, the multiplicity of congregations has resulted in a wide range of organizational structures. Nevertheless, the larger denominations share sufficient common organizational features to allow for the identification of key elements. A brief examination of two of the region's largest denominations, which in many ways occupy opposite ends of the organizational continuum, will shed light on the key factors that unite these two in their impressive growth.

The largest and one of the oldest denominations in Latin America, the Assemblies of God have adopted one of the more democratic and participatory forms of church government in a religion that manifests strong authoritarian and hierarchical tendencies. Although one of the most bureaucratized denominations with myriad ecclesial departments and professional administrators, Assembly of God polity allows for high levels of lay participation in the daily operation of the churches, particularly local ones. Numerous church offices, such as deacon, presbyter, and even doorman, permit lay members to become actively involved in the administration of their own churches. At annual general assemblies at the regional, state, and national levels, delegates discuss and vote on matters of church policy. Few other *crente* denominations can compete with the Assemblies' extraordinarily high levels of lay participation in the operation of tens of thousands of houses of worship. The ISER survey of Protestantism in Rio de Janeiro found that close to half, 43 percent, of all *Assembleianos* had served as church officers (ISER 37). My own investigation in Belem, based on a much smaller sample, discovered that an astounding four-fifths of *Assembleianos* in the Amazonian city had held church office (Chesnut 1997, 135).

Despite such high levels of lay participation and ostensibly democratic forms of decision-making, however, strong authoritarian currents flow through the church. In the Assembly of God in Belem, Latin America's oldest, the chief pastor, the *pastor-presidente*, had led the church for a quarter of a century and had concentrated ecclesiastical power to such a degree that he merits the moniker of Pentecostal pontiff. The most important decisions on church policy were made by the head pastor, often in consultation with a cabal of loyal salaried pastors. The term "participatory authoritarianism" best captures the dialectical model of the organizational structure of the Assemblies of God.

Brazil's fastest growing denomination, the UCKG, shares the Assemblies' authoritarianism but not its high levels of lay participation. In fact of all major churches surveyed in Rio de Janeiro, Universal had the lowest rate of lay engagement. Only 13 percent of UCKG members had ever held church office (ISER 37). In great contrast to lay participation in Assemblies' worship services, in which ordinary members read Bible passages, give testimony, lead hymns, and make announcements, UCKG services are notable for their complete control by pastors. Lay participation is limited to ushering duties and highly choreographed testimony. When I queried a UCKG member in Belem as to why laypersons were never invited to the altar to read a bible passage or lead a prayer, she explained that the altar is so holy that those who are not pastors risk defiling it.

The church's episcopal polity, uncommon among Pentecostals, makes for one of the most authoritarian and centralized denominations. The chief bishop, Edir Macedo, concentrating even more power than the Catholic pontiff, involves himself in all aspects of ecclesiastical policy. Yet, despite its extreme authoritarianism, the UCKG has grown to become the second largest Brazilian Pentecostal church in less than three decades. How has a denomination that is reminiscent of pre–Vatican II Catholicism in its exclusion of laity been able to attract millions of religious consumers? The answer lies both in UCKG polity itself and the larger organizational structure of Latin American Pentecostalism in general. Although it seems counterintuitive, there is obviously a demand for brands of Pentecostalism in which the laity is restricted to a relatively passive role in church life while autocratic pastors monopolize the production and administration of religious goods and services. Indeed most Latin Americans belonging to the popular classes are accustomed to such relationships in the secular world and are not necessarily looking for egalitarianism in their religious lives. And those who are can choose from other Pentecostal churches, such as the Assemblies of God, that offer greater opportunities for lay engagement.

Herein lies the second component of the UCKG's organizational success. The range and diversity of Latin American Pentecostalism has led to a high degree of specialization and niche marketing. Thus the UCKG fits the bill not only for religious consumers who prefer the traditional division between laity and clergy but also for those attracted to exorcism, prosperity theology, and aggressive combat against Umbanda and Candomblé. The Universal Church in Rio de Janeiro, for example, has the highest percentage of former practitioners of African-Brazilian religion among its ranks of any major Pentecostal denomination (ISER 18). Consumers looking for extreme asceticism and draconian moral and comport-mental codes gravitate toward God is Love or similar denominations.

In effect, there are so many varieties of Pentecostalism available in the reli-gious marketplace that consumers can choose their brands according to pref-erences in gender, class, age, musical tastes, et cetera. Membership in UCKG, for example, is the most heavily female (81 percent in Rio) in a religion in which women typically outnumber men two to one (ISER 60). In class terms, the UCKG attracts the poorest *cariocas* while the "renewed" or breakaways from the mainline churches that have Pentecostalized, such as the Renewed Presbyterian (Iglesia Presbiteriana Renovada) appeal to those with higher income levels (ISER 10). Of course, Catholicism is also offered in many variet-ies in the religious marketplace, but not to the same extent found in the hun-dreds of different denominations of Pentecostalism.

The final element of Pentecostal polity that gives this branch of ecstatic Protestantism a competitive edge over its rivals is its preference for charisma over theological training for its professional sales representatives or pastors. While larger and older denominations, particularly the Assemblies of God, have institutional-ized to the point that its salaried pastors are required to have several years of semi-nary training, Pentecostalism, as a popular religion, has historically emphasized spiritual gifts over theological education. That a male believer with not more than an elementary school education but a healthy dose of charisma can rise through the pastoral ranks of most denominations opens the ministry up to tens of thousands of impoverished male believers who would never qualify for the rigorous educa-tional requirements of the Catholic priesthood or mainline Protestant ministry. The result has been a proliferation of Pentecostal pastors, who in Brazil, the largest Catholic nation on earth, now outnumber priests by two to one.

With a larger pastorate, there are more Pentecostal preachers available to evangelize Latin Americans door to door as statistics from El Salvador dramatically reveal. In the late 1980s, 77 percent of Salvadoran Protestants surveyed had been visited at home by a pastor while only 28 percent of practic-ing Catholics and just 16 percent of nonpracticing or nominal Catholics had received a visit from a priest (Aguilar et al in Stoll and Garrard-Burnett 120). An additional advantage of Pentecostal and Protestant polity in general is its allowance for married clergy. Indeed, single pastors are often pressured to find a wife, lest they become objects of gossip or speculation about their sex lives. Given the lack of enthusiasm for celibacy on the part of Latin American men, Protestantism in general enjoys an enormous advantage over Catholicism in recruiting and retaining professional sales representatives.

If at the beginning of the twenty-first century, Latin American Christianity has Pentecostalized to the extent that the Catholic Church's most dynamic movement is its own version of Pentecostalism, it is because charismatic Protestantism has developed superior religious products and marketed them more successfully than its competitors in the free market of faith. Unlike Catholicism, which enjoyed a four-century-plus monopoly on religious production, Pentecostalism, if it were to expand in the region, had to compete for religious consumers. Thus from its arrival in the first decades of the twentieth century, Pentecostalism had to convince Catholics, predominantly nominal ones, that Pentecostal products are superior. And this it has done with such success that on this past Sunday there were more *crentes* worshiping in their churches than Catholics at Mass in Brazil, the largest "Catholic nation" on earth.

Such is the situation because Pentecostal churches, responding to popular consumer demand, developed products that offer healing of the afflictions of poverty and positive personal transformation for those who have been rejected and stigmatized by societies that have the steepest socioeconomic pyramids in the world. Amateur and professional Pentecostal sales representatives have marketed the product to religious consumers with great zeal and acumen. Finally, the organizational structure of both Pentecostalism in general and specific denominations has helped propel this ecstatic religion to its current commanding position in Latin America's religious marketplace.

NOTES

1. Pew Forum on Religion and Public Life, *Spirit and Power: A 10-Country Survey of Pentecostals.* http://pewforum.org/surveys/pentecostal/.
2. Pew Forum, *Spirit and Power.* http://pewforum.org/surveys/pentecostal.
3. Pew Forum on Religion and Public Life, "Overview, pentecostalsism in Latin America." http://pewforum.org/surveys/pentecostal/latinamerica/.
4. In their groundbreaking study of the historical winners and losers in the U.S. religious economy, Stark and Finke (1992) demonstrate that the fate of religious organizations in a free market economy depends on their products, marketing, sales representatives, and organizational structure. Translated into the ecclesiastical idiom, doctrine, evangelization techniques, clergy, and polity are the four factors that determine the success or failure of any given religious enterprise in a pluralistic environment (17). Broadening Stark and Finke's narrow pairing of the religious product with doctrine, I include liturgy or forms of worship in my definition of the religious product.
5. A native of Rio de Janeiro.
6. The ISER survey included mainline Protestants whose higher income and educational levels raised the mean. If only Pentecotals had been surveyed the gap between believers and the general population would have been substantially larger.
7. A search in May of 2007 found the following churches to be running their own websites: the UCKG, the Assemblies of God in Brazil, Luz del Mundo-Mexico (Light of the World), Deus e Amor-Brazil (God is Love), Iglesia del Evangelio Cuadrangular-Chile (Forsquare Gospel Church), El Shaddai-Guatemala, and Iglesia Crisitiana Verbo-Guatemala (Church of the Word).

4

The Growth and Development of Non-Catholic Churches in Paraguay

HENRI GOOREN

Introduction

The different varieties of Pentecostalism have generally been very successful in Latin America, where Chile, Brazil, and most Central American countries are now 15 to 30 percent Protestant. However, Colombia, Uruguay, and Paraguay are only 5 to 6 percent Protestant and only 3 percent Pentecostal[1]—a phenomenon that has received far less scholarly attention. This chapter analyzes the growth and development of non-Catholic churches in Paraguay, arguably the *least* Protestant country of Latin America, based on a literature review and on extensive fieldwork research in Asunción in July–August 2010.[2] I end with an analysis of average annual growth rates for each individual church and for the entire Protestant community in Paraguay. My main questions are: which non-Catholic churches in Paraguay have been most successful in terms of membership growth and when did this growth occur? The conclusion summarizes and analyzes why Protestantism and Pentecostalism have not been successful in Paraguay (yet?). But first I start with two counter cases: one successful and one stagnating church group.

Two Counter Cases

The Family Worship Center (Centro Familiar de Adoración, CFA) is the most successful church in Asunción, Paraguay. Its main building is imposing, immaculately white with dark windows and a cross on its tower. There is an usher to greet people at the entrance and hand out a folder with eight mini-pages of information. Inside is a new, bright, and clean reception area like in an office building, with receptionists, a vestibule, and people sitting at tables marked "Modelo 1." There are further doors into an enormous auditorium, where loud gospel music is booming from. Upon entering, one sees 2,000 people standing, singing, swaying, and holding their hands in the air. On the huge yellow-lighted stage are three young female singers in formal dress and two male singers, with one holding an acoustic guitar. At the back are a higher stage with a keyboard player and a drummer as well as a church choir of about 25 youths all dressed in white. In the center of the room are two cameras at different levels, which are continuously filming everything on stage. Their images are projected live on the two smaller screens on the sides, while the main screen in the center has an image of three lighted candle flames in close-up.

The CFA members are dressed informally, with most wearing jeans. Some women use dresses and a few men suits, which do not look very expensive. Most are younger couples between 20 and 45, although there are quite a few older people and small children. Women form a majority, as usual, with many using make-up and pants. People are asked to turn off their cell phones regularly on the center screen. The music goes on until 10:50 a.m., when there is an altar call. About 50 people come forward and are ushered into a side room for further instruction. Next an older pastor with grey hair and glasses in an expensive dark-blue suit preaches on 2 Kings 3: 9–20. All Bible quotations are projected on the big central screen and explained briefly. The pastor often invites applause or a confirming "Amen"; he is finished after only 12 minutes.

Now starts the part of the "Ofrendas" (Donations) for new church buildings and for the Marcus Witt concert on November 1 to commemorate CFA's 25 years. Tickets are 30,000 Guaranis (US $6.00). The big screen shows how to fill out the *Ofrenda* forms in much detail, and the ushers go around distributing and collecting little envelopes. During this time there are various announcements, all of which can also be found in the eight-page folder: special church meetings ("Encuentros"), the CFA Bookstore, the magazine *Revista Radicales*, and the "Escuela de Líderes." There is a special video message of church founders and central pastors Emilio and Bethany Abreu on this Leaders' School, which mentions the prices in great detail.

A second, balding pastor takes over. He announces that today is a very special Sunday, because it is Sacrament Sunday. He emphasizes the Bible quotations, saying that people who are not worthy should never partake of this or risk damnation. Nevertheless we seem to be the only people not partaking. Everybody receives a little piece of dry-looking bread and a tiny cup of purple fluid. A slow gospel ballad is playing during the distribution of the sacrament. After this, about 60 ushers in yellow sweaters stand at the back walls. At the front it has the CFA logo: a Paraguay map with a red flame and a cross. At the back it has the words "Estamos aquí para servir" (We are here to serve/help).

The balding pastor preaches for about 30–40 minutes on the importance of the sacrament, on the second coming of Jesus Christ, and on leading a righteous life. The final gospel songs start around 12:15 p.m. People start getting up immediately, with thinly disguised impatience. In less than five minutes, most of the estimated 2,000 people are gone. Some stay to pray, sway, and sing—like the man next to me. The balding pastor offers farewell prayers and best wishes.

Only half a mile away from the CFA, the central group of the Catholic Charismatic Renewal (CCR) in Paraguay meets on Wednesday afternoons. They start their meeting punctually with music at 3:00 p.m., right after reciting the rosary. The space is huge but almost completely empty, with room for over 1,500 but less than 50 visitors. They are singing CCR songs with enthusiasm. There's a huge colorful painting of Christ on the wall. I am welcomed by two female ushers with white sweaters, displaying "La virgin de paz" and a picture of Mary at the back. They introduce me to an older man. He has been a CCR participant since 1991 and is the current coordinator of all lay movements (CCR, Cursillos de Cristiandad, Legión de María, etc.) in the archdiocese of Asunción.

He tells me that the CCR arrived in Paraguay through U.S. priests in the early 1970s. For a long time it was not successful. Success came in the 1990s and early 2000s. For the past few years, participation has been down. He travels and preaches in Colombia, Ecuador, and Argentina and hears it is down there, too. Many lay leaders were formed by the CCR, only to go on to other movements. Most participants are active in their parish; almost all parishes in Asunción now have a CCR group. This is the archdiocese's central meeting group, which goes back over 20 years. In the archdiocese of Asunción, there are now 120 prayer groups of between 15 and 20 people each. On reflection he thinks the number might have gone down to 100 groups.

The leader confirms that the CCR is more urban than rural and is strongest in Asunción, Ciudad del Este, and Encarnación. Most participants are middle class and lower middle class. They tend to have more education and a somewhat higher income than the average in Paraguay. Most people in this small CCR group look well-clothed, with only a handful of exceptions.

He gives me a tour of the building, which is huge. It has room for 1,500 people below. There are also some small rooms below and a bookstore. Above are a big meeting room, a small storage room full of mattresses (for *retiros* when people sleep over), and two small offices. One is his, with a picture of former Pope John Paul II, where he does pastoral work: listening to people's problems and counseling them.

After the CCR leader has to leave, one of the old ladies in the meeting room offers herself as my guide. While the meeting downstairs continues with music, prayer, and singing, we walk along to the right, into a huge patio with room for a few hundred people. Last weekend, during the visit of a famous Peruvian priest, it was full of people. Now it looks very empty.

The mass part starts somewhat later at 4:15 p.m. There is a young Brazilian priest with a slight accent and two assistant priests. The singing, swaying, and clapping continue for a while longer. I count 72 people plus five on the stage: the three priests, one young female singer/keyboard player, and an older female speaker/singer. There are 20 men of a total of 77 participants. Only five people look poor or badly dressed or sick; there are hardly any children. Most participants are older women; there are a few older men, a few young women, and only two young men. Inside it feels just as cold as outside: 50° Fahrenheit. Everybody's cold, even though most people use big sweaters and jackets.

The main sermon by the Brazilian priest lasts only 20 minutes and begins with the question: how can we get to know God? It is very lively, entertaining, and thought-provoking, although few people are paying attention. The sermon is followed by more music, *ofrendas*, and the Eucharist (sacrament). Afterwards there is Paraguayan tea (*cocido*) and a guava (*guayabo*) pastry: delicious and very good to warm you up. I talk to some of the elderly ladies, who have all been with the group for over a decade. They cannot remember any new participants arriving in the last couple of weeks.

Theorizing Church Growth

While the Family Worship Center (CFA) was Paraguay's most successful Pentecostal church in terms of membership growth, the Catholic Charismatic Renewal (CCR) was stagnating in 2010. Why are some churches successful while others stagnate or even decline in membership? This chapter uses a model for church growth that I developed earlier for the case of Guatemala; see table 4.1 below.

Guatemala is the most Protestant country of Latin America, with estimates for the Protestant population proportion ranging from 25 to 35 percent.[3] My church growth model provides several clues as to why this is the case. The first U.S. Protestant missionaries had already arrived in Guatemala between 1900 and 1935, starting churches, schools, and clinics. Between 1935 and 1960, the first Pentecostal churches built their own institutions and gradually relied more on Guatemalan leaders. Growth was moderate in 1960–76, only to explode after the devastating 1976 earthquake. Between 1976 and 1986, six factors converged to create the Protestant explosion in Guatemala: (1) The earthquake, civil war, political repression, and a severe economic recession created an explosion of *anomie*.[4] (2) Many new Protestant churches and missionaries arrived as part of

Table 4.1 **A Model of Church Growth***

	(1) **Internal Factors**	*(2)* **External Factors**
Religious Factors	1a Appeal of the Doctrine	2a Dissatisfaction with Catholicism
	1b Evangelization Activities	2b Responses from the Catholic Hierarchy
	1c Appeal of the Organization	2c Social, Economic, and/or Psychological *Anomie*
Nonreligious Factors	1d Natural Growth and Membership Retention	2d Urbanization Process

*Adapted, with minor changes, from Gooren, "Reconsidering Protestant Growth," 177.

the earthquake relief effort. (3) More evangelization campaigns were organized than ever before. (4) The war created high urban growth in 1980–85, leading to *anomie* and a search for communities among the new city dwellers. (5) The traditional cargo system of indigenous groups had lost strength all over the country. (6) The Roman Catholic Church was slow to respond to Protestant growth, waiting until 1985 before the bishops supported the Catholic Charismatic Renewal to counter defections to Pentecostalism.[5]

My church growth model essentially analyzes church growth as a result of the interplay of eight religious and nonreligious factors, which can be both internal and external to the church under study. The internal religious factors are (1a) appeal of the doctrine and (1b) evangelization activities; the internal nonreligious factors are (1c) appeal of the church organization and (1d) natural growth and membership retention. The external religious factors are (2a) dissatisfaction with Catholicism and (2b) responses from the Catholic hierarchy to non-Catholic growth; the external nonreligious factors are (2c) social, economic, and psychological *anomie* (Émile Durkheim's concept describing a situation of chaos and a lack of established norms) as well as (2d) the urbanization process, which uproots people and is assumed to make them more susceptible to join a new church.[6]

Approaching Paraguay

In this chapter I operationalize and analyze the eight growth factors for the country under study: Paraguay. Paraguay, landlocked and isolated, forms a unique case in Latin America. Roughly the size of California, the country is mostly flat and cut in two by the Paraguay River running from north to south. West of the river, the Chaco forms a barren and dry plain with temperatures reaching over 40° Celsius (100° Fahrenheit) in the summer. Although it forms almost 60 percent of Paraguay's land, only 2 percent of the total population of almost seven million lives here.[7] Asunción sits on the east bank of the Paraguay River in the heart of the country, close to the border with Argentina. East of the river, the land is fertile, and the climate and vegetation become ever more tropical going east toward the border with Brazil.

Even since its beginnings in 1547, the isolated Catholic Church in Paraguay was poorer than in other Latin American countries and maintained a weak institutional presence, leaving ample space for the development of a strongly conservative popular Catholicism centered on the cult of the saints, faith healing, and pilgrimages. From 1609 until their expulsion in 1767, the Jesuits brought various Guaraní peoples together in over a hundred *reducciones* and baptized one million Indians in the south of Paraguay.[8] Their main heritage, apart from hauntingly beautiful ruins, was the creation of a mestizo society and the conservation of Guaraní as the second official language of Paraguay.

Paraguay's isolation and weak institutional Catholicism made early independence from Spain possible in 1811, but also created the perfect conditions for a parade of megalomaniac dictators unparalleled in Latin America.[9] The new 1870 constitution for the first time in Paraguayan history officially recognized religious freedom.[10] Only 55 priests had survived the War of the Triple Alliance, and there would not be a new bishop of Asunción until 1881, making the institutional presence of the Roman Catholic Church even weaker than before.[11] In 1871, a group of "prominent Paraguayans" sent a letter to the Methodist Mission in London, inviting them to establish a church and a school in Asunción. Although the first independent Protestant missionaries started evangelizing in 1880, the Methodist missionaries would not arrive until 1886.[12]

Between 1904 and 1940, various Liberal governments upheld religious freedom and provided modest support for evangelical churches. After 1940, however, various nationalist Colorado governments openly supported the Roman Catholic Church with funding and privileges.[13] The 1940s and 1950s also witnessed some of the worst cases of persecution of evangelicals by Catholic mobs.[14] Political infighting led to the 1947 civil war and increasingly weak and unstable governments, opening the way for the Paraguayan military to get more deeply involved in politics than they already were. In 1953, a new law was proposed that would make Roman Catholic religious education mandatory in all public schools (primary and secondary), but it was withdrawn under strong pressure from the evangelical community.[15]

From the ranks of the military, an artillery colonel would come forth to usurp power in 1954 and establish a 35-year dictatorship. Alfredo Stroessner based his rule on an iron alliance between the armed factors, the Colorado Party, and the state. His regime was characterized by widespread corruption and the use of brutal violence against the opposition. Although Stroessner was born from German Protestants, he co-opted the Roman Catholic Church hierarchy to add legitimacy to his regime. By the 1960s, however, this system was starting to break down and in the 1970s the Catholic Church would gradually become an important factor in support of the political opposition.[16] The evangelical community in Paraguay initially welcomed Stroessner's regime in the 1950s for the economic stability and religious freedom it provided.[17] This chapter aims to explain why this greater religious freedom would not lead to significant Protestant growth in subsequent years, by carefully tracking church growth in 11 main non-Catholic churches in Paraguay. Five are mainstream Protestant churches (Lutherans, Methodists, Anglicans, Baptists, and Mennonites), three are independent new Christian churches (Adventists, Witnesses, and Mormons), and three are Pentecostal: the Assemblies of God, the Church of God in Paraguay, and the Centro Familiar de Adoración (CFA).[18]

Discussing Non-Catholic Church Growth in Paraguay

My first main question was: which non-Catholic churches in Paraguay have been most successful in terms of membership growth? Based on their self-reporting in 2000, the biggest non-Catholic churches in Paraguay were the Latter-day Saints (47,850 baptized Mormons), the Mennonite groups (25,000), the U.S.-origin Assemblies of God (12,454), the Seventh-day Adventists (9,614), the Lutheran Church (9,192), the Baptist Church (7,981), the Iglesia de Dios del Paraguay (7,975), the Jehovah's Witnesses (6,883), the Anglican Church (6,400), and the Iglesia Evangélica Asamblea de Dios Misionera (6,250). Note that there are only three Pentecostal churches ranked in this non-Catholic church top ten.[19]

A somewhat different picture emerges from the 2002 census; however, based on self-reporting by the Paraguayan adult population (over 16) who were likely the more committed members of their church: Jehovah's Witnesses (11,805), Baptists (10,355), Assemblies of God (9,879), Latter-day Saints (9,374), Lutherans (8,849), Mennonites (8,445), Seventh-day Adventists (7,804), Anglicans (1,858), and members of the Iglesia de Dios del Paraguay (1,550). The census data likely underreported churches with a predominantly rural membership, like the Mennonite groups and the Iglesia de Dios del Paraguay. Members of the (Brazilian-origin) Iglesia Evangélica Asamblea de Dios Misionera did not appear at all, possibly because they were counted together with the (U.S.-origin) Assemblies of God.

My second main question concerned the chronology of non-Catholic growth in Paraguay as it appears from the (limited) available data for the 11 major non-Catholic churches. I noted earlier that the Baptist Church experienced an early boom in the 1960s, partly the result of huge evangelization campaigns with international speakers, but no data are available for the other churches in this period.[20] In the 1970s, when economic growth was strong and the Catholic bishops increasingly clashed with the Stroessner dictatorship,[21] Adventists and Mormons already had their first membership booms, whereas total Protestant growth was a modest 3 percent. However, the Iglesia de Dios del Paraguay, the Church, and the Assemblies of God all reported modest membership declines, meaning Baptist that most Protestant growth likely came from the Spanish speakers in the east and the Mennonite missionaries among Chaco Indians. The other Protestant churches still had few missionaries in the country at that time (1b).

The first Protestant boom in Paraguay took place between 1980 and 1987, when the entire Protestant community grew by 18 percent. The strongest growth occurred within the Assemblies of God (61 percent!), the Iglesia de Dios del Paraguay (33 percent), the Lutheran Church (23 percent), the Baptist Church (19 percent), and the Seventh-day Adventist Church (10 percent). Mormons (25 percent) and Witnesses (18 percent) were also experiencing a membership explosion in 1980–87, while the Anglican Church and the Mennonite groups seemed to be stagnating. Protestant growth slowly tapered off in 1987–90 (7.2 percent), 1990–93 (5.3 percent), and 1993–95 (3.2 percent), only to pick up again between 1995 and 2000.

The second Protestant boom happened between 1995 and 2000, but the data are somewhat contradictory. The total number of Protestants grew by 18.4 percent, yet there were huge variations from one church to another. The strongest growth occurred within the Lutheran Church (almost 64 percent!), the different Mennonite groups (23 percent), and the Iglesia de Dios del Paraguay (13 percent). While Mormons (34 percent) and Witnesses (19 percent) likewise continued their earlier membership explosion between 1995 and 2000, some churches only grew by about 5 percent: the Anglican Church and the Brazilian-origin Iglesia Evangélica Asamblea de Dios Misionera. Remarkably, other non-Catholic churches actually suffered a decline in membership in 1995–2000: the Baptist Church (−7.7 percent) and especially the Assemblies of God (−11 percent).

This analysis of the statistics also reveals why Pentecostal churches made up only half of the entire Protestant community in Paraguay in 2002.[22] While the main Pentecostal churches exploded during the two Protestant boom periods, so did the Baptists, Mennonites, and Lutherans. Comparing the percentage of Protestants with the percentage of Pentecostals, one can calculate that Pentecostals have made up between 17 percent (in 1970) and 53 percent (in 1995) of the total Protestant community in Paraguay. The main reason for this has been the strong membership growth in mainstream Protestant groups like Baptists, Mennonites, and Lutherans.

In order to further analyze non-Catholic church growth in Paraguay, a look at the bigger picture is fruitful. Table 4.2 allows easier comparisons of the population percentages for both Protestantism and Roman Catholicism between 1900 and 2010. The first Protestant boom (1980–87) is reflected in the doubling of the Protestant percentage, from 2.4 percent in 1970 to 4.7 percent in 1987, while the Catholic population proportion declined by 9 percent points, going down from 98.1 percent in 1970 to 89 percent in 1987. If anything, these data suggest the Protestant boom may well have started in the 1970s already, but we do not have sufficient data to support this claim.[23]

The second Protestant boom (1995–2000) is also visible in table 4.2: the Protestant percentage went up from 5.3 to 8.6 percent, while the Catholic percentage declined from 90 to 85 percent. Unfortunately, the picture of non-Catholic church growth gets murky after 2000. In the 2002 census, almost 90 percent of the Paraguayan population self-identified as Catholics and only 6 percent as Protestant. These discrepancies with the 2000 percentages are too big to be explained away after only two calendar years. It seems more likely that the 2000 percentage of Catholics was underreported and the percentage of Protestants was likely inflated by the churches reporting to Johnstone and Mandryk.

How do the two Protestant booms compare to Mormon and Witness growth? The alternate use of the terms "Protestant" and "non-Catholic" throughout the text is deliberate. Based on their unique doctrines and claims, Mormons and Witnesses are generally assigned to the non-Catholic category, while Adventists are now accepted in the Protestant community by most scholars and believers alike. Yet the three churches show some differences in their growth periods, compared to the others.[24] From 1970 to 1980, Adventists and Mormons were already booming, while Protestants had only modest growth.[25] During the years of the first Protestant boom (1980–87), Mormons were also booming (25 percent annual growth) as were Witnesses (18 percent). The Mormons maintained strong average annual growth in 1987–90 at 11 percent, while the combined average annual Protestant growth went down to 7 percent and the Adventists to 5 percent. From 1990 to 1993, Mormon growth continued strong at 15 percent, while Protestant growth tapered off, Adventists stagnated, and Witnesses actually declined. Adventist growth picked up again in 1993–95 with 11 percent, while Mormons went down to

Table 4.2 **Religious Affiliation in Paraguay in Percent, 1900–2010**

Year	Roman Catholics	Protestants (Pentecostals)	Other Religions	No Religion	Source
1900	96.7%	0.03% (0.0%)	3.27%	0.0%	Barrett, Kurian, and Johnson 2001
1970	98.1%	2.4% (0.4%)	1.7%	0.5%	Barrett, Kurian, and Johnson 2001
1987	89.0%	4.7% (N.A.)	N.A.	N.A.	Plett 1988
1990	90.9%	4.9% (2.7%)	1.3%	0.9%	Barrett, Kurian, and Johnson 2001
1993	91.7%	5.95% (2.0%)	0.8%	0.5%	Johnstone 1995
1995	90.3%	5.3% (2.8%)	1.2%	1.1%	Barrett, Kurian, and Johnson 2001
2000	85.0%	8.63% (3.65%)	0.8%	1.0%	Johnstone/Mandryk 2001
2002	89.6%	6.0% (3.0%)	0.1%	1.1%	Census 2002
2010	84–88%?	9.5% (N.A.)	N.A.	N.A.	IUDOP 2010

5 percent, Protestants to 3 percent, and Witnesses kept declining. During the second Protestant boom period of 1995–2000, Adventists grew by a modest 7 percent, Protestants increased by 18.4 percent, and Witnesses strongly regained their growth at 19.3 percent, but the Mormon Church again outperformed all other churches at 34.2 percent. Mormon growth finally tapered off after 2000, meeting Adventists in the 2.5 to 5 percent range, while Jehovah's Witnesses continued their membership explosion. The end result was that Witnesses, Mormons, and Adventists were among the biggest non-Catholic churches in Paraguay.

Finally, the Protestant population percentage mentioned in table 4.2 for 2010, 9.5 percent, comes from a huge opinion survey across Latin America, carried out by Gallup International for IUDOP and quickly reproduced by one Protestant organization in Paraguay.[26] However, I find the Protestant percentages they reported for some Latin American countries extremely high.[27] If correct, the 9.5 percentage of Protestants in Paraguay would mean that a third Protestant boom happened between 2002 and 2010, as some of my informants maintained.[28] Unfortunately, no membership statistics were available for any Protestant church in Paraguay after 2002.

Conclusion: Applying the Church Growth Model to Paraguay

The church growth model (see table 4.1 above) identified four factors that are external to the non-Catholic churches. External factor 2a, *dissatisfaction with Catholicism*, can be isolated as a root cause of non-Catholic growth in general. The popular Catholicism dominant in rural Paraguay focused on the cult of the saints, processions, and pilgrimages. In the countryside, this type of Catholicism continued to be strong in 2010, particularly in pilgrimage centers like Caacupé. The resilience of rural Catholicism explained why almost all non-Catholic churches, except the Mennonites and the Iglesia de Dios del Paraguay, were concentrated in urban areas: Asunción especially and to a lesser degree Ciudad del Este and Encarnación.

Non-Catholic growth in Paraguay could be expected to take off with the gradual development of the *urbanization process* (factor 2d), just like it did in Guatemala and Nicaragua.[29] New city dwellers were cut off from their rural Catholic roots and started looking for new moral communities to provide support.[30] However, Paraguay was one of the last countries of Latin America to become urbanized: the urban population grew from 34.6 percent in 1960 to 45 percent in 1989,[31] 55 percent in 2000,[32] and 58.5 percent in 2004.[33] Non-Catholic growth started exactly as the urbanization process gained strength: first in the 1970s (the boom of Mormons and Adventists), accelerating in the 1980s (the first Protestant boom), and exploding again after 1995 in the second Protestant boom.

However, non-Catholic growth was also strongly affected by external factor 2b, the *responses from the Catholic hierarchy*, particularly the Paraguayan Bishops' Conference. As noted above, persecution of recent Protestant converts by Catholic mobs, often led by parish priests, was strongest in the 1940s and 1950s. In the 1960s, however, under the influence of the Second Vatican Council (1962–65) and the Medellín Latin American Bishops' Council (1968), the institutional Catholic Church moderated its position on Protestants.[34] In the 1970s and 1980s, the Catholic hierarchy gradually became more critical of the human rights abuses of the Stroessner regime. The 1988 visit of Pope John Paul II supported the opposition and boosted the strength of the Catholic Church, indirectly contributing to Stroessner's fall in February 1989. After 1989, the Catholic hierarchy was more critical of Protestant churches, although they rarely denounced them in their pastoral letters. The increasing Protestant growth of the 1980s and 1990s did not move the Paraguayan Bishops' Conference to support the Catholic Charismatic Renewal as a counterweight to keep Catholics in the church, as had happened in Guatemala and Brazil. Most Paraguayan bishops were at best indifferent to the Renewal. By decentralizing the organization of the Catholic Charismatic Renewal in the late 1990s, the Paraguayan Bishops' Conference substantially weakened the movement in Paraguay.[35]

Another highly important external factor influencing church growth was 2c, *social, economic, and political turmoil* leading to psychological *anomie*. Social and political turmoil in Paraguay was highest in 1969–72 (with the radicalization of progressive Catholics in Peasant Leagues, base communities, and among some Jesuits), 1976–77 (when the start of a new guerrilla group became an excuse for the regime to crack down on opposition groups), and especially 1986–89, when the awakening of civil society supported by the Catholic Church led to increased repression and Stroessner's fall after a violent military coup by his no. 2, General Rodríguez.[36] Mormons and Adventists grew during the 1970s political turmoil, which coincided with an economic boom,[37] but Protestant growth was still modest. However, *all* non-Catholic churches grew strongly in the 1980s, the time of the first Protestant boom during the turmoil that would ultimate lead to the fall of Stroessner. This first Protestant boom also coincided with a devastating global economic recession, following the explosion of the Latin American debt crisis in 1982.[38] In 1999–2000, internal strife in the Colorado Party led to the assassination of Vice-President Luis María Argaña Ferraro.[39] The second Protestant boom, however, had already started in 1995, when the political turmoil was still moderate. However, Paraguay again suffered from the effects of a severe economic crisis after 1995, leading to a dramatic increase in poverty.[40] Paraguay has the most uneven income and land distribution of Latin America.[41] The official poverty rates were 33.7 percent in 1999, 41.4 percent in 2003, and 35.6 percent in 2007.[42] The huge number of people struggling to survive and suffering from psychological stress and *anomie* created a big reservoir of potential converts to non-Catholic churches, which helped people cope with the effects of poverty through their emphasis on individual discipline and asceticism.[43] These are part of the internal factors to the non-Catholic churches: the *appeal of the doctrine* (1a) and the *appeal of the church organization* (1c).[44] Since we lack detailed studies of converts to non-Catholic churches, we can only mention these factors in general terms.

The literature consistently shows that the churches experiencing membership growth were also the ones with the highest involvement in *evangelization activities* (factor 1b).[45] The Mormon Church had a worldwide force of 50,000 fulltime missionaries in 2007, with a few hundred in Paraguay.[46] The Jehovah's Witnesses limited their full membership status to people who were witnessing to their religion door-to-door at least a few days a week. Almost all Pentecostal churches had a strong emphasis on evangelization activities.[47] The most successful Pentecostal church, the Centro Familiar de Adoración, was also involved in the widest range of missionary outreach activities. The Assemblies of God were noted for their successful evangelization campaigns in the past. Since 2000, cooperation between Protestant churches increased and included ambitious evangelization efforts like Franklin Graham's visit in 2005.[48] This demonstrated the potential of continued Protestant growth in the future. However, at least one Pentecostal pastor thought their emphasis should now be on membership retention rather than continued growth.[49] As churches increase in size, it becomes more cost effective to keep their members in by closing their "back door,"[50] relying on natural growth through the successful socialization of children into their parental religion (factor 1d) rather than engaging in costly evangelization activities.[51]

In summary, as long as dissatisfaction with Catholicism remains low in rural areas and moderate in urban areas, steady non-Catholic growth in the future is a possibility provided certain conditions are met. External factors the churches have no control of are the urbanization process, the responses of the Catholic hierarchy to Protestant growth (for instance, more active support for the Catholic Charismatic Renewal), and political turmoil in Paraguay. Above all, Protestant churches should continue cooperating and coordinating massive evangelization activities; internal divisions will weaken growth prospects. Second, non-Catholic churches should strive to make their doctrine and internal organization appealing. Third, non-Catholic churches should aim to improve retention of new members.

Acknowledgments

Thanks to Martin H. Eitzen, Richard Flory, Armand L. Mauss, Donald E. Miller, and Kimon Sergeant for their comments on the first draft. Thanks to Karen Núñez for transcribing almost all Paraguay interviews and to Félix Seminario Fossa for conducting six interviews.

NOTES

1. See Gastón Espinosa, "The Pentecostalization of Latin American and U.S. Latino Christianity," *Pneuma: The Journal of the Society for Pentecostal Studies* 26, no. 2 (2004): 270–271, based on 2003 statistics from Todd M. Johnson and Peter Crossing at the Center for the Study of World Christianity. The data for Paraguay are based on the 2002 census; see Clifton L. Holland, "Paraguay," in *Worldmark Encyclopedia of Religious Practices: Volume 3, Countries M–Z*, ed. Andrew Riggs (Detroit, MI: Thomson Gale, 2006), 205–209.
2. My individual research project, "The Pentecostalization of Religion and Society in Paraguay and Chile" was funded by the Pentecostal-Charismatic Research Initiative (PCRI), which was sponsored by the John Templeton Foundation and administered by the University of Southern California.
3. Henri Gooren, "Reconsidering Protestant Growth in Guatemala, 1900–1995," in *Holy Saints and Fiery Preachers: The Anthropology of Protestantism in Mexico and Central America*, ed. James W. Dow and Alan R. Sandstrom, 169–203 (Westport, CT: Praeger, 2001), 170, 189–192; Instituto Universitario de Opinión Pública (IUDOP), *Crece protestantismo en América Latina* [online], retrieved December 15, 2010 from http:/radio-laprimerisima.com/noticias/general/82918/crece-protestantismo-en-america-latina. htm (press release, August 16, 2010), henceforth cited as IUDOP 2010.
4. *Anomie* can be defined as the absence—or strong erosion—of generally accepted norms and values, which threatens to cause the disintegration of society. Émile Durkheim (*Suicide: A Study in Sociology*, New York: Free Press [1897] 1966, 253) was especially worried that with the gradual unfolding of the "modernization process," human needs and desires could not be kept under control by society, leading to a situation of anomie. See also Gooren, "Reconsidering Protestant Growth," 179.
5. Gooren, "Reconsidering Protestant Growth," 190–191.
6. Emilio Willems, *Followers of the New Faith: Culture Change and the Rise of Protestantism in Brazil and Chile* (Nashville, TN: Vanderbilt University Press, 1967); Bryan R. Roberts, "Protestant Groups and Coping with Urban Life in Guatemala," *American Journal of Sociology* 73, no. 6 (1968): 753–767; Christian Lalive d'Epinay, *Haven of the Masses* (London: Lutterworth, 1969).
7. Dannin M. Hanratty and Sandra W. Meditz (eds.), *Paraguay: A Country Profile* [online] (Washington, DC: Federal Research Division for the Library of Congress, 2005), 7. Retrieved October 28, 2008 from http://lcweb2.loc.gov/frd/cs/profiles/Paraguay.pdf; Central Intelligence Agency (CIA), *The World Factbook: Paraguay* [online]. Retrieved February 25, 2011 from https://www.cia.gov/library/publications/the-world-factbook/geos/pa.html.
8. David B. Barrett, George T. Kurian, and Todd M. Johnson, *World Christian Encyclopedia*, 2nd ed. (Oxford, UK: Oxford University Press, 2001), 587.
9. Paul H. Lewis, *Paraguay under Stroessner* (Chapel Hill: University of North Carolina Press, 1980), 7–8; Dannin M. Hanratty and Sandra W. Meditz, *Paraguay: A Country Study* [online] (Washington, DC: GPO for the Library of Congress, 1988). Retrieved October 28, 2008 from http://countrystudies.us/paraguay/.

10. Rogelio Duarte P., *El desafío protestante en el Paraguay* (Asunción, Paraguay: Centro Cristiano de Comunicación Creativa, 1994), 141; Rodolfo Plett, *El protestantismo en el Paraguay* (Asunción, Paraguay: FLET/IBA, 1988), 18.
11. Hanratty and Meditz, *Paraguay: A Country Study*, "Religion."
12. Duarte, *El desafío protestante*, 50; Plett, *El protestantismo*, 31. See "Chronology of the Arrival or Start of Non-Catholic Churches in Paraguay, 1881–1988" for a chronology of the start of non-Catholic churches in Paraguay between 1880 and 1988. Accessible at http://crcc.usc.edu/initiatives/pcri/paraguay-chile.html
13. Duarte, *El desafío protestante*, 136.
14. Duarte, *El desafío protestante*, 111–118.
15. Duarte, *El desafío protestante*, 134–137.
16. Miguel Carter, "The Role of the Paraguayan Catholic Church in the Downfall of the Stroessner Regime," *Journal of Interamerican Studies and World Affairs* 32, no. 4 (1990): 67–121; Miguel Carter, *El papel de la iglesia en la caída de Stroessner* (Asunción, Paraguay: RP Ediciones, 1991).
17. Duarte, *El desafío protestante*, 137–138.
18. See "Chronology of the Arrival or Start of Non-Catholic Churches in Paraguay, 1881–1988" for a general chronology of the arrival of non-Catholic churches in Paraguay and "Historical Summaries of Non-Catholic Church Growth in Paraguay" for a detailed summary of each group's history in the country. Available at http://crcc.usc.edu/initiatives/pcri/paraguay-chile.html.
19. In Guatemala, there were no less than seven Pentecostal churches among the ten biggest non-Catholic churches (Gooren, "Reconsidering Protestant Growth," 194).
20. "Periodization of Church Growth by Denomination with Average Annual Growth Rates" summarizes the statistics in chronological order by denomination and by growth rate. Accessible at http://crcc.usc.edu/initiatives/pcri/paraguay-chile.html
21. Carter, *El papel de la iglesia*.
22. In 2003, Pentecostal churches made up 63 percent of the entire Protestant community in Guatemala, 68 percent in Nicaragua, 85 percent in Argentina, and 89 percent in Chile (Henri Gooren, "The Pentecostalization of Religion and Society in Latin America: First Findings from Paraguay," paper presented at the annual meeting of the Society for the Scientific Study of Religion [SSSR] in Baltimore, MD, October 28–30, 2010, 3).
23. See "Periodization of Church Growth by Denomination with Average Annual Growth Rates," at: http://crcc.usc.edu/initiatives/pcri/paraguay-chile.html
24. See "Periodization of Church Growth by Denomination with Average Annual Growth Rates," at: http://crcc.usc.edu/initiatives/pcri/paraguay-chile.html
25. There are no data on Jehovah's Witness growth between 1970 and 1980.
26. Red Evangélica de Comunicación (REDECOM), *686 mil evangélicos en Paraguay* [online], retrieved December 15, 2011 from http://www.redecom.org/index.php?option=com_content&view=article&id=57:686mil-evangelicos-en-paraguay&catid=1:latest-news (press release, June 26, 2010).
27. IUDOP 2010 claimed Protestant population percentages of 34.1 percent for Guatemala, 32.1 percent for Honduras, 28.4 percent for Nicaragua, and 22.8 percent for Brazil. The lowest Protestant percentages reported were 4.7 percent for Mexico, 9.0 percent for Uruguay, and 9.5 percent for Paraguay.
28. Recorded Paraguay fieldwork interviews numbers 26, 30, and 35.
29. Henri Gooren, "The Religious Market in Nicaragua: The Paradoxes of Catholicism and Protestantism," *Exchange* 32, no. 4 (2003): 340–360; Gooren, "Reconsidering Protestant Growth in Guatemala."
30. Willems, *Followers of the New Faith*; Roberts, "Protestant Groups"; Lalive, *Haven of the Masses*.
31. Carter, *El papel de la iglesia*, 144, based on United Nations statistics.
32. Patrick Johnstone and Jason Mandryk, *Operation World* (Carlisle, UK: Paternoster Lifestyle, 2001), 513.
33. David L. Clawson, *Latin America and the Caribbean: Lands and Peoples*, 4th ed. (Boston, MA: McGraw-Hill, 2006), 352. The most urbanized countries of Latin America were

also the most industrialized: Uruguay (93 percent), Argentina (90.6 percent), Chile (87.7 percent), Venezuela (88.1 percent), and Brazil (84.2 percent).

34. Carter, *El papel de la iglesia*, 62–63.
35. For a detailed analysis of the Catholic Charismatic Renewal in Paraguay, see Henri Gooren, "The Catholic Charismatic Renewal in Latin America," *Pneuma: The Journal of the Society for Pentecostal Studies* 34, no. 2 (2012): 185–207.
36. Carter, *El papel de la iglesia*, 66–68, 78–82, 108–114.
37. Carter, *El papel de la iglesia*, 80 called it the "boom of Itaipú" after the giant hydroelectric plant being constructed at that time.
38. Carter, *El papel de la iglesia*, 99–100. Guatemala and Nicaragua likewise had Protestant booms in the 1980s, coinciding with the global economic recession (Gooren, "Reconsidering Protestant Growth in Guatemala"; Gooren, "Religious Market in Nicaragua").
39. Hanratty and Meditz, *Paraguay: A Country Profile*, 5.
40. Programa de Naciones Unidas para el Desarrollo (PNUD; in English: United Nations Development Program), *Informe Nacional sobre Desarrollo Humano: Equidad para desarrollo, Paraguay 2008* (Asunción, Paraguay: PNUD, 2008), 38. The Paraguayan economy grew by a mere 0.8 percent annually between 1995 and 2002.
41. PNUD, *Informe Nacional*, 18, 194. The richest 10 percent controlled 40 percent of the Paraguayan national income, whereas the poorest 40 percent earned merely 12 percent of the national income.
42. PNUD, *Informe Nacional*, 184. Almost 20 percent of Paraguayans lived in extreme poverty, surviving on less than $1 a day, in 2007.
43. David Martin, *Tongues of Fire: The Explosion of Protestantism in Latin America* (Oxford, UK: Blackwell, 1990); David Martin, *Pentecostalism: The World Their Parish* (Oxford, UK: Blackwell, 2002); Cecília Loreto Mariz, *Coping with Poverty: Pentecostal Churches and Christian Base Communities in Brazil* (Philadelphia, PA: Temple University Press, 1994); Elizabeth E. Brusco, *The Reformation of Machismo: Evangelical Conversion and Gender in Colombia* (Austin: University of Texas Press, 1995); Henri Gooren, *Rich among the Poor: Church, Firm, and Household among Small-Scale Entrepreneurs in Guatemala City* (Amsterdam: Thela, 1999 [Latin America Series, number 13]).
44. On the relation between Pentecostal experiences and church growth, see Kay, and Poloma and Lee, in this volume.
45. Martin, *Tongues of Fire*; Martin, *Pentecostalism*; Lewis R. Rambo, *Understanding Religious Conversion* (New Haven, CT: Yale University Press, 1993); Rodney Stark and Roger Finke, *Acts of Faith: Explaining the Human Side of Religion* (Berkeley: University of California Press, 2000); Henri Gooren, *Religious Conversion and Disaffiliation: Tracing Patterns of Change in Faith Practices* (New York: Palgrave-Macmillan, 2010).
46. *Deseret News, 2009 Church Almanac* (Salt Lake City, UT: Deseret News, 2008), 4.
47. Martin, *Tongues of Fire*; Martin, *Pentecostalism*; Allan Anderson, *An Introduction to Pentecostalism: Global Charismatic Christianity* (Cambridge, UK: Cambridge University Press, 2004).
48. Recorded Paraguay fieldwork interview number 26, Asunción, August 11, 2010.
49. Recorded Paraguay fieldwork interview number 35, Asunción, August 18, 2010.
50. Rodolfo Plett, *Crecimiento evangélico en el Paraguay: Estadística, evaluación, proyección hacía el futuro* (Asunción: FLET, 2000), 3–4.
51. Recorded Paraguay fieldwork interviews 12 and 35, Asunción July 21 and August 18, 2010; see also Gooren, *Religious Conversion and Disaffiliation*.

SECTION THREE

PENTECOSTALISM AND POLITICS

Given the rapid growth and expansion of Pentecostalism over the last century, it becomes necessary to ask what, if any, social and political impact has resulted from the presence and activities of different Pentecostal groups? While we tackle the question of the different ways that Pentecostal groups engage with their societies in Section Four, this section focuses on Pentecostalism's role in and contribution to politics.

As R. Andrew Chesnut demonstrated, Pentecostalism is a significant presence in Latin America. In chapter 5, Paul Freston describes the general contours of Pentecostalism in Latin America, focusing primarily on its social impact and political involvement, especially its effect on strengthening democratic processes. He shows that while political involvement by Protestants is not recent, this trend has increased since the 1980s, especially with the involvement of many previously apolitical Pentecostal denominations. There are now over twenty political parties of Protestant (often Pentecostal) inspiration in the Spanish-speaking republics, although none has achieved great success.

Freston shows that sometimes the rapid growth of congregations and denominations can cause leaders to become more ambitious politically, thinking that they can mobilize their members to vote for them and/or their slate of candidates. However, he argues that the Pentecostal world is too divided and independent to provide a firm basis for any national-level movement that could advocate major political change.

The direct effect of Pentecostalism on politics, Freston concludes, is always less than might be hoped or feared. Latin American Pentecostals do not seem to fit the negative stereotypes often disseminated about them, that they are dangerous to democracy, potentially violent, or subordinate to American right-wing geopolitical worldviews. Nor do they live up to their own optimistic self-image as incorruptible political actors. Instead, Freston argues that

Pentecostals are basically pro-democratic political novices in their own countries. Thus, Freston sees it as unlikely that Pentecostal Christianity, economically and organizationally divided, and politically splintered, will be willing or able to play a really effective role in creating a new democratic vision of global society.

While Paul Freston focuses on the political involvement of Pentecostalism in Latin America, Robert Woodberry takes a broader view, using survey data and recent studies of Pentecostalism in several countries to explore the possible association between Pentecostalism and democracy. At the outset he notes the problematic nature of such an assertion by pointing out—as Paul Freston also asserts—that Pentecostal political leaders have been in the middle of several different scandals, suggesting that they may be as corruptible as other politicians.

However, Woodberry notes several areas in society where Pentecostals have improved or expanded opportunities, at least among "nonelites," which, he argues, may make a positive contribution to the development of democratic processes. For example, Pentecostalism has expanded civil society among groups and in areas where civil society has historically been weak. Pentecostalism seems to limit corruption at a nonelite level, leads to moderate economic and educational improvements among nonelites, and has expanded both religious liberty and the rights of organizations outside of state control. In addition to these more concrete results, the growth of Pentecostalism represents religious competition that, he argues, has forced other religious groups—such as the Catholic Church—to focus more intentionally on helping poor and ethnic minorities, thus further expanding democratic possibilities. Woodberry concludes that while the spread of Pentecostalism may not be the next best hope for democracy around the world, there is no indication that it will be a hindrance, and it is likely to make moderate contributions of its own to the development of democratic processes.

5

Pentecostals and Politics in Latin America

Compromise or Prophetic Witness?

PAUL FRESTON

Bloodsuckers in Brazil

In mid-2006, the latest in a long train of corruption scandals erupted in Brazil. Known colourfully as "the bloodsuckers scandal," it involved a three-year-old scheme by which public health authorities were overcharged for ambulances from the Ministry of Health, with members of Congress receiving 10% kickbacks. The parliamentary commission ended up implicating some 90 federal deputies (members of the lower house of the Brazilian congress), from a broad array of parties, both within and outside the government.

One aspect of the scandal that caught national attention was the disproportionate involvement of Pentecostal politicians. The number of "evangélicos," as they are commonly known, was over 30 (nearly half of the 60 plus "evangélicos" in congress), and although in Brazil the term also includes non-Pentecostal Protestants such as Baptists and Presbyterians, virtually all of those implicated were in fact from Pentecostal churches. By far the largest number were from the Universal Church of the Kingdom of God (UCKG) and the Assemblies of God (AG), two large Pentecostal denominations whose leaders present their own official candidates for congressional elections and do their best to persuade their church members to vote for those candidates. One of the congressmen implicated had even written a book called *Servindo a Deus na Vida Pública* (Serving God in Public Life), published by the UCKG.

Public reaction to Pentecostal involvement in the scandal predictably focused on the incongruousness (to say the least) of church-related politicians enriching themselves (and possibly their churches) at the expense of the already precarious public health service, and especially in view of the discourse of the moralization of public life that most of them were prone to use in their election campaigns and in congress. One major daily newspaper quoted an academic analyst to the effect that "most of the accused come from Pentecostal churches which see politics as a demonic space and advocate electing men of God, chosen by them, to exorcize it."

What of the churches themselves? The AG seemed reluctant to comment. The UCKG, far more heavily involved in the media, published a lengthy article in its main publication (*Folha Universal*), in which it enumerated "successive scandals in the public sphere, both of corruption and poor administration." Finally, tucked away in the last paragraph, came a mention of church involvement. "The Kingdom of God is comprised of order and discipline. The Universal Church is part of this Divine Kingdom and thus we emphasize morals and ethics ... Transparent disciplinary measures without fear or favor allow the people to differentiate the serious ones from the rest. We have adopted the posture of not retaining on our staff any priests, whether bishops or pastors, whose conduct has been unworthy of morality and our faith ... including the parliamentarians who received the support of the church. If they are accused of misconduct ... we suspend them until proven innocent."

With congressional elections just months away, would the scandal mean the end of the substantial Pentecostal presence? Not necessarily. As one leading charismatic wrote, the scandal "is the Lord's answer to our prayer clamor for change ... The enemies have partied over the sin of the church ... Now is the time to send [to the parliaments of the nation] men of God who have proved their uprightness." Similarly, a correspondent of a UCKG website said he was "indignant with the UCKG for not having said anything about its position" on the scandals, especially since he had voted for one of those implicated. But his "indignation" did not extend to boycotting the official church candidate for the next elections. "My candidate is Bishop Bulhões. Please don't let me down, bishop," was his plaintive cry. Even his mild protest called forth a rebuttal from church officials. One of the church journalists replied: "no-one should be considered guilty until the case is closed. Don't you think the timing [of the eruption of this scandal] is strange? Won't it cause confusion at election time for the evangelical deputies?" Or, in the words of another church member, the whole affair was a "smokescreen" designed to "stain the institution of the UCKG."

In sectors of the broader Pentecostal world, the criticism was stronger. "From the blood of the martyrs to the bloodsuckers" was the headline of one article tracing a history of ethical decline. One leading pastor from a dissident sector of the AG wrote scathingly of "wolves dressed as pastors," of evangelical politicians who were front-men for dishonest apostles and bishops who, while talking of the need to elect believers to congress to seek the interests of the Kingdom of God, "sucked the blood of poor Brazilians." Nothing, not even the argument that these congressmen are personally fallen but preach a liberating message, "justifies this indecency which has just come to light, but has long been practiced freely in the basements of the mega 'church-businesses' that trade on hopes."

A 2006 survey of Pentecostals in three Latin American countries (Brazil, Chile, and Guatemala) shows that Pentecostals are as disillusioned as other Latin Americans with regard to trust in public institutions such as governments, congress, and the military. They are also rather reticent about church pronouncements on politics; while slightly more favorable than non-Pentecostals, they are much less convinced than American Pentecostals that churches should speak out on such matters.[1]

In the end, in the Brazilian general elections of 2006 the UCKG withdrew support from all its parliamentarians implicated in the scandal and saw its representation drastically reduced. Most of the implicated AG candidates for reelection also failed at the polls. As a result, the total of *evangélicos* in congress fell from over 60 to around 40, with the reduction entirely due to the smaller number of AG and UCKG deputies.

In reality, the scandal of the bloodsuckers was far from being the first in which Pentecostal politicians had been involved in the past 20 years in Brazil, and indeed in other countries of Latin America (Freston 2001). Equally, it should not be concluded that all Pentecostal politicians in Latin America have been accused of corruption. Nevertheless, the above account points to several characteristics of Pentecostal politics in the region: the existence in some countries (notably, but not only, Brazil) of large Protestant caucuses in federal and local legislative bodies; the predominance of Pentecostals in these Protestant caucuses; the fact that most of these Pentecostal politicians are official candidates of their denominations, and if they are not relatives or protégés of the clergy they are clergy themselves, sometimes from the very top ranks; the attempt to create a denominational bloc vote, using church space for vote-getting; the spread of Pentecostal politicians in various parties; their above-average susceptibility to corruption; the negative effect on the public image of the whole community of "evangelicos"; the discourse of the demonic in public life and of a messianic project of electing "men of God" to clean it up; the divided reactions of ordinary Pentecostals (and evangelicals in general), showing that a bloc vote and a unified political project are myths; and the ambivalent effect of Pentecostal politics for still-fledgling Latin American democracies.

In this chapter I shall briefly describe the reality of Pentecostalism in Latin America today, before investigating its social impact and its political involvement, especially regarding its effect on democratic strengthening. Finally, I shall ask to what extent Latin American Pentecostalism can be compared to two other major religio-political actors in the contemporary world: militant Islamism and the American religious right. In asking about these questions,

I shall make use of the newly available survey data on global Pentecostalism gathered by the Pew Forum in 2006. This survey looked at the United States as well as three countries in each of Latin America, Asia, and Africa, providing a unique window into global Pentecostal attitudes.

Pentecostalism in Latin America

Reliable statistics are not available for all countries in the region, but it is reasonable to claim that Latin America is now the global heartland of Pentecostalism. Almost certainly, there are more Pentecostals in Brazil today than in any other country. (In this chapter, we shall consider only Protestant Pentecostals, not the Catholic "Pentecostals" of the Catholic Charismatic Renewal, which is also very large in Brazil.) People who identified with Pentecostal churches were over 10% in Brazil's 2000 census and are probably around 12% now. To them, we would have to add another 2% of people who are personally charismatic but attend "traditional" churches.

Protestantism in Spanish-speaking Latin America varies from 20% plus in Guatemala, through 15.1% in Chile (2002 census), to just over 5% in Mexico and under 5% in Uruguay. Overall, Latin America is probably around 12% Protestant, of which some 70–75% are Pentecostal, giving an estimate of 8–9% Pentecostal for the region.

Pentecostal demographic trends are upward in most of the region, both because of conversion and high birth rates. Growth rates in Brazil, which had already been high since the 1950s, accelerated even more in the 1990s and do not appear to have slackened much since then. A survey in Rio de Janeiro about ten years ago discovered that only about 30% of Pentecostals had been born into the religion, and the rest were converts. The number of Pentecostals in Chile also grows, but the Central American countries do seem to have slowed down after extremely rapid growth in the 1970s and 1980s.

Pentecostalism can be seen as part of a grassroots revitalization of Christianity (also including the Catholic Charismatic Renewal and liberation-theology base communities) that is making Christianity perhaps more rooted in the masses than it ever was when it enjoyed state protection. Catholicism, in most of the region, is no longer seen as an essential part of national or Latin American identity. The religious field is no longer similar to that of Latin Europe and has become partially (but only partially) more similar to that of the United States.

Pentecostalism is overwhelmingly an indigenous movement rather than one funded and run from the West. It also tends to be strongly practicing, rapidly expanding, fissiparous and nontraditional. It is not a state religion and rarely has an unofficial privileged relationship to governments. Usually, it does not have strong institutions; being often composed disproportionately of the poor in poor countries, its cultural and educational resources are limited. Its ecclesiastical divisions make it impossible to establish a normative "social doctrine." It is in competition for members and resources, which does not encourage reflection or costly stances on ethical principle. It often has no international contacts, cutting it off from the history of Christian reflection on politics.

Pentecostalism spread in Latin America by a variety of routes: through American missionaries in contact with home (Chile), and immigrants in the United States in contact with their homelands (Mexico) or with compatriots elsewhere (the Swedes who started the Brazilian AG and the Italian who initiated the Christian Congregation in São Paulo).

Latin American Pentecostalism is now organized in a huge number of denominations, a few of which originated abroad (such as the Assemblies of God), while the majority are homegrown (such as Brazil for Christ and the Universal Church of the Kingdom of God, from Brazil; or the Pentecostal Methodist Church and the Pentecostal Evangelical Church in Chile). The general picture is that most Pentecostal churches (unlike historical ones) were founded by Latin Americans or by independent missionaries, and only rarely by a foreign Pentecostal denomination. A different phenomenon is that of middle-class Pentecostalized groups (known in some countries as "neo-Pentecostals" and in others as "charismatics"). There were charismatic breakaways from historical denominations in the 1960s; but recent Protestant expansion in middle and even upper classes has been mainly due to charismatic "communities," part of an international trend in which traditional denominations lose importance. They have been especially successful in Guatemala.

In the last decades of the twentieth century, Protestantism (especially in Pentecostal forms) made considerable headway among Amerindian peoples in southern Mexico, Central America, and the Andes. It is too early to say what new ecclesiastical and doctrinal forms may emerge from this large-scale adoption of Protestantism by indigenous peoples.

While studies have revealed a considerable number of non-practicing Pentecostals in Chile, in Brazil levels of practice amongst Protestants remain high (over three-quarters attend church weekly). With variations, one can say that Latin American Protestantism is characterized by being highly practicing and fast growing, predominantly lower class, and organized in a plethora of nationally run and even nationally created denominations.

In social composition, Protestants in most countries are disproportionately from the poorer, less educated, and darker sectors of society. However, there is growing social diversification (greater presence among, for example, entrepreneurs, sportsmen, artists, and policemen). Membership is predominantly female, although leadership positions are largely male (some Pentecostal denominations, however, were founded by women and accept female pastors). Some recent authors have spoken of Pentecostalism's reconciliation of gender values, which serves the interests of poor women, resocializing men away from machismo.

The Pew survey of 2006 found that Pentecostals everywhere are more in favor of women religious leaders than the general populations of their countries (in Brazil by 64% to 63%; in Chile, by 61% to 57%; and in Guatemala, by 79% to 66%). As to whether men should have more right to employment than women when jobs are scarce, while American Pentecostals agree with that idea twice as much as their national average (29% compared to 14%), in Latin America Pentecostals virtually mirror their national average (29% to 25% in Brazil; 41% to 36% in Chile; and 40% to 39% in Guatemala).

In some countries there is still discrimination at certain social levels against Protestants as individuals, as well as legal discrimination against churches. Although official separation of church and state, effectuated in some countries in the nineteenth century and in others only in the 1990s, is now almost universal (only Bolivia, Argentina, and Costa Rica still have an official religion), there are countries where Protestant churches do not enjoy the same legal rights as the Catholic Church. Even where tolerance and freedom of worship are secure, there is often some way still to go before full equality takes hold in public life and civil society.

Social Impact

There has always been some Pentecostal social involvement; there were orphanages and other projects right from the beginning. But only on a relatively small scale. The theological emphasis was very much on evangelism, and sometimes the strong feeling of living in the "last times" inhibited social concern. In Latin America, until recently people used to say that the "traditional" Protestants had social projects but the Pentecostals did not. That has changed considerably in the last 15 or 20 years. There is now quite a lot being done, possibly because of worsening social conditions, the weakening of the state, the effects of globalization, and also because of the growing numbers of Pentecostals and the growing expectation (from Pentecostals themselves and society in general) that those numbers should result in greater social impact. Some of the newer denominations, both at the lower-class and middle-class levels, have become heavily involved in social programs of quite varied types.

This involvement is often of a rather "assistentialist" type rather than more sophisticated projects of "conscientization," community mobilizing, and empowering. But over time there has been a growing reflection on what has worked and what has not worked. In some cases that leads to a growing reflection on politics, perhaps out of frustration with lack of results, or wondering about why things are the way they are, a growing awareness of social reality and its structural dimensions. Gradually some Pentecostals come to realize that not everything can be solved simply by converting individuals and transforming them into altruistic people, but there are also other dimensions that need to be tackled through lobbying, social pressure, community mobilization, and perhaps direct involvement in the political system.

The Pew survey of 2006 found that Pentecostals generally reflect national opinion regarding a free market economy (78% of Brazilian Pentecostals agreeing that most people are better off in a free market, compared to 72% of the general population; in Chile, the respective figures were 47% and 52%, and in Guatemala 74% and 72%). On whether government should guarantee food and shelter to every citizen, Pentecostals are as or more affirmative as their fellow-citizens (95% to 93% in Brazil; 90% to 87% in Chile; 92% for both categories in Guatemala).

On the whole, the Pentecostal approach to social action has been a straightforward one based on the "holistic" ministry of Jesus (teaching, helping, healing). Occasionally still, social work is done as a pre-evangelistic strategy, an underhand way of evangelizing, but most Pentecostal social involvement cannot be classified in this way.

There are a lot of grassroots initiatives that often reinvent the wheel and are not linked in to global Christian reflection on social involvement, although sometimes such initiatives do later make connections with national or international Christian NGOs. Some scholars are starting to talk of "progressive Pentecostalism," a new wave of social ministries carried out by Pentecostal and charismatic churches in the name of a gospel "holism."

However, specific social projects are not the only way that Pentecostals might be promoting economic and social development. Another way is through their effect on people's economic attitudes. While Pentecostals do not usually have the classic Protestant Ethic based on the theological idea of vocation, they do usually cultivate hard work and honesty. The process of conversion helps many disoriented people on the margins of society to take control of their own lives and to progress modestly within the constraints of the harsh economic reality of Third World societies. Through personal experience of the Holy Spirit and through community support, they help people to overcome vices that may be disastrous for people living on the edge. They teach economic disciplines and change attitudes toward economic chances. Pentecostalism is not fatalistic; on the contrary, it tends to regard poverty as something to be overcome if possible, not just accepted and endured. It tends to make people more optimistic about the possibilities of change in all dimensions of their lives. Some churches explicitly encourage members to find new economic opportunities, especially to become self-employed, even advising them on how to set up for themselves in small-scale business. There also seems to be a positive relation to migration and even to emigration for economic reasons; in addition, many Third World migrants in the global north become Pentecostals after migrating.

Another dimension of Pentecostal promotion of development is through networking, especially helping people who depend on the informal economy in the megacities of the Third World to build up networks of information and employment. Churches also provide community safety nets for the especially hard times. In addition, the church community acts as maintainer of the disciplines necessary to help people get better jobs, gain a reputation for honesty and hard work, helping people to avoid the vices and moral looseness that can be fatal for survival (even physical survival) at that level. Pentecostalism purveys both an unmediated individual experience of God and a strong moral code upheld by a strong community life. Involvement in the church can also develop skills that can then be transferred to the economic arena. Literacy is one example. People learn to read because of the Bible, but once learned, the skill can be applied to other areas and one's economic options are expanded. Some people develop leadership skills that are applied in other social spheres.

Another Pentecostal contribution is in marginal areas virtually untouched by other sectors of civil society or indeed the state, such as the shanty-towns. In Brazil, it is said that only two institutions really function in the shanties: organized crime and Pentecostal churches. Other forms of organized religion are generally absent or weak, and so is the state. This is Pentecostalism's "civilizing" mission, providing people with ways of escape from criminality, prostitution, and drug addiction. The same applies to the vibrant Pentecostal work in many Third World prisons (as, until its dismantling, in the notorious São Paulo prison of Carandiru), sometimes creating whole prison wings inhabited by prisoners who have become Pentecostals, transformed in their behavior within the prison and, so it is claimed, with considerably better rates of reintegration into society afterward.

A major indirect Pentecostal contribution to development is through the restoration of the family, largely through the reformation of the male and the elimination of the double standard of morality. From this can flow economic betterment and, especially, better chances for the next generation. A fascinating documentary film *Santa Cruz*, on the first year in the life of a small Pentecostal church on the periphery of Rio de Janeiro, Brazil, tells how in one neighborhood virtually everyone has become Pentecostal and property values have risen. The location is considered safe, people concern themselves with the well-being of their neighbors, families are more structured, the men no longer drink and beat their wives, and it is generally considered a more desirable place to live, despite the visible poverty that still reigns there.

Another aspect is that Pentecostalism appeals disproportionately to women (even more so than most forms of religion). Sometimes this is a puzzle to scholars because they perceive in Pentecostalism what seems to be a very traditional patriarchal discourse. But in fact the effects on the ground for poor women in the Third World are usually very positive, especially in domesticating their menfolk, weaning men off the machista culture and helping them value the same things as the women themselves do, especially in terms of how money and time are spent. Inasmuch as few things encourage development more than the education of women and releasing them for more significant roles, this may turn out to be the greatest Pentecostal contribution to development in the long run.

At the same time, there are limits to the Pentecostal effect on development. Sometimes in the long run, in the next generation, people make considerable advances, maybe into the middle class, especially through investing in their children's education. But there are very few cases of spectacular advance (notwithstanding the testimonies peddled by the "prosperity gospel" churches). For most people, the economic effect of conversion takes them from absolute destitution to dignified poverty. But even this, of course, can mean a tremendous amount to the people involved and can be the basis for more significant advance over one or two generations.

Political Involvement

The political involvement of Latin American Pentecostalism is based on its social embeddedness and legitimacy (in most of the region, as opposed to some other parts of the Third World); and on the extension of political democracy, both as part of the "third wave" of democratization stemming (in Latin America) from the 1980s and as a region traditionally linked to the worldwide Catholic Church, which has, since the 1960s, officially embraced religious freedom, human rights, and democracy.

Political involvement by Protestants is not recent (they were disproportionately active in the Mexican Revolution), but since the 1980s this trend has increased, especially with the involvement of many previously apolitical Pentecostal denominations. Two charismatic Protestant presidents have governed Guatemala, and there have been large Protestant (mainly Pentecostal) congressional caucuses in several countries, notably Brazil. Over 20 political parties of Protestant (often Pentecostal) inspiration have been founded in the Spanish-speaking republics, though none has achieved great success (Freston

2004). Much Protestant political activity has been oriented to institutional aggrandizement, leading to a worsening of the public image of Protestants as a whole in some countries. Another factor in this is the lack, in most countries, of a strong representative Protestant body; an exception is in Peru, where the National Evangelical Council (CONEP) has had a notable role in the defense of human rights since the 1980s.

The political operationalizing of Protestant (rather than generically Christian) identity is more pronounced than in other parts of the global south. As a variant of the dominant religion, it effectively entered the region on the Anabaptist principle of separation of church and state and even of total rejection of politics. Most Pentecostal churches had scant possibility of playing surrogate oppositions to military regimes in the 1960s and 1970s, as the Catholic Church sometimes did, although a few medium-sized Pentecostal denominations in Brazil and Chile did voice criticisms. In some countries there is still discrimination at certain social levels against Protestants, as well as mild legal discrimination against their churches. "Religious freedom" (in the fuller sense of equal treatment in the public sphere) has been a rallying cry for some Protestants in politics in recent years. Ethnic "minorities" (indigenous, mixed race, black) tend to be well represented in Pentecostalism, which can open up new channels to political participation. A recent poll in Rio de Janeiro showed that Pentecostal women were more interested in voting than were women of other religions or none.

Democracy

Pentecostalism, like other forms of Evangelical Protestantism, arrived in Latin America largely with a critique of Catholic or non-Christian "confusion" of religion and politics. However, with its numerical burgeoning and rise to political influence, the political restraint implied in acceptance of religious disestablishment and the democratic rules of the game is less evident in some quarters.

The political implications of Pentecostalism have been appraised in very varied ways by scholars. On the one side are authors (e.g. D'Epinay 1969 and Bastian 1990) who emphasize the repressive and corporatist nature of the Pentecostal churches and see them as reproducing traditional authoritarian political culture and social control. Other authors (e.g. Willems 1967 and Martin 1990) stress its democratizing potential, talking of a vibrant civil society. They contend that Protestant churches offer a free social space, an experience of solidarity and a new personal identity, as well as responsible participation in the community and, for some, the development of leadership gifts.

Theorists who favor the latter interpretation often go back to Tocqueville's (1988) study of American democracy in the 1830s. The question is whether Latin American Pentecostalism has the characteristics Tocqueville viewed as beneficial to democracy, especially clerical self-restraint in avoiding direct political involvement and doctrines that moderate the people's taste for material well-being. Many Pentecostal churches fall short on one or both of these criteria.

Regarding democratization, there is no simple yes or no answer. Democratization itself is complex; one can distinguish, for example, between democratic transition and democratic consolidation. In transitions, Pentecostal churches are often not much use. For standing up to dictatorships, it is more helpful to be a traditional, hierarchical, transnational church with elite connections. (e.g., the Catholic Church's role in Brazil under the military regime). It is not so easy for a Pentecostal church, especially for those founded locally and with no transnational or elite connections, deprived of intellectual resources and vulnerable to repression. However, in the phase of democratic consolidation that comes afterward, the long haul of creating a democratic culture and instilling certain virtues and practices, these churches might be more use because they encourage certain activities and initiatives: they encourage economic development, which indirectly helps democratic deepening; they are anti-fatalistic; and they instill skills of leadership and public speaking, which can be transferred to the public sphere.

However, it is also possible that churches may be extremely wrapped up in an apocalyptic mentality that regards the world as hopeless and not worth bothering about. Such a mentality of withdrawal is at best not helpful to democratization and may indirectly harm it. That withdrawal mentality is now becoming less common, especially in churches with a slightly higher social level. One now sometimes finds the opposite of that, a triumphalistic mentality that "we are the children of God, the cream of society, and should be governing." So theocratic ideas are emerging that say believers should govern their countries in the name of God. In some places (e.g., Guatemala) it is better-off charismatics, used to having a political role in society, who entertain such ideas. In other places (e.g., Brazil) it is more the older lower-class Pentecostal churches that have grown so much that their leaders become ambitious. This especially happens when democracy takes hold, because democracy is the numbers game and they see themselves as controlling vast numbers of votes. So they try to transform their religious leadership into political leadership, either simply to help their own churches as institutions, to get benefits by milking the state, or by dreaming of exercising political power themselves, or at least by electing a "person of God" as president who will then channel the blessings of God onto the country. Of course, that dream has serious anti-democratic potential, but in practice it does not happen because they do not control the votes of all their members as they imagine, and in any case the churches are too divided among themselves and cannot unite behind a single political project. The Pentecostal world is inherently divided and cannot agree on very much, still less on how to exercise political power.

The Pew survey showed ordinary Pentecostals to be encouragingly affirmative of the value of democratic processes. They stress the importance of honest multiparty elections as much or slightly more so than their national average; and they are generally more inclined than other religious believers to think that God's will is achieved through the democratic process (especially in Chile, 32% compared to 13%). When asked whether, to solve a country's problems, it would be better to have a more participatory government or a strong leader, Pentecostals always prefer a participatory government. But in Guatemala (following the national tendency) over 40% would like a strong leader, whereas Pentecostals in Brazil and Chile are less interested (under 30%) in the strong-leader solution. Brazilian Pentecostals (25%) are less favorable to that idea than their fellow Brazilians (29%).

So the direct effect of Pentecostalism on politics is always less than might be hoped or feared. It is a pluralist form of organization, which can be seen as inherently compatible with democracy. These are voluntary communities that people enter or leave at will, and Pentecostalism is perceived in many countries as helping to create a vibrant civil society. But at times it is a civil society that is bound up in its own limited projects and unable to look beyond and develop a more universalist reflection on public life and public morality such as characterizes, for example, the Catholic tradition of social doctrine. Very often Pentecostals are cut off from the 2,000 years of Christian reflection on politics. In some countries the result has been damage to the public image of Pentecostalism, associating it with political naivete and vulnerability to manipulation, and even sometimes with corruption and hunger for power.

I think one can definitely say that Latin American Pentecostal politics is a phenomenon *of* democratization. Whether it is also a phenomenon *for* democratization—deepening it—is an important query. But it has certainly played a role in incorporating grassroots sectors into the democratic process and has provided a significant route for individuals of lower social origin to achieve political visibility (e.g., some of the congressmen in Brazil or Nicaragua).

The fiercely independent spirit that characterizes Pentecostalism (and evangelicalism generally) results in opting out of social "sacred canopies" and the creation of autonomous social spaces and an unending pluralism. The results for democracy are paradoxical. Totalitarian movements are firmly resisted, but authoritarian regimes that do not impinge on evangelical religion may not always be. The Pentecostal world is too fissured and independent to provide a firm basis for any national-level movement advocating major political change in whatever direction. Pentecostalism is thus of less "use" during phases of democratic transition than during the more extended periods of democratic consolidation. Indeed, the Pentecostal concept of voluntarism and the right and duty to propagate the faith bears more than a resemblance to Habermas's concept of the public sphere and communicative action. The massive daily practice of *convincing*, at the grassroots level, even by Pentecostal groups that are not internally democratic, may be vital for the quality of democracy that is possible in the public sphere. At the same time, it is institutionally vulnerable to manipulation by political leaders (as with the Fujimori regime in Peru).

Within the broad middle ground (between helping processes of democratic deepening and supporting existing authoritarianisms), the prevailing tendencies have to be constantly verified. While circumscribed by certain broad parameters, actual Pentecostal politics is very hard to predict. One implication of Pentecostal decentralization is that imitation may prevail: local patterns of religion-state relations may be absorbed by Pentecostals as they gain in political ambition. In Latin America, the fading (but still visible) heritage of a monolithic Catholic model may modify aspirations somewhat; but the more democratic and pluralist present will almost certainly keep Pentecostals broadly within the democratic and non-confessional track.

In most countries, Pentecostals have only been politically active for 15–20 years at the most, and they are in the early stages of a steep learning curve. But the growing involvement in social projects sometimes leads to more critical political involvement oriented more to the good of society as a whole. No religious movement is frozen in time. Just as the Catholic Church has changed politically several times during the last 100 years, so the Pentecostal movement is evolving.

Leftward Shift?

As an example of such an evolution, one can even see, to a certain extent, a Pentecostal shift to the left, or at least to the center left, in parts of Latin America. In part, this shift is due to changes in the politics of the Catholic Church, no longer seen as occupying the left so much and therefore opening up space for another religion to do that. There are also, of course, class aspects: one finds, for example, that Pentecostals in Venezuela tend to be quite favorable toward Hugo Chávez, as are other members of the lower classes. In addition, growing involvement in social projects sometimes leads to more critical political involvement, oriented more to the good of society as a whole, and a perception that many transformations cannot be achieved at the purely individual level.

Also, and increasingly, Pentecostalism's attraction as a religion of personal salvation means that there are more and more left-wing militants converting to Pentecostalism and continuing their left-wing militancy.

And it should not be forgotten that the new left in Latin America is usually extremely nationalist, and Pentecostals are often very nationalist as well. Thus, there is often considerable doubt about the idea of a free-trade area of the Americas. Another factor is evangelical penetration of the indigenous communities in the Andes, Central America, and southern Mexico, and that also has taken a strong political connotation in many areas.

Finally, I would say that at the level of civil society, very often the contribution of evangelicals has a rather different feel to it from what one might perceive looking at the parliamentary and party level. Pentecostals are having an impact on communities that are largely ungoverned and crime-ridden, a presence that is based very much on the idea of exorcizing the demons of violence, addiction, and so forth. Exorcism seems more effective at this level than at the level of the political system, where charismatic ritualism functions rather as a substitute for the steep learning curve that most Pentecostals still need to go through. The intense Pentecostal self-belief that is positive for personal transformation becomes a liability in politics.

Can Latin American Pentecostalism Be Compared to Islamism?

Since Islam and Pentecostalism are the two most popular religions among the poor of the global south, some authors see a terrorist potential in the latter, especially in Africa. Exposed to similar poverty and marginalization, does grassroots Protestantism turn violent?

There is certainly in Pentecostal political militancy some use of violence. There are one or two marginal examples in Central America of Pentecostal vigilante groups, in a general context where vigilante groups are proliferating because the state is unable to guarantee law and order, but it is not quite clear to what extent these groups are supported by their churches. There was also a lot of Pentecostal involvement in the peasant patrols in the highlands of Peru against the Shining Path guerillas in the 1980s and early 1990s. And there have been some Pentecostals involved in the Zapatista guerilla movement in Mexico.

Not least, of course, the presidency of the charismatic evangelical general Ríos Montt in Guatemala in the early 1980s was extremely violent. However, he was a recent convert and it is difficult to see exactly how his new religion made his brutal military repression any different from other, non-Pentecostal, military leaders in Central America at the time. The relationship between Pentecostalism and state violence cannot, therefore, be decided solely on the case of Ríos Montt. What is certain, however, is that his Pentecostalism did not *prevent* him acting in that way, since he was held in high esteem by his church.

There are theocratic tendencies among some Latin American Pentecostals. However, since they do not have a sharia to implement, their ideas of theocracy generally boil down to little more than their supposed God-given right to rule (i.e., a Pentecostal hierocracy). The tendency of some Pentecostal groups to consider one's religious opponents as demon-possessed could well be explosive in some locations, and there is also a worrying tendency in some new theologies toward a return to ideas of territoriality and even to a rule of the saints. However, it should be remembered that Pentecostal Christianity, as compared to Islam, has had a very different historical relationship to the state, to territory, and to the use of force. Pentecostalism sees itself, among other things, as a recovery of primitive Christianity. And primitive Christianity, of course, was largely pacifist. It was persecuted, not persecuting. So even though there are increasingly some Pentecostals moving in other directions, they have greater difficulty justifying that tendency on the basis of primitive Christianity.

Religious Conflict

Pentecostal assertiveness does contribute to religious conflict in some places just by the fact of being what it is, an actively proselytizing faith based on the principle of voluntary individual adherence. So sometimes it is met by resistance on the part of other churches and religions that function on different principles. And on occasion Pentecostals even reply with physical force, although that is not very common. What is more common is religious conflict and "bad feeling" on the part of other groups who are losing out because people are converting to Pentecostalism. Thus, in parts of Latin America there is tension between Catholics and Pentecostals (and even violence, as in the southern Mexican state of Chiapas). Sometimes this may be connected with ethnic assertiveness on the part of ethnic minorities (e.g., some indigenous groups in Latin America).

There is also concern about a growing tendency on the part of some (not all) Pentecostals and charismatics to demonize their religious rivals and some social groups and movements that they regard as degenerate. Although this demonization is not necessarily incompatible with peaceful coexistence and participation in democratic life, it is potentially worrying in regions where democratic norms are not soundly embedded. However, the danger can be exaggerated: many analysts jump from the discourse to the supposed effects, without any empirical evidence. In practice, the language of demonization functions largely as an internal language of justification, a manichaeism of people and not of ideas ("we must elect men of God").

Yet despite fears of wars of religion in Latin America, these have not in fact happened. Guatemala would be the place for one; it has the largest proportion of evangelicals in Latin America. But even there, there has not been a war of religion, if only because evangelicals conspicuously lack unity. In Brazil, there have been two types of religious conflict. One is regarding ownership of important media stations—the Globo television network against the Record television network that the Universal Church of the Kingdom of God has acquired. And second, there has been a conflict between Pentecostal churches and the Afro-Brazilian religions. But that conflict has rarely been violent. It has been, if you like, a full-blooded religious dispute between social equals at the grassroots level.

The 2006 Pew survey data on such issues is broadly encouraging. To the question of whether it is important that there be freedom for religions other than one's own, Pentecostals are as affirmative as the general population of their countries (e.g., 94% of Brazilian Pentecostals, compared to a national average of 95%). When asked whether government should make our country a Christian country or whether there should be separation of church and state, Pentecostals reject the "Christian country" idea, notably in Chile (23% in favor, versus 62% favoring separation) and Brazil (32% versus 50%). However, everywhere except Chile Pentecostals are more inclined to the idea than other religious believers in their country.

Comparison with US Evangelicalism

What about a comparison between Pentecostals from Latin America and their evangelical co-religionists in the United States? Far perhaps from being a constituency for international terrorism, does global Pentecostalism constitute an extension of American soft power? Does it mean that there will be a commonality of geopolitical worldviews that will extend the power of the United States throughout the world? Once again, this is dubious. The war on terror, and especially the war in Iraq, has revealed a deep fissure within global Pentecostalism. Before the invasion of Iraq, a television program in Brazil featured several Brazilian Pentecostal congressmen discussing this issue. However conservative the political parties that these congressmen represented, and however new and unconventional some of the churches that they were involved in, all of them were unanimous in condemning the imminent invasion of Iraq.

While not monolithic, the majority current in Brazilian Pentecostalism seems far closer on these questions to Christian currents in the United States, which might be labeled mainstream. As for Spanish-speaking Latin America, a surprising diversity of Latin American churches made official pronouncements against the war, including many churches usually thought of as politically conservative, or which like to imagine themselves as nonpolitical.

The stance of church leaders mentioned above seems to be in line with that of ordinary Latin American Pentecostals, according to the Pew survey, which asked whether respondents favored "the US-led efforts to fight terrorism." Compared to 72% support from American Pentecostals, only around one-third of their Latin American co-religionists are supportive of the "war on terror." In all three Latin American countries surveyed, Pentecostals are actually slightly less favorable to it than their general populations.

More data casting doubt on the idea of Latin American Pentecostalism as a strengthening of US geopolitical "soft power" emerges from the question that asked respondents whether they sympathized more with Israel or the Palestinians. It is well known that American evangelicals have, on the whole, been strongly "Christian Zionist," not merely sympathizing with Israel but favoring its geographical expansion. In all ten countries surveyed, Pentecostals are above their national average in sympathy for Israel, considerably so in the American case (60% compared to 41%). Over 40% of Guatemalan Pentecostals sympathize with Israel, a percentage that falls to around a third in Brazil and Chile. "Sympathy" for Israel does not necessarily mean Christian Zionism, of course, but the other three replies certainly preclude it (sympathy for the Palestinians, both, or neither). Only 18% of American Pentecostals come in these categories, versus 56% of Pentecostals in Chile and almost as many in Brazil. Christian Zionism, therefore, seems to be much weaker in Latin American Pentecostalism than in the United States.

We thus see how risky it is to read third-world Pentecostalism either through the lens of contemporary Islamic politics or through the lens of the American religious right. Pentecostalism in Latin America is unlikely to become either the next constituency of recruits for geopolitical terrorism or an extension of American soft power.

As for American-style "culture wars," these are on the whole not reproduced in Latin America, despite the well-funded efforts of American proponents. This is partly because most of society (and current legislation) would be on the side of the Pentecostals regarding issues such as opposition to easy abortion and to gay marriage. So these issues do not usually have the political salience that they have for white American Pentecostals.

The Pew survey asked two questions on abortion. First, whether abortion is ever morally justified. In the United States, 64% of Pentecostals answered

no, well above the 45% of the general population. Latin American percentages are higher, but there the Pentecostals merely slightly reinforce the strong
general opposition. The second question asked whether government should
interfere with a woman's ability to have an abortion. Pentecostals are more
nuanced on this than often imagined. American Pentecostals are now divided,
with only 54% favoring government intervention, but this is still way above
their national average. In Latin America, they reflect the average quite closely.
Little more than a third of Guatemalan Pentecostals think government should
legislate against abortion.

Thus, Latin American Pentecostals do not seem to fit the negative stereotypes often disseminated about them (dangerous to democracy, potentially
violent, or subordinate to American right-wing geopolitical worldviews). Nor
do they live up to their own optimistic self-image as incorruptible purveyors
of political blessings. They are basically pro-democratic political novices in
their own countries. Inasmuch as they are linked into transnational faith networks, it might be attractive to think of this new grassroots Protestantism of
the global poor as a faith that straddles global divides and might therefore offer
a different vision of what globalized society could be, with its more privileged
members acting as amplifiers for the voices of their less privileged brethren far
away. But it is unlikely that Pentecostal Christianity, economically divided,
organizationally riven, and politically fractured, will be willing or able to play
a really effective role in such questions for the foreseeable future.

NOTES

1. Pew Forum, *Spirit and Power*, 2006.

6

Pentecostalism and Democracy

Is There a Relationship?

ROBERT D. WOODBERRY

Although no one knows exactly how many Pentecostal and charismatic Christians there are in the world, this cluster of "Spirit-filled" movements is clearly one of the largest and fastest growing religious movements in the world.[1] The World Christian Database estimates that there are about 550 million of them (Grim 2009; Johnson 2007; Johnson 2009). In the United States Protestant charismatics and Pentecostals made up over 12% of the total population in mid-1990s (Smidt et al. 1998 and grew to 23% of the population by 2006 (Pew Forum 2006)—although some of this "growth" may be because of better measurement. In Africa, Asia, Oceania, and Latin America this cluster of movements often constitutes even a larger percentage of Christians (Jenkins 2002; Pew Forum 2006; Grim 2009; Johnson 2009).

Moreover, Pentecostal worship styles and spiritual emphases have spurred charismatic movements in other Protestant denominations and in the Catholic Church. For example, in Latin America, there are now about twice as many charismatic Catholics as Protestants (Cleary 2011). Thus, some scholars argue if we include charismatic Catholics as part of the movement, it will soon become the predominant form of Christianity (Casanova 2001).

Given the massive size and rapid growth of these movements, intellectuals and officials should be interested in their social impact. But although Pentecostal growth has spurred jubilations and jeremiads, it has not spurred much careful empirical research—at least until recently (Manglos and Weinreb 2012). What research exists is mostly qualitative (ethnographies or broad discussions of political movements and actors); very little is statistical. Moreover, the published statistical research is mostly based on cross-sectional, non-probability samples, which makes statistical inference problematic.

This chapter explores the possible association between Pentecostalism and democracy.[2] However, given the available evidence, any analysis must be tentative. The chapter begins with an example from Peru that illustrates the complex association between Pentecostalism and democracy. However, generalizing from specific cases are difficult because Pentecostalism in an individual context is associated with so many other factors, such as marginalized class background and past experiences of discrimination. Thus, the rest of the chapter is more comparative.

Because research about the relationship between Protestantism and democracy is more developed, I first discuss this research and then discuss reasons why research on Pentecostalism and democracy lags behind (particularly statistical research). I then analyze mechanisms through which Pentecostalism might influence democracy: in other words, by instilling rule of law and mitigating corruption, by facilitating volunteerism and civil society, by expanding education among nonelites, and by promoting economic development in marginalized groups. Although these mechanisms are indirect, past research suggests that they are associated with greater democracy.

In each section I first summarize the research about Protestantism's and church attendance's social impact, and then use available research to analyze whether these patterns generalize to Pentecostals. In general, it seems that Pentecostalism is likely to have only a moderate influence on democracy.

Pentecostalism and Democracy in Peru

The complexity of Pentecostals' engagement with democracy can be seen even in the same country—for example, Peru.[3] One the one hand, Pentecostals were crucial to the development of civil society among marginalized groups. Rural Evangelicals (many of whom were Pentecostals) were disproportionately involved in the formation and leadership of so-called survival organizations such as Mothers Clubs, the Glass of Milk Committees and the Self-Run Canteens. These organizations became vehicles through which the popular classes expressed their social and political interests. The honesty and integrity of many of these Pentecostal leaders in managing organizations and funds in a context of high corruption helped spread democratic norms and enable marginalized communities to organize for their interests.

Similarly, Evangelicals (many of whom were Pentecostals) disproportionately participated in peasant patrols that limited the ability of the Shining Path (a brutal Maoist revolutionary group) from dominating rural areas and also limited human rights violations by the military. In this violent context, Catholic clergy often fled, other forms of civil society disappeared, and most acquiesced to violent groups for fear of being killed. These peasant patrols helped create both some stability and local-level democracy in an otherwise chaotic environment.

However, Pentecostal involvement in higher-level electoral politics is more complex. In 1990 Alberto Fujimori was elected president of Peru. He initially received widespread support from Pentecostals and other Evangelicals—several of whom were elected to parliament. However, in 1992 Fujimori instituted a self-coup and began restricting democracy. In 1995 he passed an Amnesty Law, which exonerated police and soldiers from responsibility for human rights violations during their struggle with the Shining Path. Finally, in 2000 he organized a fraudulent election in an attempt to extend and consolidate his power. By this time it was clear that the Fujimori regime was deeply involved in corruption.

During this process a number of Pentecostal pastors and parliamentarians continued to support him. Of course, some Evangelical parliamentarians withdrew their support from Fujimori, the major Protestant denominational association CONEP[4] (which included Pentecostals) condemned restrictions on democracy and directly criticized Fujimori, and the evangelical vote was split. However, elected Pentecostal parliamentarians were apologists for Fujimori, and FIPAC,[5] an association of independent Pentecostal pastors (mostly from "health and wealth" mega-churches) criticized CONEP for its public censure of the Fujimori government.

Most of the Pentecostals elected to national office and many of the mega-church pastors focused their political involvement on gaining resources for their constituencies and seemed to believe that Pentecostal voters owed them their votes based on shared religious loyalties. At least at the national level, Pentecostals did not play a significant role either in criticizing abuses of the Fujimori government or in expanding democratic space for non-evangelicals.

However, it is difficult to generalize from one case; the sections that follow attempt to determine if there are relatively consistent patterns across counties that help us understand the association between Pentecostalism and democracy in general. We start with an overview of research on Protestantism and democracy.

Protestantism and Democracy Overview

A substantial body of research suggests a relationship between Protestantism and both the development and spread of representative democracy. For example, Protestantism seems to have spurred the development of some democracy-friendly theories and institutions (Woodberry and Shah 2004;

Woodberry 2004; Woodberry 2012) and statistical research suggests an association between the percentage of Protestants in a country and both the level of political democracy and the stability of democratic transitions (Bollen 1979; Bollen and Jackman 1985a; Bollen and Jackman 1985b; Hadenius 1992; Lipset 1994; Gasiorowski and Power 1998; Midlarsky 1998; Karatnycky 1999; Woodberry 1999; Treisman 2000; Clague, Gleason, and Knack 2001; Kurzman and Leahey 2004; Karatnycky 2003; Woodberry 2004; Woodberry 2012; Woodberry and Shah 2004).

However, in recent decades the Catholic Church has increasingly advocated democracy (Philpott 2004); several "Confucian societies" have democratized (Hahm 2004) and some Muslim societies have experienced democratization movements. Given these changes, Protestants are less likely to stand out as disproportionately democratic. Moreover, little statistical research examines whether Pentecostalism fosters democracy in ways previous forms of Protestantism seem to have.

Reasons for Lack of Research on Pentecostalism

Several factors have hampered social research on Pentecostalism. First, there are few Pentecostal scholars at research universities in the social sciences. As a result, few scholars have the knowledge and interest to study these groups carefully.

Second, few surveys contain any questions with which to identify the "Spirit filled." Even in the United States where surveys are conducted regularly and many social scientists study religion, only a handful of surveys have even a single question useful for identifying Pentecostals and charismatics.

Internationally the situation is even worse. Outside North America, most surveys ignore religion entirely and almost none ask anything about "Spirit-filled" Christians. Longitudinal surveys are especially negligent. Outside Europe and North America I have found only one longitudinal survey that asks about religion (let alone Pentecostalism): *The Malawi Diffusion and Ideational Change Project (MDICP) Survey*. There are a few surveys from Latin America and Southern Africa that ask about Pentecostals (see, e.g., Steigenga 2001; Sherman 1997; Smilde 2007; Garner 2000). But these are cross-sectional studies and focused on only one country or region at a time; thus, it is difficult to differentiate contextual factors and differential conversions from consistent influences of Pentecostalism per se. Moreover, these surveys do not have probability samples—which makes any statistics based on them problematic.[6] This huge data-void makes measuring the impact of Pentecostalism difficult.

Fortunately, the Pew Forum survey of Pentecostals (Pew Forum 2006) uses probability samples, asks detailed questions about Pentecostals and charismatics, and allows more systematic study. Although it is still a cross-section, it allows scholars to compare identical questions in ten countries at the same time. If Pentecostal responses are consistently different regardless of context, the differences are more likely to be caused by something intrinsic to Pentecostalism, rather than unmeasured factors correlated with Pentecostalism. Moreover, *The World Christian Database* and its successor *The World Religion Database* contain estimates of the proportion of Pentecostals and charismatics in each country, which allow cross-national analyses. Unfortunately both sources are still underutilized.

A third factor that hampers understanding the relationship between Pentecostalism and democracy is that much of the growth of Pentecostalism has been since the second half of the 20th century. Thus, the tradition has had little time to change existing institutions and cultural patterns. Both political institutions and patterns of corruption and income distribution are already in place and resist change. Pentecostals must work within these dominant patterns and often conform to them.

Fourth, there is substantial diversity within what we label Pentecostalism. Statements by neo-Pentecostal/"health and wealth" elites may not reflect the attitudes and behaviors of ordinary believers—especially those in different Pentecostal traditions (e.g., Freston 2001). Yet statements by these elites get much of the attention in published literature. "Pentecostal" groups vary widely in theology, from "Jesus-only" Pentecostals who deny the Trinity, to historic Pentecostals like the Assemblies of God, to neo-Pentecostals who stress God's material blessing in the here and now, to various locally initiated groups. Moreover, Pentecostal groups vary politically from those who ban participation in politics to those who actively endorse political candidates.

Fifth, Pentecostal groups compete within a changing religious field. Thus, we must differentiate the current direct effects of Pentecostalism, from their long-term indirect effects on other religious groups and on political actors. For example, historically the Catholic hierarchy in much of the world was resistant to democracy and religious liberty—although this has changed radically over the 20th century (Philpott 2004; Woodberry 2004). Competition with Pentecostals spurred some of this transformation in Catholic policy. For example, in Latin America the conversion of large numbers of poor people and indigenous minorities to Pentecostalism pressured the Catholic Church to send more priests to work among the poor and opened space for both the development of Liberation Theology and a Church that was more responsive to non-elites (Smith 1991; Gill 1998; Trejo 2009; Trejo 2012; Woodberry 2012).

Once the Catholic Church is focused on promoting democracy and expanding political participation of nonelites, it has many institutional advantages that make "speaking truth to power" more feasible for Catholics than for Pentecostals. The Church is financially secure, has few problems getting permission to build religious structures, has access to academic, financial, and political elites, and has an international hierarchical organization with the resources to punish governments that kill or imprison their religious leaders.

Pentecostals generally have more recent and direct experiences of government harassment, such as the inability to get building permits and the inability to get their schools or marriages recognized by the state. Moreover, in most countries Pentecostals are disproportionately from marginalized communities: that is, poor, less educated, and darker skinned (Freston 2008: 15).[7] Pentecostals are also fractured into hundreds of distinct groups. If the government kills or imprisons a Pentecostal minister, there is less chance the international community will know about it and less chance the government will suffer consequences than if they kill or imprison a Catholic priest. This makes Pentecostals more vulnerable to local political pressures. Thus, while the Catholic Church may currently take a more active role in fostering both democratic transitions and political organization by nonelites in Latin America, historical evidence suggests this is not unrelated to the threat created by Pentecostal competition. Research that merely contrasts the behavior of Catholics and Protestants in the late 20th and early 21st centuries is likely to miss this.

Moreover, Protestant Pentecostalism has helped spur a major charismatic renewal within the Catholic Church (Cleary 2011). These charismatic movements often have substantial lay involvement and leadership. Thus, these Catholic charismatic movements may spur similar lay civic skills to Protestant movements, further diminishing any distinction that may have previously existed.

Mechanisms through which Pentecostalism May Influence Democracy

The rest of this chapter explores mechanisms through which Pentecostalism may influence the development and stability of democracy. Because the research on Protestantism and democracy and on religiosity and some of these intervening mechanisms are far more developed, each section begins with this broader literature and then examines how well it applies to Pentecostalism.

Rule of Law, Corruption, and Honesty

One way a religious tradition can help foster democracy is through fostering the rule of law, but some religious traditions seem to foster rule of law more than others (Woodberry 2004; Woodberry 2012; Woodberry and Shah 2004; Stark 2001).[8]

On an individual level, quantitative evidence suggests that regular church attenders are less involved in criminal activity—although this effect is primarily in areas with high overall religiosity and when parents and children share the same religiosity (Johnson et al. 2000; Lipford, McCormick and Tollison 1993; Donahue and Benson 1995; Hull and Bold 1995; Pearce and Haynie 2004; Regnerus 2003; Regnerus and Elder 2003). Moreover, regular church attenders and Protestants are less accepting of bribery, cheating on taxes, buying stolen goods, et cetera (Guiso, Sapienza, and Zingales 2003), and regular church attenders and conservative Protestants are less likely to misappropriate resources at work—for example, workers calling in sick when they are not, using company supplies for personal benefit, and so forth (Sikkink and Smith 1998). In Latin America, employers often seek out Protestants because they are perceived to be more trustworthy and reliable workers (Robbins 2004: 136).

Ethnographic research on Pentecostalism mirrors the patterns described above. Ethnographies consistently suggest that active involvement in Pentecostal congregations helps strengthen moral character and moderate infidelity, drug use, and alcohol abuse (Brusco 1993; Englund 2007; Smilde 2007; Aaron 2009; Budijanto 2009; Chan 2009; Lim 2009; Lumsdaine 2009: 18).

Available quantitative data is consistent with this. The Pew Forum survey (Pew Forum 2006) does not measure corruption-related behavior directly, but it does suggest that Pentecostalism may moderate corruption. First, Pentecostals attend religious services far more often than the general public in all ten countries surveyed.[9] Other research suggests church attendance is related to resistance to corruption (see above). Second, Pentecostals place more value on fair elections than others members of their societies in Africa, Asia, and the United States (although in Latin America and Kenya, Pentecostal attitudes are roughly comparable to others).[10] In all ten countries Pentecostals have a level of concern about corrupt political leaders comparable to other members of their societies.[11]

On a national and community level, societies with more Protestants have less corruption and more efficient governments (Clark 1975; Heidenheimer 1996: 337; La Porta et al. 1997; La Porta et al. 1999; Lipset and Lenz 2000; Sandholtz and Koetzle 2000; Treisman 2000; Paldam 2001; Stulz and Williamson 2003; Nieuwbeerta, De Geest, and Siegers 2003; You and Khagram 2005). These results remain strong when scholars control for a wide variety of other factors—including economic development and democratic experience.[12]

The results also hold for all the different measures of corruption scholars have used: external ratings of corruption constructed from surveys of international businesspeople, surveys of citizens' perception of corruption in their own society, surveys of citizens' victimization by corruption, measures of corruption by judges, policemen, politicians, and bureaucrats, and so on. Protestantism also correlates with multiple measures of government efficiency (La Porta et al. 1999), with protection of investor rights (Stulz and Williamson 2003), and with a number of factors that are also correlated with corruption—and controlled for in the previous regressions—including GDP per capita, consecutive years of democracy, and so on (e.g., Treisman 2000: 427; Grier 1997; Woodberry 2004; Woodberry2012).[13]

However, if a causal relationship exists between Protestantism and corruption, it is not automatic or perpetually necessary. Northwestern Europe has sustained low levels of corruption despite declining religiosity. Moreover, in the late 20th century large segments of Africa and Latin America have become Protestant with minimal impact on corruption rates. Clearly religion is not the only factor that influences corruption, and once social expectations and institutions are in place, they do not rapidly change.

The impact of Pentecostalism on corruption is less clear than the impact of classical Protestantism on corruption. Pentecostalism often has a moralistic tone and anticorruption campaigns have mobilized Pentecostals into politics (Freston 2001: 36). Yet many high-profile Pentecostal leaders and politicians have been mired in corruption scandals (Freston 2001; Freston 2008; Woodberry and Shah 2004; Levine 2008; Lumsdaine 2009: 33; Hong 2009; Lim 2009). The pattern of the first wave of Pentecostal politicians being linked to corruption is so consistent between countries in Latin America, Asia, and Africa that it does not seem accidental. There are also high-quality, noncorrupt, Pentecostal government officials (Lumsdaine 2009: 33; Hong 2009; Lim 2009), but to date, Pentecostal politicians have not proven more resistant to corruption than others (Levine 2008: 217).

Over time this pattern may change as Pentecostals gain more political experience and sophistication. Pentecostals have disproportionately mobilized poor and marginalized groups into politics, and just like other political movements by marginalized groups, they have often initially tried to link to patronage networks to "get their share of the pie." (Serbin 1999; Lim 2009). However, the resultant scandals have tarnished the image of Pentecostals and other Evangelicals, and these religious groups have increasingly become more careful and reflective in their political involvement (Lumsdaine 2009: 19–20; Lim 2009).

However, the beliefs and organizational forms of some Pentecostal groups may make undermining corruption more difficult. Some Pentecostal groups have strong individual leaders with little denominational or lay oversight; some neo-Pentecostal groups teach that God materially blesses those who have true faith and give "seed money" to the church. In these groups, the wealth of pastors is often viewed as a sign of God's blessing (e.g., Maxwell 2000). This may foster conditions where corruption develops even within the church (for example, the Brazilian "Universal Church of the Kingdom of God").

Thus, neo-Pentecostal ("health and wealth") churches may differ from other forms of Pentecostalism. Many of the major Pentecostal political leaders involved in corruption scandals came from neo-Pentecostal congregations. Moreover, wealthy elite Pentecostals may differ from ordinary believers. As mentioned earlier, studies of small Pentecostal congregations typically note their ethical rigor and avoidance of corruption rather than visa versa (e.g., Brusco 1995). Thus, elite-level scandals do not mean the overall impact of Pentecostalism does not inhibit corruption.

The influence of Pentecostalism on corruption may also be indirect through religious competition. Widespread conversions of poor and marginalized people to Pentecostalism have motivated the Catholic Church and others to increase work among the poor and open positions of lay leadership (e.g., Trejo 2009; Trejo 2012; Gill 1998; Smith 1991; Cleary 2011). In contexts of religious freedom, people may leave a church when leaders are perceived to be corrupt, creating pressure for leaders and politicians to act more ethically.

However, research about corruption suggests that it is highly resistant to change. Major programs by the IMF and World Bank have had minimal impact and even years of continuous political democracy have little influence on corruption (Treisman 2000). Our expectations for the transformative power of Pentecostalism should be proportional.

Volunteerism and Civil Society

A substantial branch of research suggests that civil society facilitates the stability and proper functioning of democratic regimes (e.g., Putnam 1993) and that religion influences the development of civil society. In the West, empirical evidence suggests that highly religious people tend to volunteer more time and give more money to support both religious and nonreligious voluntary organizations and to help people informally (Verba, Schlozman, and Brady 1995; Regnerus, Smith, and Sikkink 1998; Putnam 2000; Brennan and London 2001; Lam 2002; Smidt 2003; Cadge and Wuthnow 2006). Similarly, a recent study conducted in Mozambique concluded that Pentecostal groups were more efficient at sharing social services and assistance among the poor than internationally funded NGOs (Pfeiffer 2004).

Religious groups are also central to forming humanitarian organizations, private schools, and private hospitals, even if over time these organizations loose religious ties (Young 2002; Woodberry 2004; Smith and Woodberry 2001; Anheier and Salamon 1998). However, religious traditions vary substantially in the amount of organizational civil society they foster with Christians—especially non-state Protestants—being the most active in forming voluntary groups (Woodberry 2004; Woodberry 2012; Anheier 1989; Salamon and Anheier 1996; Salamon and Anheier 1997; Anheier and Salamon 1998; Ecklund and Park 2007).

I know of only one published study that differentiates the voluntary activity of Pentecostals from other Protestant groups. In South Africa, Pentecostals and Apostolic Christians give a higher percentage of their income than mainline Protestants, Zionists, and non-Christians (Garner 2000: 326). However, these results should be viewed tentatively because they represent only one context and the sample is not random. Still, The Pew Forum survey (Pew Forum 2006) partially confirms these results. Typically Pentecostals are more likely to be involved in voluntary organizations related to "education, arts, music, and cultural activities," "women's groups," and "other groups" than other members of their societies and have comparable levels of participation in other voluntary organizations.[14]

Pentecostal groups are likely to foster voluntarism because they are not funded by the state, thus they must instill voluntarism and charity in their congregants in order to survive. Moreover, Pentecostal leaders are not sacramentally distinct from other congregants and do not need formal education to be ordained; this opens organizational initiative to much of the congregation—in other words, anyone who has "the gifts of the Spirit." By working in congregations, people gain skills that are useful for organizing other types of civil society (Verba, Schlozman and Brady 1995; Robbins 2004: 134). Still, the focus on evangelism and the "spontaneous" moving of the Holy Spirit *may* make Pentecostals less likely to create formal, non-church, social organizations than some other Protestant groups. Moreover, competition with Protestantism has spurred major growth in lay organizations among Catholics', Buddhists', Hindus' and Muslims' organizations (Woodberry 2004; Woodberry 2012; Dunch 2001; Oddie 1978; Tejirian and Simon 2002; Gombrich and Obeyeskere 1988; Grayson 2002). Thus, distinctions between Protestants and others may diminish over time.

Religious groups and other forms of civil society can instigate transitions to democracy or protest abuses of power. But internationally, Pentecostal groups have often been less willing to publicly confront dictators than Catholic and mission/mainline Protestant groups. In Ghana, Malawi, Kenya, Congo, El Salvador, Taiwan, et cetera, Catholic and mission Protestant groups (such as

Methodists and Presbyterians) were more likely to publicly condemn abuses by dictators (e.g., Freston 2001; Gifford 1998; Kuo 2002). However, this may have to do more with their differential power than with a greater predilection for democracy. International religious denominations have international resources and networks that enable them to punish governments that kill or restrict their religious leaders. Pentecostal groups are less likely to have these links (Freston 2001: 15).

In addition, established denominations often have inside information. When I interviewed the former General Secretary of the Christian Council of Ghana, David Asante Dartey, he told me that he was able to speak out against the government when others did not "because I knew if something happened to me, there would be an international protest," whereas other religious leaders could disappear with little international notice. He also said that he had inside information because religious schools had trained most of the senior bureaucrats. Thus, friends in the administration would tell him what was going to happen before the government announced it, and he was able to plan what to do. Friends also warned him when it was OK to criticize and when it was not. Less established groups did not have the same insider information.

Until recently many Pentecostal groups have eschewed politics as "worldly." However, in countries like Korea and the Philippines, Pentecostals have swelled the ranks of democratization movements initiated by Catholics and mission/mainline Protestants. Pentecostals have mobilized many marginalized groups into electoral politics—often for the first time. Moreover, Pentecostals have become increasingly sophisticated and civic in their political involvement (Lim 2009; Hong 2009; Lumsdaine 2009: 19–20; Burdick 1999; Burdick 2010; Marsh and Tonoyan 2009; Freston 2008: 31).

In addition, Pentecostal religious groups seem especially able to spread in poor communities and in politically oppressed societies—where both hierarchical religious organizations and organizations that require clergy to have academic degrees have often floundered (e.g., Freston 2008: 31). In Guatemala and Colombia when civil war forced Catholic priests and foreign missionaries to flee, Pentecostal groups spread widely in the vacuum. They provided basic civil society and social services in contexts that would otherwise have had far less (Brusco 1995; Garrard-Burnett 1998). Thus, the civil society created by different religious groups may promote democratization better in different circumstances.

Education

A substantial quantitative literature argues that mass education promotes both the level of political democracy and the stability of democratic transitions (Bollen 1979; Crenshaw 1995; Gasiorowski and Power 1998; Kamens

1988; Barro 1999). Other research suggests that religion influences both the demand for and supply of education (Woodberry 2004; Woodberry and Shah 2004; Woodberry 2006; Zhai and Woodberry 2011) —although the educational context seems to influence whether Pentecostals get more or less education than those around them.

In North America, regular church attenders tend to have higher education rates—although few of them seem to end up as professors in the social sciences. Between religious traditions in the United States, Jews have the highest education rates. Conservative Protestants are often perceived as having less education than other religious respondents, but much of this depends on how theological conservatism is measured (Hackett and Lindsey 2008; Woodberry et al. 2012). Moreover, lower education rates among conservative Protestants seems to apply primarily to women—who tend to get married and have children early in theologically conservative communites and thus do not go on for graduate education (Glass and Jacobs 2005; Fitzgerald and Glass 2008; Fitzgerald and Glass 2012). However, the one study that disaggregates conservative Protestants finds that in the United States Pentecostals are the least educated religious group of all (although the difference with fundamentalists is not statistically significant) (Beyerlein 2004).

However, church attendance has the same positive impact on educational outcomes for "biblical literalists"/conservative Protestants as it does for other religious groups (i.e., in regressions predicting education the interaction term between attendance and Biblical literalism is positive) (Woodberry et al. 2012). If biblical literalism hampered education, we would expect the interaction term to be negative and significant—that is, either people who are most committed to "literalist" beliefs would have less education or attendance would be less beneficial for "literalists" than for other religious groups.

Still, two caveats are important. First, the surveys mentioned above analyze probability samples of the general US population, and thus the positive association between church attendance and education is primarily driven by graduation from high school and college, and the negative association between Biblical literalism and education is primarily driven by graduate education. Second, the United States has a long history of Protestantism, religious competition, and state-sponsored education. Thus, the impact of Protestantism on mass education is already institutionalized in the United States, masking old differences and allowing other differences to become more important, particularly distinctions in gender role ideologies, age of marriage and child bearing, resistance to some emphases within academia, or regional variations in religious traditions and educational institutions.

Christianity has a more strikingly positive association with educational outcomes outside the West. In both sub-Saharan Africa and India, Christians are disproportionately educated (Woodberry 2004), and in Latin America Protestants seem to invest more in educating their children relative to others in their economic circumstances (Tax and Hinshaw 1970; Early 1973; Sexton 1978; Annis 1987; Brusco 1995; Sherman 1997—although also see Steigenga 2001). However, this data is qualitative or from cross-sectional, non-probability samples, and thus difficult to generalize.

In Taiwan, Protestants have more education than members of other religious groups and have higher educational expectations for both their sons and their daughters than parents in all other groups. This result is based on nationally representative probability sample and remains strong even after controls for the education of the parents and other relevant social factors. The positive effect of Protestantism on educational expectations is especially strong for parents who have little formal education themselves (Zhai 2006; Zhai and Woodberry 2011). Thus, in the Taiwanese case, the disproportionate education of Protestants seems to be related to the expectations of Christian parents, not just more educated people converting to Protestantism.

Many of the Protestants and Christians in the studies mentioned above are Pentecostals, although the studies seldom differentiate them. Two studies that do differente them have mixed results. In Latin America, traditional Protestants and Mormons seem to have higher education rates than most Pentecostals (Steigenga 2001), although this may be due to the class background of converts and the length of time these other Protestant traditions have been in Latin America. Among South African blacks, Pentecostals and Apostolic Christians seem to put the highest priority on education (Garner 2000). However, neither of these studies uses a full probability sample which makes any statistics based on them problematic.

Religion also seems to influence the supply of education. Protestant missionaries and religious competition were crucial for expanding mass education throughout the Global South. Countries that had more religious liberty, earlier Protestant missionary activity, and more Protestant missionaries per capita still have higher education rates (Woodberry 2004; Woodberry 2012).

However, Pentecostalism developed in the 20th century, after other Protestant groups had already invested in mass education and spurred competing traditions to do the same. By the time Pentecostalism became a major force, states were providing mass education and religious groups (which did not have the power to tax) provided a smaller proportion. Moreover, because most Protestants no longer perceive higher education as a natural preparation for conversion to Christianity and because Pentecostal church leadership is based more on having the gifts of the Holy Spirit than on having a degree from a seminary, Pentecostalism may not have the same tendency to found higher educational institutions as earlier Protestant groups had.

Still, as cited above, in Latin America Pentecostals from marginalized backgrounds seem to invest more in the education of their children than non-Protestants from similar class backgrounds. Where we have evidence from Africa and Asia, Protestants (who are disproportionately Pentecostal) typically invest more in the education of their children than members of most other religious groups. In West Africa there are growing Pentecostal associations among university faculty and Pentecostals have formed a number of colleges. Thus, to the extent that broader education fosters democracy, we would expect a long-term positive association between the spread of Pentecostalism in countries with low education rates and later political democracy.

Economic Development

Research also suggests that there is an association between the level of economic development in a country and both the level of political democracy and the stability of democratic transitions (Bollen 1979; Burkhart and Lewis-Beck 1994; Londregan and Poole 1996; Gasiorowski and Power 1998; Lipset 1994). Much democratic theory also emphasizes the importance of a large middle class for stable democratic transitions—although this has not been tested as rigorously in the quantitative research (see e.g., Lipset 1994).

Most of the current literature on the topic also argues that Protestantism, including Pentecostalism, may have a moderate positive impact on economic growth (for a summary of this literature see Woodberry 2006; Woodberry 2008; Potter, Amaral, and Woodberry 2011). Some researchers argue that Protestantism fosters a work ethic or a greater commitment to family (e.g., Brusco 1995), others suggest that Protestants have beliefs that are more "friendly" to economic growth (e.g., Guiso, Sapienza and Zingales 2003) or that in Latin America both Protestants and Charismatic Catholics have attitudes friendly to economic growth (Sherman 1997).

However, The Pew survey does not suggest these "economically friendly" attitudes extend to Pentecostals (at least "economically friendly" from the perspective of neo-classical economists). Pentecostals do not typically have a greater generalized trust than other members of their society (except in South Korea).[15] On average 0.9 percentage points fewer Pentecostals think "most people can be trusted"—which in most countries means they are statistically indistinguishable from others (i.e., there is a high probability the differences are due entirely to chance and not real differences in the population).

Pentecostals do not have more positive attitudes toward the free market either. When asked how strongly they agree with the statement: "Most people are better off in a free market economy, even though some people are rich and some are poor," Pentecostals had more moderate attitudes than the general public in Latin America,[16] more negative attitudes in the United States, Kenya, India, and the Philippines, comparable attitudes in Nigeria and South Korea, and more positive attitudes only in South Africa. This inconsistent pattern suggests contextual factors matter more than Pentecostalism per se.

Pentecostals typically view government redistribution more favorably than other members of their societies. Pentecostals are more likely than the general public to agree that "[t]he government should guarantee every citizen enough to eat and a place to sleep" in 7 of 10 countries. On average, 3.2 percentage points more Pentecostals than others "completely agree" with this statement.[17] Pentecostals also have a strong sense that Christianity has "a responsibility to work for justice for the poor." On average, 10.7 percentage points more Pentecostals than other religious people agree with this statement. The contrast is particularly large in societies with large non-Christian populations. In South Korea, 29 percentage points more Pentecostals than other religious respondents "completely agree" that their religion has a "responsibility to work for justice for the poor," and in India 19 percentage points more Pentecostals do.

While many neo-classical economists think government redistribution may hamper economic growth, improving the conditions of the poor and expanding the middle class may help democratization. However, it is not clear how much these attitudes influence the economy.

On an individual level, the Pew Survey suggests that Pentecostals typically have a more positive assessment of their own financial situation. In Africa and Asia, Pentecostals rate their financial situation much better than the general public. On average 11.5 percentage points more Pentecostals than others rate their personal finances as "excellent" or "good." In the United States and Latin America the percentages are roughly equal. However, in all countries surveyed fewer Pentecostals than others rate their personal finances as being "poor"—on average 6.3 percentage points fewer Pentecostals do. Pentecostals are also more hopeful about their future financial situation. Ten percentage points more Pentecostals than others think their financial situation will "improve a lot" over the course of the next year.

Moreover, a non-random sample of South African blacks suggests that mainline Protestants, Pentecostals, and Apostolic Protestants save a higher portion of their incomes than Zionists or those who do not belong to a church. Pentecostal and Apostolic Protestants are also less likely to use money to pay for animal sacrifices or to consult the spirits of ancestors (Garner 2000). Perhaps saving, abstention from drinking, and so on are related to the greater intergenerational mobility for Pentecostals and Apostolic Protestants in this sample. Similarly, research about Brazil suggests that when we link micro-units between waves of the Brazilian census, the incomes of non-whites with limited education disproportionately increases in areas with greater conversion to Protestantism (in this case mostly Pentecostalism) (Potter, Amaral and Woodberry 2011). However, the jury is still out on how much, and in which contexts, Pentecostalism fosters economic growth and how much this fosters later democratization.

Violence and Intolerance

Some scholars suggest that religion may encourage violence and intolerance—particularly monotheistic religion (Moore 2000). However, any association between religion and violence is complex since religion is often merely a marker in conflicts spurred by ethnic competition, economic exploitation, reactions to colonial occupation, or political calculation (e.g., Wilkinson 2004; Cavanaugh 2009). Moreover, religious violence is clearly not limited to monotheistic faiths (e.g., Tambiah 1993; van der Veer 2001: 83–105; Macfarquhar 2003; White 2009; Jerryson and Juergensmeyer 2010). However, if particular types of religion accentuate violence, this could hamper economic development and democracy.

Yet, although Muslims, Hindus, Buddhists and others have killed or attacked converts *to* Pentecostalism (e.g., Stafford 2004; Grim and Finke 2011), I am not aware of Pentecostals using violence against people who convert *from* their faith. Thus, violent intolerance is not a particularly Pentecostal-initiated phenomenon. In fact, on average, religious liberty is higher in areas with more Protestants (Marshall 2000: 27; Freedom House 2004; Woodberry and Shah 2004). However, in societies where there is discrimination against Pentecostals, violence and discrimination could hamper democratization.

Despite Pentecostal support for such things as declaring Zambia a "Christian nation" (Freston 2001: 158), Pentecostals have not advocated laws that activity restricted other religious groups—with the possible exception of witchcraft. The rapid spread and diversity of Pentecostal groups have also created pressure throughout Latin America and elsewhere to expand religious liberty, remove restrictions on minority religious groups, and remove subsidies of dominant religious groups—such as the Catholic Church. Pentecostals have also organized coalitions with other religious groups to expand religious liberty (Chan 2009).Freed from state patronage, the Catholic Church has been more willing to critique abuses by the state (Woodberry 2004; Woodberry 2012; Philpott 2004; Trejo 2009).

The Pentecostal belief that only *true* faith can save someone implies that faith cannot be compelled by the state. Moreover, the religious diversity within Pentecostalism prevents them from establishing a state church. These two factors foster the "twin tolerations" so crucial to the development of liberal democracy, that is, freedom from both government restriction of religion and religious control of the state (Stepan 2000).

Data from The Pew survey confirms Pentecostals' support for religious liberty, but also reveals tendencies that make others uncomfortable. On the one hand, Pentecostals are more supportive of the government taking "specific steps to make our country a Christian nation"—an attitude Pentecostals often associate with fostering God's blessing. On average, 10.9 percentage points more Pentecostals support this than others in their country. On the other hand, Pentecostals typically put higher emphasis on both religious freedom for themselves and for others than the general public. On average, 5.5 percentage points more Pentecostals say it is "very important" for them to live in a country where they can practice their religion freely. Moreover, on average 3 percentage points more Pentecostals say that if is "very important" that "there is freedom of religion for religions other than [their] own." Pentecostals are also typically more concerned than others about conflict between religious groups in their country. On average, 4 percentage points more Pentecostals perceive religious conflict as a "very big problem." Together these results suggest that Pentecostals are likely to support symbolic statements of Christian nationhood, but unlikely to restrict the religious liberty of others.

Conclusion

Thus, existing evidence suggests the global spread of Pentecostalism has a moderate positive impact on the spread and stability of democracy. However, this relationship is not unproblematic. For example, a number of Pentecostal political leaders have been involved in vote selling and corruption (Freston 2001: 35). Moreover, initial Pentecostal forays into politics are often clamorous. But, this is often the case with movements that have traditionally been excluded from power (see for example, Freston 2001: 45).

However, Pentecostalism has expanded civil society among groups and in areas where civil society has historically been weak. It seems to limit corruption at a nonelite level, lead to moderate economic and educational improvements among nonelites, and expand both religious liberty and the rights of organizations outside state control. Moreover, the threat of Pentecostal conversion has spurred other religious groups—such as the Catholic Church—to focus more intentionally on helping the poor and ethnic minorities. This has created alternative means for nonelites to influence political outcomes. Thus, while the spread of Pentecostalism may not be a panacea for democracy, it is unlikely to hamper the process and is likely to make some moderate positive contributions of its own.

Acknowledgments

This work has been made possible through funding by the Spiritual Capital Research Program, sponsored by the Metanexus Institute on Religion and Science with the generous support of the John Templeton Foundation.

NOTES

1. Some scholars dislike the "Pentecostal" label because it too easily implies that these diverse set of movements can all trace their origins to the Azusa Street revival and other related movements in the United States around the beginning of the 20th century. In fact, "Spirit-filled" movements began in Chile, India, and elsewhere either before or concurrently with the revivals in the United States. Moreover, the label Pentecostalism applies a western category to a diverse set of nonwestern churches, many of which have local origins and respond to local issues (Robert 2000; Kalu 2012).
2. Following Larry Diamond (1999: 10–11) I define democracy as "a civilian, constitutional system in which the legislative and chief executive offices are filled through regular, competitive, multiparty elections with universal suffrage" in a context where there is no "reserved domains of power for the military or other actors not accountable to the electorate" and there are "extensive provisions for political and civic pluralism as well as for individual and group freedoms, so that contending interests and values may be expressed and compete through ongoing processes of articulation and representation beyond periodic elections." However, research on democracy does not consistently use such an expansive definition. Typically statistical research uses some type of scale that attempts to enumerate the level of liberal democracy in a society: e.g., Polity IV (2012) and Bollen (2001).
3. The following example is based on Freston 2001; Österlund 2001; and López Rodríquez 2008.
4. Concilio Nacional Evangélico del Perú (National Evangelical Council of Peru).
5. Fraternidad Internacional de Pastores Cristianos (International Fraternity of Christian Pastors).
6. Each person in the respective populations does not have a known probability of inclusion in the samples. Some randomization is used in Steigenga's sample, but it is combined with convenience samples of congregants and neighborhood residents. Thus, there is no way to know the relationship between sample statistics and the population parameters or know if the samples from different groups are comparable.
7. Although there is a growing segment of wealthy and highly educated Pentecostals.
8. Internationally the link is primarily with monotheistic religious traditions, especially Protestantism. In North America, the link is strongest with theologically conservative traditions.
9. The Pew Survey data can be downloaded at www.thearda.com. Crosstabs showing the association between Pentecostals and the variables discussed in this chapter for each of the 10 countries in the sample are available at (http://pewforum.org/surveys/pentecostal/). I report differences when Pentecostals seem to be distinct in most of the countries sampled.
10. If we combine mean differences from all 10 countries surveyed, on average 3.6 percentage points more Pentecostals than the general public say "honest elections held regularly with a choice of at least two political parties" is very important.
11. Showing this pattern in all ten countries for each question would require substantial space. To see the exact percentages see Pew Forum, *Spirit and Power*, (http://pewforum.org/surveys/pentecostal/).

12. For example, Sandholtz and Koetzle (2000) control for GDP/capita, economic freedom, democracy, years of democracy, and trade. Treisman (2000) controls for common law tradition; British colonialism; never being a colony; ethnolinguistic divisions; fuel, metal and mineral exports; log GDP; federal system; uninterrupted democracy 1950–1995; imports/GDP; state intervention; government wages; government turnover; degrees latitude from the equator; and continent.

13. The relationship with other religious traditions may change over time (see Bourgault and Dion 1993 for a suggestive example).

14. Pentecostals are more likely than the general public to belong to voluntary organizations related to "education, arts, music, and cultural activities" in 7 of 10 countries and virtually identically in 2 countries. The mean difference is 4.3 percentage points. Pentecostals are more likely to participate in "women's groups" in 9 of 10 countries and the mean difference is 3.5 percentage points. They are also more likely to participation in "other" voluntary organizations in 7 of 10 countries and the mean difference is 4.5 percentage points.

15. The question is, "Generally speaking, would you say that most people can be trusted or that you can't be too careful in dealing with people?"

16. Fewer completely agreed or completely disagreed.

17. Pentecostals' concern for redistribution may be partially driven by the socioeconomic background of Pentecostals (Pentecostalism has typically grown disproportionately among the poor).

SECTION FOUR

PENTECOSTALISM AND SOCIAL ENGAGEMENT

Although Pentecostalism is often characterized as primarily a religion of personal experience, in recent years there have been an increasing number of Pentecostal churches that have established significant social outreach ministries. Many of these efforts can best be understood as "mercy ministries" that provide such things as food, clothing, and shelter for those in need. Although these kinds of approaches are probably the most prevalent types of Pentecostal social engagement, there are other developments that suggest that Pentecostals are becoming more engaged at all levels of their societies, linking Pentecostal spirituality and their understanding of biblical teaching to being active and engaged citizens and bringing their religious beliefs and experiences to bear in the public realm.

Timothy Wadkins provides a view from El Salvador, where Pentecostalism has not only grown exponentially in a very short period of time, but where new models of social engagement have also developed as it has spread through the population. Wadkins details three ideal types of engagement with society and among Salvadoran Pentecostals: those who are *separating* from culture, those who are *consuming* culture, and finally, those that are *engaging* culture in new and creative ways. What these different orientations share is an immersion in a biblical worldview that is grounded in a supernatural understanding of continuous divine intervention in their lives.

Wadkins shows that Salvadoran Pentecostalism is individualistic, emphasizing a personal experience of being filled with the Spirit, but this then leads believers to adopt a lifestyle in which individuals feel empowered and directed by God, believing that God enters into every part of their lives as they seek his guidance and direction.

However, while the dominant trend in Salvadoran Pentecostalism has been social withdrawal, coupled with the idea that social change will only come through the cumulative effects of evangelism, Wadkins shows that there are emerging groups that are seeking to become effective agents of social structural change. In this, Wadkins says, their experience tells them that heaven can be realized on earth as they become agents of the power of the Spirit in their communities and the larger society. Thus, similar to what Juan Martinez argues about transnational Latino Pentecostal mission work (see chapter 10), Wadkins suggests that Salvadoran Pentecostals become agents of their own personal and social renewal through the power of the Spirit.

While there are emerging Pentecostal groups in El Salvador whose work may start to bring about social structural change, according to Danny McCain, these efforts are well underway in Nigeria. McCain describes the growing movement of Nigerian Pentecostal leaders who have developed a more holistic worldview in which they are as concerned for social transformation as they are for personal transformation. McCain argues that this movement is the result of an emerging worldview that is being influenced from two directions. First, the new social awareness is being encouraged by *internal* religious factors such as biblical values, an emerging "kingdom theology" (that is, an emphasis on improving this world as a reflection of Jesus ruling over all aspects of life, thus implementing the kingdom of God on earth), and a disappointment with the results of contemporary Nigerian Pentecostalism that has tended to employ an emphasis on the "health and wealth" gospel. It is also being advanced by *external* factors related to education, upward mobility, and the massive transfer of ideas—including religious ideas—taking place internationally as a result of globalization.

McCain shows that leaders of this new movement tend to have college degrees in professional fields, as well as experience in the business world rather than seminary degrees and church experience. Their lack of "sophisticated" biblical exegesis often leads them to literal interpretations of biblical passages that instruct believers to care for the poor, the sick, and the widows. McCain argues that not only do these leaders think differently, they have had more exposure to the many problems of Nigerian society than more traditionally trained ministers. Finally, the social capital that has accrued to these leaders, through their business, educational, and social-class location, has provided them with different types and amounts of social capital than the traditional church leader. The result, as McCain shows, has been that these leaders have made significant inroads in different segments of Nigerian society—in some cases extending to the president's family—in the effort to bring about change.

These new types of social engagement raise important questions about the ultimate influence that Pentecostals can and may have in their societies. And while the ultimate results remain to be seen, identifying and tracking this newer trend toward Pentecostal social engagement, and how it is expressed and pursued in different social settings, remains an important task. As Timothy Wadkins asks, owing to the belief among Salvadoran Pentecostals that they have been empowered to move out into the world to become witnesses of Christ and the Spirit's agents of transformation, what effects will such a perspective and motivation have on society?

7

Pentecostals and the New World Order in El Salvador

Separating, Consuming, and Engaging

TIMOTHY H. WADKINS

In the gang-ridden and very poor Salvadoran barrio of San Bartolo, some 6,000 people have gathered for the Saturday evening celebration at Tabernáculo de Avivamiento Internacional (TAI), the palatial, newly constructed, corporate-looking, mega-church that sits high on a hill overlooking the urban sprawl of greater San Salvador.[1] Within ten minutes it is holy bedlam— high-energy guitar music, electronic-generated images on two big screens, girls waving flags, hands raised, people dancing in the aisles, crying and singing so loud the windows vibrate. Some people are speaking in tongues; others have fallen to the floor, apparently slain in the Spirit. On stage, periodically add-ing to the frenzy by blowing a Jewish shofar, and crying out to *Señor Jesus* and *El Spirito Santo*, is Carlos Rivas, the fiery preacher and politically left-leaning founder of this church, which in a decade has grown to almost 8,000 members, 70% of whom are under the age of 35.

What takes place at TAI is replicated all over El Salvador in dozens of Pentecostal and Evangelical churches that are just as large, and often, much larger. Misión Cristiana Elim in Illopango, for example, has a membership that exceeds 75,000, not counting its various satellite churches scattered around Central America and its growing network of churches among the Salvadoran Diaspora in North America.[2] Despite the proliferation of mega-churches like these, however, most Salvadoran Pentecostals still worship in churches of a hundred or less. It is virtually impossible to walk through any village or barrio and miss hearing the pulsating music and shouts emanating from these store-front, or, often, half-finished cinder block, churches.

This movement has commonalities in belief and practice, but it is also diverse. Most of its churches are characterized by fervent tongues-speaking, faith healing, and sundry charismatic manifestations of the Spirit. A few congregations, however, have significantly muted the boisterousness in their worship. The diversity in this movement is also seen in the rituals of clothing and gender boundaries. In many of the small, indigenous denominations women come to church in long dresses and white veils, and they sit separately from their husbands, who, in church, always wear long-sleeved shirts. In the more affluent Assemblias de Dios churches, however, men wear what they want, and women arrive in Calvin Klein jeans, heels, and dangly earrings.

What factors can account for the rapid growth and diversification of these kinds of Christian expressions, especially since El Salvador has been predominately Roman Catholic since the sixteenth century? How do Salvadoran Pentecostals relate to and live within the various social and cultural contexts of modern and increasingly urban life? In this essay I will suggest that the answers to these questions must be sought in the inextricable connections between Pentecostal religiosity on the one hand and recent patterns of cultural change on the other.

It is not a coincidence that during the same time period that El Salvador began to modernize its economy and take steps in the direction of a more participatory democracy, the hegemony of Roman Catholicism began to erode and Pentecostalism exploded.[3] The most recent polls indicate that in the two decades between 1988 and 2009, while mega-malls and economic trade zones were being erected, and freely contested elections were increasingly taking place, Catholic allegiance dropped from 88 percent of the population to just over 50 percent and of these, only half professed to being practicing Catholics. Meanwhile, Evangelical and Pentecostal allegiance rose from 15 to 40 percent with a majority attending church more than twice per week.[4] What exactly is the relationship between Pentecostalism and this transition toward what I refer to as El Salvador's new world order? To begin to answer this question I will present three case studies. These cases are mostly composites drawn from over one hundred videotaped interviews that I conducted in 2010 and backed up with survey data. Each case is an ideal type that represents divergent Pentecostal tendencies to *separate from, consume,* and *critically engage* culture. The boundaries that distinguish these ways of being Pentecostal are certainly porous. In many cases all three could be found in one church. Nevertheless, they are also distinguishable. Considered together these portraits will help us to better account for the growth, the mutation, and especially the reciprocating influences that take place between Pentecostal faith and practice and the multiple cultural niches within El Salvador's increasingly modernized landscape.

Separating from Culture: Alberto

Alberto was born in Chalatenango, a region in the North West of El Salvador, which was fiercely contested during the civil war. He was raised in a large family of nine children, overseen by a single mother. Alberto was raised Catholic, received his first communion, but rarely went to mass, apart from Easter and Christmas. "I just could not relate to all the idols … and I hardly even heard about the Bible." In desperation over unemployment, when the war ended in 1992, Alberto left his family to go to San Salvador. He was only sixteen. But he could not find work and began to run with street gangs, committed several armed robberies, and became addicted to crack cocaine. Only one year after he left home his mother became very ill and died. Alberto fell into a tailspin of depression.

One day, while playing basketball with his amigos, an elderly woman along with other women from a cell group associated with Misión Cristiana Elim approached him. She told him that he needed to pray with her, and when he refused to kneel with her and pray, she kicked him and demanded that he kneel. Her authoritarian ways actually convinced him that she might have actually been sent by God, and so he knelt. The very next day, while riding on a bus, he heard an evangelist on the radio who seemed to know his needs. "I know where you are," the evangelist said. "You are in despair over the death of a loved one, you are trapped by life in the streets, and you think there is no way out. God wants to heal your heart right now." "I do not know what came over me," Alberto told me. "But right there on the bus I got on my knees and prayed the way the evangelist told me to. I asked to be forgiven and for Christ to come into my heart."

This initial experience led him to the gang ministry Alcance Victoria in the town of Santa Tecla, where during a church service he formally "went forward" and accepted Christ.[5] The results were profound. "Christ immediately took away my desire for crack and helped me feel like I was loved, a feeling I never received in my family." It was during the early days of his residence at Alcance's halfway house that he was baptized in the Holy Spirit. "I cried for days, and could hardly keep from speaking in tongues all the time," reported Alberto. After eighteen months, Alberto re-entered the world, developed his skills as a creative artist, and started a bus-painting operation. He also met Sylvia, who two years later he married.

Although Sylvia was a Christian, soon after the wedding she began to plunge into depression and had to be hospitalized. Eventually she began to completely give her heart to the Lord, and as she did she was healed of her illness and was able to return home from the hospital.

Supplemented by his wife's income from sewing at a Korean-owned textile factory in San Bartolo, they earn just enough to keep their six children in school and the bills paid. His goals are simple—to make sure his children get an education and have a better future. Their lives are almost completely dominated by their involvement in a small inner-city Assemblies of God church, whose pastor is an elderly woman who inherited the church from her late husband. The church is considered Alberto's extended family. "Some people think we are strange because the men wear long sleeve shirts to church, and the women wear dresses and veils and sit separately from the men. But we take the scriptures seriously and we believe strongly that we should not be conformed to the world." As a Pentecostal, Alberto regularly speaks in tongues and hears the Lord speaking to him through dreams. He feels completely surrendered to the Lord and is following His will.

Had Alberto been born at the beginning of the twentieth century, he most likely would have grown up as an illiterate, landless farmer who worked on any number of agricultural haciendas or coffee *fincas* owned by a small number of families that composed a ruling oligarchy. His world would have been ordered according to a kind of sleepy feudalism that favored elites and locked him firmly in place. Even his Catholic religion would have normalized and legitimated this social order. Much like the authority of the aristocracy, the church was the location of sacred authority that was passed down by the clergy, reinforcing the immutable fact that not only was there no salvation outside its domain, but also that there was no society beyond this one.[6]

It is different today. A century later, with several brutally crushed uprisings and a bloody civil war under its belt, El Salvador has gradually begun to open its doors to greater levels of democratization. Much of the infrastructure has been deregulated thanks to the seductive strategies of neoliberal capitalism. With the welcoming of structural reforms, the dollarized economy, and the *maquila* sector, which escalated after the ratification of the Central American Free Trade Agreement (CAFTA), this tiny country has increasingly been absorbed into the globalizing processes engineered by the first world, especially the United States.

Such changes have not been altogether positive. El Salvador is now nearly 70 percent urbanized, and 45 percent of the Salvadoran population earns less than two dollars per day. It is difficult to feel optimistic about the future. With the steep plunge in the living standards of the mostly urban poor, the only hope for many is to illegally immigrate to the north. Over two million mostly poor Salvadorans now live in the major cities of the United States. Despite the resulting influx of remittances that are helping those who remain in the mother country, migration has led to the disintegration of the Salvadoran family and to the escalation of gangs and violence.

It is in this context that the most typical expression of Salvadoran Pentecostalism can be understood. Like Alberto, most Pentecostals in El Salvador are poor.[7] Their embrace of Pentecostal religiosity involves a series of breaks from former connections in favor of something altogether new and more stabilizing.[8] It begins with conversion. From the perspective of Pentecostals, these are gut-wrenching, dramatic turns, resulting from the excruciating psychological pain and guilt over a life lived with few choices other than those of the street. While conversion is often a slow process and not necessarily as dramatic as St. Paul's Damascus-road experience, it amounts to a profound individual experience of finding personal solutions for the chaos of modern existence. But it also extends to the collective life in church communities where believers take care of one another and where they learn to live with their minds "set on the things above."

It always involves a rupture from the past. Whether suddenly or gradually, the profound gospel message comes to make sense to converts: that all humans are infected by sin, and, like a spreading cancer, sin has pervasively metastasized throughout the modern, impoverished, and violent social body in such a way that every individual is in need of divine intervention. Conversion then is a dramatic solution to the personal and structural problem of sin and the consequent suffering it has created. It is a decision to separate from an old life and enter in to the embrace of a new one. It amounts to a fundamental reorientation toward something new and different that helps to heal psychological wounds, to bring release from guilt over personal failings, to spawn the development of a disciplined and even more productive way of life, and perhaps even leads to social lift.

For Pentecostals, conversion is also complemented by an infusion of supernatural power. Pentecostals like Alberto are saturated by the experience of the miraculous. This begins with an initial experience of divine power, a "filling" of the Spirit that is accompanied by manifestations of supernatural power such as speaking in tongues, physical healing, dreams, visions, prophetic words, dancing, singing, crying, or being slain in the Spirit. Different from the observations of Max Weber, who latched on to an austere segment of Protestants to build a theory that Protestants look to worldly success as signs of election, Pentecostals look for such assurance through emotional experiences that they often describe as feeling like heat or pulsating electrical current, and that are outwardly expressed in charismatic displays. Such manifestations are not just personal signs for the believer, however. They are collective, even ritualistic experiences that draw people together in a series of embodied, sacred "languages" that, like *glossolalia* itself, transcend human categories of communication. Congregants report that a good or bad worship experience depends upon the prevalence of these manifestations and the level of emotional and charismatic intensity.

A major driving force throughout Pentecostalism is healing, which in many ways is another dramatic rupture. In a country where medical care is limited, it is understandable that the poor would gravitate toward spiritual communities where direct healing by God was an expectation and a common occurrence. This is certainly true in El Salvador. More often than not, converts described a personal healing of themselves or a family member as the instrument that led to their conversion. Yet healing extends beyond the physical, and includes such things as ending domestic abuse, gambling, frequenting of brothels, gang violence, alcohol and drug addiction, and especially the healing of self-perception. Respondents often report that the Holy Spirit gave them a sense that they were fundamentally important to God. Whether gradual, like the cure for Sylvia's depression, or instantaneous, like Alberto's freedom from drug addiction, healing is a break from the material or psychological effects of sin into something totally new and whole.

Neither conversion nor empowerment eliminates life's problems for the Pentecostal, but it does change directions in both outlook and behavior. Converts no longer associate with gangs. They stop going to bars and brothels. They begin to invest themselves in morally responsible tasks like family life and gainful employment. Despite the distress of underemployment, congregants typically feel optimistic about the future. They also join communities of like-minded believers, where, lashed together on these rafts of the redeemed, they feel empowered to navigate the perilous seas of poverty and corruption and the crosscurrents of temptation that could potentially pull them under.[9]

Such communities are withdrawn, alternative enclaves of spiritual support, separated from a demonic world. But they are also more than that. They frequently take care of one another financially. One pastor told me that if someone in the church has a need that cannot be taken care of in the context of a cell group, it goes to the board of deacons "where there is a budget for taking care of the needy among us."[10] If Pentecostal churches really function this way, then they represent a fairly large series of faith-based NGOs in the midst of a nation that lacks the infrastructures to adequately help the poor.

The kinds of churches represented by Alberto's spirituality are egalitarian organizations as well. It is true, as some scholars point out, that some of the larger churches are run by autocratic pastors reminiscent of the hacienda *Patrón*. Yet, unlike the Catholic Church, where priests are trained formally in seminaries and then appointed to serve in a particular parish, almost every Pentecostal pastor has been brought up and trained within the structures of the local church, symbolizing the extent to which this movement is formed from below. Even when there is one dominant personality in charge, there is nevertheless a sense that all forms of service in the church are shared ministries, whether someone is a janitor, a secretary, a song leader, a cell-group leader, or a pastor.

The by-product of such egalitarian cloisters is that congregants learn the values of moral responsibility and the various skills of participatory democracy.

Women in these churches are becoming especially empowered, and many emerge in positions of pastoral leadership. Despite the overarching canopy of biblically based patriarchy, women often lead men into the faith. Once the men cross over into the household of faith, they abandon the more blatant aspects of *machismo*, and become husbands and fathers who forsake the streets and turn inward toward their families, sometimes even submitting to the authority of a woman pastor.[11] Family life becomes more stable and the family unit becomes valued and more socially productive. Children begin to stay in school and small-scale property ownership begins to take place, coupling redemption with at least the possibility of social lift.[12] Many scholars want to know whether Pentecostals are engaged in social projects. It is fair to say that in Alberto's subculture they *are* the project.

Consuming Culture: Tanya

Tanya is an attractive thirty-five-year-old woman who owns a very successful real estate brokerage. She has been a Christian for almost as long as she can remember, having been raised in a strict Baptist home. When her parents migrated to Brazil during the civil war she stayed in El Salvador to finish her college education. During this time she turned away from God and became a model. But increasingly the lifestyle of parties and drinking felt empty.

Two years ago she accepted an invitation from a friend to attend the affluent church, Templo Internacional Evangelistico (TIE) in San Salvador.[13] TIE was founded by a former businessman who received a call into ministry through a vision. In just six years TIE has grown to 3,000 members, and it intentionally caters to educated and upwardly mobile members of the professional classes. Its services are lively, but in comparison with other Pentecostal churches they are intentionally toned down. There is, however, an abundance of highly choreographed praise music, led by an accomplished song leader and accompanied by one of several different bands with backup singers. While TIE supports those churches who are engaged in ministries with the poor, its ministry is to help TIE's members become the "fragrance" of Christ to those in more affluent sectors of society. Most members in this church did not enter through the doors of conversion. In fact most are long-time Christians who have migrated to TIE because they felt somehow "abused" by the legalism in other Evangelical churches.

In the nurturing fellowship of TIE Tanya's life dramatically changed. She loved the fact that the church was clean, orderly, and clearly designed by someone with affluent tastes. She liked the Pentecostal atmosphere that was much less demonstrative than other mega-churches she had visited. Through the ministries at TIE she renewed her commitment to Christ, got out of the party lifestyle, and with the help of some business associates at the church she started her real estate business. Now her social center is TIE. She sings in one of the bands that lead worship and she goes to a weekly Bible study. At TIE she also experienced the filling of the Holy Spirit, but not in the conventional way. She has never spoken in tongues, but she has very deep mystical experiences, has witnessed healings through her touch, and frequently God speaks to her through dreams.

Tanya also believes fervently that God has a very distinct plan for her life that has been marvelously revealed to her. Two years ago she began to pray for a husband. She wanted someone who was educated, a working professional, who spoke English like her, and, she admitted, even someone who had brown eyes like hers. "If you have enough faith, you can ask God for anything, and he will give it to you." In the airport in Rio, en route back to San Salvador after visiting her parents, she met the man of her dreams: a brown-eyed British citizen who plays professional soccer for one of the Salvadoran pro teams. They dated briefly back in San Salvador and were married last year.

Tanya and her husband are not without problems, however. She laments the fact that he is not yet a Christian. She is also obviously worried about their inability, thus far, to have children. Medical tests have revealed that the infertility problem lies with her, and she has been earnestly praying about it. "I know that God will give us the desires of our heart and allow us to have children," Tanya told me. Even though she recently had an expensive surgery, the problem was not corrected. Undeterred, she continues to believe that God has given her a promise through the biblical story of Abraham and Sarah, who, because of their faith, in their old age were rewarded with an heir.

While Alberto's separatist subculture is an other-worldly asceticism of converts who perceive the world as a domain of sin and suffering, Tanya's is very different. It consists primarily of second- and third-generation Evangelicals who have not experienced radical conversions, but like many members of Evangelical, but traditionally non-Pentecostal churches, have become *pentecostalized.* They perceive the world as a relatively safe environment where God's blessings can be enjoyed. They are not ascetic, but they are nevertheless characterized by a supernatural spirituality and depend on God to help them navigate through all the complex possibilities that the world offers.

Virtually all Pentecostals in El Salvador talk about knowing the will of God for their lives. In our survey, 99% affirmed that God has a plan for every believer's life and that they were supernaturally directed by God in the details of life.[14] In this attitude, they identify deeply with the supernatural worldview embedded in the stories of the Bible that depict God changing historical circumstances, such as opening the Red Sea, providing Abraham with an heir in his old age, or even punishing Jonah, who was swallowed by a big fish because he did not want to go to Ninevah. Pentecostals like Tanya and Alberto believe that the pattern of God's direction revealed in such stories is normative for today. This direction often comes through an important insight while reading scripture, or by being led to read a particular biblical text. It is often heard through the medium of dreams, in visions, during prophecies at church, or in deep mystical states of prayer.

In Tanya's Pentecostal circles however, the revealed will of God often coincides with a consumerist orientation—a mechanized spirituality that connects the will of God with the abundant desires of the believer. This attitude bears an uncanny resemblance to the need for "on-time delivery," so characteristic of the modern globalized world, where information, products, and experiences are consumed in virtual time, as fast as a text message can be sent or Amazon can download a book on an e-reader.[15] In the spirituality of Tanya's subculture, the present and future are typically collapsed, and heaven can be realized on earth in the expectation that God will deliver whatever one desires when one wants it. With the coins of faith and surrender to God, you can order up anything—a husband with brown eyes, a new car, a better job, fertility to conceive—and like a transcendent vending machine, God will deliver.

Not everyone in Tanya's Pentecostal circle articulates his or her relationship with God in exactly the terms outlined above. Nor does everyone get what he or she wants from God always and immediately. I have interviewed numerous individuals who have experienced difficult physical ailments, a loss of employment, or near financial ruin. But in every case, the stories moved in the direction of victory. These individuals believed that God wanted them to stop suffering and to give them the desires of their hearts. But they were tested by God until they learned the formulae of faith and surrender. After all, when Abraham finally learned to believe the promises of God, his elderly wife conceived.

Tanya's subculture also represents a more collectivist consumer orientation. As this movement has mutated more and more in the direction of large mega-churches it has rapidly taken on the symbolic structures of transnational market society. New churches are springing up that look more like malls than traditional churches and usually have *internacional* in their name. Preachers dress like American businessmen and mimic the flamboyant preaching style projected on the cable channel *Enlace,* which is part of the Global Trinity Broadcast Network. Churches are filled with the latest in high-tech equipment, which can project on big screens, keep congregates entertained, and "manage" the way in which the Spirit is moving. They are also acquiring airtime on television, buying their own stations, and actively marketing their own look that will appeal to broad, worldly wise sectors of the population. Virtually every large church has a sophisticated website that is user friendly, features musical concerts, *YouTube* videos of the pastor preaching, and announcements about upcoming events. Through the social media, younger Pentecostals are connecting to the music and message of a transnational Pentecostal culture that, like the McDonalds golden arches, has become a monolithic global brand and is increasingly dissipating their interest in older, poorer, more localized versions of Salvadoran Pentecostalism.

Engaging Culture: Pedro[16]

In many ways Pedro is a self-made man. Born in La Poppa, a very poor barrio within metro San Salvador, he was abandoned by his father at the age of two. Although his mother took him to his first communion, they never practiced the Catholic faith. His family was very poor and in order to finish high school Pedro had to work fifty hours per week on night shifts. After high-school graduation he acquired a job at a beer-making enterprise and through his hard work, he rose fairly high into management levels.

In 1980 Pedro went with his wife to church at Misión Cristiana Elim. He was struck by the deep emotionalism he experienced at the church, and the pastor's message cut into him. When the time came he was the first to go forward. His life changed very quickly. After he was baptized in the Holy Spirit, he began to devote himself to ministry. At that time, Elim was still a church of only about 1,000 and was meeting in a tent. He became a deacon within eight months, and as Elim began to embrace organization through cell groups and to grow rather rapidly, he became a cell leader and within two years a supervisor of cell groups.

Pedro began to feel conflicted about his work at a brewery when El Salvador was a country with high rates of alcohol addiction. "It was like we were making atomic bombs," Pedro said. His problems were solved in 1990 when he was asked to become a full-time zone pastor at Elim. By that time Elim was growing very rapidly. Under the leadership of Mario Vega, and influenced by cellular methods of the Yoido Full Gospel Church in Seoul Korea, it had become one of the largest churches in the world.

Increasingly Pedro's ministry led him to Comunidad Iberia, one of the most violent and gang-ridden sectors in San Salvador. He wanted to do something different than just preach to the kids of Iberia and try to win them to Christ. "These are barrios of immense poverty, with people who feel alone, with families at risk, with escalating episodes of violence ... It does no good to tell them of the love of Jesus unless we practice that love ... We need to help make this neighborhood safe, we need to help this community become transformed so that people can regain a sense of identity, their children can go to school and they can find work that will help them out of poverty."

In the winter of 2009 he began to develop a plan for Iberia, which eventually led to a Christmas dinner with gang leaders and their families attended by Pastor Pedro and Pastor Mario Vega. *"There we were breaking bread and eating chicken with some of the most violent young men in all of Latin America." Shocked by such compassionate attention, the gang leaders and pastors together strategized about what sorts of programs would help them get some of their material and economic needs met. What came from this was the development of a profitable bakery where gang members are trained as bakers, distributors, and bookkeepers, as well as the creation of a small bleach factory where they make and sell bleach as a cleaning supply. Now, two years later the gang violence has been neutralized in that neighborhood, and just this year they opened up a thriving elementary school as well. In addition, several gang members have become Christians and are actively participating in cell groups.*

Pedro is often critical of his Pentecostal tradition. *"They live in a bubble of emotionalism that has no windows that look outward … It is not enough just to make Jesus our Savior, or to have a deep experience with the Holy Spirit. These are both important … but we must also wake up to the fact that the Holy Spirit moves, not just inside of us, but wherever there is chaos, violence, and poverty as well. Evangelism is therefore not just about soul winning … it is about an integrated, redemptive engagement with all spheres of society, whether anyone becomes a Christian or not."*

Pedro is an example of the egalitarian, bottom-up nature of this movement. Like virtually all the pastors in the Elim church, Pedro became a Christian at Elim and as his leadership skills began to be recognized, he moved up the ranks into pastoral leadership. However, Pedro also represents a growing number of Pentecostal leaders who have moved out ahead of their congregations and have become deeply engaged with the problematic social realities of El Salvador and increasingly critical of the evangelical and Pentecostal tendencies toward otherworldly social separation.

Mario Vega, pastor general of Misión Cristiana Elim, told me that he and many of his staff are beginning to address structural evil in the country. "It is not enough just to preach the gospel or even give aid to the poor," Vega told me, "We must speak out against and attempt to change those conditions that cause poverty."[17] In recent radio broadcasts and newspaper advertisements, Elim has denounced policies that are contributing to such things as gang violence and poverty. In addition, the church is now engaged in job-training programs, promoting recycling as a form of Christian concern for the environment, and, at the risk of severe criticism, testing for HIV. Its media outreach ministries have also begun to move away from an exclusive emphasis on evangelism or Christian nurture, to addressing issues of social and cultural importance, especially those that concern youth.

In recent years, this kind of orientation toward social ministry has been growing, thanks primarily to an emergent theological literacy among Pentecostal leaders. It is hard to overestimate the rather quiet influence of the

Latin American Theological Fraternity in this process.[18] Based in Argentina, this organization has been led by such well-known theologians as Renee Padilla, his daughter Ruth Padilla, Samuel Escobar, and the Methodist evangelical Jose Miguez Bonino. Several of the more left-leaning Pentecostal leaders have been in continuous dialogue with the Fraternity over the past decade. In El Salvador, hundreds of pastors, including the entire staff at Elim, have been trained by Semillas de Nueva Creación, an affiliate of the Theological Fraternity, directed by Eliberto Juarez.[19] Semillas' theological orientation is toward ministry that is always social and even political at the same time that it is spiritual. In their two-year training program they emphasize what they call integral ministry—an emphasis on God's comprehensive, incarnational intention of not leaving any human and any corner of the earth untouched by His love, thus integrating every aspect of life into the redemptive message of good news.

Pentecostals like Pedro represent the birth of a Pentecostal intelligentsia in El Salvador. They are increasingly educated, theologically trained, culturally engaged in ministries that focus on structural issues, and they are pushing fellow Pentecostals in decidedly new theological directions, primarily toward a different way of reading the Bible. Every Salvadoran Pentecostal affirms that the Bible is God's inspired revelation. But most Pentecostals are wedded to a personalized focus on those biblical narratives that highlight the miraculous works of God. Ignoring the social ministry of Jesus, they reduce the Bible to a mere manual for personal spirituality and morality. Pentecostals like Pedro are challenging this hermeneutic. They have moved toward a reading of the Bible that is Christ-centered and expands the notion of personal salvation to include all aspects of the created order—social, cultural, political, and ecological. Pentecostals involved in this movement continue to embrace the gifts of the Spirit and miraculous intervention of God in their lives. But this is now just one corner of their spiritual orientation.

Individual Empowerment in the New World Order

The portraits of Alberto, Tanya, and Pedro represent the most significant tendencies in Salvadoran Pentecostalism and help us to appreciate its ability to fit into different cultural contexts. Alberto's separatist orientation is still the most dominant Pentecostal expression in El Salvador, and Tanya and Pedro represent newer ways that the movement has mutated and adapted to differing social and cultural contexts, primarily in those sectors with greater degrees of wealth, social mobility, and education. What is it about Pentecostalism that makes it so adaptable to the complex structures of modernity?

As noted earlier, a massive cultural shift has taken place in El Salvador at almost the same pace and during the same time period as the Pentecostal surge. Perhaps its greatest indicator is the rapid decline in numbers of Catholics. At the beginning of the twentieth century, El Salvador's population was primarily rural and poor. In the hacienda culture of the campo, power and authority were vested in the distant, aristocratically controlled institutions of government and the military, and locally in a wealthy oligarchy of landholders who wielded power and exploited the poor for their labor. The poor were hardly more than indentured servants within this often-harsh hierarchical structure. But with the exception of an occasional, violently crushed revolt over sequestered property, they were mostly unaware of any other life or alternative social structures. Thus they were "dwellers" in a system that held them in place and demanded acquiescence to their social superiors and passive conformity to a prescribed way of life.

The church did not dehumanize the poor in the same way. In fact it assured them that, if they were obedient to the sacramental requirements of the faith, their present sufferings would be offset by future rewards in heaven. But the church was still an explicit extension of the static hierarchical social order. For one thing, its theologians taught that social inequality was part of the divine and immutable created order. For another, every parish church was a concrete symbol of such inequality. A typical Catholic grew up with the awareness that, like the Jewish temple in ancient Israel, holiness and divine power were institutionally embodied in the church and could be accessed only vicariously. Throughout their lives the faithful would frequent this holy of holies, touch its relics, adore its images, pray to its saints, participate in its local festivals, and above all else receive the sacramental host at the hands of God's vicars, the clergy. But the church was a static institution not a dynamic organization of like-minded and equally empowered believers. The church was not considered to be, as it would be after Vatican II, "the people of God." Catholics who came to mass were passive recipients of what this institution provided in the same way that they related to the social order to which they belonged by virtue of birth. For the typical rural peasant, self-determination in religious, political, or economic matters was still mostly inconceivable in a society that corralled the many and held them in place, but was *controlled* by a few.

Over the past century, however, a break has occurred. It began slowly with the break from Spain, the liberalization of the constitution, and the theoretical separation of church and state in the late the late nineteenth century. It continued with the bitter and violent land-rights rebellions of the 1930s, especially the massacre at La Matanza, with the opening of doors to Protestant missionaries and the resulting onset of Christian pluralism, and especially with the violent crucible of the twelve-year civil war that finally ended in 1992. The hacienda culture of the past is now increasingly dismantled and is being replaced by emergent market capitalism, transnational *mequilas*, agribusinesses, and globalized networks of communication such as television and the internet. In these processes, the families that comprised the traditional ruling oligarchy have not disappeared but have moved away from landed wealth into financial markets. Increasingly, new generations of Salvadoran citizens have emerged as well. These individuals, who are children and grandchildren of rural *campesinos*, are now typically urbanized wage earners who take their autonomy for granted. Even though still poor and underemployed in a market economy, they are "masterless" people who can move freely and make choices for themselves. For these individuals, the Catholic Church and the social order it represents often seems alien, antiquated, and irrelevant. It does not easily adapt to the multiple versions of modernity created by these new sorts of individuals. And as the polls suggest, they often walk away from the church with little angst about their decisions.

No doubt many devout Roman Catholics would take exception to this analysis. Indeed there were Pentecostals in El Salvador long before Toyota dealerships, Kentucky Fried Chicken restaurants, and call centers. Likewise there are Catholics now who are still flourishing members of the traditional church in the midst of these symbols of modernity. The arrows of causation and conditioning certainly fly in many different directions, and the historical sketch offered above remains somewhat general. But despite the connective ambiguities, a pervasive kind of individualism has increasingly enveloped El Salvador at the same time that Evangelicalism and Pentecostalism have surged. The key to understanding this connection is the fact that Pentecostal spirituality empowers individuals and becomes a religion almost tailor-made for the modern era of personal autonomy and social portability. Spirit-filled religiosity is individualized in various ways. First of all, it is absolutely person-centered rather than institution-centered. In Evangelicalism there can be salvation outside the Catholic Church. There is no necessity for a building, a priest, or a sacrament. The presentation of and response to God's message can take place anytime, anywhere, and is not mediated by anything. Alberto's conversion began on a basketball court and culminated on a city bus. Numerous Salvadorans got their first taste of the gospel from radio or television. This person centeredness translates very quickly into the idea that all persons are equal before God. The elderly woman who kicked Alberto into praying with her was his equal in every way. Given such a priesthood of all believers, it follows that Evangelical and Pentecostal Christianity develops person to person, creates voluntary social spaces, and evolves into organizations from the bottom up, literally leveling the old social order.

Evangelical and Pentecostal Christianity is also word based. Unlike the Catholic statues, which St. Bernard famously described as "books for the unlearned," the gospel must be personally understood by the individual and mentally appropriated as a message of good news. Such news comes via different media—personal communication, radio or television, books, and especially the Bible—but it is always the word—spoken, written, or heard—that informs and persuades the individual. Protestantism at the time of the Reformation spawned a literacy and information revolution by virtue of its emphasis on understanding the written word of God. One of the constant refrains in my interviews with Salvadoran converts from Catholicism is that they were never introduced to the Bible, and thus were prevented from understanding its message. I have also interviewed others who remain functionally illiterate and who deeply desire to learn to read so as to better understand the text.

Pentecostalism is also grounded in free choice. Since the evangelical gospel is not confined to an institution, it freely and frequently jumps over boundaries. It moves best in a cultural ethos where individuals are free to choose, not only what they might want to do or buy, but also what kind of religion they might want to embrace. The notion of free choice not only led to the modern dance between buyers and sellers, but it was also the launching pad for modern methods of evangelism. The foremost antecedent for this might be the nineteenth-century evangelist and president of Oberlin College, Charles Finney, who argued that with the right methods of persuasion, a revival could be engineered.[20] It is not too far from this basic gospel entrepreneurialism to today's high-tech marketing of the message that dominates so much of the Salvadoran mega-church ethos. Freedom of choice is primarily about mobility and Evangelicals and Pentecostals are on the move, constantly canceling what came before in favor the new. Most of the early members of Tanya's church were originally Baptists until they began to see visions and have dreams that moved them away from their roots. Historically, Protestantism has upheld the notion of *sola scriptura*, but not everyone interprets the scriptures in the same way, and some individuals get entirely new revelations under the influence of the Spirit. Like procreating rabbits, this tradition continuously gives birth to new charismatic visionaries who are gifted with the art of persuasion. The result is the continuous reincarnation of new churches and ministries in a process that mimics the frenetic pluralism of modern market societies and forms what sociologist Birgit Meyer describes as the "logic of spread" in Pentecostalism.[21]

Harvey Cox suggests that in its current manifestations Pentecostalism might be a protest or reaction to the "ecstasy deficiency" created by the technological and scientific rationality that characterizes the post-enlightenment world.[22] From a social scientific perspective this is a poignant suggestion. However, I think Salvadoran Pentecostals would disagree. They understand this eruption not as some kind of reactive effort to reach upward from below. This, after all, is what took place in the Genesis story of Babel. Instead, they would argue, the Day of Pentecost radically reversed the direction of Babel.[23] It was the "latter rain" predicted by the Prophet Joel, when God *poured* out His Spirit, and it *descended* into the realm of humanity. This was no reaction. It was a reception. Moreover, what took place on the day of Pentecost was not just the display of tongues. Tongues were just the outward sign that the Holy Spirit had entered into the history of the new people of God and that nothing would ever be the same again.

As we have observed, for some more affluent Pentecostals, this reception of the Holy Spirit becomes frosting on the cake of upward mobility. But most Salvadorans are very poor. They feel like economic vagabonds who wander from one informal job to another in the wastelands of the urban-industrial complex. They are crippled by a power deficiency. The poor Pentecostals I have interviewed are empowered. They are saturated by a biblical worldview that is grounded in a supernatural understanding of continuous divine intervention in their lives. It is of course individualistic. Beginning with the overwhelming experience of being filled with the Holy Spirit, it proceeds to become a lifestyle wherein the believer feels personally directed by God. Such power is also a collective experience, as churches become reservoirs of spiritual recharging, where the gifts continue to be manifested, where the redeemed can unburden their souls, get prayed for, and even are healed. The power in such communities creates in people the sense that they are God's elect and therefore uniquely important persons. Just as important, they are people who experientially know that heaven is not just about gold streets and mansions in the future. It is about heaven realized on earth as God's unbounded love and power breaks into every cultural niche and corner of their existence. Perhaps individual autonomy is one of the more important hinges upon which the door of the new world order of modernity hangs in El Salvador. If so, the supernatural individualism and with it, the almost limitless, life-giving adaptability of Pentecostal spirituality is one of the more powerful forces making it swing.

Acknowledgments

The project is part of the *Pentecostal and Charismatic Research Initiative* (PCRI), funded by the John Templeton Foundation and administered by the Center for Religion and Civic Culture (CRCC) at the University of Southern California. I wish to thank Tracy Daub, Patricia Christian, and Michael Gent for their comments on an earlier draft of this essay.

NOTES

1. The website of Tabernáculo de Avivamiento: www.tabernaculodeavivamiento.org.
2. The website of Misión Cristiana Elim: www.elim.org.sv.

3. Aside from Timothy Wadkins, "Pentecostal Power: Conversions in El Salvador," *Christian Century*, November, 14, 2006, 26–29, and "Getting Saved in El Salvador: the Preferential Option of the Poor," *International Review of Mission* 9.384/385 (2008): 31–49, post–civil war aspects of this revival have not been examined in any detail.

4. Patricia Christian, Michael Gent, and Timothy Wadkins, "The Advance of the Spirit in El Salvador: Twenty Years of Survey Evidence of Pentecostal Growth," Figure 3: Average Monthly Church Attendance (unpublished manuscript, under consideration by *Latin American Research Review*).

5. The website of Alcance Victoria: www.alcancevictoriasansalvador.org.

6. The best overview of the "old order" is Howard J. Wiarda, *The Soul of Latin America: The Cultural and Political Tradition* (New Haven: Yale University Press, 2001).

7. According to Informe 122- *Encuesta sobre la Religion para Las y Los Salvadorenos*, 72% of Salvadoran Protestants earn less than $307 per month and 35% earn less than $153. See Christian, Gent, Wadkins, "Advance of the Spirit in El Salvador," Table A.

8. Cf. Joel Robbins, "Anthropology of Religion," in Allan Anderson, Michael Bergunder, Andre Droogers, Cornelis van der Laan, eds., *Studying Global Pentecostalism: Theories and Methods* (Berkeley: University of California Press, 2010): 156–178.

9. David Martin, "Evangelical and Charismatic Christianity in Latin America," in Karla Poewe, ed., *Charismatic Christianity as a Global Culture* (Charleston: University of South Carolina Press, 1994), 85.

10. The Rev. Mario Vega, interview by author, 2 June 2006.

11. See Elizabeth Brusco, "The Reformation of Machismo: Asceticism and Masculinity Among Columbian Evangelicals," in Virginia Garrard-Burnett, David Stoll, eds, *Rethinking Protestantism in Latin America* (Philadelphia: Temple University Press, 1993): 143–158.

12. Many of my interview subjects reported better living conditions as a result of super-natural agency and/or better life style choices that resulted in better living conditions.

13. TIE is not an actual congregation. It is a composite description of similar churches.

14. Instituto de Opinion Publica, *El Pentecostalismo y la Cultura en El Salvador,* (Questions 23, 24, 25, 26).

15. See Sturla J. Stalsett, "Offering On-Time Deliverance: The Pathos of Neo-Pentecostalism and the Spirits of Globalization," in Sturla Stalsett, ed., *The Spirits of Globalism* (London: SCM Press, 2006): 198–212.

16. Pastor Pedro Landeverde is an actual pastor at Elim. The information in this story is used with permission.

17. Vega, Interview, 2 June 2006.

18. The website of La Fraternidad Teológica Latinoamericana: www. ftl-al.org.

19. The website of Casa Semillas de Neuva Creacion: www. casasemillas.org.

20. Charles Finney, *On Revivals of Religion* (1835), lecture 3, "How to Promote a Revival."

21. Birgit Meyer, "Pentecostalism and Globalization," in Allan Anderson, Michael Bergunder, Andre Droogers, Cornelis van der Laan, eds., *Studying Global Pentecostalism*, 113–130.

22. Harvey Cox, "Spirits of Globalization: Pentecostalism and Experiential Spiritualities in a Global Era," in Stalsett, *Spirits of Globalization*, 20, 21.

23. See Waldo Cesar, "From Babel to Pentecost: A Social-Historical-Theological study of the Growth of Pentecostalism," in Andre Corten, Ruth Marshall-Fratani, eds., *Between Babel and Pentecost: Transnational Pentecostalism in Africa and Latin America* (Bloomington: University of Indiana Press, 2001), 22–40.

8

The Metamorphosis of Nigerian Pentecostalism

From Signs and Wonders in the Church to Service and Influence in Society

DANNY MCCAIN

Introduction

"No one will go from this service today without being blessed." Pastor Wale Adefarasin of the Guiding Light Assembly, an upscale Pentecostal church in Lagos, was speaking after a Sunday morning service filled with body-shaking music, energetic preaching, and a spirit of warmth and friendship.[1] "Have you been blessed?" he continued. A loud roar went up along with the spontaneous raising of hundreds of hands. Pastor Adefarasin smiled and said, "Is there any-one here who has not been blessed today?"

I was shocked when a tall sober-looking woman in the balcony stood up and raised her hand. The pastor also looked a little surprised, but said to her, "Please come down." This first-time visitor to the church made her way to the pulpit and spoke quietly with the pastor for a few seconds. I then received my second shock in two minutes. Pastor Adefarasin picked up one of the large containers that had been used earlier to take up the offering, placed it in front of altar and said, "Our sister has not been able to enjoy the blessings of this service because of many heavy burdens in her life. However, we will make sure she goes from this place today with a blessing." He pulled a wad of bills from his pocket and placed them in the container. "I want you to come forward and help bless our sister this morning." Dozens of middle-class, well-dressed Nigerians streamed forward to deposit a financial blessing in the container.

This incident illustrates a broader change of emphasis within the Pentecostal churches in Nigeria. As a 24-year resident of Nigeria, I have visited dozens of Pentecostal services. I have seen offerings taken up for missions, evangelism, church buildings, and even church members who had some specific need. However, witnessing this special offering for a visitor unknown to the congregation was a new experience for me. It represented a shift from the internal spiritual focus on the church and its members to an outward focus on the practical needs of society. This small incident is a living metaphor for an increasingly socially conscious Pentecostal movement that aims to mend what it sees as a broken world. In a simple way, Pastor Adefarasin's gesture illustrates the thesis of this chapter—that a growing movement of Nigerian Pentecostal leaders has developed a worldview equally concerned with assisting a hurting world as with achieving a home in heaven. My findings are based on personal observations, interviews with these leaders, and their written statements and documents. I will further suggest that this movement is shaped by two key forces. First, this new social awareness is encouraged by internal religious factors such as an emerging kingdom theology, subjective spiritual experiences, and a disappointment with the results of contemporary Pentecostalism. It is also influenced by external, nonreligious issues related to education, upward mobility, and the transfer of ideas facilitated by globalism.

Early Focus of Pentecostalism in Nigeria

One of the paradoxes of the Pentecostal and Charismatic movements in Nigeria is that though they have been quite conservative in many ways, they have also shown a willingness to change. The theology and worship style of the Roman Catholic Church and the Anglican Church in Nigeria 100 years ago were not substantially different from what they are now. A person from a century ago would feel quite at home in one of these churches today. However, Pentecostalism is a much more dynamic movement. It has adapted to its various host communities and evolved under the influence of powerful leaders and its social context.

The movement that might be loosely called Pentecostalism came to Nigeria in three major waves. First, an indigenous movement in Nigeria and West Africa exhibited Pentecostal characteristics such as an emphasis on dreams, visions and prophecy, a special focus on the supernatural, a literal interpretation of the Bible (including a heavy dependence upon the Hebrew Bible) and little or no association with the missionary-planted churches. This movement developed within an African society that was closer to the worldview of biblical times than the culture of the Western missionaries. Thus, its adherents accepted the reality of the spirit world and God's supernatural intervention in life. It was led by people like William Wade Harris of Liberia, Garrick Braide from southeastern Nigeria, and Joseph Babalola from southwestern Nigeria.[2]

The first two international Pentecostal groups to enter Nigeria were invited by people who had already experienced indigenous Pentecostal-type phenomena. One of these groups was Faith Tabernacle from Philadelphia, which later affiliated with the Apostolic Church from the United Kingdom and formed the Apostolic Church Nigeria.[3] The Assemblies of God came to Nigeria when invited by five young men who had been expelled from the True Faith Tabernacle for speaking in tongues.[4] The Foursquare Gospel Church entered Nigeria in the 1950s.[5] These churches represent mainstream or classical Pentecostalism in Nigeria today.

In the early 1970s, a strong revival movement emerged on Nigerian university campuses through ministries led by the Student Christian Movement, Christian Union, Evangelical Christian Union, Scripture Union, and others.[6] This movement exhibited many of the traditional characteristics of Pentecostalism including speaking in tongues, an emphasis on the supernatural, and a commitment to evangelism, missions, and church-planting.

The first two waves of Pentecostalism in Nigeria were largely grassroots, working-class movements that built their worship style on a literal interpretation of the Bible. At times, biblical words and phrases were used like traditional African proverbs to teach and inspire. It was more important for pastors to be able to speak with power than to be good expositors of the Bible. The university movement, however, produced leaders with better educations. They continued to reflect the same emphases, although with more energy, enthusiasm, and greater articulation.

Up to the 1980s, all three waves of Pentecostalism in Nigeria were characterized by three major emphases:

Personal Salvation

Like all evangelicals, the most important thing to the traditional Pentecostal was personal conversion or being "born again," which prepared a person to go to heaven at the end of life.[7] Hence, evangelism was an essential responsibility for all Christians. Of course this emphasis is not unique to Pentecostals. Most churches in Nigeria in the early and mid-twentieth century were equally committed to evangelism.

Pentecostalism was often introduced to Nigerians through massive outdoor crusades. In September 1988, I attended an event in Port Harcourt in which a soccer field was packed with people who stood four hours in the rain to hear the preaching and receive healing from Reinhard Bonnke, the popular German Pentecostal evangelist. The 2006 Bonnke crusade in Lagos attracted at least two million people.[8] Such crusades illustrate that Pentecostalism has traditionally been almost synonymous with evangelism.

Intense Worship

One of the most distinctive characteristics of Pentecostals in Nigeria is an intense and emotional style of worship. This includes enthusiastic and repetitive singing, physical expressions like raising of hands and dancing, loud, energetic preaching (with a lot of audience response), prophecy (speaking as if God were communicating through the voice of the prophesier), and speaking or praying in tongues.[9] Choral praying, wherein the entire congregation prays aloud at the same time, is also a common practice in Pentecostal churches.

Supernatural Experiences

One of the appealing aspects of Pentecostalism, especially to Nigerians, is its claim to cultivate the same type of supernatural experiences described in the New Testament. Those who are sick, for example, are prayed for with the expectation they will be supernaturally healed. Pentecostals have also claimed to replicate Jesus's practice of casting out demons, and deliverance services are common within Nigerian Pentecostalism.

The most recent Pentecostal movement broke out of the traditional grassroots mold to include the middle and upper classes. Organizations like the Full Gospel Businessmen's Fellowship International made remarkable gains among businessmen, educators, medical and legal professionals, and civil servants, including politicians. Notably, in this group, better educated than earlier adherents, there was little if any reduction in the emphasis on the supernatural. This new movement did not stop emphasizing what earlier Pentecostals had stressed; however, over the years they slowly shifted those emphases and added new ones.

Earlier Changes within Pentecostalism

Religious movements seldom remain static, and Nigerian Pentecostalism is no exception. The new focus on charismatic gifts that surfaced in the 1970s further reshaped Pentecostalism in Nigeria.

Greater Emphasis on Healing

Although Pentecostals have traditionally emphasized healing, the new charismatic movement used healing as one of the attractions to bring people to the faith. The large crusades that started in the 1970s attracted people primarily because of the message of healing. The healing service began to overshadow the invitation to salvation. In public crusades, the invitation to salvation would last perhaps five or ten minutes, but the invitation to healing and deliverance would last an hour.

Emphasis on Prosperity

Neo-Pentecostals developed an optimistic worldview stressing not only God's will for believers to be healed in their bodies, but also that they should experience financial prosperity. This positive message of hope in an atmosphere of poverty stimulated even more rapid church growth. Advertisements for crusades began to stress the possibility of "financial breakthroughs" and "fulfilling your destiny," and the faithful were encouraged to demand the "blessings" that were their divine right.

New Emphasis within Pentecostalism

The Pentecostal and Charismatic movements in Nigeria have continued to change in the 21st century. Most modern Pentecostal leaders have retained previous emphases on evangelism and healing, but some have added a new approach to health and prosperity that has been emerging since about the beginning of the new century.[10] This emphasis is consistent with what Miller and Yamamori call "Progressive Pentecostalism."[11] This kind of ministry includes a much more deliberate and focused engagement in society. Paul Adefarasin, the founder and pastor of the House on the Rock in Lagos, has established branches in the United Kingdom and the United States. At the biannual Pentecostal Fellowship of Nigeria Conference in February 2011, he remarked, "I did not get born again to go to heaven. That is a by-product. I got born again to bring heaven to earth."[12] Early Pentecostalism focused more on bringing outsiders into the church. The emerging brand of Pentecostalism in Nigeria is more focused on implementing the claims of Christianity outside of the church.

To illustrate this ongoing change, I examined three specific spheres of society where Nigerian Pentecostals have been active: poverty alleviation, economic empowerment, and national transformation. I selected and interviewed 15 leading Pentecostal pastors who model this emerging Pentecostal emphasis in their personal lives, and whose ministries are addressing these issues.

Poverty Alleviation

Wale Adefarasin, brother of Paul Adefarasin and the pastor referred to in the opening story, is also the current general secretary of the Pentecostal Fellowship of Nigeria (PFN), a large but loose coalition of Pentecostals in

Nigeria. He was reared in the home of an Anglican judge and trained in management studies. His church services include the normal range of enthusiastic singing and preaching characteristic of Pentecostal churches, and he continues to emphasize evangelism as well as supernatural signs and wonders. However, in the last few years, Pastor Adefarasin and his church have tackled some of the social and infrastructure problems that afflict the city of Lagos.[13]

A few years ago Adefarasin visited a prestigious secondary school he had attended as a teenager. Obalende, the community surrounding the school, had become one of the worst slums in Lagos. The pastor decided that if he was going to positively influence the society, this was a good place to begin. He mobilized his church and embarked on a fivefold strategy to change that community:

1. Education. Adefarasin went to the local public school in Obalende and discovered that in a school with over 2,000 students, there was just one toilet and no running water. The roof leaked, and the teachers appeared to have little motivation. Adefarasin and his church decided to renovate the school. They repaired buildings, painted walls, installed blackboards, and built a bank of toilets. They sank a borehole so that the staff and students could have potable tap water. They supplied books and other materials. To help motivate the staff and create a more professional atmosphere, they added an additional stipend to their meager government salary. All of this was provided for a government-owned school over which they had no real authority or control. The goal was simply to help the people in the community.

2. Health Care. The church also renovated the local government-owned health clinic. They send medical teams to the community every two weeks to provide free health care. When doctors refer patients for more advanced treatment, the church picks up the medical bill if the patient cannot afford it.

3. Nutrition. The church has also created a feeding team that goes into Obalende every Saturday to feed about 800 children. They also provide uncooked food to the 70 widows in the community that they have so far been identified.

4. Environment. Members of the Guiding Light Assembly discovered that one of the biggest problems in Obalende was a lack of water. Most people purchased water from commercial water sellers who pushed around carts with water in 25-liter plastic jugs. In response, the church installed boreholes in six strategic areas in the community. Any person who takes a bucket to one of the wells can get water without charge. Commercial water sellers are also allowed to get water, but they are required to pay for it. Adefarasin has handed over the supervision of the boreholes, including the collecting of revenue and maintenance of the generators that pump the water, to the local women's organization in Obalende. None of the revenue

comes back to the church. Because refuse was simply thrown out on the street, Adefarasin convinced corporate sponsors to place large bins in the community to collect the refuse and conducted training sessions to educate people about how to maintain a clean environment. Once a month, the church pays a team to work with local residents to help clean the streets and clear out the gutters to keep water flowing freely.

5. Rights and Responsibilities. The church has created a team to go into the area and use various venues to teach the people their civil rights and responsibilities. Adefarasin freely admits this is the least successful of the five-part agenda. However, they are continuing to experiment with the best ways to get the "rights and responsibilities" messages to the communities.[14]

Pastor Adefarasin is also teaching the principles of civic engagement and social responsibility to his congregation and urging them to get involved on a personal basis. In response, one of his church members has created a ministry with corporate sponsorship to build public toilets all over the city of Lagos.

When Pastor Adefarasin first articulated this idea, his church members asked how they would pay for it. He replied, "Let's go in there with our five loaves and two fishes."[15] The pastor said that within six months of starting this project, without his doing anything different in the way of fund-raising, the income in his church doubled and has continued to rise ever since.[16]

Guiding Light Assembly does not have a branch in the Obalende community. Very few if any of the people in Obalende attend the church that sponsors these activities. There appear to be few tangible benefits for the church or its members from investing so much time and energy into this community other than their sense of obedience and fulfillment in following what they perceive to be the teachings of Jesus. Obviously, the team leaders are happy to receive converts who may show interest, but they claim that the services rendered to this community are not restricted to Christian believers and are not used as evangelistic bait. They are simply cleaning up God's kingdom. Paul Adefarasin said that where there is poverty, starvation, deterioration, and no education, the one in charge of that territory looks bad. He says, "We make God look bad by not taking responsibility and not going deeper than just the salvation gospel that speaks only to salvation after life."

Economic Empowerment

Sam Adeyemi is the pastor of the Daystar Christian Assembly, a large Pentecostal church in Lagos with multiple services on Sunday. According to him, "Some people say, 'O Lord, do it.' And what they are asking God to do is what he has asked them to do."[17] This encapsulates the slowly changing understanding of the path toward financial success presented in some of the Pentecostal churches in Nigeria.

Despite the export of about two million barrels of oil per day, many in Nigeria live in squalor and destitution. The cities are filled with restless people trying desperately to break out of the cycle of poverty. Great sacrifices are made by families to send their children to universities, but when they graduate, hundreds of thousands of them remain unemployed. These conditions help to explain why the Pentecostal prosperity message has been so appealing in Nigeria during the past 30 years.

Sam Adeyemi was a young unemployed university graduate feeling the pains of Nigeria's depressed economy. One night he meditated on the biblical story in which God swore that Abraham would be blessed. "My heart burned as I asked for the same oath to be pronounced over my life." He said he received a powerful internal message that he would always have anything he needed to fulfill any assignment God gave him. "That moment, I became a new person," he said. "The limits were taken off my mind. Nothing could stop me since God's resources were now available to me. My excuses for not making progress died. I began to tell people that I can never be poor again … My self-image changed. And that literally changed my life."[18]

Developing a Teaching Ministry

Although this sounds like a typical prelude to a homily about acquiring wealth supernaturally by faith, it did not turn out that way. Adeyemi began to examine the Bible for ways to address the needs of the society. The first thing he observed was that while the masses were expecting a king who would fight against the Roman government, instead Jesus taught them principles of life. Jesus's model of presenting the power of truth simply and clearly helped to shape Adeyemi's calling. He realized that he had the gift of teaching, so he began to utilize this gift to empower Nigerians to make their world a better place. He has used several creative educational approaches.

First, he started teaching financial principles in his local church. In his study of economic development, he said he discovered that successful nations usually build their prosperity on small businesses. Business owners and their employees pay taxes that provide revenue for the government, and they also spend money, which stimulates the economy. Adeyemi developed multiple venues for his teaching ministry.

Sunday Morning Teaching. At that time Adeyemi was conducting four Sunday services in his church in Lagos. He decided to turn the first service into an entrepreneurship class. He received a lot of criticism in the early days for using a Sunday morning service to teach about business. However, he says now there are a number of churches doing the same thing because they observed that his church members soon became financially empowered and, this in turn, helped the financial buoyancy of his church.[19]

Teaching in the Media. In 1995 Adeyemi started a radio program called "Success Power" and added a TV component some years later. The program is nonreligious. He does not pray or quote scriptures even though he sometimes uses biblical illustrations and stories. He describes this program as "purely motivational." His goal is to motivate people to be successful in their lives and businesses. He believes that if people will live by the principles and standards taught in the Bible, they will prosper spiritually, financially, intellectually, and in other ways even though they may not have a personal faith in Christ.

Teaching in Daystar Leadership Academy. Students enroll in courses for three weeks at a time to learn more about being successful in life. Courses like financial management, project management, systems development, organizational growth, entrepreneurship, and building an excellence-oriented organization are taught in the school, which meets in his church with Pastor Adeyemi serving as the main lecturer.[20]

Modeling Proven Business Principles

In addition to teaching financial and business principles, Adeyemi models successful business principles. He started Pneuma Publishing Ltd., which publishes and distributes his books and other Christian literature.[21] Tuition from his teaching programs also generates money for the church and makes it less dependent upon traditional giving-type revenue.

Emphasizing a New Philosophy of Prosperity

Pastor Adeyemi is also an example of the slowly changing prosperity gospel among Pentecostal leaders in Nigeria. The early message about prosperity was largely based upon divine right and acquired by faith in God. Paul Adefarasin explained, "In the old days, prosperity was postulated as a miracle of giving and receiving, and it didn't require much responsibility from the individuals. It was a 'bless me' cup." Tony Rapu observed that the earlier prosperity preaching in Nigeria was "a message of prosperity without the balance of hard work, integrity, and productivity," and so was in his words "a little skewed."

However, the new generation of Pentecostal leaders, though respecting their spiritual mentors who first began to preach prosperity, promotes a broader version of prosperity. Paul Adefarasin refers to prosperity as stewardship. His brother, Wale, said it is "a means to achieving success at whatever you are supposed to do." Adeyemi described prosperity as "wholesomeness—living a life that is whole and fulfilling." The emphasis of this evolving prosperity theology includes spiritual, financial, intellectual, and relational wholeness.[22]

National Transformation

William Okoye was a young trader in Eastern Nigeria when he was "born again" in December 1971.[23] Although he never finished secondary school, he started preaching and even founded several churches. He entered the full-time ministry on March 4, 1974. He eventually started a Pentecostal church named All Christians Fellowship Mission, which now has over 150 congregations throughout Nigeria.

In 1976, Okoye had an experience that eventually launched him into a ministry of national transformation. On the 21st day of the 30-day fasting and prayer program, in preparation for an evangelistic crusade, Okoye had a dream. In the dream, he testified that God revealed to him what he was going to do in Nigeria and the role Okoye would play in national transformation. Okoye explained that this dream was so clear and convincing, that he moved his headquarters to Abuja, the capital of Nigeria, in anticipation of this ministry of national transformation.

Chaplain to the President

One day in 1999, over two decades after he had had the dream and shortly after Nigeria returned to democracy with the election of Olusegun Obasanjo as president, he heard a knock on his door. Standing in front of his house was the new chaplain of the Aso Rock Villa Chapel, a Baptist minister, whom Okoye had never met.[24] In a very brief meeting, the chaplain invited Okoye to join him in ministering to the president of Nigeria. For the next six years, Rev. Okoye served as the deputy chaplain of Aso Rock, which meant that he met with the president and his family every morning from 6:30 to 7:30 for a prayer meeting. He advised the president and other senior government officials on moral, ethical, and spiritual issues and also ministered in the Aso Rock chapel where President Obasanjo and many top government officials worshipped. In 2006, Rev. Okoye became the senior chaplain and served in that capacity for the next two years.

Okoye did not shy away from offering his opinion on policies, especially those related to justice for the poor. He said that he quickly learned that "while you are having a simple discussion with the president, drinking tea or whatever, those little things you say there can become policies and affect the lives of millions of people." His official duties and informal contacts with government officials made him more committed to issues of governance and politics when he saw the positive impact one could have in ministering to the political class.

African Forum on Religion and Government

In addition to serving senior government officials, Rev. Okoye has helped to get the church in Nigeria engaged in governance in other ways. For example, in 2006, he suggested a plan to the president that eventually developed into a continent-wide conference called the African Forum on Religion and Governance (AFREG). The purpose of the conference was "to build a movement of African leaders of integrity who are committed to transforming Africa into a First World continent shaped by God-centered values."[25]

About 200 leaders from 27 African countries attended the Abuja conference in 2006, including church and denominational leaders and senior Christian government officials. Okoye personally raised the money for the conference from non-government sources to make sure that the delegates could attend at little or no expense. Included among the participants were two heads of state, several ministers and ambassadors, along with dozens of bishops, archbishops, general overseers, academics, and heads of para-church organizations. The second AFREG conference was held in Kenya in 2009 with over 300 attendees from 33 African countries. The AFREG members have gotten directly involved in the political process by interviewing political candidates in Nigeria at both the national and state level. In these interviews, political candidates, including Muslims, were asked to declare their beliefs and plans about issues that were important to Christians. Though envisioned and led by Pentecostals, AFREG is by no means exclusively a Pentecostal movement; it has appealed to Christian leaders from a broad spectrum.

Government Projects

Rev. Okoye has also used his position and his influence to get government involved in projects that would not normally be considered religious. For example, for many years there had been a major erosion problem in his home state. Because he believed that the earth belonged to God and should be properly cared for, he decided to address the issue. He was able to get the president to visit the area and commit 400 million Naira (about $2.5 million) to address the problem that had plagued the area for decades.

In 2010, Rev. Okoye became concerned about kidnapping and other social problems created by unemployed youth in the southeastern part of Nigeria. He approached the governor of Anambra State with a plan to train 5,000 youth in a three-step process. The governor not only approved the plan but also invested

50 million Naira (about $320,000) in the first phase. First, Rev. Okoye brought young men together for a 21-day camp where he and others taught principles of honesty, justice, hard work, respect, and success found in the Bible and the book *The Purpose Driven Life* by Rick Warren. The second phase of the program involved placing these young men in apprenticeship programs of their choice. The Anambra State government invested another 50 million Naira in this apprenticeship program. The third phase makes low-interest loans available to trainees after they have completed their apprenticeship and are ready to start their own businesses.

William Okoye is not the only Pentecostal who is focused on national transformation. Wale Adefarasin, referred to earlier, has a similar conviction but has used different strategies. He believes Christians must inject positive Christian values into governance and society; consequently, he created the Centre for Values and Social Development. One of his projects was a public lecture in Lagos in May 2010 entitled "The Values that Brought Obama to the White House." The lecture was presented by former U.S. ambassador to Nigeria, Walter Carrington. Joining him to talk about traditional values in Africa was Dr. Christopher Koloade, former Nigerian ambassador to the United Kingdom. Many of the political and business elites of Lagos attended the function, including the popular Muslim governor of Lagos State, Babatunde Fashola. This was not an overtly Christian gathering, but it did highlight the moral and religious values that Adefarasin believes are necessary for national transformation.

Sunday Adelaja, from southwest Nigeria, demonstrates that the impact of Pentecostalism on government and the society is not restricted to Nigeria. Adelaja studied journalism in the Soviet Union before settling in Kiev, Ukraine, and founding the Embassy of God, which has been described as the largest church in Europe. His story of exporting Nigerian Pentecostalism by building his church and helping to establish thousands of NGOs to impact society is told in his book *Churchshift*.[26] One of Adelaja's key objectives is national transformation. He helped to create a political party and counts the mayor and 30 percent of the parliament of Kiev as members of his church. He was crucially involved in Ukraine's "Orange Revolution," which helped to bring down a government and install a new one.[27]

The kinds of social ministries that Okoye, Adefarasin, and Adelaja have initiated are not necessarily new ideas in nation-building, but they do illustrate that Nigerian Pentecostal leaders are developing successful programs for national transformation that go far beyond the evangelism and prayers for miracles of their predecessors. Pentecostals are taking advantage of the non-secular atmosphere in Nigeria to create partnerships between the church and government that were unheard of in the past.[28]

Motivations for the New Focus

The stories of social engagement in this chapter have demonstrated a changing worldview among some Pentecostals in Nigeria, particularly related to the Christian's responsibility to society. What accounts for this greater social awareness? What motivates these agents of change? I will address these questions by looking at both internal and external factors.

Internal Factors

The Pentecostal and Charismatic movements have strong opinions about God, sacred writings, faith, prayer, rituals and other spiritual beliefs and practices. Therefore one must begin to look for answers within the faith community itself.

Pentecostalism. To what extent have the distinctive doctrines and experiences of the Pentecostal leaders shaped this phenomenon? The only leaders who said that their Pentecostal faith seriously affected their social engagement were Sunday Adelaja and his associate Vincent Anigbogu.[29] The others tend to play down the impact of Pentecostalism on their social awareness. Tony Rapu sums it up best: "I could jolly well be a Roman Catholic and do the same things." William Okoye says he has even been accused of not being a Pentecostal because he has not "seen the difference between the evangelicals and the Pentecostals" on these issues. Adeyemi admits he did not acquire social consciousness growing up as a Pentecostal, but says Pentecostalism did predispose him to use the power of God to solve the social problems. He thinks this kind of social consciousness is still weak in most Pentecostal churches but is growing "at a very fast rate."

Biblical Values. Though socially engaged Christianity may not be linked directly to Pentecostalism, there is certainly a linkage between these beliefs and the Bible. Pentecostals historically have taken a more literal approach to interpreting and applying the Bible. As a result, certain biblical passages and events have shaped this new social awareness.

Wale Adefarasin uses the words of Jesus as the foundation of his work: "The Spirit of the Lord is on me, because he has anointed me to preach good news to the poor. He has sent me to proclaim freedom for the prisoners and recovery of sight for the blind, to release the oppressed" (Luke 4:18). He said that the modern application of this kind of freedom is giving people deliverance from water-born diseases by providing good water and helping to rescue the continent from AIDS. He refers back to his Pentecostal roots in saying "I believe we have the Spirit of God so that we can change the world."

Sam Adeyemi has worked out a philosophy of social engagement that he believes is very biblical. "When it comes to the formation of society and the structures of society," he says, "I believe the values of the Christian should still impact those aspects of life." He explained that people form governments because they need to leverage their collective resources. Christian values need to guide that process, including "the value of human life, the value of truth, the value of work, the value of generosity, and the value of humility." He said, "Without those values we are unable to work together as a team to achieve God's purposes."

Pentecostals have historically used the Hebrew Bible to find allegorical models for what they are doing. Adeyemi sees in Israel's journey from Egypt to Canaan a "template for nation-building." He describes it this way: "You have people who had been slaves and now they were free. What were they supposed to do? They were creating a new nation and with that God gives Moses revelations and instruction how to set up the military system, the justice system, and a health care system that advises on hygiene, including what to eat and not to eat. And they appoint judges. And then there is management coming in. So you see God introducing different things like that." He summarizes his theology by saying, "I believe that it is the church, building on the righteousness that God has given us, that can bring peace and order to society." He does not advocate that the church attempt some kind of spiritual coup, but he believes it is the church's business to propose the values of God's kingdom as the underpinning of the society.

Kingdom Theology. One word I heard repeatedly from the Pentecostal leaders I interviewed was "kingdom." The following are some key examples:

- "We want to see those values of God's kingdom thoroughly interposed upon the policies that regulate our economy" (Paul Adefarasin).
- "The dimensions of society and government and politics and education ought to be influenced by the message of the kingdom" (Tony Rapu).
- "This issue of influencing the society with the values of the kingdom of God is part and parcel of the Great Commission" (Sam Adeyemi).
- "We need to get Christians who are mature to work in medical work and in the media and bring a kingdom culture to the media, into education and government" (Wale Adefarasin).
- "So seeking the king, as far as I am concerned, means to seek to be like Christ. That is the kingdom of God for me. Seeking to be like the king in character, in nature, in behavior, in values. Seeking to inculcate the nature of Christ himself into myself. Seeking to be his image. Seeking to carry his personality" (Sunday Adelaja).

This emphasis obviously reflects a proliferation of kingdom theology among the socially engaged Pentecostals. This view looks at the world from a broader perspective than just the church. It believes that Jesus desires to rule in all parts of society, including government, education, media, entertainment, the health sector, and the environment. Therefore, it expands Jesus's commission to go into the world and make disciples of all nations to include not just evangelism, which restores one to a relationship with God, but the restoration all the systems of this world back to the sovereign control of God and the rules and principles within which God designed them to function. Adeyemi asked, "Is the Great Commission only about getting them to accept Jesus as the Lord and Savior?" He answered, "It seems to me that it is more than that. I think that accepting Christ as Lord and Savior is the process of becoming part of God's kingdom. But when you become a part of that kingdom, you should function within that kingdom."

Subjective Call. At least two leaders indicated that their move in the direction of greater social engagement was related to a subjective experience. William Okoye had a dream that he would be involved in national transformation. Sam Adeyemi also had a spiritual encounter in which he felt God promised him he would be used to provide Christians with more financial resources. Such subjective experiences are very common to Pentecostals in Nigeria.

Failed Expectations. A final internal issue that has prompted some Pentecostal churches to move in a new direction is the failure of many Pentecostal aspirations to materialize as expected. Vincent Anigbogu, director of the Institute for National Transformation, believes that Pentecostalism lost sight of socially engaged values like education and community betterment and got stuck in its own special interests.[30] Members are "burnt out" and "disgruntled" hearing the miracles message because they have waited long and have not yet experienced them.[31]

Bishop Abraham Olaleye, the speaker on the national TV program "Revival in the Land," is even more adamant that the Pentecostal movement of the last 30 years in Nigeria has stalled. He believes the typical prosperity message has only brought greed and corruption and made Nigeria the "laughingstock of the world." Many of those who were originally attracted from the traditional churches are returning to their old denominations because of the emptiness of much of modern Pentecostalism. He believes that the new emphases outlined in this chapter embody a post-Pentecostal movement that God has raised up to move the body of Christ to a higher level.[32]

External Factors

Pentecostal leaders are not only affected by religious convictions and experiences but also by other parts of society, which help to shape their worldview. These external factors have pushed them toward greater social engagement.

Traditional Family Values. Wale Adefarasin said that his parents insisted that an education is the best legacy parents can give their children. His parents also stressed such simple values as "honesty is the best policy" and "cleanliness is next to godliness." Later when he saw firsthand the lack of education and the deplorable hygienic conditions in Lagos, the values his parents had instilled in him motivated him to do something about those problems. When leaders see that the loss of traditional values results in chaos and poverty in their communities, they are often motivated to help restore those values.

Exposure to Needs. When Tony Rapu was asked why he is engaged in social ministries, he said people are normally disappointed in his answer. They expect him to talk about the books he has read, the people who influenced him and how his theology developed. He said, "I don't have any of those answers. I am just sort of inspired to do what I do. You see something wrong and you have a desire to put it right. It is just that simple." He frequently used the term "broken world" and stressed that Christians must seek for solutions "to make life better for humanity."

Non-Theological Education. Churches like the Assemblies of God and the Foursquare Gospel Church have sponsored Pentecostal seminaries in Nigeria for many years, and most of their senior leaders have passed through those institutions. However, the men and women who are leading the new wave of Pentecostalism have largely been educated in the public universities.[33] Of the six most prominent Nigerian Pentecostal leaders referred to in this chapter, their academic backgrounds include business management, architecture, civil engineering, medicine, journalism, and trading. It is arguable that those educated in the traditional theological seminaries and other pastoral training institutions have been so shaped in the traditional way of doing things that they have difficulty seeing alternatives. However, without the hindrances of traditional theological education, these new leaders are able to see problems in the church and society through new social lenses and, therefore, be more creative in addressing social problems.

Secular Professions. Closely connected to this is the fact that many of the Pentecostal leaders moving in this new direction are also employed in professions outside the church. Most of the mid-level pastors and overseers in the Redeemed Christian Church of God are bi-vocational, working in their profession during the week and in the church on the weekend. Adeyemi said, "I think it was a huge positive thing that God pulled people in from the professional class into the church to lead churches in Nigeria. There was a little more depth that was brought into ministry and the ability to build systems."[34] Paul Adefarasin said that this phenomenon has led to a "lot of innovation in the contemporary church in the last twenty years" and "is beginning to give some organization to the body and portends some good things for the country and the church."

Upward Mobility. All of the churches described in this chapter are filled with middle-class, upwardly mobile members. Though there is no evidence that wealthy people are more generous than poor people, more affluent people often have more social capital to invest in things to which they are committed. Further research is needed on this, but it is reasonable to argue that the mixture of skills, assets, and funding sources that professionals bring to socially engaged projects will help them to be successful in those endeavors.

Expanding Globalism. The Internet and various forms of social media have created an awareness of other parts of the world and a blending of social values and practices that is unprecedented in human history. This is true in Pentecostal circles as well. The Nigerian congregations that are demonstrating the greatest interest in social engagement are also the ones that have the greatest access to the Internet, cell phones and other electronic networks. This supports the thesis that great exposure to a wider array of people and ideas, coupled with an attitude molded by religious experience, expands one's commitment to social responsibility. This increased exposure within Pentecostalism can be illustrated in several ways.

First, Pentecostalism is not the only branch of Christianity that is becoming more socially conscious. For the last three or four decades, evangelicalism, of which Pentecostalism is a substantial part, has generally been moving back toward the "social gospel," which the more fundamentalist branch of Protestantism repudiated in the early part of the 20th century. During the Lausanne Conference in Cape Town in November 2010, 73 percent of the evangelical leaders said that it was essential for a good evangelical to reach out to poor, and 84 percent said that Christians should express their views on political matters.[35] Since Pentecostalism is inseparable from evangelicalism, it is understandable that these overlapping movements would cross-fertilize each other and experience a common tendency toward greater social engagement.

Second, Nigerian Pentecostal churches are not the only Pentecostals engaged in social programs. Over a four-year period, Miller and Yamamori visited Pentecostal ministries in 20 countries and found "progressive Pentecostals" engaged in activities similar to those described in this chapter.[36] It is assumed that these fraternal Pentecostal leaders will have interacted and influenced each other. One likely source for a common link between these Pentecostal leaders is the International Coalition of Apostles (ICA), a worldwide network of senior Pentecostal leaders. This body explicitly embraces the kind of social engagement represented by progressive Pentecostals.[37] Wale Adefarasin, one the prominent Nigerian Pentecostal leaders described in this chapter, is an active member.

Third, though there are now no known Western missionaries with traditional Pentecostal agencies in Nigeria, Ware, Ware, Clarke and Buchanan illustrate that a similar social shift is developing among Western Pentecostal missionaries serving in Southeast Asia. By interviewing a dozen long-term missionaries from nine Pentecostal mission agencies from five Western countries they demonstrated that social ministries were not designed primarily as bait for evangelism. They summarized the motivations behind such social engagement as observing the practices of other Christian organizations doing compassionate ministries, seeing the needs of humanity in a different light and re-assessing the compassionate ministry of Jesus.[38]

Fourth, the influence of Sunday Adelaja, the dynamic Nigerian pastor in Ukraine, cannot be overstated. In 2004 Adelaja had a meeting in Lagos with several Pentecostal leaders that helped to provide strategies for implementing his version of kingdom theology and national transformation.[39] In addition, several of the Pentecostal leaders mentioned in this chapter have attended his History Makers Training (HMT) program in the Ukraine.[40] In recent years, it has been difficult for Nigerians to get visas to attend such seminars. However, Adelaja has worked around that obstacle by continuing to influence Nigerian leaders with his books and by extensively using the Internet. John Enelamah, senior pastor of the End Times Revival Ministries in Lagos and the executive director of the Apostles in the Market Place, clearly states that the movement of the "impact of Christianity in society" started with Adelaja's 2004 visit.[41]

Conclusion

The case studies presented above demonstrate that the new Pentecostalism in Nigeria is indeed having an impact on society beyond the four walls of the church. It has evolved from a conservative movement in the early 1970s—one that wanted little to do with society and whose objective was to draw people into their insular church world—to one that thrives on engaging society. Twenty years ago, in the Pentecostalism I observed in Nigeria, the emphasis was primarily on the spiritual and supernatural. Rev. N. C. Thompson, one of the pioneers of Pentecostalism in northern Nigeria, summarized a particular outdoor crusade in his autobiography by stating simply, "The message went on, souls were saved and the sick healed."[42] "Saving the lost" and healing the sick were the primary ministries of Pentecostals, but the current generation of Pentecostal leaders is pushing the movement in a new direction.

A More Human Face. Are the pastors I have described outliers? Wale Adefarasin is the national secretary of the Pentecostal Fellowship of Nigeria (PFN), the organization that brings Pentecostal churches in Nigeria together under one umbrella. Two of the others, Paul Adefarasin and William Okoye, were selected to speak at the PFN national biennial conference in February 2011. Though most of them are younger leaders, they have gained the respect of the national Pentecostal leadership as well as the Pentecostal communities they are leading. Thus compassion and service outside the church building are becoming the face of Pentecostalism in Nigeria.

A Longer Reach. The new Pentecostal leaders are not just reaching out to the downtrodden; they have goals to expand the impact of Christianity in their communities and in their nation. These Pentecostals are no longer satisfied just to hold evangelistic crusades to "save souls." They now organize government consultations to save the society. They are no longer satisfied just to build churches. They now want to rebuild nations. They are no longer content to sing and dance and speak in tongues. They now want to change the discourse of society.

In this chapter, I have attempted to demonstrate that while Pentecostalism came to Nigeria with signs and wonders, it is now expanding within and beyond Nigeria with service and social engagement. It came as a grassroots movement; it continues as an upwardly mobile movement. It came with a focus on evangelism, emotional worship, healing, and deliverance; it continues by claiming all human institutions as part of the kingdom of Christ.

What do the new generation Pentecostal leaders want to accomplish in Nigeria? Paul Adefarasin summarized their aims well:

> We want to empower our people. We want to give them skills of understanding and a deep sense of vision and purpose and mission. We want to tell them it is possible to do great things for God, in turning around, reforming and rebuilding and building a nation. We can rebuild our infrastructure. We can create private, public and faith-based partnerships to deliver our infrastructure and education and health care. We can access the grace and might and majesty of God and be his representative priesthood and kingship in the earth so that he is the God of the universe and we are his regency.

Notes

1. I observed this event while attending the Guiding Light Assembly on Sunday, May 1, 2011.
2. For information about William Wade Harris, see Jonathan Hildebrandt, *History of the Church in Africa* (Achimota, Ghana: Africa Christian Press, 1981), 153–154. For information about Garrick Braide, see G. O. M. Tasie, "The Church in the Niger Delta" in *The Nigerian Story*, ed. Ogbu Kalu (Ibadan: Daystar Press, 1978), 326. For information about Joseph Babalola, see Ogbu Kalu, *African Pentecostalism: An Introduction* (Oxford: Oxford University Press, 2008), 41. In this book Kalu has an excellent summary of most of the significant movements of Pentecostalism in Nigeria.
3. Matthews A. Ojo, *The End-Time Army: Charismatic Movements in Modern Nigeria* (Trenton, NJ: Africa World Press, Inc., 2006), 34.

4. Kalu, *Nigerian Story* (1978), 42.

5. Ojo, *End-Time Army* (2006), 35.

6. See Ojo, *End-Time Army* (2006), Chapter 2 for a comprehensive survey of the university student-led Pentecostal movement in Nigeria in the early 1970s which he personally observed and participated in as a university student at the time.

7. "Born again" is a phrase used by Jesus during his interactions with Nicodemus in John 3:3, 7. It has become a common phrase among evangelical Christians to refer to the transforming experience that happens when a person repents and makes a personal commitment to Christ. The theological equivalent for "born again" is regeneration.

8. See footage of the masses who attended the Lagos Bonnke Crusade at Dave Dempsey's My Space, video entitled "Reinhard Bonnke- Millenium Crusade, Lagos, Nigeria" released January 16, 2008. http://www.myspace.com/video/vid/26207250.

9. Invitations similar to those used for evangelism were given and special prayer sessions were held to encourage people to receive the baptism of the Holy Spirit with the primary evidence being speaking in tongues. According to Pentecostals, the ability to speak in tongues ensures a richer worship experience.

10. Dr. Gary Maxey, an American missionary, is the founder of West Africa Theological Seminary (WATS) in Lagos and has been involved in theological education in Nigeria for 30 years. Maxey believes that there has been "a notable decrease in evangelism" within Pentecostal circles during the last 30 years. He believes the upward social mobility within the Pentecostal churches is partially responsible for this. "As you get increasing numbers of more advanced sophisticated people, I think there has tended to be a lessening focus on personal evangelism and also, related to this, more focus on reaching out to the social needs around them." Gary Maxey, interview by Danny McCain, May 2, 2011.

11. Donald E. Miller and Tetsunao Yamamori, *Global Pentecostalism: The New Face of Christian Social Engagement* (Berkeley: University of California Press, 2007), 2. Tony Rapu, the highly respected Pentecostal pastor of This Present House in Lagos, said, "I am a Pentecostal in the sense of the Holy Spirit and the expressions of Pentecostalism but often times I consider myself post-Pentecostal." Tony Rapu interview conducted by Danny McCain on June 9, 2011. All subsequent quotations or references to Tony Rapu come from this interview, unless otherwise noted. For more information about Tony Rapu and This Present House, see This Present House website (copyright 2013) http://thispresenthouse.org/.

12. Paul Adefarasin, interview by Danny McCain, May 1, 2011. All subsequent quotations or references to Paul Adefarasin come from this interview, unless otherwise noted. For more information about Paul Adefarasin and his church, the House on the Rock, see the House on the Rock website (copyright 2010) http://houseontherockng.com/. Adefarasin is also ambivalent about the label of Pentecostal. He said, "I struggle to define myself as a Pentecostal. I embrace Pentecostalism. I am leader in the Pentecostal Fellowship of Nigeria but I cannot be limited to Pentecostalism."

13. Wale Adefarasin, interview by Danny McCain, May 2, 2011. All subsequent quotations or references to Wale Adefarasin come from this interview, unless otherwise noted. For more information about Pastor Wale Adefarasin and the Guiding Light Assembly, see Guiding Light Assembly website (copyright 2012) http://guidinglight.org.ng/index.html.

14. Paul Adefarasin says that there is still room for preaching civil rights because of the abuse of civil rights in Nigeria, but it is becoming imperative for a relevant church to preach "civil responsibilities."

15. This is a reference to the story of Jesus using five loaves of bread and two fish to feed 5,000 people. This is the only story about Jesus found in all four gospels. See Matthew 14:15–21; Mark 6:35–44; Luke 9:12–17; John 6:5–13.

16. The Guiding Light Assembly is not the only church in Lagos cooperating with communities and government institutions to combat poverty. Pastor Sam Adeyemi of the Daystar Christian Assembly has also adopted and renovated public schools. His church has spent 250 million Naira (about $1.6 million) rebuilding five government-owned schools that were destroyed by an accidental explosion at a military weapons depot.

17. Sam Adeyemi, interview by Danny McCain, June 9, 2011. All subsequent quotations or references to Sam Adeyemi come from this interview, unless otherwise noted. For more information about Sam Adeyemi and his church the Daystar Christian Assembly, see the Daystar Christian Centre website (accessed February 8, 2013) http://daystarng.org/.
18. Sam Adeyemi, *We Are the Government*. (Lagos: Pneuma Publishing, Ltd., 2010), 8.
19. The House on the Rock has followed Adeyemi's example. Paul Adefarasin is currently building a multimillion dollar National Reformation Training Centre. This building will serve as a 10,000 seat auditorium for his House on the Rock headquarters and have 24 classrooms that will house four schools, including the International Institute of Business and Government. Adefarasin's goal is to teach people to be "God's priests in the market place."
20. The website of the Daystar Leadership Academy describes 25 courses related to business, leadership, and family taught in the academy. See Daystar Christian Academy website (copyright 2008) http://www.dlaonline.org/courses/acc.asp.
21. Bishop David Oyedepo's Living Faith Church has also created a publishing company. His personal books are widely published by its Dominion Publishing House, and members are encouraged to buy and read them.
22. Not every Pentecostal leader supports this new emphasis on prosperity. Many TV preachers continue to preach the "divine right" prosperity. And, on the other side, some believe that teaching people how to make money is not the church's business. Apostle Geoffrey Numbere is founder and international director of the Greater Evangelism World Crusade. While giving the keynote address to the 400th Anniversary Celebration of the King James Version of the Bible in Port Harcourt, he said, "In Greater Evangelism World Crusade, we do not teach people how to make money; we teach people how to make heaven. Our Number One emphasis is heaven. Our Number Two emphasis is heaven. Our Number Three emphasis is heaven." For a comprehensive overview of his evangelistic ministry, see Nonyem E. Numbere, *A Man and a Vision: A Biography of Apostle Geoffrey D. Numbere* (Diobu, Nigeria: Greater Evangelism Publications, 2008).
23. William Okoye, interview by Danny McCain, May 4, 2011. All subsequent quotations or references to William Okoye come from this interview, unless otherwise noted.
24. The Aso Rock Villa Chapel is located inside the presidential compound in Abuja. It holds Sunday services, weekly Bible studies, and functions much like a local church except it ministers primarily to senior government officials.
25. See African Forum on Religion and Government website (copyright 2012) http://www.afreg.org/African_Forum_on_Religion_%26_Government/Purpose.html. See AFREG I Declaration at http://transformingleadership.com/files/PDF%20Files/AFREG%20I%20Abuja%20Final%20Final%20Declaration.pdf.
26. Sunday Adelaja, *Churchshift* (Lake Mary, FL: Charisma House, 2008).
27. See Sunday Adelaja, *Spearheading a National Transformation* (Kiev: Fares Publishing House, 2008). Most of the Pentecostals leaders described in this chapter say that Sunday Adelaja has had a major influence on their thinking and strategies. For more information on Sunday Adelaja and the Embassy of God, see The Embassy of the Blessed Kingdom of God for All Nations website (accessed February 8, 2013) .
28. Wale Babatunde is another Nigerian living abroad who has attempted to influence government. He is the senior minister of the World Harvest Christian Centre, London. He has written two books in his attempt to persuade the church in England to work toward national transformation, including *Great Britain has Fallen* (Chichester, UK: New Wine Press, 2002) and *Awake! Great Britain* (Chichester, UK: Xpression Books, 2005). For more information on Wale Babatunde and his church, see World Harvest Christian Centre website (copyright 2013) http://www.worldharvest.org.uk/.
29. Adelaja said, "Without the Pentecostal faith and the Pentecostal gifts I do not think I would have a ministry but thanks to the Pentecostal expression, I was able to able to believe … that I could do something through ministry. It is the Pentecostal experience that cemented that in me. I have seen God in action. I believe that God could do miracles." Sunday Adelaja, interview by Danny McCain, November 7 and 9, 2011.

30. The Institute for National Transformation is a training organization in Nigeria affiliated with Sunday Adelaja.

31. Vincent Anigbogu, interview by Danny McCain, June 30, 2011.

32. Abraham Olaleye, interview by Danny McCain, September 24, 2011. He uses this analogy to describe the contemporary Nigerian Pentecostal movement: "We (Pentecostals) are just living on borrowed time. Assuming a ceiling fan is here and the electricity goes off. The ceiling fan does not stop on the spot. There is still motion until it comes to a final end. Perhaps we are still having some motion but I believe that God is done with this movement … He is bringing a new movement." For more information about Bishop Abraham Olaleye and his ministry, see Abraham's Evangelistic Ministry website (copyright 2011) http://aem-revival.com/tv.php.

33. In their book *Out of Africa* (Ventura, CA: Regal Books, 2003), Peter Wagner and Joseph Thompson describe 11 successful Nigerian Pentecostal "apostles." The training of those leaders includes: graphic design; journalism, advertising, education, marketing, management, architecture, and medicine. Only one had a graduate degree in theological studies.

34. Adeyemi also recognizes that there are some "potential disadvantages" to leaders who have limited theological education and admits that a seminary lecturer whom he engaged to help teach him theology had pointed out quite a few of his "goofs." Gary Maxey has a much less enthusiastic attitude toward Pentecostal leaders without formal theological education. He said, "There is a high degree of uncertainty about the theological and hermeneutical orthodoxy of leaders who come almost straight out of the secular professions into church leadership, without the benefit of any traditional ecclesiastical training." He also said that he has heard some sermons from such leaders that are "truly scary" in the way they use the Bible.

35. *Global Survey of Evangelical Protestant Leaders* conducted by the Pew Forum on Religion and Public Life, 2011, 20, 31. See Pew Forum on Religion and Public Life website (copyright 2010) http://www.pewforum.org. One-third of the evangelical leaders from the Global South identified themselves as Pentecostals. 22.

36. Miller and Yamamori, *Global Pentecostalism* 6.

37. See International Coalition of Apostles (ICA) website (accessed on February 8, 2013) http://www.coalitionofapostles.com/. In part, the doctrinal statement of the International Coalition of Apostles on the Great Commission says, "We believe in the practical application of the Christian faith in everyday life and the need to minister to people everywhere and in every area of their lives, which includes not only the spiritual, but also the social, commercial, political and physical." The statement entitled "Governments in the Work Place" reflects the kingdom theology emphasized by the new generation Pentecostal churches.

38. See Vicki-Ann Ware, Anthony Ware, Matthew Clarke and Grant Buchanan "Why Western-based, Pentecostal Mission Organisations Undertake Community Development in South East Asia," "*Handbook of Research on Religion and Development*, ed. Matthew Clarke, (Cheltenham, UK: Edward Elgar Publishing 2013.

39. Wale Adefarasin, interview by Danny McCain, December 3, 2011.

40. Pentecostal leaders mentioned in this chapter who have attended the HMT training in Ukraine include Wale Adefarasin, Tony Rapu, Sam Adeyemi, Vincent Anigbogu, John Enelamah, and Abraham Olalaye.

41. John Enelamah, interviewed by Danny McCain, September 24, 2011. Wale Adefarasin and Abraham Olalaye both said that Adelaja pushed them in the direction of social engagement.

42. N. C. Thompson, *Journey into Destiny* (Jos: TONAJO Publishing House, 2009), 127.

SECTION FIVE

TRANSNATIONAL PENTECOSTALISM

With the global growth and spread of Pentecostalism as the focus of this volume, one might conclude that Pentecostalism has gone from the West to the rest of the world. However, that particular directional flow is only part of the story. A development that has received significant scholarly attention recently is the so-called "reverse missionary" movement, in which missionaries from the Global South are sending missionaries to Europe and the United States.

Afe Adogame enters this discussion via his investigation of African Pentecostalism and challenges the assumption by some scholars that Pentecostalism, as a new form of African Christianity, was packaged in the United States and delivered fully formed to Africa. Adogame argues instead that such assumptions fail to take into account the diversity and complexity of African Christianity and gloss over indigenous religious creativity and innovation. Adogame describes how internal religious characteristics and self-financing dynamics and strategies act as significant stimuli for Pentecostal growth and demographic spread in Africa and around the world—including in the United States.

If images of a (reverse) unidirectional transnational flow of Pentecostalism come to mind from Afe Adogame's descriptions of Nigerian Pentecostal churches in Houston and Dallas, Texas, Juan Martínez provides a somewhat different model of transnational Pentecostalism. The mission activities described by Adogame, and earlier by Anderson and Robeck, generally assume a primarily religious motivation to bring Pentecostal Christianity to a particular region. Martínez however describes Latino Pentecostals who are already moving to and from the United States and/or within their own countries looking for better economic opportunities, but who bring their religion along with them. Thus as they are migrating for economic reasons, they bring their churches with them, start new churches, or join churches they know of through their family, kin, and friendship networks. Then, utilizing these networks, they establish mission activities that provide them a presence in both their new and old home communities. These are "poor to poor" mission efforts that are not dependent on large mission organizations or denominational support, but instead are pursued through the remittance networks that already exist and that reflect their presence as transnational actors. For these Latino Pentecostals, the borders of the modern nation-state are a mere nuisance to their economic and missionary efforts, and do not prevent them from pursuing better economic opportunities or mission activities.

These chapters suggest a rethinking of how Pentecostals are approaching their mission activities in a "globalized" world. While certainly many groups pursue global mission activities primarily from a religious motivation—as with the original Azusa Street missionaries—others simply bring their churches along or set up new efforts that happen to be located in the United States, or elsewhere in their own countries, because they are migrants seeking out better economic opportunities. As more countries become included in the global capitalist system and workers seek opportunities abroad, Pentecostalism is sure to follow, but what forms will it take?

9

Reconfiguring the Global Religious Economy

The Role of African Pentecostalism

AFE ADOGAME

Introduction

Since 1998, the annual Holy Ghost Congress assembled by the Redeemed Christian Church of God in Nigeria has drawn a sharply increasing number of participants. The six-day event currently attracts four to five million worshippers, rivaling the Hajj in Mecca as the world's largest yearly religious gathering. The combination of Pentecostal modes of worship and sermons inflected with themes of "health and wealth" may initially suggest that this phenomenon is an example of a transplanted religious movement that has dramatically flourished in African soil. But a closer examination of the RCCG and its culture will show that it is, at root, an indigenous form of spiritual expression.

In this rapidly globalizing era, significant religious transformations and developments are re-sketching the traditional religious maps. One significant development reshaping global Christianity is the growth of Pentecostal and Charismatic movements. Recent demographic statistics such as those from the Pew Forum survey on Pentecostalism,[1] Jenkin's *Next Christendom*,[2] and *The World Christian Encyclopedia* (by Barrett, Kurian, and Johnson)[3] are indicators of the shift of Christianity's center of gravity from the North to the South. Pentecostal and Charismatic Christianity has become one of the most rapidly proliferating segments of world Christianity; descriptors like "Pentecostal power"[4] and "a religion made to travel"[5] illustrate this trend as well as the dynamic nature of the phenomenon.

The criteria for categorizing these movements as Pentecostal or Charismatic can be confusing. The Pew Forum's appropriation of the concept "renewalist" as an umbrella term that refers to both Pentecostals and Charismatics as a group is suggestive of this complexity. However, as the Pew survey indicates, "By all accounts, Pentecostalism and related charismatic movements represent one of the fastest-growing segments of global Christianity. At least a quarter of the world's 2 billion Christians are thought to be members of these lively, highly personal faiths, which emphasize such spiritually renewing 'gifts of the Holy Spirit' as speaking in tongues, divine healing and prophesying."[6] The survey provides analyses of the religious demography of 10 countries—including Nigeria, Kenya, and South Africa—and demonstrates how Africa, Asia and Latin America are becoming significant global players in the development of world Christianity.

Further critical scholarly probing of Pentecostalism should focus on the provenance and character of these new forms of religiosity; their growth dynamics and social impact; whether, how, and to what extent the emerging renewalist phenomenon in the Southern Hemisphere is homegrown or linked to external influences. The basic contention of this chapter is that the strand of argument that privileges "ecclesiastical externality" and "'extraversion" in explaining the public role and demographic profile of African Christianities is lacking in depth and scope. Specifically, the assumptions that underlie such arguments fail to take into account the diversity and complexity of African Christianities, thus glossing over indigenous religious creativity and innovation. Drawing from recent religious ethnography, this chapter therefore explores how internal religious characteristics, dynamics, and strategies act as stimuli for Pentecostal growth in Africa and in the African diaspora, which in turn shapes the global religious economy.

Revisiting the Narrative of Ecclesiastical Externality and Extraversion

A controversial debate to which this chapter critically responds is summarized here as the narrative of "ecclesiastical externality" and "extraversion." The most prominent proponents of this argument, at least in reference to Africa, are Brouwer, Gifford and Rose, and Paul Gifford.[7] The main thrust of their argument is that Pentecostal Christianity's evolution in Africa is not a genuinely African phenomenon arising out of African experience and meeting African needs. First, such studies speculate that African churches generally have been reduced to a state of penury as a result of the collapse of African economies; and second, that the continent has become increasingly receptive to a form of Christianity that is new, fundamentalist, and American. The appeal of this imported form of Christianity—and the marker of its American-ness—has to do with the abundance of resources, personnel, and technology that it brings and which make a powerful impact on the African religious landscape. In this paradigm, American congregations and missionaries are systematically proselytizing the African continent and sparking an African religious revival.

According to Gifford, "For all the talk within African church circles of localization, inculturation, Africanization or indigenization, external links have become more important than ever. Through these links the churches have become a major, if not the greatest single, source of development assistance, money, employment and opportunity in Africa."[8] Gifford also asserts that "Africa's current evangelical revival is directed from the U.S., and U.S. evangelicalism is made up of two really distinct streams, Pentecostalism and fundamentalism."[9] Brouwer, Gifford and Rose corroborate this view, claiming, "A new kind of Christian fundamentalism once thought to be unique to the U.S. is spreading across the globe .... While the leaders of the new Christian faith come from various nations, the message is predominantly American."[10] Even though Gifford makes a clear distinction between fundamentalism and Pentecostalism in general, he and Rijk van Dijk occasionally conflate the characteristics of Pentecostal developments in Africa and Christian fundamentalism more broadly understood.[11]

Furthermore, Gifford and other scholars describe the "prosperity gospel" as external to African religious sensibilities, again attributing its presence in Africa to the influence of American Pentecostalism. As Gifford suggests, prosperity was a novel, foreign element in African Christianity that arrived with the current wave of U.S. evangelical revival sweeping the continent.[12] As he describes it, "The essential point of this Gospel of Prosperity is that prosperity of all kinds is the right of every Christian. God wants a Christian to be wealthy. True Christianity necessarily means wealth; it inevitably brings wealth. Conversely, poverty indicates personal sin, or at least a deficient faith or inadequate understanding."[13]

He goes on to argue, "This Gospel of Prosperity does not belong in Africa's revival. It did not originate in Africa. It originated with the media evangelists of the U.S.... The fact that it is so commonly preached in Africa shows the degree to which this current revival is directed from the U.S.A.... It is spreading because of these [African] evangelists' attention to and investment in all areas of the media."[14]

Gifford reasons that black Africa responds to the gospel of prosperity because it offers the prospect of material wealth to Africa's poor who despair over the absence of secular solutions to Africa's persistent crises of health and wealth[15] He also maintains that the gospel of prosperity suits white Christians in South Africa and Zimbabwe because it suggests that their disproportionate wealth is nothing to feel guilty about. Rather, it provides divine assurance that

wealth is a blessing from God and has nothing to do with the unjust structures that Tutu, Hurley, Boesak, and Naude have challenged their churches to
acknowledge and rectify.[16]

By exploring the complex relationship between Pentecostalism and globalization, Droogers challenges the assertion that external factors explain
Pentecostalism's flourishing in Africa.[17] Instead, he argues that explaining the
growth, expansion, and impact of these religious movements must begin with
an examination of their internal particularities before the influence of external social processes can be properly understood. Specifically, the diversity that
African Pentecostalism exhibits must be taken into account in an attempt to
assess its nature, practice, vitality, and provenance.

To be sure, some "born-again" churches rely or depend partially on
American Pentecostal organizations for external funding and resources (Bible
Belt literature, for example). But there are also several Pentecostal movements
in African countries such as Nigeria that are self-financing and that demonstrate a high degree of indigenous religious vitality and innovation.

Using the example of the Redeemed Christian Church of God (RCCG), this
chapter revisits the "prosperity gospel" in order to compare its characteristics
in the African context with the broader contours of the global phenomenon. In
particular, Ojo's earlier critique of Gifford will provide a fuller and deeper perspective on the origins of the prosperity gospel in Africa. As Ojo observed:

> Prosperity and success as religious ideas were not introduced to
> Africa by American tele-evangelists, and they are not "foreign ele-
> ments" in African Christianity as Paul Gifford (1990) has asserted ...
> [T]he emphasis was indigenously developed as a response to the
> socio-economic changes of the 1980s. African Charismatics have
> been associated with American evangelists from the mid-1970s, yet
> did not develop this teaching until the mid-1980s when many African
> nations began to feel the impact of the IMF-inspired Structural
> Adjustment Programmes. The reality, therefore, is that Charismatics
> have read the Scriptures on their own and have appropriated its mes-
> sage to suit their contemporary socio-economic situation.[18]

In other words, Ojo situates the quest for material resources partly in the dete-
riorating economic situation in Africa. Charismatics, he argued, were incorporating the economic exigencies of their societies into the existing narrative of
their religious experience.[19] Thus, while a rereading of the scriptures produced
a distinctive perspective on the prosperity discourse, the indigenous culture
within which the message is preached has shaped prosperity teachings in the
African context.[20]

Gifford seems subsequently to have tempered his arguments in favor of external influence. He argues elsewhere that

> In Africa it is obvious that the faith gospel builds on traditional pre-occupations. Africa's traditional religions were focused on material realities ... But Africa's current Pentecostalism is increasingly articulated in terms of the faith gospel normally associated with a standardized American form ... I suggest that in the form which it is widely heard in Africa the African preoccupation with material realities has been subsumed into this standardized formulation.[21]

Still, this shift was not as evident in Gifford's later writings.[22] The rest of this chapter focuses on the RCCG, providing a brief overview of its history, growth, demographic spread, global impact, and tendency toward transnationalization. It also explores the health and wealth, or prosperity discourse within the context of the church, while examining the factors that shape RCCG's economic base.

The Redeemed Christian Church of God: A Brief History

The RCCG is a typical example of an indigenous African Pentecostal/charismatic church, one which has spread globally from Nigeria to about 120 countries with over five million members, scattered across Africa, the Americas, Europe, Asia, Australia, and the Middle East.[23] The RCCG was founded in Lagos in 1952 by Pa Josiah Akindayomi, who claimed to have experienced a divine call to a special mission. Pa Akindayomi became popular for his charismatic qualities and healing activities, although the church did not witness any large-scale expansion under his leadership. Most parishes (branches) were limited to western Nigeria with only a few in eastern and northern Nigeria. He was succeeded as the general overseer in 1980 by Enoch Adejare Adeboye, a former university professor of applied mathematics, who increased the national stature of RCCG and launched the church onto the global religious map. Adeboye's charismatic qualities and healing ministries largely accounted for the organizational and numerical growth as well as the geo-ethnic spread within Nigeria and beyond. The RCCG is considered to be the fastest growing Pentecostal church in Nigeria today. The official RCCG website states:

> Since 1981, an open explosion began with the number of parishes growing in leaps and bounds. At the last count, there are at least about 2000 parishes of the Redeemed Christian Church of God in Nigeria.

On the International scene, the church is present in other African nations including Cote D'Ivoire, Ghana, Zambia, Malawi, Zaire, Tanzania, Kenya, Uganda, Gambia, Cameroon, and South Africa. In Europe the church is spread in England, Germany, and France. In the United States there are parishes in Dallas, Tallahassee, Houston, New York, Washington, and Chicago and also in the Caribbean states of Haiti and Jamaica.[24]

Current information gleaned from the RCCG website parish directory even suggests an underrepresentation of the geographical spread. The church offers a conservative estimate of over five thousand parishes with large memberships in several other countries across the globe.[25] The RCCG parishes worldwide are organizationally structured into "areas," with each area subdivided into "zones" for administrative purposes. Each zone is made up of several parishes and is assigned a coordinator.[26] For example, the RCCG North America area is divided into ten zones, and comprises the United States, Canada, and the Caribbean islands. At the RCCG North America (RCCGNA) Annual Convention held in Dallas, in 2003, over 120 parishes were listed.[27] The first RCCG parish in the United States was founded in 1992 in Detroit. From 1994 onward, new parishes sprang up in Florida, Texas, Massachusetts, and other states. During one of his visits to the United States, Pastor Adeboye was in contact with James Fadele, an engineer employed by Ford Motors and living with his family in Detroit. In Nigeria, he was an RCCG church worker. Adeboye instructed him: "Listen, we need to start doing something in order to execute the program of God for this church, especially in North America."[28]

A fellowship group comprising a few Nigerian families commenced in Detroit as a consequence of this instruction. Due to the enlargement of its membership, the group grew to become a substantial parish. In Dallas, the initiative to establish a parish was initiated by Nigerian employees and trainees with oil companies based in Dallas. Many of these workers could not find a place of worship "where they could feel at home." A fellowship group comprising twelve families formed, leading to its registration as a parish in October 1994.

The RCCG General Overseer Enoch Adeboye was invited and flew in from Nigeria to attend the parish's inauguration ceremony. Soon after, the abrupt decision of the first leader to return home required a new pastor directly from Nigeria. In November 1994, Pastor Dr. Ajibike Akinkoye moved with his family to Dallas to oversee the new parish. From this pioneer parish, the Dallas metroplex eventually nurtured fourteen full-fledged RCCG parishes. There are also twelve parishes in Houston and other locations in Texas. The push to establish parishes in North America is closely related to the vision and goals of members as expressed in RCCG's "Mission Statement":

It is our goal to make heaven. It is our goal to take as many people as possible with us. In order to accomplish our goals, holiness will be our lifestyle. In order to take as many people with us as possible, we will plant churches within five minutes walking distance in every city and town of developing countries; and within five minutes driving distance in every city and town of developed countries. We will pursue these objectives until every nation in the world is reached for Jesus Christ our Lord.[29]

In the case of RCCGNA, this statement suggests how contextual factors can shape the growth of a religious movement and serve as the impetus for change in a new context: "We believe in positioning our worship centers close to the people hence in North America we are challenged to establish parishes in every State, County, City and in fact within 30 minutes driving distance."[30] RCCG Pastor Samuel Shorimade offered this perspective on American evangelism in the RCCGNA, "The United States was often described in some circles as God's own country, but this country has become very slack morally and spiritually. So God is making us bring worship and praise to them as well as in rediscovering God."[31]

The Redemption Camp—RCCG North America

One of the significant ways in which the RCCG is gradually being imprinted on the American cultural landscape is through the reproduction of Nigeria's Redemption Camp.[32] The Redemption Camp (a.k.a. Redemption City), located along the Lagos-Ibadan Expressway, doubles as RCCG's international headquarters and the church's most important sacred space. The venue hosts their most popular religious programs and festivals such as the Holy Ghost Service, an all-night prayer, healing, and miracle event. It has metamorphosed, first, into the International Holy Ghost Festival, which drew at least a million participants each year.[33] It was recently renamed the Holy Ghost Congress and housed at the Holy Ghost arena at the Redemption City.[34] The Camp is located on ten square kilometers of land acquired since its inauguration two decades ago. Much like a small city, the site also boasts a maternity center, an orphanage, a post office, a gas station, bookstores, two banks, supermarkets, bakery, canteen, a secondary school, and a Bible school. The significance of the Redemption Camp lies not only in the religious needs it meets. Moreover, it constitutes a nexus for the social, economic, cultural, and political interests of the vast, extended community it serves.

In 2003, the RCCGNA acquired over four hundred land hectares near Dallas with plans to build a replica of the Redemption Camp in Nigeria.[35] The new

Redemption Camp now serves as RCCGNA headquarters. Significantly, most of the resources used in developing the Redemption Camp were generated from within the church. The impulse to build a new Redemption Camp was contextualized as part of religious experiences reported by Enoch Adeboye and Ajibike Akinkoye at different times. Narrating his prolonged spiritual experience during the formative years of the RCCG parish in Dallas, Akinkoye claimed:

> In the 1990s I heard a voice speaking to me. First, I was not sure what it was. The voice came repeatedly afterwards and then I recognized that it was God speaking to me. The voice was telling me "You are not going to build a mega church here yet, you will plant little churches around the Dallas metroplex and then I will give you a Camp. And each of these little parishes can then become a mega church" ... I kept this to myself although I continued to hear this voice ... I recounted this vision to Enoch Adeboye, the General Overseer during one of his pastoral visits to Dallas. Adeboye nodded afterwards and said "Yes, you are right. About ten years ago, when I was passing through Dallas to attend a church meeting in Oklahoma, God showed me that He would give us (RCCG) a camp in Dallas."[36]

The quest for land, the contacts with the landowners, the actual acquisition, selling rates, and the payment procedure are all part of a Pentecostal testimony. Such narratives are believed to be the manifestation of God's vision and miracle-working.[37] Duplication of the Nigerian camp in Dallas is important for a number of reasons. On the one hand, it represents the decentralization of church programs such as the Holy Ghost Festival, annual conventions, and ministers' conference. The reenactment of such events at the Dallas Redemption Camp reduces logistic and financial problems associated with RCCG members' having to travel the long distance to attend similar programs at the international headquarters. Furthermore, restrictive immigration policies prevent members with illegal status from attending such programs outside the United States. The Dallas camp also regrounds the sacred space of the RCCG, allowing the rituals and community to be shared by members in the diaspora.

The RCCG and the Transnationalization of New African Churches

One feature that distinguishes this new movement from the religiosity transmitted through previous immigration waves is the transnational network, the hallmark of what Stephen Castles and Mark Miller describe as "the age of migration."[38] The transnational nature of many African churches in the diaspora challenges the assumption that immigrants often sever links with their homeland after integration into the new host context. Most new African migrant churches are rooted locally *and* in the land of origin, but also into an intra-communal web linking them with different places across the globe. Specifically, these communities are connected through various ties of religion, economy, friendship, kinship, and politics. Cell phones, websites, and social media have become central features of the construction and growth of diasporic identities. In an article on "New Black Pentecostal Churches in Britain," Hunt and Lightly argue that:

> The importance of the "new" black African churches within the framework of globalization is not merely with reference to a unique expression of African Christianity. Rather, they are noteworthy in that they constitute international ministries, which have implications on a worldwide scale. As part of an increasing phenomenon of what might be termed "reverse proselytization," these new West African churches have systematically set out to evangelize the world. In the case of the RCCG this has meant establishing churches in as far-flung places as India, the Caribbean, Hong Kong, the U.S.A. and Europe. The impact and significance of the exportation of a fiercely evangelical Nigerian church such as the RCCG, driven by a vision of winning converts, is that it offers a unique opportunity to analyze its impact at a local level, in this case the Western context.[39]

The importance of local and global networks among African churches in both home and host contexts cannot be overemphasized. Such networks assume increasing significance for new African migrants. The ties these networks provide include new ecumenical affiliations, pastoral exchanges between Africa, Europe, and the United States, special events and conferences, prayer networks, Internet sites, international ministries, publications, audio and video elements of worship, and televangelism. The linkage and "flow" is two-directional; that is, information constantly circulates within the networks, allowing global influences to penetrate locally, and vice versa.

The proliferation of these networked relationships among new African migrants—and between migrant churches, host churches and their home base—has important implications that must be contextually understood. Some of these groups frequently organize programs that are local in nature, but that also have a global focus that links the local church with other churches globally. The mobility of religious leaders, freelance evangelists, and church members between the homeland and diasporic spaces is another vital component of these networked movements. The RCCG is one of many African churches that are now sending missionaries to evangelize Europe, the United States of America and other parts of the globe. Many of the African missionaries are commissioned by their home churches and provided with financial and material resources to pursue their evangelism. While this "reverse-mission" initiative is not unique to African Christian movements, the important consideration for the argument of this chapter is that African churches are creators—not merely passive consumers—of contemporary Christian culture.

Changing Austerity to Prosperity: RCCG Prosperity Discourse

One central discourse prevalent in the RCCG worldview is "health and wealth." The emphasis on prosperity teaching, the epistemologies of health and wealth, and the ritual attitudes they invoke in members are integrally linked to how the economic base of the church is shaped, reconfigured, and sustained. Health, for these religious communities, encompasses physical, spiritual, mental, material, psychological, and social well-being. It also includes belief in the right to gainful employment, fair wages, residence permits, and a safe environment that nurtures a life of dignity and decency. The networked culture of RCCG means that indigenous epistemologies of health and wealth—in other words, the quest for "the good things in life" as local iterations of prosperity—blend seamlessly with external discourses on prosperity.

The holistic perspective of RCCG on health and wealth also means that illness is understood as a potent manifestation of poverty, even as wealth is perceived as potentially leading to another kind of poverty. The RCCG's ritual tradition includes strategies through which members are inoculated against, and equipped to exorcise, what they perceive as the demons or spiritual maladies of poverty. Honing his theological argument about prosperity, Adeboye remarked in a sermon during the July 2004 Holy Ghost service:

> I don't preach on prosperity often because some preachers have preached on it as if it is the only counsel of God. But prosperity is only one of the whole counsel of God and I believe that the Almighty God wants me to preach the whole counsel of God. That's why once a year I talk about prosperity. That is why tonight our topic is "anointed to flourish." There are five categories of people: the poor, the comfortable, the rich, the wealthy and the flourishing. Which one do you want to be? ... This may be one of the greatest messages you ever heard in your life so I'm not going to be in a hurry .... If you fully understand

what I'm going to tell you tonight I'm sure by this time next year you will be smiling....[40]

Adeboye deploys one of his trademark opening remarks as a strategy to draw each congregant's attention to his sermon. Illustrating his initial remarks with the parable of "Jesus feeding 5,000 people with the lunch of a small boy," he announced, "There is someone here today, between now and tomorrow your austerity is going to be changed to prosperity provided if for the next few minutes you are going to—like nobody else—lift your eyes to the Almighty God and just thank Him, thank Him...." Such "prophetic utterances" often prompt a chorused "Amen" from an excited crowd of worshippers and participants. The sermon text then illuminates a dimension of the "official" discourse on prosperity, revealing the hermeneutics of poverty, health, and wealth. Adeboye then highlights what he sees as the root source of poverty:

> There is no greatness in poverty because poverty is a curse pronounced by God on those who are disobedient. There is nothing glorious about poverty. It brings hunger. In Proverbs 10:15 the Bible says the destruction of the poor is their poverty. Poverty is a destroyer, and everything that is trying to destroy your destiny, I command that they be destroyed tonight in Jesus name ... Anybody who is sickly, all is not well with him so that when you are sick, it doesn't matter how much money you have, you are poor.[41]

Adeboye tightly integrates this argument about prosperity with the hermeneutics of health and wealth. In what also seems to be a critique of "holiness" and "pietist" Christianity, he underscores the significance of wealth and holy living in both a this-worldly and other-worldly orientation:

> Health and wealth, they go together. In fact they say health is wealth. 3 John 2 the Bible says I wish above all things that you prosper and be in health. God wants you to be healthy as well as prosperous. Barrenness is another kind of poverty, that is why I am praying for all those who are trusting God for the fruit of the womb. This month God will answer you. Let's look at some of the forms of poverty because some people glorify poverty. They think you have to be poor to make it to heaven. I used to believe that and I have discovered, you can be the poorest man on earth, if you are not born again and you don't live holy you are not going to see God, you will just suffer for nothing here. I've also discovered you can be the richest man on earth, if you are born again and you are living holy, there is a room, a mansion reserved

for you in heaven. I say I don't know about you—In this world I will enjoy. And then I will go and enjoy in heaven. Does that surprise you? So shall it be in Jesus' name (*Amen!*) [42]

This view rebuts the claim made by some scholars that African Christianity is only concerned with this-worldly goals to the neglect of other-worldly orientations. In this case, the biblical parable of the rich young man—"I tell you the truth, it is very hard for a rich man to get into the kingdom of heaven ....It is easier for a camel to go through the eye of a needle than for a rich man to enter the Kingdom of heaven" (Mt. 19: 23–24)—is rephrased in a way that makes it less problematic for a rich, holy man to gain access. The sermon text is often interspersed with "prophetic utterances," which suggests immediate resolution of existential problems.

Adeboye asserts in an imperative tone, "But God has a cure for poverty." He announces, "And I decree to somebody here today, you may find it difficult to pay your house rent but very soon you'll be drinking tea with the president (Amen!). How can that be? I know it can be because I'm a living example."

Toward the end of the sermon, he hints further, "Here we are talking about prosperity, and the Lord is solving the problem of one fellow. He said that somebody is getting a brand new brain (Amen!) Thank you Father!"[43]

One way of understanding the nature of prosperity discourse in African Pentecostal Christianity is to probe the complex factors that account for its attractiveness to congregants. What attracts people to these churches, and why the unprecedented proliferation of Pentecostal and Charismatic churches in sub-Saharan Africa? Results of our ethnographic study show that many people are drawn to these churches precisely because of the possibility that their ailments might be cured. Our interviews with RCCG informants detail illnesses described by members, their accounts of treatments received in the church, and the social situation in which they live.[44] Through participant observation in their services and programs, we documented hundreds of "testimonies" in which subjects recount their conversion narratives or their history of affiliation.

The questionnaire asked for demographic information of members, their reasons for joining a local church, as well as certain aspects of church life. The interviews, testimonies, and questionnaire provided ample healing narratives over and above any quest for prosperity in the popular sense of becoming rich and wealthy. Other reasons for seeking membership varied from acceptance of a friend's or family member's invitation; attendance at a program such as a revival or crusade; the appeal of the music; a desire to receive or witness a miracle; and a directive from the Holy Spirit.

If the prosperity or faith gospel simply entails the desire for material success and the blessings of health and wealth, then it is not new to indigenous worldviews and mission churches that have been ritually preoccupied with the pursuit of the "the good things in life." For members, the failure to realize these objectives largely motivates their seeking a new religious affiliation. The Yoruba phrase/song, *Owo, Omo, Alafia Repete* ("money, children, good health in abundance") sung by Yoruba Christians at thanksgiving rituals best embodies the significance of health and wealth for believers. The general preoccupation with the quest for the good things in life is therefore "rebranded" with the label of prosperity gospel within Pentecostal discourse. These mechanisms of this reconfiguration are apparent in the religious principles of the RCCG.

Tithes and Offerings: The Malachi Rhetoric and RCCG Economic Base

Tithes (from the Hebrew *maaser*) and offerings (from *minchah*) represent one of RCCG fundamental belief codes, the giving of which forms an essential part of worship and constitutes a potent way of invoking the blessings of God. As the church claims:

> Regular payment of tithe and offering is obligatory because it is God's command. It is God's way of providing for the Ministers in the Church. The ministers and other church employees are paid their food, allowance through tithe. The offering is used to cater for the needy in the Church. Tithe and Offering must be paid on every income e.g. salary, profit from business transaction, gifts, etc. Mal. 3:8–12; Gen. 14:19–20; Num. 18:20–21; Deut. 26:12–13; Lev. 27:30; Heb. 7:2–5; I Cor. 16:2; Matt. 23:23. Tithe is exclusively for the minister's welfare.[45]

Thus practice of tithes and offerings is linked to Hebrew scriptures in which God enjoined the Israelites at different periods of their religious history to pay tithes and offerings. For instance, one of the notable works of Abraham was to pay tithes to Melchizedek, the priest-king of Salem (Gen. 14:17–20; Heb. 7:4–10). In the Hebrew political economy, one-tenth of the income of the people was set apart to support public worship of God (Lev. 27:30; 32; Gen. 28:22). And in the New Testament, what taxes symbolize for the state is what tithes represent for the church (I Cor. 9: 13–14).

In the RCCG, tithes have continued to represent one-tenth of a members' total or gross income. While a tithe means 10 percent of all benefits that come a member's way, such as salary, inheritance, gifts, and even the interest earned on bank accounts, the offering is essentially different. Offering goes beyond the 10 percent tithes and could be in cash or property. The giver takes the initiative on what to give toward needs of the church or an individual. Several biblical references are also evoked to support the giving of offerings (Gen. 4:4–5; Exo. 23:15; Exo. 34:20; I Sam. 2:30; Lev. 22:17–25 and 29; Psa. 50:14, 23; Eph. 5:10; Rom. 12:1–2; II Cor. 9:6–8; Gal. 6:7–9). The RCCG worship services and programs include thanksgiving rituals for childbirth, naming, marriage, job promotion, recovery from sickness, procurement of visas, passing examinations, New Year and Christmas celebrations, safe journeys, buying a new car, building a new house, as well as other rites of passage. As a member remarked: "Today we do not bring sin or burnt guilt offerings as in Old Testament times because Jesus has done it all for us. However, we still bring thanks offering. It is an expression of gratitude to our God. More so, He is honored."[46]

Tithing is perceived as a solemn covenant between God and his people (members of the church). Two of the frequently quoted biblical references used to legitimize this practice state:

> Will a man rob God? Yet you rob me. But you ask, How do we rob you? In tithes and offerings. You are under a curse—the whole nation of you—because you are robbing God. Bring the whole tithe into the storehouse, that there may be food in my house. Test me in this and see if I will not throw open the floodgates of heaven and pour out so much blessing that you will not have room enough for it. I will prevent pests from devouring your crops, and the vines in your fields will not cast their fruits, says the Lord Almighty. Then all the nations will call you blessed, for yours will be a delightful land, says the Lord Almighty (Malachi 3:8–12).
>
> Remember this: Whoever sows sparingly will also reap sparingly, and whoever sows generously will also reap generously. Each man should give what he has decided in his heart to give, not reluctantly or under compulsion, for God loves a cheerful giver (II Corinthians 9:6–7).

While the RCCG strongly encourages its members to engage in tithing, members are not compelled to do so. Still, the liturgical structure makes ample space for the collection of tithes. And within the sermons, the oft-cited biblical references are recited as a way of calling members to wake up to their responsibility. It is believed that unfaithfulness in the area of tithing can make a member lose God's blessing, because he is perceived as stealing directly from God. The failure to pay tithes is believed to automatically bring a curse on a member and his or her business.

In one of his writings, Adeboye enjoined members to attach utmost priority to payment of tithes: "What you have stolen from God, I appeal to you, restore and He will surprise you … God says when you begin to pay your tithes, all the devourers that have been eating up your money and all the abortive efforts that you have been making, He will silence."[47] In one of his sermons, he outlines the intricate correlation between the acquisition of wealth and giving offerings to God: "If you want a double portion of wealth, you have to do something greater than what Solomon did. You have to give an offering the kind that you have never given before. God is a God of principles: Do what nobody had done before; He will respond by giving you something that nobody had ever got before."[48]

On one level, the tithe and offering discourse suggests a pathway from poverty to prosperity. It is even literally described as a formula: "If you need money, make sure you pay tithes and give offerings. Money begets money." When you pay tithes, you are not expecting the returns from man's limited ability but from God's unlimited supply.[49]

The importance of tithes and offerings is evident in members' adherence to these imperatives both in their giving as well as in their testimonies about tithing. One member's testimony suggests the significance attached to it. He says:

> I am a natural hard worker and I make a lot of money. However, with all my hard work and the money I make, there is really nothing to show for it. One day, I listened to Pastor Doyin Oke preached on tithes and offerings. I said to myself, "What's this man talking about? With the 100 percent I keep to myself, I find it difficult to live, now he says God demands at least 10 percent in tithes and offerings." Anyway, because he had earlier taught on the benefits of obedience, I decided to start tithing and giving generous offerings. To the glory of God, my financial situation is a lot better than it used to be. Even though I have more expenses, I can still afford to give and give and save.[50]

Some tithing testimonies indicate that the tithing discourse and popular beliefs surrounding the practice generate controversial interpretations. The testimonial below entitled "Must read for all brethren! Praise God!!!" illustrates the tenacity and enthusiasm that some members bring to the practice of tithing. Ola says:

> Hello Brethren, I heard this wonderful testimony and I said to let you hear of it. I heard on a Christian radio channel that a Christian sister had her credit card stolen and weeks later she found her credit card account buoyant with money she did not put there! When she got the monthly statement she found out that the thief who had stolen the card had used her card to bet on a race on the Internet and the thief

had been winning very big money which was being deposited in her credit card account all the time! Talk about blessings from heaven! The Lord has said that the riches of gentiles are laid up for the righteous! Maybe this sister had been paying her tithes and God had said to everyone of us to test him with our tithes and see if he would not open up the window of heaven on us! That is shower of blessings from heaven! I believe that this sister is reaping what she had sown. I just praised the Lord when I heard this. My God is a covenant-keeping God and his words can never fall to the ground. It was wonderful! Praise the living Jesus! Halleluyah![51]

The enormous financial resources generated through tithing are primarily geared toward the welfare of ministers and church employees, as well as for the poor and the needy within the church. In spite of this, only a very small percentage of RCCG parish pastors earn their pay from the church. Several of the local pastors operate as honorary pastors, while others are supported materially by local parishes.

Every RCCG parish is autonomous, yet there is a reasonable degree of cohesion without uniformity. Each individual parish is linked to the RCCG international headquarters in Lagos through an evolving hierarchical administrative structure.[52] At the central organizational level, local parishes are required to make monthly financial remittances through administrative zonal headquarters to RCCG's international headquarters. This includes 10 percent of total tithes and offerings of all RCCG fellowships, and 10 percent of tithes and offerings of all parishes dedicated by the general overseer. Each local parish is expected in addition to submit a comprehensive financial report. In the case of RCCG North America, each parish is required to send a portion of its monthly income to the Finance Coordinating Center in Houston. The funds accumulating there are used to assist new, young, or weak parishes that need financial help for a time, and also for international missions.[53]

While the RCCG's primary source of internal revenue is tithes and offerings, other sources include Sunday worship offertory, thanksgiving offerings, special program offerings, donations, vows, pledges, and special levies for projects such as building construction. The huge monies generated from these diverse sources and events form the economic bedrock of the church.

The RCCG expansion and proliferation in diaspora is now characterized by parishes founded out of the initiative of local parishes in Nigeria. Such local parishes not only establish new branches in diaspora, but also take financial responsibility by sending a missionary pastor and providing facilities and infrastructure for the new parish. Coordinating pastors sent directly from Nigeria also have their salaries paid from the local Nigerian parish while the new parish gets on its feet. All of this calls for a further reexamination of explanations that privilege ecclesiastical externality in explaining the success of African Pentecostalism.

Conclusion

This chapter has demonstrated, with the case of RCCG, how internal religious dynamics in tandem with external social processes are crucial factors in explaining the growth of African Pentecostalism. It underscores how explanations that prioritize external factors, over and above internal characteristics, obscure rather than illuminate how and to what extent indigenous African Pentecostal and Charismatic churches are creating distinctive identities through their indigenous epistemologies of health and wealth (prosperity teaching). This distinctiveness also is evident in healing rituals and in their reconfiguration of the global religious economy through self-financing strategies, including the emphasis on tithes and offering, volunteerism, and other internal fund-raising mechanisms. Thus, the dependence on external funding and resources by African churches is an exception rather than the norm. In the case of the RCCG and several other indigenous African Pentecostal and Charismatic churches, the spiritual and material resources they generate, their social relevance, and their globalizing and transnationalizing tendencies and strategies act as stimuli for growth and mobility in Africa and beyond.

NOTES

1. See Pew Forum on Religion and Public Life, *Spirit and Power: A 10-Country Survey of Pentecostals*. Washington, DC: Pew Research Center. (http://pewforum.org/surveys/pentecostal/). (Accessed March 3, 2007.)
2. Jenkins 2002.
3. Barrett, Kurian, and Johnson 2001.
4. See Pew Forum, *Spirit and Power.*
5. Dempster, Klaus, and Peterson 1999.
6. Pew Forum, *Spirit and Power*, 1.
7. Brouwer, Gifford, and Rose 1996; Gifford 1998, 1990, 2001, 2004.
8. Gifford, 1998: 308.
9. Gifford 1990: 373.
10. Brouwer, Gifford, and Rose, 1996: 1.
11. Van Dijk 2000.
12. Gifford 1990: 373–388.
13. Gifford 1990: 75.
14. Gifford 1990: 382.
15. Gifford 1990: 383.
16. Gifford 1990: 382.
17. Droogers 2001: 41–61.

18. Ojo 1996: 106.
19. Ojo 1996: 106.
20. Kalu 2000; Adogame 2004a, 2004b, 2005a, 2005b; Asamoah-Gyadu 2005: 203.
21. Gifford 2001: 64.
22. Cf. Gifford 2004.
23. Adogame 2004a.
24. From "Foundation" posted on Redeemed Christian Church of God website: http://rccg.org/foundation.php.
25. A conservative list of parishes worldwide is available at the RCCG Internet Outreach: http://www.rccgnet.org. This list is far incomplete. There are several existing parishes that are yet to be included in the directory.
26. The Zonal Coordinator heads a local parish but also performs special functions in issues of doctrine, protocol, finance, legal and immigration matters, special programs and projects, etc. See details in RCCG 2003.
27. "The Latter Rain" 7th Annual RCCG North American Convention Program, Dallas, June 2003.
28. Personal Interview with Pastor Dr. Ajibike Akinkoye at the RCCGNA Headquarters, Dallas, Texas, on 7 March 2004.
29. Redeemed Christian Church of God, "Our Vision and Mission," available at http://www.rccg.org/our_vision_mission.php. (Accessed March 4, 2013.)
30. See "Addendum—Our Poise," The Redeemed Christian Church of God, North America and Caribbean Statement of Fundamental Truths, a publication of RCCGNA, n.d., pp. 39–40.
31. Personal Interview with Pastor Dr. Samuel Shorimade at the RCCG Cornerstone Worship Center for All Nations parish, Cambridge, Massachusetts, on 23 November 2003. Pastor Shorimade is the founder and current pastor of the parish.
32. For a detailed discussion, see Adogame 2004a.
33. See a brief account of the Holy Ghost Service, see "Holy Ghost Service" description, available at http://liveway.tv/channels/holy-ghost-service/about. Statistics of attendance at the Holy Ghost Congress are rather guesstimates. For instance, foreign media such as the CNN estimated the attendance for the event tagged "Divine Visitation," on December 18–19, 1998, at seven million, while the local media gave varying figures. See also "Holy Ghost Congress: A Wonder in a Jungle": http://rccg.org/congress2011/holy_ghost.html (Accessed December 22, 2011).
34. The Holy Ghost congress presently attracts a tremendously huge attendance estimated at over two million, thus leading some observers to describe the religious festival as the largest Christian gathering on earth. See Grady 2002.
35. Personal Interview with Pastor (Dr.) Ajibike Akinyoye at the RCCGNA Headquarters, Dallas, Texas, on 9 March 2004. Cf. Akande 2003. Also available at: http://odili.net/news/source/2003/apr/3/100.html or http://www.rccgna.org/news.htm.
36. Personal Interview with Pastor (Dr.) Ajibike Akinyoye at the RCCGNA Headquarters, Dallas, Texas on 9 March 2004. See also "Redemption Camp, Texas USA," in RCCG 2002: 2–5.
37. Personal Interview with Pastor (Dr.) Ajibike Akinyoye at the RCCGNA Headquarters, Dallas, Texas on 9 March 2004. See also "Redemption Camp, Texas USA," in RCCG 2002: 2–5.
38. Castles and Miller 2003.
39. Hunt and Lightly 2001: 121.
40. Sermon text of Pastor E.A. Adeboye, RCCG General Overseer at the Holy Ghost Service, RCCG Redemption Camp, Lagos-Ibadan Expressway on 2 July 2004. Available at: http://main.rccg.org/holy_ghost_service/2004_hgs?hgs_Jul_04.htm.
41. Ibid.
42. Ibid.
43. Ibid.
44. Field survey and results from RCCG parishes in Bonn and Hamburg, Germany 2001–2005.

45. See "RCCG Fundamental Beliefs", available at: http://home.rccg.org/ChurchHistory/FundamentalBeliefs3.htm.
46. Personal Interview with Richard Olaiya (pseudonym) at RCCG parish, Hamburg, on 18 November 2003.
47. Adeboye 1989: 16–17.
48. Sermon text of Pastor E. A. Adeboye, RCCG General Overseer at the Holy Ghost Service, RCCG Redemption Camp, Lagos-Ibadan Expressway "God of Double Portion," at the Holy Ghost Service, RCCG Redemption Camp, on 1 March 2002. Available at: http://rccg.org/Holy_Ghost_Service/Monthly_Holy_Ghost%20Service/mar2002.htm.
49. Ibid.
50. See Akin A., Testimony, "End of Financial Struggle," available at: http://www.rccgsalvationcenter.org/testimonies-pg2.htm. (Accessed December 22, 2011.)
51. Testimonial available at RCCG Testimony Page: http://www.rccg.org/testimony/_disc3/000002c1.htm. (Accessed December 22, 2011.)
52. See "RCCG: Past, Present and Future. The Structure, Administration and Finance of the Redeemed Christian Church of God in North America," 7th Annual RCCG North America Convention Program, June 18–20, 2003, pp. 15 and 30.
53. RCCG 2001.

10

Remittances and Mission

Transnational Latino Pentecostal Ministry in Los Angeles

JUAN FRANCISCO MARTÍNEZ

Introduction

Latino Protestant pastors in immigrant communities are increasingly becoming involved in ministry patterns that include commitments not only in their local area, but also beyond their "parishes" and even beyond the borders of the United States. The ministry focus of these churches in Los Angeles is created and expanded by the extended family and friendship networks of the church members and often follows the same patterns as their remittance commitments. Because many pastors and members maintain strong links to countries in Latin America, and beyond, these links become one of the means by which they attract new members and also expand the ministry outreach of their churches.

Due to the constant and multidirectional migratory patterns of many Latinos, Latino churches are increasingly developing a "network" understanding of their church's ministry. Because these ministry links are created by local church-based networks they do not fit the traditional definition of "mission" usually understood as something initiated "here," but done "out there." Pastoral care and ministry outreach often include church members that live "transnational" lives, so that pastors find themselves providing pastoral care across national boundaries and involved in ministries in various countries.

These tendencies are particularly evident among Latino Pentecostal churches, which are the fastest growing among Latinos in the United States and which continue to expand in Southern California. The globalized migratory patterns that connect Los Angeles to Latin America and the world are changing the way these churches view Christian mission and are having an impact on the religious landscape of Pentecostal Christianity in the United States.

Latino Pentecostal churches are not only changing how they do mission; they are also at the vanguard of the changing face of the church and its mission. This study will demonstrate that poor immigrants who are committed to Christian mission are leaving behind traditional ways of doing Protestant mission and are using models that reflect how they live their transnational lives. These models are the work of the poor to the poor; they provide the poor ways of doing mission that neither require a great deal of money nor much formal education. Mission follows their familial and social networks, based on the "leading of the Holy Spirit." Because more and more poor migrants are becoming involved in mission they are becoming the cutting edge of Christian mission and growth. Even though traditional Protestant mission work will continue, much of the growth of the church will happen through the work of migrants like those described in this chapter.

These migrants come from churches in the global south or are part of the "global south" in the United States. They are part of the growing edge of the church, a poor church that looks more like the working class and poor believers of the first century than the Protestantism of the last century. They are practicing a model of mission born in the Azusa Street revival, one in which the poor have taken the message to the poor using models of mission that were often linked to relational networks. Their models of mission also have more in common with the mission advancement of the first century than with modern Protestant mission. As such the mission model used by these Latino Pentecostal churches is representative of the most common model of mission of the global south. It will likely be the predominant mission model of the churches of global south.

Migration studies have demonstrated that in today's globalized environment, immigrants are developing and maintaining kinship and social networks that are creating transnational identities and commitments.[1] Hanciles has demonstrated how migration is changing the face of the church throughout the Western world.[2] Vásquez and Friedmann Marquardt have described how many churches in North America are changing because of the transnational links throughout the Americas.[3] Migration is also changing the face of religion in the United States because the immigrants are bringing new religions and different understandings of Christianity. Books like *Immigrant Faiths Transforming Religious Life in America*,[4] *God Needs No Passport: Immigrants and the Changing Religious Landscape*,[5] and *Migración y Creencias Pensar las Religiones en Tiempo de Movilidad*[6] invite people both in religious studies and in migration studies to rethink how migration in a globalized world is changing the religious landscape in the United States, and around the world, even as immigrants' religious understandings are being changed by migration. Specifically, "Immigrant Religion in the City of Angels" has described this impact in Southern California.[7]

This study analyzes how immigrant-based Latino Pentecostal churches in Southern California minister in transnational networks and how such networks are changing these churches' understanding of their mission. Because most Latino Pentecostal churches, and many non-Pentecostal churches, in Southern California are involved in some type of transnational network–based ministry, this study focuses on five churches that can serve as examples of what others are doing. It is an ethnographic study of these five churches and their transnational mission efforts. These churches were chosen through a three-step process. First, an initial list was created of Latino Pentecostal churches that have pastors with formal seminary education. Ten of the pastors on this list were sent an initial survey, asking questions about their current transnational mission efforts. The five churches chosen are actively involved in transnational mission projects and agreed to participate in the study.[8]

The pastors each chose one project that they felt best exemplified their transnational efforts. We visited each project together and interviewed the leaders involved in the projects, both in the United States and in Latin America. After visiting each mission project the pastors were also invited to analyze their work in light of migration theory and to reflect on how their work is changing their understanding of mission.

This study demonstrates that migration is not only changing the face of Protestant Christianity in the United States; it is also affecting how Christians understand mission. The US churches and denominations, which have traditionally seen immigrants as objects of mission, are finding that these immigrants from the global south are establishing their own churches and are seeing themselves as missionaries. These churches are using their remittances not only to help their relatives and friends in their countries of origin. They are also following those same transnational networks to become involved in mission projects in the various countries of origin of which they are a part. These immigrants are not only taking their faith with them as they migrate, they are following their transnational networks to participate in Christian mission.

The Changing Face of Protestant Mission Work

The story of the modern Protestant missionary movement is one of missionaries from the centers of Christendom (mostly Europe and the United States) going out to the non-Christianized world preaching and inviting people to become Christians. Mission has been commonly understood as going beyond the borders of the Christian world, from the center to the periphery. It has also usually been understood as a task of those who had financial resources to those who are poor, or perceived to be poor. Though most missionaries made major sacrifices to go "to the ends of the earth" they usually served among people who were much poorer than them.

This model and understanding of mission became "normative" among Protestant missionaries during the modern missionary movement of the 18th, 19th, and 20th centuries. Mission was the task of those who had the means to do mission. The "missionized" poor might be able to do mission are some time in the future, but that future always seemed to be "in the future."

The modern Pentecostal movement expanded with an alternative model of mission. Most of the early missionaries that came out of the Azusa Street revival in Los Angeles did not fit the traditional Protestant mold. They were simple people who had an encounter with God and who decided to invite others to share in the experience. Many of the converts preached to their relatives, even if it meant returning to their home countries, particularly Mexico. (There were also some converts who went beyond "their own" and became transcultural missionaries.)

The Pentecostal movement has expanded from Los Angeles all around the world, mostly because of converts who have shared their experience with others. Pentecostals from around the world are now returning to Los Angeles, changing the face of the church, but also creating a new generation of Pentecostal missionaries from Los Angeles to the world.

Latino Pentecostal Immigrants as Transnational Missionaries

The five churches chosen for this study are not exceptional among Latino Pentecostal churches. Most of the churches in Los Angeles have some type of formal or informal transnational relationships with churches or ministries outside of the United States. The congregations in this study were chosen because they have clearly defined ongoing mission projects based on transnational familial and friendship network links. All five of the pastors have a US-based seminary education, which gives them tools to reflect on their experience based on migration theory and missiology.

A three-step process was followed with each congregation. First, the pastors were invited to write an initial self-study in which they described all of the transnational ministries in which their churches were involved and identified one project that best modeled what they hoped to accomplish as a church. Second, I visited the selected project with the pastor and key leaders from the Los Angeles congregation. While there I interviewed the key local leaders. In each case I was a participant observer. I preached during four of the trips, taught a pastoral seminar, and helped with a building project. In the third part of the process each of the pastors was invited to reflect on what their church was doing in light of migration theory and traditional Protestant missiology.[9] One of the goals of the third part was to give the pastors a new vocabulary to reflect on their ministry.

Misión El Redentor—Colonia Todos Santos

A congregation with people from many nations has multiple familial networks. But mission does not always follow the most obvious and direct links. Misión El Redentor has been committed to mission for many years, but its strongest link developed in a roundabout way.

Rev. Urías Mendoza completed his Master of Divinity at Fuller Theological Seminary and was a Doctor of Ministry student when he became a part of this study.[10] He is the pastor of Misión el Redentor, a network-based Assemblies of God church ministry in Monrovia, California. The congregation was founded in 1972 and has moved many times because of they have not been able to obtain a permanent building.[11] Currently the congregation has a regular attendance of about 100 adults. These people are from all over Latin America, including Brazil, though the pastor is from Nicaragua and about half the congregation has Mexican roots. (Interestingly for this project, many of the church members are involved in the house building industry.)[12]

Javier Villalobos migrated to Los Angeles in the 1980s. While in Los Angeles he had a conversion experience and worked alongside Ramón López in various ministry projects. Javier learned the building trade during his years in Los Angeles. Later both wandered from the faith for a while. Ramón got divorced and Javier was deported in 1998.

Javier ended up in Ensenada where his wife is from. While there he reaffirmed his faith commitment and he and his wife began a church in Colonia Todos Santos, a community of people who had migrated north hoping to work in the United States. The government zoned the area so that poor people could buy a small plot of land to build simple housing. Most of the people are very poor, so many live in makeshift houses made of discarded lumber, cardboard, and tarps. People hope to build more permanent housing, but many find it impossible to improve their situation due to limited resources.

Villalobos and his wife, Alba, started a church and developed a preschool and feeding program for the children of poor working families, who could not afford childcare. "We believe that faith is not something we have, but something we do," according to Villalobos. When he saw the housing situation he determined that God had given him building skills so that he could help the people of the area. With help from friends in the United States he had already built a simple church building and facilities for the preschool using wood frame construction that he had learned in Los Angeles, even though the common construction style in the area is concrete block. Villalobos developed an Asociación Civil (nonprofit civil association to legally handle donations), Manos en la Obra, so that they could receive financial support from both the United States and Mexico. They chose that name because "we want to put our hands at the service of the gospel and at the service of our needy people."

Villalobos developed a simple wood frame house model that could be built with less than $2500 worth of materials. His wife, who could travel legally to the United States, went to Los Angeles to contact friends and churches that might be interested in supporting this project. They made contact with María Bonilla, Ramón López's ex-wife, who had since remarried. She and her husband, Moisés Bonilla, began supporting the work of Manos en la Obra on a personal level. María informed Ramón, who had also remarried. Since then Ramón has become a member of Misión el Redentor. He invited the pastor to visit the project. After a visit from Alba Villalobos, the congregation decided to become a part and sent a group to Ensenada to take supplies and to help with various projects. According to Rev. Mendoza they decided to become a part because "we are collaborating with someone who already has the vision of helping the community. We like that very much."

Later the church decided to work with the church in Ensenada to build one house, called Proyecto Paola, because it was built for an ex-prostitute by the name of Paola. Since many of the members of the church are involved in the building trade, those who have legal documentation and can travel to Ensenada went to build one of the houses. Church members raised the funds through offerings and sales and the builders travelled to Ensenada on several weekends to work with local church builders to complete the house. The group includes people who are originally from Ensenada, people from several Central American countries, and even several people from Brazil. "Because we know what it is like to be poor we also know the joy that a person will have when they obtain their own home, to feel more secure" (Rev. Mendoza).

The congregation is one of several churches that have helped build sixteen houses, to date, and to help fund the preschool. Manos en la Obra has also bought a property near the church where they plan to develop a park for the children of Todos Santos. Another project that Misión El Redentor hopes to support is a rehab program for abused women.

Rev. Mendoza sees this project as a natural part of how the church views its ministry. Their members invite others to be part of their church through their family and friendship networks. According to Mendoza "many of our churches (Latino Assemblies of God) do this type of mission." They have followed these links to various parts of Mexico and anticipate following the pastor's familial links to work in Nicaragua in the future.

The first reading Rev. Mendoza makes of what is happening is theological. He is convinced that God is in the middle of the global migration movement. God is working through migrants, even those who have been deported. So that even "deportability" can be part of how God works through the undocumented.[13]

Immigrant and border officials make the task more complicated, but God even uses immigration officials to "move" people to those places where they can serve most effectively. Migration theory confirms for him that migrants are subjects of their own reality, even in the religious realm. Poor immigrants do not necessarily need to be the objects of mission of US churches; they can develop their own ministries and be key players in God's mission in the world. And though Misión El Redentor is a poor church it can work alongside other projects that have a clear missional vision, like they do. This makes it possible to avoid developing a dependency relationship between their "richer" church and the "poorer" congregation in Ensenada. "Since we do mission from the bottom up, we also do not need all the machinery, all that large organization, all those large budgets" that formal mission agencies need to function.

Misión El Redentor has finally obtained a building permit so will need to work on their own building during the next few months. But Rev. Mendoza anticipates that their church will expand their work with Manos en la Obra and also begin work in Nicaragua using his own familial links. By being open to what they understand as the Spirit's leading they have first done mission in a roundabout way, but anticipate following more direct links in the future. Their model of mission is not strategic; it is about following opportunities that develop.

Iglesia Palabra de Fe—Proyecto Angelito

Hugo Mora (Costa Rica) and Bertha Segura (Mexico) met in Los Angeles in a church pastored by Mora and were married in 1998.[14] By 2000 they were pastoring Iglesia Palabra de Fe, an independent Pentecostal congregation with links to the Church of God of the Prophecy, in Monrovia, California. During a visit to Bertha's family in Jiquilpan, Michoacán, Rev. Mora saw the needs of abandoned children in that city and proposed starting a program to meet those needs to Bertha's family. When they returned to Monrovia they also presented the idea to the congregation and convinced them that they should be a part.

Family and friends in Jiquilpan established an Asociación Civil (AC) named Proyecto Angelito (Project Little Angel) which refers to the children, but also to Angel Chávez Campos, an early supporter of the project who passed away. Bertha's mother donated a property to build an orphanage and feeding center for these children. The local church in Monrovia had a special dinner and raised $15,000 to begin the building project. Because Protestants are such a small minority in the region, there was strong initial opposition from the Catholic Church and the building project was stopped for several months. But eventually the city authorities allowed the project to continue. A couple was hired to direct the orphanage, and Mexican government officials helped them with the legal paperwork necessary to begin the orphanage. Family members also joined the team as cooks and support staff.

The orphanage continued for over a year, but had to close temporarily when the couple in charge was not able to continue leading it. The AC decided to continue the feeding center while they identified a new couple to lead the orphanage. They also continued building larger facilities on the site so as to be able to house more children once they hire new directors.

Proyecto Angelito has played an important role in the Jiquilpan area. The Protestant population is extremely small, only 12 small congregations, with a total of about 500 adult members in a region with a population of about 500,000. What is uncommon is that six of the congregations are oneness Pentecostals, including a congregation pastored by Bertha Mora's brother and another one where another brother is a member. Because of this it has been difficult for the congregations to work together, even though they are so small (several have less than 20 members). But because Hugo is from a Trinitarian church, and works well with the oneness churches, most of the other churches have been willing to work with Hugo and have developed several joint projects, including leadership development and evangelistic services. The local AC also hopes that some of their Catholic friends will become involved in Proyecto Angelito, because some of them have seen what is happening and have shown interest in giving to the project. The familial links have taken Rev. Mora and the congregation into areas where they never expected to be. But by following those networks they have arrived where they believe God wants them to be.

Iglesia Pentecostal Esmirna—Iglesia Pentecostal Yo Soy la Voz de uno que Clama en el Desierto

Iglesia Pentecostal Yo Soy la Voz de uno que Clama en el Desierto of San Luis Río Colorado, Sonora, was born in the second marriage of two older people.[15] It is a church planting project that includes a feeding program for poor children and that is also working with another project in the area to develop an after-school program for the children of neighborhood. Transnational mission became the natural response of people attentive to the need, following the relational links that their lives had created.

Ariel Fernández, who is originally from Cuba, married Mercedes, from San Luis, in Los Angeles. Ariel was retired and often travelled to Tijuana to help needy families. During a visit to Mercedes' family (2005) they discovered a newer colonia made up of people who had migrated north with hopes of entering the United States, but had ended up in the border town of San Luis. The city had zoned the area so that people could become owners of small plots of land for building a house with a minimal down payment. But the people there were all very poor. Ariel and Mercedes were touched by what they saw and they began to visit the area regularly, providing food and clothing to the people.

After several months of work they decided to build a church building to support a small congregation that was meeting in the area. Ariel and Mercedes, who were members of Iglesia Pentecostal Esmirna, an Assemblies of God congregation in Highland Park, presented the project to Pastor William Rodríguez, who is originally from El Salvador. Because Ariel was a faithful member, the congregation decided to support him. Since Ariel had been a builder he led the building project (interestingly, also using wood-frame construction). A church member, Roberto Savedra, was named director of missions, in charge of raised funds for San Luis. People from the Highland Park congregation traveled to San Luis to help with the construction and provided other funds for the ministry. Initially, they attempted to work with the AG of Mexico, but found that the requirements for working under the denomination would make their ministry impossible.

Every two or three months a core group travels to San Luis, often with other church members. According to Rev. Rodríguez "the first visit is almost always what I believe impacts them, it leaves a burden on their heart to return." The Highland Park church continues to support the work at the church. Churches' members raise funds, make pledges, and have sales. The teams that go take materials and help with specific projects. This is one of four projects funded by the church in this way.

The Fernández family decided to move to the San Luis area to work with the church and expand the ministry. The Highland Park congregation provides some financial support to the Fernándezes, but they are using retirement funds to support themselves. The newest project is a daily feeding center for poor children in the area. The Highland Park congregation has 200 adult members and assumes that they will need help from other congregations or people from other churches to fully fund the new project.

Pastor Rodríguez recognizes that their congregation is developing a multidirectional transnational network. People from Cuba, several Central American countries, and Mexico are working together in this project. "I [Rev. Rodríguez] do not know if it is because we live in Los Angeles where we live among so many people from Mexico (my wife is also Mexican), but for me going to Mexico is almost like going to my people. I believe that maybe the experience of being Latino in the United States causes me to do mission in Mexico very differently than if I came from El Salvador to do mission in Mexico. I would feel like a stranger as a Salvadoran in Mexico. But because I am in Los Angeles and we live among some many people from Mexico, we travel to Mexico and we feel like we are a part and not so strange, at least that is my perspective."

The key leader is a layperson that would never qualify as a missionary if the followed AG protocol. Yet the church is convinced that God is working through this "unqualified" layperson, even though they support denominational projects and believe in the importance of educated leaders. Their Pentecostal sense of evangelistic urgency makes it important to go forward when someone has a sense of God's call.

But Pastor Rodríguez recognizes the danger of creating dependency. Even though they are a poor church they know that the people they are helping are poorer than they are. He knows that members of his church send remittances to Latin America and sometimes create dependency among their friends and family. Yet, since he was once poor, he feels they are best prepared to avoid dependency. They work, not principally from a sense of compassion for the poor, but of identification with the poor.

The fact that they are small and are immigrants is not seen as any type of deficiency. They are convinced that God is working through them and that God has often used immigrants in what He is doing in the world. The fact that they are also poor makes them particularly apt to work among the poor. According to Rodríguez: "Migration is a way of doing mission that is not intentional, but there is movement and [mission] is being done...As people come from Latin America to the United States, to reside here, they live their lives here but do not forget the people over there and they return. This has created an opportunity to do a different type of mission."

Ministerio A la Luz de la Palabra—Iglesia Rey de Reyes y Señor de Señores

Iglesia Rey de Reyes y Señor de Señores in El Salvador (Caserío El Cerezo, Cantón Nancistepeque, Dept. Santa Ana) is linked to Ministerio A la Luz de la Palabra (Assemblies of God) in Compton, California, through a father-and-son relationship.[16] Vicente Salamanca came to Los Angeles after a failed marriage in El Salvador. Here he had a conversion experience and became a lay pastor with his new wife, Marina. They began a church in 1995, but soon decided to return to El Salvador. Vicente followed his own relational links and left the congregation under the responsibility of his son, Mario Salamanca (the current pastor).

Vicente and Marina returned to Marina's hometown. There they sensed from God that they needed to start a church and ministry to help the poor of the area. They began working in 2000. In 2006 several of Vicente's children,

Mario and some who live in El Salvador, helped them put together the down payment for the current church property. Vicente made several trips to Los Angeles to earn some extra income and to raise offerings for the project at the church pastored by Mario.

Though most of the congregation has roots in Mexico, the church in Compton followed their pastors' relational links and decided to formally adopt the congregation in El Salvador as a mission project. They sent a work team to help them put a block fence around the property and set up an open-air meeting area. Rogelio Romero, a Mexican immigrant, went with the group and returned ready to spearhead the support. He is now the mission director and works with the Compton congregation to raise funds by having car washes and selling pupusas and tamales. "I [Rogelio] find it incredible because if I had written the story of my life I do not think that any of the paragraphs would have included where I am walking now, specifically in El Salvador . . . It is a privilege for me because I can call this project mine because it was born in my heart."

Their goal is to help the congregation complete a church building and to help them start an after-school tutoring program by paying for a Salvadoran teacher to work with the local church. They also anticipate starting a program to provide basic services to the extremely poor of the region. An interesting unintended consequence has been that the congregation in El Salvador has become a point of unity among the various Protestant churches of the area. Most of them are independent and they have found in Vicente and Mario Salamanca leaders that they trust, so they are now developing a number of projects together.

The congregation in Compton is composed largely of people who earn little more than the minimum wage. According to Rev. Mario Salamanca the average income of this church of about 150 members is less than $20,000 a year; nonetheless, "they feel they are rich giving something to the work of the Lord." Though most of the church people are originally from Mexico, they have made this project their own. The congregation also supports other projects in Mexico, but currently this is their principal commitment.

Interestingly, the church in Compton has never owned a building and has had to move many times, as they have lost leases. They see themselves as a migrant church even in the sense of needing to constantly find a new meeting place. That constant movement has created a sense that they are "pilgrims" and that God is calling them to serve without significant resources. Yet, they are committed to making sure that the congregation in El Salvador has its own facilities.

According to Rev. Mario Salamanca the congregation in Compton supports denominational mission projects of the Assemblies of God, but this project is "theirs." It is his perception that they would never be able to do what they are doing if they had to go through the denominational missionary structure.

This project follows the north-south movements of the Salamanca family, but has also begun to include people who are not originally from El Salvador, such as Rogelio. Pastor Mario is very proud of the commitment of his church and he sees them as subjects of God's mission in the world. Though, because of his seminary education, he recognizes that sometimes they work with more zeal than strategy and that this may not always be the best way to do mission. Nonetheless, says Mario, "a Pentecostal wants to feel useful. Pentecostalism, the gospel as we see it, at least, gives us potential, gives us the idea that we have the capacity to do what we can, that God blesses us and that this pleases God. So this, then, is a combination of theology, and maybe even eschatology and the Pentecostal concept."

Centro Familiar Cristiano—Asamblea Apostólica, Cancún

The Apostolic Assembly of the Faith in Christ Jesus is a Latino denomination that was born among the "Mexican" converts at the Azusa Street revival. They have been involved in network-based transnational mission work into Mexico since early in the 20th century. According to Bishop Ismael Martín del Campo, the Apostolic Assembly and its sister denomination the Apostolic Church of Mexico have been most successful in mission when they have followed this model.[17]

Bishop Martín serves the national denomination as bishop in charge of Christian Education. But he is also the pastor of Centro Familiar Cristiano (South Gate), an Apostolic Assembly congregation of about 300 members. The membership is 70% either Mexican or Mexican-Americans.

Bishop Martín is originally from Mexico City and still has relatives there. He grew up in the Apostolic Church of Mexico and joined the Apostolic Assembly when he moved to the United States. Six years ago, he proposed to his brother Elicio that he become part of a church-planting project in Mexico City, something they planned for 2004.

During a vacation trip to Cancún, Quintana Roo, Bishop Martín saw the need among the new immigrants to the city. He encouraged his brother to move to Cancún and study the possibility of starting a church among the new migrants to the city. Soon after he arrived Hurricane Wilma hit the region (October 2005). The church in South Gate worked with Elicio to provide emergency help and supplies to people who suffered losses because of the hurricane. Through the contacts made because of this help a congregation was started.[18]

The church in South Gate committed itself to providing Elicio with minimal financial support and they helped the new congregation obtain a meeting place. The Apostolic Assembly had not previously had churches in the area. But Ismael and Elicio had several friends and acquaintances in Quintana

Roo who had an Apostolic background. Through the initial work with Elicio and subsequent contacts a number of these people also became involved in church planting in the state. The Apostolic Assembly now has six congregations in Quintana Roo and a Bible Institute. The congregation in South Gate is committed to continue supporting the congregation started by Elicio until it completes its building. Bishop Martín also hopes that the Bible Institute will become the basis for a national training program of the Apostolic Assembly in Mexico.

The Apostolic Assembly is the only Pentecostal denomination that has made network-based mission work a key part of their mission effort. Their sister denomination, the Apostolic Church in Mexico, was started by Mexicans Ramonita de Valenzuela and Antonio Nava who returned to Mexico from the Azusa Street revival to preach to their relatives. Because of the migration patterns between the United States and Mexico this model served to start many churches in both Mexico and the United States. (Mary I. O'Conner has studied this pattern among Apostolics in Santa Barbara County.[19])

According to Bishop Martín the history of the Apostolic Assembly is about this type of transnational mission. Up to about 1980 all congregations started this way in Mexico were later joined to the Apostolic Church, based on an agreement between both groups. Once the agreement lapsed the Apostolic Assembly started organizing new churches as part of the Assembly. Since that time the Assembly has started 150 churches, mostly in Mexico, though also a few in El Salvador, through this method. "Any person that says 'I have a relative and I want to go share' does not have to have a ministerial position, they just take a Bible study there. If they have success it is very common for the pastor to assign a deacon and that begins to develop. Sometimes the pastor himself embraces this and begins to visit [the area]."

The Apostolic Assembly sees itself as following the model of the book of Acts. They usually do not train people to become church planting missionaries; "it is in the apostolic subconscious." The common church planting model is that a convert in the United States senses a need to preach to their relatives in their country of origin. Variants on this model are when people are deported or when someone decides to return to their hometown, be it for mission or because they decide not to remain in the United States. According to Rev. Martín del Campo "any time someone was deported from the United States, he or she immediately understood that they had to go and share or participate in the formation of a church." They travel on their own initiative, so there is no expense to the church or denomination. If a Bible study develops the person invites their US pastor to visit.

The US pastor and church decide whether or not to support the new project. If they go forward the congregation takes on the responsibility of providing funds for a building and potentially for some limited pastoral support. These churches raise funds through food sales or similar projects. The method used depends "on the vision of the pastor. For example, it is common that the pastor will decide to designate funds generated from a kitchen commission or from a specific vending machine or that a specific commission raise funds for the project. This is to support what we usually call our mission, our work... Others take it out of the general fund."

Congregations in the United States know that their goal is to help the young congregation become established as a self-supporting church. Therefore, financial support is specific and short term, though with no set period. Once the congregation is ready to be recognized as a church then the local bishop is informed and the church is joined to the denomination.

The Apostolic Assembly has seen this model work in other parts of the world where they have been able to follow familial or network links. When they have used the "traditional" missionary model the results have been much more limited, though Bishop Martín is sure that this model is necessary in secularized societies or in places where they do not have existing links. But both the Apostolic Assembly and its sister denomination, the Apostolic Church, are the result of mission efforts that followed familial and relational links into Mexico and later into Central and South America.

How Latino Pentecostal Immigrants are Redefining Protestant Mission

Latino Pentecostals from the south are subjects of their own reality and do mission from that perspective. Though most Protestants in the United States see them as objects of mission, they perceive themselves as subjects of God's mission in the world. God has worked in their lives and has called them to be subjects of their own reality. From their perspective global migration is one of the ways that God is working in the world, and migrants are one of God's tools for mission in the world. Because of this understanding, they do not assume that mission has to be from the center to the periphery or from rich to poor. They never "got the memo" about needing to be rich to do mission. These Christians are following a model of mission that has become common among migrants from the south.

These churches do not minister in a geographic parish. They follow the networks of their people to serve and minister. Because they are transnational people, their networks cross national borders. They do not see a fundamental difference between their local networks and their international ones. Therefore, they have no problems crossing international borders in their mission projects as they respond to needs, nor is that move seen as something different than when they work more locally.

From the perspective of these people, international borders are a nuisance, but they do not define mission. These are transnational people who follow their transnational networks. Because they are migrants they sometimes have to deal with immigration officials, particularly if they have "creative" paperwork. They live transnational lives, sometimes as a matter of choice and sometimes when they are deported. National laws obligate them to take borders into account when they plan their mission efforts and sometimes make their work more complicated. But because home and host society (and sometimes other societies) have become a "single arena of social action," national borders do not define their ministry.[20] In many cases these projects have not only taken people back to their countries of origin, they have also encouraged them to venture into new countries, as their networks expand because of the new links created in Los Angeles.

This is not a new model of mission among Latino Pentecostals, though it is becoming more common as Latino Pentecostalism continues to grow in the Los Angeles area. The Apostolic Assembly (United States) and Apostolic Church (Mexico) have used this as one of their principal methods of church planting since they began almost 100 years ago in the Los Angeles area. Most US-based Pentecostal groups have "traditional" missionaries, but a large number of Latino churches from these denominations have these types of ministry efforts "on the side."

These poor people do mission very organically, following familial and network links. They do not follow strategic plans, but what they understand as the leading of the Spirit. They do mission in much the same way that they send remittances to their families and friends. These networks are "permeable, expanding, and fluid" and so become an effective way to experiment with mission projects, particularly with short-term, concise projects.[21] The Apostolics have incorporated the model into their mission strategy, but the pastors from the other denominations sense that they would never get these projects off the ground if they followed denominational protocol.

Denominational structures on both sides of the border find it difficult to integrate these projects in ways that make sense to the people involved. Though all of the churches in Los Angeles are linked to denominations, most of them do these projects "off the books" denominationally, on both sides of the border.

These projects reflect the impact of economic globalization. All of them exist because of emigration to the United States and/or internal migration (particularly Cancún, San Luis, and Ensenada) of people looking for better economic opportunities. The region around the church in El Salvador was particularly impacted because the farms in the region cannot compete with the subsidized agriculture of the United States.

Because this is mission from the poor to the poor they are able to avoid many of the problems of dependency common among Protestant mission projects in Latin America. The local congregation or project is expected to take some level of economic responsibility from the beginning.

An interesting side note is that these projects seem to be able to serve as means for unity among the local churches. These new works do not seem to be perceived as threats to the existing churches. Quite the contrary, in several places the LA-based leaders are seen as fair power brokers and are trusted when they call local churches to work together.

The lay leaders have limited mission expertise, so they have not always thought through the implications of their impact. But because they have long-term relationships with the local population some of the potential negative impact seems to get absorbed in the process of walking together.

Even as these transnational people are blurring and reconstructing the concept of a territorialized "national" identity, they are also reconstructing the traditional sense of Protestant mission that has framed its work based on the nation-state. They are living and doing mission in a world that may not yet be totally deterritorialized, but certainly one that is territorialized in very different ways than the traditional nation-state. [22]

Conclusion

Pentecostalism expanded from Los Angeles through people who experienced the revival at Azusa Street and decided to go around the world to share what they had experienced and to invite others into that experience. They were not trained missionaries and most went out without any church or agency supporting them. Many of the "Mexicans" that participated in the Azusa Street revival returned to their country of origin to preach to their friends and relatives.

Latino Pentecostal immigrants continue that model, breaking the mold of how to do Protestant missions. Though traditional Protestant missions will continue being done, most church growth around the world will come from informal missionaries, like those in this study.

The migration of a new generation of Latino Pentecostals to Los Angeles is changing how ministry and mission are being defined in Los Angeles, even though they are also part of the periphery, like their theological ancestors 100 years ago. Because these are the types of groups that are growing in Los Angeles today they are changing the face of the church in Southern California. Even as the traditional churches in Los Angeles, and the United States, continue to shrink, churches like these Pentecostal congregations will become more normative of what it means to be a Christian in Los Angeles and around the world.

Notes

1. Caroline B. Brettell and James F. Hollifield, eds., *Migration Theory: Talking Across Disciplines* (New York: Routledge, 2007) includes several articles and references that demonstrate how newer studies of immigrants are not merely looking at their adaptation or assimilation, but are also recognizing the importance of the transnational links they are developing.

2. Jehu Hanciles, *Beyond Christendom: Globalization, African Migration, and the Transformation of the West* (Maryknoll, NY: Orbis Books, 2008).

3. Manuel Vásquez and Marie Friedmann Marquardt, *Globalizing the Sacred: Religion across the Americas* (Piscataway, NJ: Rutgers University Press, 2003).

4. Karen Leonard, Alex Stepick, Manuel Vásquez, and Jennifer Holdaway, eds., *Immigrant Faiths Transforming Religious Life in America* (Lanham, MD: Altamira Press, 2005).

5. Peggy Levitt, *God Needs No Passport: Immigrants and the Changing Religious Landscape* (New York: The New Press, 2007).

6. Olga Odgers Ortiz and Juan Carlos Ruiz Guadalajara, eds., *Migración y Creencias Pensar en las Religiones en Tiempo de Movilidad* (Tijuana: El Colegio de la Frontera Norte and San Luis Potosí: El Colegio de San Luis, 2009).

7. Center for Religion and Civic Culture, University of Southern California, 2001. Project funded by the John Randolph Haynes and Dora Haynes Foundation.

8. I decided to work with pastors who had a seminary education because I wanted them to be able to interact with migration theory and its implications for how they understand their task.

9. Due to personal problems Rev. Hugo Mora was not able to participate in the third part of the process.

10. He completed his D.Min. and graduated in June 2011.

11. That is now changing since they obtained a building and the permits to begin remodeling.

12. This section is based on interviews with Urías Mendoza (April 14, 2011, in Pasadena), Ramón López (August 27, 2010, in Ensenada), and Javier Villalobos (August 27, 2010, in Ensenada). It also uses information from the self-study Rev. Mendoza wrote during the first-stage self-assessment. I also visited Manos en la Obra on August 27 and 28, 2010, and helped with the building project of the Proyecto Paola house and gave a financial donation to the project.

13. Nicholas De Genova argues that "deportability" is an important function of the US legal system that seeks to regulate the flow of migrants (*Working the Boundaries: Race, Space and "Illegality" in Mexican Chicago* [Durham: Duke University Press, 2007], 8). Latino Pentecostals like Rev. Mendoza see God using even this in the process of working through migrants.

14. This section is based on interviews with Jesús Núñez (October 20, 2010, in Jiquilpan, Michoacán), María Luisa Segura (October 20, 2010, in Jiquilpan, Michoacán), Leonel Segura (October 20, 2010, in Totolán, Michoacán) and Elvira Zacarías (October 20, 2010, in Totolán, Michoacán). It also uses information from the self-study Rev. Mora wrote during the first-stage self-assessment. I also visited Proyecto Angelito on October 19–21, 2010. I also led a seminar for most of the pastors in the región at the church in Totolán led by Leonel Seguro.

15. This section is based on interviews with Ariel Fernández (July 31, 2010, in San Luis Río Colorado), William Rodríguez (September 3, 2010, and April 11, 2011, in Pasadena, CA) and Roberto Savedra (September 3, 2010, in Pasadena, CA). It also uses information from the self-study Rev. Rodríguez wrote during the first-stage self-assessment. I also visited the congregation and preached at the church on July 31 and August 1, 2010.

16. This section is based on interviews with Mario Salamanca (June 9, 2010, and April 28, 2011, in Pasadena, CA), Vicente Salamanca (June 9, 2010, in Pasadena, CA), Marina Alcira Salamanca (October 31, 2010, in El Salvador) and Rogelio Romero Méndez

(Oct. 31, 2010, in El Salvador). It also uses information from the self-study Rev. Salamanca wrote during the first-stage self-assessment. I also visited the congregation in El Salvador during anniversary services on October 29–31, 2010.

17. See "Un esbozo de lectura misionológica sobre la Asamblea Apostólica" by Ismael Martín del Campo. Unpublished document, 2011.

18. This section is based on interviews with Ismael Martín del Campo (October 9, 2010, in Cancún and April 21, 2011, in Pasadena, CA) and Elicio Martín del Campo (October 7, 2010, in Cancún). It also uses information from the self-study the bishop wrote during the first-stage self-assessment. I also visited two of the congregations in the Cancún area and taught a course in the Bible Institute October 7–10, 2010.

19. "La Iglesia/Asamblea Apostólica: una iglesia transnacional" in Ortiz and Guadalajara, *Migración y Creencias*, pp. 485–502.

20. Caroline B. Brettell, "Theorizing Migration in Anthropology: The Social Construction of Networks, Identities, Communities, and Globalscapes" in Brettell and Hollifield, *Migration Theory*, p. 120.

21. Ibid., p. 124.

22. Ibid., p. 123.

SECTION SIX

GENDERED PENTECOSTALISM

From its beginning, Pentecostalism has been much more welcoming of women and people of color in its leadership ranks than its evangelical and fundamentalist cousins. As has been noted elsewhere in this volume, the Azusa Street Revival was led by an African American minister, and many of the participants and missionaries who went out from Azusa Street were women and people of color. Yet fairly early on in the development of Pentecostalism, different denominations were formed around racial and ethnic identities and, with some few exceptions, many of the efforts spearheaded by women were taken over by men as they became successful, self-sustaining mission organizations. Thus Pentecostalism has somewhat of a mixed record in regard to the role of women in churches and other organizations. As such, scholars have raised questions about just what role gender plays in global Pentecostalism, asking, for example, whether it actually allows women more freedom and individual agency than other competing religious movements.

Estrelda Alexander sets the stage for thinking about the role of gender within Pentecostalism by providing a broader historiographical view of the role of women since its emergence in 1906. Alexander profiles 11 women from different spheres and eras of global Pentecostalism, each of whom managed to avoid having their efforts taken over by men, at least until they either stepped down of their own accord or passed away. In this, she demonstrates that women were not only present at the beginning of the global Pentecostal movement, but also were crucial to its formation and development around the globe. She argues that although the contribution of women is starting to be recognized by scholars, there is still much to be done to uncover how they managed to negotiate the gendered religious territory and remain in control of their mission activities.

Utilizing two case studies from Pentecostal groups in South Africa, Katherine Attanasi takes up the more recent question regarding how gender currently operates within global Pentecostalism. She focuses on two questions that scholars of Pentecostalism and gender have pursued: first, whether Pentecostalism has a feminine or masculine ethos; and second, whether Pentecostalism is good or bad for women. In this second question are included arguments that characterize Pentecostalism as either a regressive fundamentalist movement or one that empowers women. Attanasi points to the importance of paying attention to the sociocultural contexts within which women's lives are lived, in order to make conclusions about these questions. She argues that Pentecostalism should not be essentialized as either masculine or feminine, but rather that studies should focus on how it may contribute to women's "agency, flourishing, and freedom," within their particular sociocultural and religious context. Thus for Attanasi, whether Pentecostalism has a particularly gendered ethos, or whether it holds women back or empowers them, is contingent on their particular context and experiences.

Together these chapters provide a good perspective on current issues and debates among scholars of Pentecostalism and gender and offer an excellent starting place for other studies that seek to unravel the relationship between the two. For example, what are the specific conditions under which women in Pentecostal churches are able to flourish? And what conditions were necessary for the women described by Alexander to be able to hold on to the ministry organizations they founded while many other women had to give up control of their organizations once they became viable operations?

11

Beautiful Feet

Women Leaders and the Shaping of Global Pentecostalism

ESTRELDA ALEXANDER

> *How lovely on the mountains*
> *Are the feet of [the one] who brings good news,*
> *Who announces peace*
> *And brings good news of happiness,*
> *Who announces salvation,*
> *And says to Zion, "Your God reigns!"*

—Isaiah 52:7

The predominance of male voices within a dynamic Christian tradition often characterized as among the most egalitarian within modern Christian history is unmistakable. No less striking is the privileged position of American voices in the stories of a global movement whose roots draw from every corner of the earth. Understandably, these particular biases could initially be traced to the predominance of Anglo-American male scholars in developing the movement's earliest historical record. Within the last several decades, however, that sustained prominence has given way to more balanced portrayals of the variety of contributors from other constituencies. In this emerging shift, the inclusion of previously marginalized voices has significantly enriched a once flat narrative and provided a fuller, more authentic portrait of the phenomenal growth of the movement.

Certainly, the genuine contribution from North America, generally, and from Los Angeles, specifically, cannot be ignored. In some respects, the city's Azusa Street mission served as an authentic center, as seekers flowed in and out of it, imbibing the spiritual fervor of its fires and spreading its embers onto the ashes of souls that had long seemed to have grown spiritually cold. However, a balanced portrait of the movement's unfolding reveals the faithful not only going out from Azusa Street, or even the United States, but also coming to the United States, with flames still warm from other centers of revival that were breaking out in locations that most of the Azusa Street faithful would never see.

Of course the rich contribution of the numerous men whose names have become synonymous with early Pentecostalism in the United should not be overlooked. Their efforts were significant within the explosive spiritual climate that fueled the rapid spread of the Pentecostal movement. Yet no less deserving of mention are the numerous women in the United States and other parts of the world who undertook their exploits at a time when Pentecostalism was scorned by respectable people as a religion strictly for the disinherited and marginalized.

Over the last several decades, as the movement has gained global prominence and respectability, an abundance of primary resources from pioneering leaders and their followers has become known. Scholars and laypeople have also developed numerous secondary sources to help interpret Pentecostalism for a wider audience. Together, these sources highlight the significance of Pentecostal spirituality for the broader Christian tradition, especially in the arenas of missions and revivalism. Still, the majority of this material focuses on the contribution of North American men, to the neglect of the sizeable contribution of women and those from other cultures who have participated in every phase of the growth of Pentecostalism.

Neither the international import of the Pentecostal revival nor the significance of women's role was lost to the believers at Azusa Street. Even before the revival began in earnest, while Seymour was still holding prayer meetings at the Bonnie Brae Street house,[1] women made up the bulk of the faithful. Soon after the revival moved into full swing, women were involved in every aspect— they preached, led worship, prayed with unbelievers for salvation, and prayed with believers for Holy Spirit baptism and divine healing. They served in church administration—on the ministerial board, as editors of the newspaper, and as overseers of new works. After a few months, when the mission began publication of the *Apostolic Faith* newsletter, reports poured in from around the world about miraculous outpourings of the Spirit, healings and other signs and wonders. Many of these reports were from women who acted as freelance correspondents, regularly filing stories to the newspaper reporting personal testimonies, revivals, and other similar events.

In these earliest days, women were active as both indigenous leaders and missionaries on every continent where the force of renewal was felt. They moved out across the United States, sometime alone, sometimes as members of husband-and-wife teams, sometimes as members of or at the head of evangelistic teams, spreading the message of Pentecostal Spirit-baptism. They preached in camp meetings and revivals, to small congregations and large crowds, in rural townships and in large cities. Their collective ministry garnered thousands of converts to Pentecostal faith and left in its wake new congregations of every type. Still, their pioneering exploits have been largely neglected in the movement's historiographical record.

This chapter focuses on the important contributions of women to global Pentecostalism. In the first part of the chapter, I outline the role of key women at the Azusa Street Revival and how they launched out from that revival onto the evangelistic trail to touch most corners of the globe. Following the brief background, I survey the lives and ministries of eleven women missionaries, evangelists, and teachers from very different spheres. Some women were contemporary with Azusa Street, yet had little knowledge of that revival, while others came on the scene at a later period. Yet all shared a sense that they were drinking from the same well of Pentecostal spirituality and constructed ministries that dynamically engaged the empowerment of their experience of Pentecostal Spirit-baptism to accomplish deeds for God.

Each of these women are significant because their work had a lasting impact on the growth of Pentecostalism in arenas where it might not have otherwise flourished—or at least, not as quickly as it did. The ministries, schools, churches, and denominations they founded are still viable institutions today. These women would not settle for the narrow roles often proscribed for them as the movement drifted away from its egalitarian roots. They did not generally seek permission to carry out what they saw as their God-ordained missions, but decided for themselves what God had called them to do and did it—with or, as often, without the support of male colleagues or denominational infrastructure. Their examples stand as a testimony that early Pentecostal women were not only capable of playing a supportive role in ministry, but also could successfully head organizations in a culture that often relegated women to secondary or very minor roles and generally reserved leadership roles for men.

Importantly, each of these women escaped a common pattern that developed within early Pentecostal culture in which once a woman had founded a ministry and brought it to some semblance of viability, it was taken over by a denominational leader. As new works grew to any size that could economically sustain the leader's support—as well as other financial obligations—denominational leaders often replaced the woman leader with a man. These leaders then sent the woman to another community to dig out another new work. Over several decades, a woman might start or renew several congregations, missions, or institutions in this manner, but would never be allowed to take any of them past that point. The women that I highlight in this narrative, however, were able to hold on to the institutions they built until they decided to step down or died. In this way, they carried their visions through to the point that they could leave their lasting imprint on the work that they started.

Telling the stories of these women is what theologian Elisabeth Schüssler Fiorenza would call an act of recovery.[2] It allows us to understand that women always played a vital part—not just a minor role—in the growth of global Pentecostal spirituality. Through their stories, we can better understand the ways that women worked to build the Pentecostal movement and correct the perspective that women were God's second choice, achieving ministries of only minor impact, employed only when men were not available.

From Azusa Street

As early as the Azusa Street Revival, home and foreign missionary endeavors were a central focus of Pentecostal ministry, with women an important element of those efforts. Within months of the revival's outbreak, several teams fanned out across the continent and the world taking with them the message of Pentecostal Spirit-empowerment. Many of the same women who had been integral to the revival's internal workings now found themselves as integral members of these teams.

For example, Lucy Farrow knew William Seymour in Houston, Texas, before he moved to Los Angeles and provided two important introductions for Seymour. First, Farrow introduced Seymour to the experience of speaking in tongues when he witnessed her engaging in the practice in a worship service at the little Holiness congregation she pastored. Secondly, she introduced Seymour to Charles Fox Parham. Once the Azusa Street Revival got underway, Farrow left Parham to join Seymour where she became one of the most important women in the early days of the revival. She left Azusa Street for a while, moving across the country to hold revivals in a number of cities and plant two congregations in Virginia. Afterward she led a team of missionaries to Liberia, where she was, reportedly, able to use her xenolalic[3] gift to preach in the Kru language.

Another woman central to Azusa Street was Julia Hutchins, who issued the original invitation that brought Seymour to Los Angeles. Although she was initially opposed to his teachings, she introduced Seymour to local Los Angeles Holiness leaders who generally agreed with her assessment and asked Seymour to refrain from causing discord within Holiness congregations through his teachings. Hutchins was eventually won over to Seymour's understanding of Pentecostal Spirit-baptism and to the Azusa Street Revival. As a result, she traveled as a missionary, preaching in several cities across the United States before leading an evangelistic team that took the Pentecostal message to Liberia.

Other Azusa Street women such as Lucy Leatherman led missionary expeditions to seemingly exotic lands such as Israel/Palestine and Egypt.

After joining the Church of God, Leatherman moved to Chile and Argentina to help to establish the denomination in that region. Other women who came out of Azusa Street were part of husband-wife teams. Some, such as Mexican immigrants Abundio and Rosa de Lopez, remained relatively close to home. The couple was probably among the first Hispanics to visit the Azusa Street Mission. Once there, they became active in its ministry, holding street worship services in the Hispanic sections of Los Angeles and in their adopted hometown of San Diego. For a short period, Rosa was sidelined with a debilitating tumor, but was healed through the ministry of famed evangelist Maria-Woodward Etta, who herself had moved from the Holiness movement into the embrace of Pentecostalism. The couple later pastored one of the budding Los Angeles Hispanic Pentecostal congregations.

May Evans had been the first white women among a "group of colored people" to speak in tongues at the Bonnie Brae Street prayer meeting that preceded the Azusa Street Revival. Her testimony and several stories about her and her husband's ministry appear in the 1906 fall and winter editions of the *Apostolic Faith* newspaper. She worked with her husband, G. W., primarily in the northwestern United States, accompanying Florence Crawford as members of her evangelistic teams. Though G. W. was the more prominent preacher among the pair, May was always at his side assisting in the ministry of prayer and altar work.

Lillian Anderson Garr, the daughter of a Methodist Bishop and Asbury College board member, was initially repelled by the "uncouth" atmosphere surrounding the revival. But she eventually acquiesced to the request of her husband, A. G. Garr, to attend one meeting to see the goings-on. Within weeks, the couple had each individually received a Pentecostal Spirit-baptism, and they were ready to assume their evangelistic ministry. After a short series of revival meetings in Danville, Virginia, they embarked on a missionary tour that would take them to India and China.

Lillian was actively involved in preaching and teaching alongside her husband and was an advocate for women's rights in China. She was also committed to actively seeking social reform regarding some of the harsher practices of Chinese culture related to women such as foot binding. In Hong Kong, she challenged the tradition through her preaching and by confronting the Chinese and British governments until she convinced both the people and the British government to outlaw the practice in that colony.[4] Her story exemplifies the heavy personal toll early missionaries often paid. While on the mission field, she lost two daughters and a nurse to smallpox. She, herself, was only thirty-eight years old when she died from complications from an operation.

To the World

Pandita Ramabai (1858–1922)

The Garrs' work in India was not the initial foray of Pentecostalism into that country. Several months before the Azusa Street Revival got underway, a revival broke out in Mukti Mission,[5] in Western India, that was characterized by people being slain in the Spirit and experiencing a burning sensation tagged as "the Holy Ghost and fire." This meeting was led by a woman who did not perceive herself primarily as a religious leader, and it is not in that arena that she is most remembered. As a young girl, Pandita Ramabai's father, a devoted Hindu, defied Indian culture by teaching his daughter to read and write, and she became a Sanskrit scholar. While a student in England in the late 1870s, Ramabai had a conversion experience. She was already a social reformer who used her position as a woman of standing within the Brahmin upper caste to champion the cause of women and children among India's poor.

Ramabai led an explosive revival in her mission that unfolded at the same time that Azusa Street was getting underway, although there is no indication that this was precipitated by events in Los Angeles. The mission was home to abandoned women and young children, among whom the revival broke out, the fervor of which rivaled that of the Los Angeles meeting. Young Indian women had the same intense experiences as many in America. They saw visions, fell into trances, and spoke in tongues. Ramabai saw the outpouring at her compound as the Holy Spirit creating an independent Indian Christianity. Like Azusa Street, the revival in Mukti was sustained and intense, as day after day seekers come into "fullness of blessing." Some of the young women received the gift of healing, which they exercised by visiting the hospital and praying for the sick.

Ramabai, as other early Pentecostal leaders, was linked to the Azusa Revival through the *Apostolic Faith* newspaper. More than one article detailing the miraculous occurrences and spiritual intensity in Mukti graced its pages from time to time.[6] Just as at Azusa Street, missionaries went out from Mukti after receiving their Pentecostal blessing, carrying the message of the revival to other communities throughout the region and seeing many converted to the Christian faith.

Ramabai's revival lasted only several months, but her work in India lasted for several decades. Her ministry at the Mukti compound however was comprised of elementary and secondary schools, a Bible institute, an industrial school, a printing office, and a hospital. At the time of the revival, about 1,400 female students were enrolled. It is for that work, rather than for her spiritual influence, that most of the world acknowledges her. In 1989, the Indian government acknowledged Ramabai's contribution to social reform in that nation by issuing a commemorative postage stamp in her honor.

Minnie Abrams (1859–1912)

In 1887, the Woman's Foreign Missionary Society of the Methodist Church commissioned American evangelist and revivalist Minnie Abrams as a "deaconess-missionary" and deployed her to India where she expected to be involved in evangelistic efforts to reach the Indian community with the Gospel. Instead, her male colleagues, convinced mission work was their domain and that women should be relegated to support roles, assigned Abrams to teaching the children of other missionaries. For the next ten years she faithfully carried out that assignment during the day, but in the evenings, she independently ministered to people of all ages in the opium dens of the city.

Finally, after a decade of attempting to balance the expectations of her colleagues and her desire to be fully engaged in ministry, Abrams moved 100 miles away to join Ramabai at the Mukti Mission for an opportunity to openly pursue evangelistic ministry and help train hundreds of Indian women as evangelists. Abrams was working at Mukti when the 1905 Pentecostal revival occurred there. Shortly after that, she began traveling with "praying bands" of young women to hold services and spread the "fire of the revival" to other mission stations. News of her activities appeared in two major Christian newspapers in India, the *Bombay Guardian* and the *Christian Patriot*. The Methodist periodical *The Indian Witness* also tracked her ministry. She sent her 1906 publication, *The Baptism of the Holy Ghost and Fire*, to her friends Willis and May Hoover, Methodist missionaries in Chile, and it fueled interest in Pentecostalism in Chile. Methodist churches in Valparaiso and Santiago prayed for and expected a similar revival, which began in 1909, and led to Willis becoming the leader of the new Chilean Methodist Pentecostal Church. Her publication deemphasized the Holy Spirit as providing languages for the mission field and emphasized this baptism as an outflow of missionary love, holiness, and zeal.[7] Her work, which preceded the writings of Charles Fox Parham, is considered the first written Pentecostal theology of Spirit-baptism.[8]

Leaving India in 1908 for a promotional tour in the United States, Abrams preached at many important centers of Pentecostal activity, including Carrie Judd Montgomery's Home of Peace in Oakland, California; Upper Room Mission in Los Angeles; Stone Church in Chicago; the regional camp meeting at Homestead, Pennsylvania; and the headquarters of the Christian Workers Union in Massachusetts. In 1910, several women from the United States accompanied Abrams back to India where she founded the Bazaleel Evangelistic Mission, the only known Pentecostal women's missionary society. Upon her return to India, Abrams had a premonition that her missionary work would be complete within two years. She died from malaria in 1912.

Ellen Wharton Hebden (?–1923)

At the age of fifteen, Ellen Wharton had a conversion experience and came under the teachings of the Keswick Holiness movement regarding cultivating a "higher Christian life" and seeking the "fullness of the Spirit." That year, Wharton sensed the Holiness experience of sanctification that she described as a "bright conversion" in which the Lord "gave me the Holy Spirit as my Sanctifier." When her father, a highly respected churchman and local police constable, objected to her new religious fervor, Ellen travelled to London to be mentored by renowned Keswick leader Elizabeth Baxter. Living there, she had two encounters that would color the rest of her life and ministry. First, she observed many people suffering spiritual and economic poverty, and, second, she was introduced to Holiness teaching regarding divine healing.

In the early years of her marriage to James Hebden, Ellen repeatedly shared with him her dream of serving Christ on the mission field. In 1904, the couple moved their family of eight to Jamaica, opening a mission in Tarrant, near Kingston. By the end of that year, however, the family saw little results in the ministry and had resettled in Toronto, Canada. By the spring of 1906, the Hebdens established the East End Mission as a faith-healing home.

One day, while in prayer, Ellen had experienced Pentecostal Spirit-baptism. In her dramatic encounter, she felt a divine presence taking over her hands and she began to speak in tongues. Following this episode, she began using her glossolalic[9] gift within the worship services of the mission, singing and delivering messages in tongues. Within a month, her husband James also experienced Pentecostal Spirit-baptism. Within six more months, seventy members of the congregation had had the same experience. Subsequently, the mission became a hub of Pentecostal revival in Canada, with people coming from all over the country and along the West Coast of the United States to participate in the revival.

The Hebden mission sent out twenty-five missionaries, and by 1910, there were fourteen Pentecostal missions in Canada that were in some way connected to it. Moreover, many who would be important to the establishment and spread of Pentecostalism in Canada were at one time affiliated with the mission. Among them were Robert and Aimee Semple, several leaders within the Pentecostal Assemblies of Canada,[10] and Charles W. Charner, a missionary leader who was the first Canadian Pentecostal missionary to South Africa.

Many elements of the Hebdens' mission paralleled those of the Azusa Street Mission. Like Azusa Street, the Hebdens produced a monthly periodical: the first Pentecostal journal in Canada. The mission and the revival, dubbed by some as "the Canadian Azusa," were as egalitarian as was the Los Angeles mission. James and Ellen shared the leadership of the mission.

Further, Ellen, who is regarded by many as the first known person in Canada to have the Pentecostal experience of speaking in tongues, is revered as much as—and in many accounts more than—James, as an early leader of Canadian Pentecostalism. The mission also operated without racial or ethnic discrimination; people of all cultures came to the meetings, and people went out from the meetings to minister to people of all races and cultures in every corner of the globe with the message of Pentecostalism.

Alice Belle Garrigus (1858–1949)

In 1907, while serving as an itinerant preacher for the Congregational Church in New Hampshire, Alice Garrigus accepted the doctrine and experience of Pentecostal Spirit-baptism when she met Frank Bartleman, an Azusa Street veteran and unofficial chronicler of the Pentecostal movement, at a Christian and Missionary Alliance camp meeting in Maine. Following the meeting with Bartleman, she continued preaching throughout New England, but began sensing an urging from God to go to Newfoundland to minister.

By 1910, Garrigus was ready to carry the Pentecostal message to St. John's Newfoundland, and she joined with a retired missionary couple, William Fowler and his wife, and together they introduced Pentecostalism to the island. On Easter Sunday 1911, the team opened the Bethesda Mission in downtown St. John's. The Fowlers and Garrigus saw only modest growth as they worked side by side for the first year, and at year's end, the couple was tired of the harsh northern conditions, which had been harmful to their health.

The Fowlers returned to the United States, leaving Garrigus to, more or less, fend for herself in maintaining the work. Under her leadership, the mission slowly grew from a single congregation to become an organization of churches—the Bethesda Pentecostal Assemblies—and was officially recognized by the provincial government in 1925. By 1930, it had become Pentecostal Assemblies of Newfoundland.[11] Though her own mission remained small and local, Garrigus and her Pentecostal doctrine found a following among Methodist businessmen, and with their financing her efforts reached into all corners of the colony, primarily drawing members from the Methodist tradition.

Though Garrigus was already fifty-two years old when she arrived in Newfoundland, she led her congregation and denomination for almost forty years, until her death in 1949. Little more than twenty years later, the Pentecostal Assemblies of Newfoundland had such an impact on the territory that the province had the highest percentage of Pentecostals of any in Canada.[12]

Alice Eveline Luce (1873–1955) and Florence Murcutt (1868–1935)

British born, Alice Luce served as a missionary on three continents—Asia, North, and South America. In 1896, Luce became a missionary with the Anglican mission organization, the Church Missionary Society (CMS). The group sent her to Azimgarh, India, where she worked in a school and among women isolated in harems or "zenanas." While in that country, she reportedly sought and received her Pentecostal Spirit-baptism experience in 1910. Not long after that, Luce became seriously ill because of drinking contaminated water. After a period of convalescence, she returned home in 1912. The next year, CMS loaned Luce to the Zenana Bible and Medical Mission to undertake secretarial work in Vancouver. Within two years however, she had resigned on medical grounds. And then, a year later, she was ordained by the newly formed Assemblies of God denomination, with which she remained aligned and worked for the remainder of her life.

Luce's work with the Assemblies of God was exhaustive. She worked with Henry Ball, Sunshine Marshall, and Rodolfo Orozco to evangelize Mexicans along the Texas border in 1915. Their efforts resulted in the ordination of a number of Mexican American women who served with their husbands as co-pastors. In Los Angeles, her pioneering work established the Latin American District Council of the Assemblies of God by conducting open-air evangelistic services and street ministry.

One of Luce's most important contributions was establishing a Spanish-language Pentecostal department as part of the Berean Bible Institute in San Diego, California, for training indigenous Hispanic clergy. In the first 20 years with the institute, Luce wrote most of its curriculum. This program, established in 1926, served as the foundation for the Latin American Bible Institute, now located in La Puente, California.

Luce's work throughout California was assisted by Florence Josephine Murcutt, who helped her organize, teach, and minister to the physical and spiritual needs of the students. The two also worked together to plant Spanish and English congregations in central and southern California. Murcutt was a British missionary doctor and Jewish convert to Christianity. She encountered Pentecostalism in Vancouver through the ministry of Lillian Garr. After having her own Pentecostal Spirit-baptism experience in 1912, she worked in Palestine, distributing Hebrew and Arabic New Testaments to Jews before joining Luce to establish Spanish and English congregations in central and southern California. In 1918, the two held meetings in the Mexican Plaza District, the area in which Azusa Street missionaries Rosa and Abundio de López, had preached twelve years earlier. Through her work with Luce, Murcutt became the first female Pentecostal medical missionary to Mexican Americans and

Mexicans. The friendship between the two women lasted for nearly a quarter of a century until Murcutt died after being struck by an automobile in 1935.

Luce was among the few women who widely influenced Assemblies of God doctrinal thought. Her writing included Bible school curriculum, intermediate and senior lessons and commentary for Sunday School quarterlies, evangelistic tracts, several books, and regular contributions to Ball's *Apostolic Light* magazine. In 1921, she wrote a series of articles, "Paul's Missionary Methods," for the *Pentecostal Evangel* that was to have a huge influence of Pentecostal missiology. Her advocacy was instrumental in the incorporation of indigenous church-planting principles as part of the missions strategy of the Assemblies of God.

Lillian Thrasher (1887–1961)

Lillian Thrasher was among the most fruitful early Pentecostal missionaries of either gender. Her ministry in Assiut, Egypt (230 miles south of Cairo) was so successful that two major Pentecostal denominations—the Church of God (Cleveland, TN) and the Assemblies of God—later claimed her efforts as part of their missionary legacy. Thrasher served in Egypt for fifty-one years, from 1910 until her death in 1961, working first under her own auspices, then with the Church of God, and finally with the Assemblies of God. Yet, while she never received substantial financial support from either body, one historian credits her with being the first Church of God missionary to go to a foreign land.

As a young woman in the United States, Thrasher served in an orphanage, pastored a small Pentecostal congregation, and traveled as an evangelist. In 1910, at the age of twenty-three she broke her engagement to a young preacher, and defying her family's wishes, with less than $100 to her name and accompanied by her sister Jennie, she sailed to Africa where they served as missionaries for decades.

Though initially licensed by the Church of God from 1912 to 1919, Thrasher financed her maiden trip to Egypt from her own funds. Her ministry centered on children and women, and she initially housed orphans and homeless and abused women in her own home. By 1916, her home had become a shelter for fifty orphans. Thrasher's involvement with the Assemblies of God began in 1914. That denomination also provided little financial support to Thrasher, but occasionally sent food and clothing.

Thrasher served her last twenty-five years in Egypt—from 1929 to 1954—without a single furlough, sustained by donations from wealthy Coptic Christian supporters that allowed her to purchase land and begin construction on the first building of the orphanage. By the time "Mama Lillian" died, the compound that bears her name had expanded to thirteen buildings including a church, a clinic, and an elementary school. Her work was revered by the Egyptian leaders and community, even among many in the Muslim sector. After her death, she was buried at the site of her orphanage.[13]

Aimee Semple McPherson (1890–1944)

Though most early Pentecostal leaders were roundly ignored by the mainline church and the secular press, Canadian-born Aimee Semple McPherson attracted a surplus of coverage from a variety of sources. Her evangelistic and pastoral ministry was concentrated in Los Angeles, yet she was widely recognized during the 1920s and 1930s as one of the most gifted preachers, teachers, and faith healers in the entire United States and perhaps the world. More material has been developed about her extravagant exploits than any other Pentecostal woman—and most other Pentecostal men.[14] McPherson received her early ministry training at the Hebden Toronto mission and served for a short period as a missionary in China with her husband, Robert Semple. After Robert's untimely death, the young mother returned to North America and withdrew from ministry for several years.

McPherson's dramatic flair attracted people from all walks of life and regularly placed her on the cover of the nation's most prominent periodicals. Her legacy includes building the 5,300-seat Angelus Temple (one the nation's first megachurches), being the first woman to broadcast a sermon on the radio or receive a license from the Federal Communications Commission to operate a radio station, and establishing L.I.F.E. Bible College,[15] one of the earliest Pentecostal institutions of higher education. Today, the denomination she founded—the International Church of the Foursquare Gospel—has more than one million members and is, perhaps, the largest and most influential Protestant body established by a woman.

At McPherson's death, her son Rolf took over as head of the Foursquare Church. For the remainder of the twentieth century, while the denomination has generally remained open to women in pastoral ministry, the higher positions of authority have remained, de facto, the province of men. Moreover, while women remained active in Foursquare ministry, the number and proportion of women pursing pastoral ministry declined significantly. At the end of that century, the denomination began making a concerted effort to draw more women into leadership positions. The first decade of the twenty-first century has seen the denomination taking bold steps to recognize the giftedness of women within their ranks, and women are again involved in all levels of leadership within the denomination.

Zelma Argue (1900–1980)

Zelma Argue was a young child from North Dakota by the time her family settled in Winnipeg, Manitoba, Canada in 1906. She was only an adolescent when
she attended the Arroyo Seco camp meetings near Los Angeles several years
later and received a Pentecostal Spirit-baptism. From that time, Zelma exhibited a zeal for God much beyond her years, and in 1920, at the age of twenty,
she was ordained in the Assemblies of God denomination. For over a decade
after that, when her mother's fragile health limited her travel, Zelma regularly
accompanied her father, Andrew Harvey (A. H.), and brother, Watson, to minister throughout the Canadian provinces.

Part of the family's work was establishing two congregations—Calvary
Temple in Winnipeg and Evangel Temple in Toronto. During a period in the
1920s when her mother's illness and the church responsibilities of her father
and brother curtailed their travels, Zelma and her sister Beulah held revival
meetings throughout the United States and Canada that drew coverage from
both the Pentecostal periodicals and the secular press.

Over a sixty-year period, Argue, like Luce before her, added to the store of
Pentecostal theology, writing more than two hundred articles for the *Pentecostal
Evangel*, the *Canadian Pentecostal Testimony*, and *Latter Day Rain Messenger*,
and authoring several full-length manuscripts, including nine books authored
between 1923 and the 1940s. Even more than Luce, among early Pentecostal
women, Argue comes closest to developing an authentic theological frame-
work. She exhibited an egalitarian impulse in her work, and though ordained
in the Assemblies of God, she developed a more Wesleyan understanding of
sanctification than is generally held in that denomination.[16]

Ellen Moore Hopkins (1921–2000)

Ellen Moore Hopkins was neither a pastor nor a preacher, yet the work of
this indigenous missionary in her homeland of Liberia had a major impact on
Pentecostal missions in that country. As a young girl, Moore came to America as
the adopted daughter of Samuel Grimes, the presiding bishop of the Pentecostal
Assemblies of the World, who had served with his wife, Katherine, as a West
African missionary. Their support allowed Moore to pursue her education,
earning several degrees including a B.S. in public health nursing education,
a master's degree, and a doctorate of divinity. After completing her education, Hopkins, a licensed midwife, returned to Liberia where she established
an educational program for students from primary school through junior college. In 1946, Moore established the Samuel K. Grimes Child Welfare Center
in Kakata in a renovated warehouse. That work gradually developed into an

organized Christian community of fourteen buildings including schools, a thousand-seat church, a maternity hospital, two medical clinics, three dormitories, and two cafeterias. In thirty-three years of service in Liberia, Hopkins cared for seven hundred orphaned and indigent children, delivered approximately five thousand babies, and trained over a hundred nurses who served all over that country.

Hopkins launched an aggressive health education effort aimed at reducing disease by teaching mothers to care for their children's health needs and youth to care for their own needs. Her extensive work gained recognition in both Liberia and United States. In the United States, both the white and black media took note of her work. She was featured in such diverse publications as the *Saturday Evening Post* and in *Ebony Magazine* and was listed in *Who's Who of American Women.*[17] In her homeland, Hopkins was awarded the Tubman Liberian National Award. Like so many others however, Hopkins was forced to flee during the Liberian civil war. She returned to the United States and continued to minister and publish work that encouraged women's physical and spiritual health.

Mary Louise Coore (1879–1964)

Jamaican born, Mary Coore converted to Christianity as young girl, and from that time on, had a passion for evangelistic ministry. As a young woman, Coore had embarked on a ministry of teaching and praying for the sick to such an extent that she was dubbed "the girl with the healing hands." In the early 1900s she joined Raglan Phillips, a white, British Salvation Army clergyman who had been evangelizing Jamaica for a quarter century with only limited success. Phillips recognized Coore's spiritual ability and leadership qualities and chose her to open his ministry to the native Jamaican community, which had proven to be somewhat suspicious of outsiders. The respect and acceptance that Coore had garnered in Jamaican society gave his ministry the credibility that it had been lacking, allowing him to make substantially greater progress in his evangelistic effort. Working together, the two formed the Pentecostal City Mission movement and traveled throughout Jamaica with the fourfold message of salvation, healing, holiness and the Second Coming of Christ. At the time of Phillips's death, the City Mission movement was localized within the fourteen parishes of Jamaica. Before his death, he transferred leadership of the organization to Coore who, in 1929, had become the first woman in Jamaica to be ordained.

Coore expanded Phillips's vision by establishing new congregations throughout Jamaica and, in 1939, pioneered the first international branch of the City Mission Church in British Honduras.[18] Under her leadership, the movement pioneered the hand-clapping, foot-stomping style of worship in Jamaica. More important, Coore took it upon herself to mentor women in Pentecostal ministry. The denomination pioneered the ordination of women in the island, and Coore was instrumental in placing several women pastors in different congregations. After her death, Coore was succeeded by another woman, Delrose Lucille Walters. As a young woman, Walters dreamed of becoming a medical doctor. She was converted at age ten within the Pentecostal Mission congregation pastored by Phillips and became active in the church as a young woman. Walters was influential in expanding the ministry of the City Mission Movement to the United States. For several years, she pastored a congregation in Los Angeles.

The City Mission movement accomplished several firsts for Jamaican women. Both women broke historical ground during the 1940s when they became Jamaica's first female bishops. (Coore also introduced the rank of bishop into the organization.) In 1945, Coore was also appointed Jamaica's first female marriage officer. The two women collaborated with the Jamaica Women's Federation and other women of political and social standing within the society to promote Jamaica's first mass wedding. This effort was an attempt to raise the moral climate of the society by reducing high rates of children born out of wedlock and the high rate of common law marriages in the country.[19]

Conclusion

As an effort at developing a more balanced portrait of early Pentecostalism and reinserting the history of women's contribution to the movement, I have presented the stories of eleven largely unsung women leaders who span the history of the Pentecostal movement. Although Pentecostal denominations in the United States have been dominated by male leadership since their earliest days, women in both the United States and in the broader global arena found venues in which they could exercise both their spiritual prowess and their leadership skills. Similarly, while the Azusa Street Mission in Los Angeles served as an important starting point for American Pentecostals, the early global spread of the movement provided women's leadership with greater opportunities than they might have found by confining themselves to the American context.

Courageous women such as I have highlighted in this chapter contributed greatly to Pentecostalism's global reach. They had the daring to evangelize, plant churches, serve as pastors of congregations, and found denominations in large metropolitan areas and small towns across the United States and Canada. They also had the courage to set out on their own and carry out a variety of missionary endeavors in the cities and villages of Africa, South America, and Asia. Significantly, much of their effort was focused on the temporal needs of women and children in societies that did not always take those needs seriously or did not have the resources to address them adequately. They built orphanages, schools, clinics, and hospitals. They advocated for women's rights. They fed hungry women and their children. In addition, they ministered healing to the sick through both spiritual and temporal means. Their work saved the lives of thousands of women and children or delivered them from living with the demeaning realities of being poor and female in cultures where both were prescriptions for marginalization.

Yet, as mothers of the faith, these women did not shrink away from preaching a Gospel message focused on the eternal needs of both men and women or from exercising their spiritual gifts of prophesying, exhorting, and praying for divine healing. The intensity and fervor of the revivals that broke out under their leadership often rivaled that of Azusa Street and drew thousands of converts into the movement over the first half of the twentieth century.

Importantly, several of these women took the initiative to record their personal experiences of Pentecostal Holy Spirit–empowerment and the exploits that such empowerment brought about through them. They also recorded their understanding of Pentecostal faith and what it means to be baptized in the Holy Spirit. In doing so, they added to the store of primary material. Unfortunately, until recently, much of this material has been ignored by scholars of Pentecostalism, who have only now begun to pour through the store of newly unearthed primary sources, including such as I have included here, suggesting that the remnants of a prejudice for male voices still lingers within the Pentecostal academy.

Yet new scholars are emerging with greater sensitivity to biblical feminist demands for a full, more inclusive, picture of the Christian tradition. New voices from the two-thirds world continue calling for a broader lens to view the global import of Pentecostalism on major Christian movements. The convergence of these two realities provides an opportunity to create a richer portrait of the beginnings, development, and contemporary context of this dynamic movement.

NOTES

1. The Bonnie Brae house was where William Seymour held prayer meetings and first gathered a following. The house is located at 214 North Bonnie Brae St., in Los Angeles.
2. See Elisabeth Schüssler Fiorenza, *In Memory of Her: A Feminist Theological Reconstruction of Christian Origins* (London, UK: SCM Press, 1995).
3. Meaning the ability to speak in a language she did not previously know. This is the original meaning of speaking in tongues, as described in the New Testament book of the Acts of the Apostles, chapter 2, verses 1–4 (eds.).

4. For a more thorough discussion of the contribution of women to the Azusa Street Mission and Revival, see Estrelda Alexander, *The Women of Azusa Street* (Cleveland, OH: Pilgrim Press, 2006).

5. "Mukti" means salvation.

6. See for example, Max Wood Moorhead, "Pentecost in Mukti, India," *Apostolic Faith* 1:10 (December 1907), 4.

7. Gary McGee, "Pentecostal Strategies for Global Mission: A Historical Assessment," in Murray Dempster, Byron D Klaus; Douglas Petersen, eds., *Called and Empowered: Global Mission in Pentecostal Perspective* (Peabody, MA: Hendrickson Publications, 1991), 210.

8. Allan Anderson, "To All Points of the Compass: The Azusa Street Revival and Global Pentecostalism," *Enrichment Journal* (Spring 2006), http://www.enrichmentjournal. ag.org/200602/200602_164_AllPoints.cfm.

9. Gift of speaking in tongues (eds.).

10. The PAOC is the largest Pentecostal denomination in Canada.

11. PAON operates primarily in that province and neighboring Labrador. Though the two provinces have been annexed into Canada, the organization founded by Garrigus never formerly aligned itself with the Pentecostal Assemblies of Canada, though the two bodies work closely together.

12. Garrigus's life story was serialized from 1938 to 1942 in *Good Tidings*, the official magazine of the Pentecostal Assemblies of Newfoundland.

13. See Beth Prim Howell, *Lady on a Donkey* (New York: E. P. Dutton, 1960) and Lillian Thrasher, *Letters from Lillian* (Springfield, MO: Assemblies of God, Division of Foreign Missions, 1983).

14. See for example, Robert Bahr, *Least of All Saints: The Story of Aimee Semple McPherson* (Englewood Cliffs, NJ: Prentice-Hall, 1979). Alvyn Austin, *Aimee Semple McPherson* (Don Mills, ON: Fitzhenry and Whiteside, 1980).

15. Lighthouse of International Foursquare Evangelism.

16. Rather than a "finished work" understanding of sanctification as a process that begins at regeneration but progresses throughout the life of a believer. For a discussion of Argue's theology, see Pamela M.S. Holmes, "Zelma Argue's Theological Contribution to Early Pentecostalism," in Michael Wilkinson and Peter Althouse, eds., *Winds from the North: Canadian Contributions to the Pentecostal Movement* (Boston: Brill, 2010), 129–149.

17. See "The House that Saves Lives," *Saturday Evening Post* 225 (1953); "The Lady with the Lamp," *Ebony Magazine* 6 (1951); and "Nurse Hopkins, Thirty Years Later." *Ebony* 32: 6 (8/1977): 80–87.

18. Now Belize.

19. Tracy Robinson, "Taxonomies of Conjugality," Global Law Working Paper, New York University School of Law, November 2006, 11.

12

Constructing Gender within Global Pentecostalism

Contrasting Case Studies in Colombia and South Africa

KATHERINE ATTANASI

A pair of questions often preoccupy studies of global Pentecostalism and gender: Does Pentecostalism have a feminine or masculine ethos? Also, is Pentecostalism good or bad for women?[1] The latter question arises because Pentecostalism is often characterized as "a 'regressive,' 'fundamentalist' Christian movement" that seems to oppress women but may actually empower them.[2]

This chapter examines three case studies of gender and Pentecostalism, one in Colombia and two in South Africa. First is Elizabeth Brusco's landmark study, *The Reformation of Machismo*.[3] Brusco describes a feminization of Pentecostalism because churches meet in domestic spaces, which are culturally coded as feminine. Moreover, according to Brusco, Pentecostalism is good for women because of the "reformation of machismo," whereby newly converted husbands redirect needed attention and resources into the family. The women Brusco studied were married to husbands who had also converted to Pentecostalism.

In the second case study, Maria Frahm-Arp argues for a masculinization of South African Pentecostalism insofar as the churches adopt the language and ethos of a male-dominated corporate culture as a means of fulfilling God's purposes in the world.[4] Moreover, Frahm-Arp considers such masculinized Pentecostalism to be good for women because it empowers them to achieve success in their professional lives. Single women figure most prominently in Frahm-Arp's study.

There is much in common among the Pentecostal teachings of Brusco's Colombian churches and Frahm-Arp's South African ones—enough so as to call into question whether to essentialize the religion as masculine or feminine in any given culture. As a third case study, my own fieldwork in South Africa seeks to avoid such gendered generalizations. Married Pentecostal women whose husbands were non-Christians constituted the largest demographic of my participants. Their stories reveal that Pentecostalism both impedes and enhances their capabilities, and so I recommend refocusing on women's agency, flourishing, and freedom rather than asking simply whether global Pentecostalism is good or bad for women.

Elizabeth Brusco on the Feminization of Pentecostalism in Colombia (1980s)

Since its publication in 1995, Brusco's *The Reformation of Machismo* has become a standard-bearer for studies of women and Pentecostalism.[5] Her work is based on sixteen months of fieldwork in Bogotá and a rural community north of the capital during 1982 and 1983. In this time, Brusco conducted participant observation, gathered life and family histories, and carried out open-ended interviews, close-ended interviews, surveys, and archival research.

Brusco's scholarship considers "women in the Pentecostal movement in Colombia."[6] Although her participants identify themselves by the term *evangélico*, the descriptor "Pentecostal" is preferable to "Evangelical";[7] the terms "Pentecostal" and "Charismatic" are rarely used in Colombia, and yet Brusco's congregations affiliated with classical Pentecostal denominations such as the Assemblies of God and Foursquare Gospel Church. Most distinctively, Brusco's participants shared a set of behavioral restrictions (e.g., no drinking, dancing, extramarital sex, etc.), a focus on reading the Bible, and a rejection of Catholicism.[8]

Colombian Pentecostalism had experienced its greatest time of growth during a period of persecution (called "La Violencia") by Roman Catholics.[9] From 1946 to 1966, an estimated 200,000 people were killed for political and religious reasons. *Evangélicos* were threatened, stoned, imprisoned, and killed; proselytism and reading the Bible could lead to execution. Non-Catholic church buildings closed, and most international missionaries left the country. Under these conditions, it became extremely dangerous to practice Pentecostalism in the public sphere. Consequently, Pentecostals began meeting in private homes. Even at the time of Brusco's study in the early 1980s, churches as large as 600 people divided into multiple services in order to meet in the main room of a pastoral couple's home.[10]

In the Spanish language and in Colombian cultural life, the "home" (*la casa*) is gendered female. Homes are considered women's domain and part of the private sphere, and thus the activities conducted there are gendered female as well.

The preeminence of the home as meeting places for Colombian Pentecostal congregations constitutes Brusco's primary evidence that the movement has a feminine ethos. Additional evidence include the following: the congregations are predominantly female; sermons emphasize the importance of the home and the family; and the most successful evangelistic outreaches take place in women's homes—as opposed to open-air rallies or preaching to strangers in the marketplace.[11]

The feminization of Colombian Pentecostalism provides the context for the "reformation of machismo," by which converted men reject cultural constructions of masculinity (machismo) and embrace Pentecostal values such as attending to, and financially supporting, the domestic sphere. Prior to male conversion, gender relations in Colombia are shaped by a complex interplay of expectations known as machismo, which Brusco describes as "the culturally constructed aggressive masculinity" characteristic of Colombia and Latin America.[12] Typically, traits include "hypersexuality, *cuatismo* (male camaraderie), violence, risk taking, courage or stoicism, authoritarianism, independence."[13] A key aspect of machismo is the construction of separate male and female spheres: men dominate the public domain, and women are in charge of private household life. The separation of domains restricts men's involvement in the household as both husbands and fathers.[14] Since each partner is responsible for a different sphere, the husband's and wife's goals and spending habits do not align. The matter of resource allocation is of particular concern because women in the study generally had a lower earning capacity and relied on male contributions to care for their families. Men earn more but are expected to spend their wages on themselves and their "public" activities, not on the home.

Colombian Pentecostalism contrasts sharply with machismo by emphasizing asceticism and family responsibility. Churches teach believers not to drink alcohol, smoke cigarettes, or participate in extramarital relationships. Sermons regularly emphasize that husbands are responsible for providing and caring for their families. For Brusco, these guidelines signify Pentecostalism's radical redefinition of the masculine role in the Colombian family. Regarding a husband's conversion to Pentecostalism, Brusco concludes that:

> machismo is replaced by evangelical belief as the main determinant of husband-wife relations. The machismo role and the male role defined by evangelicalism are almost diametrical opposites. Aggression, violence, pride, self-indulgence, and an individualistic orientation in the public sphere are replaced by peace seeking, humility, self-restraint, and a collective orientation and identity with the church and the home.[15]

The significant "reform" after conversion entails the reorientation of male attention to the family. Machismo prescribes that males dominate the public sphere, but Colombian Pentecostalism insists that husbands make decisions that will benefit the household. As a result, a husband's aspirations for the family's well-being begin matching more closely with his wife's, and the family's material quality of life improves as resources the husband once spent on vices in the public sphere are redirected back into the family and the domestic sphere.[16]

Brusco shows that Pentecostal women benefit financially and relationally from the reallocation of their husbands' attention and resources. When men's aspirations and resources are reoriented toward the family, women are better able to fulfill their own goals of caring for their families. Pentecostalism does good for women, and the churches are predominantly female. Accordingly, Brusco construes Pentecostalism as a kind of "female collective action" that challenges gender inequality, reforms gender roles, and addresses women's strategic concerns.[17] Unlike other women's movements, Pentecostalism does not address traditional power structures or underlying political inequalities; however, Pentecostalism does inspire changes to the family unit that improve women's circumstances.

Maria Frahm-Arp on the Masculinization of Pentecostalism in South Africa (2000s)

The second case study is Maria Frahm-Arp's *Professional Women in South African Pentecostal Charismatic Churches.* Her work is based on fieldwork conducted in two Pentecostal Charismatic churches outside of Johannesburg in 2004; the majority of the congregants were women. Frahm-Arp utilized participant observation, focus groups, and qualitative interviews.

The churches spend considerable time teaching about marriage and family life. In particular, teachings center on a man's role as the head of the household, which entails providing financially for the family and being a faithful husband and a good father.[18] Male pastors take pride in being "successful patriarchal heads of families who did not need the props of the shebeen-street culture to prove their masculinity."[19] To complement the husbands' roles of protector, leader, and provider, wives are to be nurturing, supportive, and caring helpmates.[20] Frahm-Arp found that such complementarian teachings prove attractive to women and men alike: women appreciated the emphasis on a husband's faithfulness and responsibility to his family, while men found the messages attractive "because it placed them in a good light [and] gave them authority."[21]

Aside from marital and familial roles, the churches are predominantly concerned with Christians' roles in professional work environments. In particular:

> By offering leadership training courses, personal empowerment
> seminars, group counseling and individual mentoring the churches
> in [Frahm-Arp's] study actively tried to equip members to become
> leaders in their workplaces and social spheres of influence so that
> Christian values would become implemented in all sectors of South
> African society.[22]

Frahm-Arp characterizes both churches as masculinized.[23] That is, these South African churches borrow language from the male-dominated corporate environment to convey their main message of personal empowerment, and the churches' teachings emphasize "purpose, achievement, leadership, competiveness, excellence, domination, wealth and victory"—qualities typically associated with masculinity rather than femininity in South Africa.[24] Nevertheless, these messages equip both men and women to pursue positions of influence in the workplace and broader society, particularly in education, health, and politics.[25]

Frahm-Arp's main focus is on young black women's professional lives, and the majority of her participants were single. She examines the connections between religious participation and economic mobility by asking why "politically and economically emancipated women choose to join a form of Christianity that ideologically seems to oppress them."[26] Frahm-Arp persuasively argues that Pentecostal Charismatic churches provide women invaluable and otherwise unavailable social capital such as mentoring, skills development, and positive affirmation. Such resources enable women better to navigate life in the corporate world.

Frahm-Arp found Pentecostalism to be attractive to women, but not because it promised advantages in the domestic sphere. Instead, young professional women join Pentecostal Charismatic churches to help themselves negotiate their opportunities in the workplace. Among others, Frahm-Arp identified two key advantages for Pentecostal women: they gain familiarity with the masculine rhetoric of the corporate world; also, they are not restricted to being wives, mothers, and homemakers but can also excel on their own in professional society.[27]

South African Pentecostalism as Neither Masculinized nor Feminized: Women's Agency in Good Times and Bad

As a third case study, I draw on my own fieldwork in South Africa in 2008. The fieldwork consisted of participant observation, qualitative open-ended interviews, follow-up interviews, and focus groups. I surveyed two Pentecostal churches, one in an urban township and the other in a rural village. In each location, more than three-quarters of congregants were women. In all, I interviewed fifty black South African Pentecostal women. More than three-quarters of these women were married, divorced, or widowed; over half of the husbands were non-Christians. Many of the married couples spent considerable time living apart in order to find work.[28]

My research fills a gap in the existing literature. Frahm-Arp focused on single Pentecostal women, and Brusco studied Pentecostal women whose husbands also convert to the religion. I highlight Pentecostal women whose husbands were non-Christians because this was the most common scenario I encountered among my participants. Bernice Martin has made the general claim that even for those women whose husbands do not convert, global Pentecostalism provides a familial system of sorts in which women acquire belonging, standing, and responsibility.[29] My participants reveal that Martin's claim is only partly true: women's belonging and standing are more precarious when their husbands are outside of the church; moreover, women remarkably remain within Pentecostalism even when even when they do not accrue the benefits detailed by Brusco, Frahm-Arp, and Martin.

Pentecostal Teachings about Conversion, Marriage, and Divorce

Brusco and Frahm-Arp encountered very similar teachings about behavioral regulations in Pentecostal churches in Colombia and South Africa respectively. Given these commonalities, which recur in my research, I avoid categorizing Pentecostalism as one gender or another—Brusco and Frahm-Arp having offered opposing designations.

I studied South African Pentecostal churches in which conversion entails rejecting drug and alcohol use and maintaining fidelity in marriage. My participants said that many men reject Pentecostalism because they will not adhere to such behavioral restrictions. The women often connected South African masculinity to drug and alcohol abuse, marital infidelity, unsafe sex, domestic abuse, and authoritarian decision-making.[30]

The churches teach a complementarian view of marriage.[31] Pastors emphasize male headship and the wife's obligation to submit to the husband's divinely sanctioned authority over her. The husband's authority over the wife applies even if he is not a Christian. Relatedly, the churches' teaching on divorce comes very near to an absolute prohibition.[32] My participants repeatedly cited the Bible as saying that God hates divorce, a paraphrase of the Hebrew prophet Malachi: "'I hate divorce,' says the Lord God of Israel" (Mal. 2:16). Even the divorcées among my participants, including one female pastor, stated that divorce was wrong and that they would not advise other women to get divorced. This strong prohibition affects women whose non-Christian husbands commit acts of adultery and domestic violence.[33] In one congregation, more than half of the women had non-Christian husbands; more than half of those husbands committed adultery; and more than a quarter of those husbands physically abused their wives.[34] I found that Pentecostalism impedes women's flourishing by commanding them to submit to, and not to divorce, physically abusive and/or adulterous husbands.[35]

Five Women's Narratives

In what follows, I relate five narratives by Pentecostal women whose husbands were non-Christians.[36] Four of the husbands physically abused the women, and the fifth husband was an adulterer. All of the women remained part of their Pentecostal congregations. These stories provide a complex view of women's agency and resiliency that shows darker and more complicated aspects of gender in global Pentecostalism than previous literature has reflected. The churches provided the women varying levels of support, and the women negotiated various responses to their struggles.

A first woman, Violet, personally experienced domestic violence but recommends wifely submission and prayer instead of divorce or legal protection. Violet is now in her early fifties, and at age eighteen she married her first boyfriend, with whom she had one son. Her husband was a police officer who regularly—sometimes daily—beat her with his nightstick, which resulted in many hospitalizations, at least two miscarriages, and permanent disfigurement to her leg. Her entire family and neighborhood knew of the ongoing abuse, but no one came to her defense. Violet never reported her husband's abuse to authorities because he was a policeman. She said, "In those days they would just come to our house and talk to us. They would tell us it would look bad if their top officer was abusing his wife. It would just disappear."

Violet's husband did not want her to attend her Pentecostal church, and he even burned some of her belongings as punishment for her doing so. Nevertheless, Violet believes in traditional gender roles and said that toward the end of her marriage (before her husband died of a heart attack) she would submit and remain silent, such that her husband would eventually grow tired of beating her. Violet admits that that her situation was difficult but emphasizes that wifely submission improved her condition. She would recommend the same course of action to other women in similar situations. Despite the challenges Violet faced in her marriage, she also said that she would not recommend divorce because prohibitions of divorce "are God's laws, not ours" and because "(God) hates divorce." She enjoys her life now and says, "I am living because of God. God has made me to be free. For thirty-two years, my marriage was hell, but now I'm free."

Violet also highlights the importance of prayer for overcoming marital difficulties. She participates in a prayer group and said that they have prayed for the restoration of marriages in which partners have already filed divorce papers: "Then we deal with it, and we pray hard. We tell God, 'You say in your Word people must never divorce—you hate divorce.'" Through the group's faith and prayers, Violet says, women are testifying that their marriages are being saved.

A second woman, Caroline, shows that taking legal action to protect herself from her abusive husband placed her at odds with her male pastor. Caroline, who is in her early fifties, was married to a prominent leader in the township. They had several children, and the husband physically abused the family for over a decade. As the violence escalated, Caroline initiated paperwork with the local police to file a restraining order against the husband. The husband then threatened Caroline with a gun in the middle of the night and said he was kicking her out of the house. The next day while Caroline was at work, one of her sons shot and killed his father. Caroline openly shared her story with other women as a testimony of God's deliverance from an abusive husband.

In a separate interview, Caroline's male pastor told the story very differently. He left out entirely that the abuse had already lasted a decade before escalating to the point that the son believed his father would murder his mother. Instead, the pastor said that Caroline's legal intervention had instigated the violence that led to the murder. That is, in the pastor's estimation, Caroline's husband felt threatened because his wife had filed a restraining order. The pastor said, "At the end of the day, (Caroline) went to get the court order against (her husband)..... The abuse increased, and eventually one of the sons killed the father. At times the interdiction helps, but other times it fans the flames." By seeking police protection, Caroline was not submitting to her husband's authority and thereby incurred her pastor's disapproval.

Caroline's pastor was not alone in viewing women's legal action as aggravating men's anger and instigating their violent abuse. An additional pastor explained:

> Another cause [of violence against women] is that women will go for protection orders. Now that to me is ... a big source for this domestic violence, because men will not succumb to the protection order. They ignore it, and then they end up even killing their spouses and so on. These (protection orders) may be working other places—in England, for example—but you cannot just take it and apply it in South Africa.

Both male pastors voiced strong disapproval of government-sanctioned restraining orders as means of protecting wives victimized by domestic violence. Both Caroline's husband and her pastor are significant male figures within her social sphere, and both men agree that legal protection is provocative and unwarranted, even though Caroline and her children suffered such physical violence.

A third woman, Nichole, was ostracized when she separated from her husband because of his aggression and "serialized domestic violence." Nichole is in her late forties and is a nurse in the rural village's local clinic. When she separated from her husband, she sought the counsel of the pastor's wife, who holds a prominent position in the congregation. Nichole confided in the pastor's wife and shared her feelings a couple of times very early on in the separation. However, Nichole found the pastor's wife unsupportive; that is, throughout Nichole's eventual two-year separation, the pastor's wife ignored Nichole and her troubled marriage. After the separation, Nichole reconciled with her husband, and she gives assurances that her marriage is very good now. She remains part of the congregation despite her dismay over the church's lack of support during her time of need. Yet Nichole says that she would not advise other women to separate from their husbands. Instead, she would advise a woman to have faith and stay—not to quit her marriage—unless she was being severely abused on a daily basis.

A fourth woman, Mrs. Nkabinde, found herself in conflict with her Pentecostal prayer group because of her daughter's troubled marriage. Mrs. Nkabinde, a mother of six, is in her early sixties. She shared that one of her daughters suffered regular beatings from her husband, who also threatened to kill his wife and had even sent his nephews with axes to underscore the seriousness of his threats. Mrs. Nkabinde told the daughter to come home to her. When Mrs. Nkabinde told her women's prayer group of this decision, however, they disapproved. The prayer group recommended that the wife submit and not divorce the husband. These women said instead that the daughter should remain with her husband while they prayed for her safety. Mrs. Nkabinde affirmed her strong belief in the power of prayer, but she disagreed with her prayer group's recommendations. Moreover, Mrs. Nkabinde was uncomfortable that the group disapproved of her course of action, as though she had shown a lack of faith in God and distrust in the efficacy of the group's prayers. Mrs. Nkabinde remains a part of the prayer group even though her daughter took her advice by separating from, and eventually divorcing, her abusive husband.

A fifth woman, Barbara, strictly followed the church's teaching by remaining with her husband despite very trying circumstances, and through prayer her marriage finally improved. Barbara, a mother of four, is in her early sixties. Barbara's husband disapproved of her membership in the Pentecostal church, and many times he would leave for extended periods and carry on adulterous affairs. This pattern went on for a decade. Barbara never sought a divorce and said that she would not seek the counsel of anyone who might advocate for divorce. She simply prayed for her husband. After ten years the husband's mother became sick. In addition to seeking medical care for her, he asked Barbara to pray for her mother-in-law. The woman's health improved, as did Barbara's marriage. The couple remains together, the husband remains a non-Christian, and Barbara continues to pray for his salvation.

Each of these women suffered from violence or infidelity on the part of her husband. The women's responses varied, as did their congregations'. Violet followed church teachings on wifely submission and avoiding divorce; she endured her husband's beatings until they stopped and her husband died. Caroline sought legal protection, against the will of her pastor, and eventually her son shot her husband. Nichole separated from her husband and was ostracized by the pastor's wife; ultimately Nichole did not divorce her husband but reconciled with him. Mrs. Nkabinde recommended separation and divorce to her daughter whose husband abused her; because Mrs. Nkabinde recommended transgressing her women's prayer group's marital norms, her advice created a rift within the prayer group. Just as her church regulates, Barbara remained faithful to her adulterous husband by praying for him and not divorcing him, despite years of his infidelity; eventually their marriage improved. None of these women left their churches, and yet certain courses of action can definitely diminish one's social standing within the group.

Summary and Implications

The foregoing analysis, based on my fieldwork in South Africa, has focused on Pentecostal women whose husbands do not convert. Unlike Frahm-Arp and Brusco, I have eschewed the question of whether Pentecostalism is feminized or masculinized. Instead, I have highlighted the Pentecostal teachings regarding behavioral restrictions (e.g., avoiding alcohol) and marriage (e.g., avoiding adultery and emphasizing wives' submission to husbands' authority) that all the case studies share. As distinct from Brusco and Frahm-Arp's studies, the prohibition of divorce figured prominently in the South African churches I observed. This prohibition was not easily maintained, as exemplified by five of my participants' stories.

Brusco has called Pentecostalism a kind of "female collective action" that challenges and reforms certain types of gender inequality;[37] yet the majority of the married women in my study have non-Christian husbands whose authoritarianism goes largely unchallenged by their wives and by their wives' churches. My participants' narratives complicate the simplistic question of whether Pentecostalism is good for women.[38] Also, previous scholarship on gender and global Pentecostalism too often has been preoccupied with describing the ways the religion benefits women (e.g., by offering social support), and the scholarship tends to explain women's conversion in terms of accruing such benefits. My work not only provides the qualification that these benefits are in fact conditional but also shows that women remain within the church even when they lose their standing and the church's social support.

Rather than asking, "Is Pentecostalism good or bad for women?" I find it preferable to assess global Pentecostalism and gender in terms of agency, flourishing, and freedom.[39] More nuanced questions then include, "In what ways does Pentecostalism promote and impede women's flourishing?" Similarly, "How does Pentecostalism contribute to and constrain women's freedom?"[40] Simply put, this is a both-and approach rather than an either-or. For even when the religion impedes flourishing and constrains freedom, one need not essentialize Pentecostal women as victims, for women still have agency. At the same time, although Pentecostalism can promote flourishing and enhance freedom, one need not romanticize that women have absolute agency to chart their own destinies. In these regards, I am deeply indebted to R. Marie Griffith, whose analyses of Charismatic women in the United States seek to "render such women with the depth and complexity that their lives warrant and thereby dispute the flat, stereotypical terms to which so many ... still cling;"[41] also, "to see beyond simple antitheses of liberation versus repression" is an important achievement of Griffith's work,[42] one that should be replicated in future studies of gender and global Pentecostalism.

My study focused on South African Pentecostal women's experiences of adulterous and/or physically abusive husbands. Without exception, the churches taught that wives should submit to their husbands and pray for them. Although these churches constrain women's freedom by disallowing such choices as restraining orders, separation, and divorce, three of the women in my study broke with the church's norms. Caroline initiated a restraining order against her husband. Soon thereafter her son shot and killed her husband, and so the extent of Caroline's flourishing is difficult to ascertain; according to her, though, God freed her family from her husband's abuse. Nichole's home life flourished when she separated from her husband; however, her relationship with her pastor's wife suffered as a result of that choice. Similarly, Mrs. Nkabinde recommended that her daughter divorce her husband. While the daughter flourished, Mrs. Nkabinde's relationships with her prayer group were strained.

Women's agency may be more readily apparent when the women break with the norms of Pentecostalism, but women who abide by the church's teachings are still exercising agency. Violet's husband beat her and cheated on her while she submitted to him and prayed for him. This cycle only ended when her husband died, yet today Violet praises God for her freedom, which she compares to Israel's deliverance from Egypt. Similarly, Barbara refused to divorce her husband, and her marriage eventually improved; she would say that God blessed her on account of her faithfulness. At the most basic level, women demonstrate their agency by voluntarily participating in the life of the church. Moreover, women are free to choose whether, or to what extent, they will adhere to their churches' teachings. In the end, though, there is no guarantee that any given choice will lead to a woman's flourishing.

Conclusion

I started this chapter by noting a scholarly tendency to characterize Pentecostalism as having a masculine or feminine ethos. Brusco described Colombian Pentecostalism as feminized because churches in the early 1980s met in private homes,[43] which are considered female-dominated spheres, and because churches "domesticated" men by reforming machismo. In the early 2000s, Frahm-Arp characterized South African Pentecostalism as masculinized because churches empower women and men to succeed in the corporate world, which is considered a male-dominated sphere. In both studies, however, Pentecostalism laid down the same kind of regulations for men and women. The problem, then, is that Brusco and Frahm-Arp label Pentecostalism with opposite metaphorical genders. In my estimation, these labels prove misleading insofar as they distract from strong cross-cultural similarities in Pentecostal teachings.

Regarding women's status and progress, Martin has asserted that "if there is a 'women's movement' among the poor of the developing world, Pentecostalism has a good claim to the title."[44] Brusco shows that Pentecostalism empowers women by elevating their roles in domestic spheres. By contrast, Frahm-Arp shows that Pentecostalism enhances women's ability to succeed in professional contexts. As I see it, these would constitute such different types of collective action that it may be inaccurate to generalize global Pentecostalism as a women's movement.

To guard against overgeneralizations, I echo Brusco's recent call for additional "contextualized case studies" to contribute to the knowledge of women and Pentecostalism.[45] In other words, we need more landmarks to map the field of gender and global Pentecostalism. On a related note, I have focused on Pentecostal women throughout this chapter, and yet there are at least two genders. Although masculinities studies are well established in many fields, they are not yet prevalent in Pentecostal studies. There are initial insights, given the similar ways Pentecostalism proscribes behavior typically associated with Colombian and South African men. Further studies could include men's perspectives and consider the ways men construct and perform their gender, understand their sexuality, and negotiate tensions between religious and cultural norms. Another area of inquiry could couple sociological and theological analyses of the sources and norms behind Pentecostalism's behavioral regulations.[46]

In conclusion, I also began this chapter with the question of whether Pentecostalism is good or bad for women, but my aim has been to reframe that question in terms of women's agency, flourishing, and freedom. I do not deny that Pentecostalism affords women the benefits Brusco and Frahm-Arp describe. I do, however, question the extent to which women affiliate with Pentecostalism because of these benefits. That is, I strive to complexify women's involvement within Pentecostalism based on the experiences of my participants, who resiliently embrace a religion that simultaneously impedes and enhances their flourishing, and constrains and promotes their freedom.[47]

Notes

1. For example, after listing a dozen studies, Bernice Martin epitomizes that "research on evangelicals/Pentecostals in the developing world has repeatedly found that women …are advantaged in new and crucial ways by the movement" (Bernice Martin, "The Pentecostal Gender Paradox: A Cautionary Tale for the Sociology of Religion," in *The Blackwell Companion to Sociology of Religion*, ed. Richard K. Fenn [Malden: Blackwell, 2001], 52–66, here 54).

2. Martin, "Pentecostal Gender Paradox," 57.

3. Elizabeth Brusco, *The Reformation of Machismo: Evangelical Conversion and Gender in Colombia* (Austin: University of Texas Press, 1995); more recently see also Brusco, "Gender and Power," in *Studying Global Pentecostalism: Theories and Methods*, ed. Allan Anderson and others (Berkeley: University of California Press, 2010), 74–92.

4. Maria Frahm-Arp, *Professional Women in South African Pentecostal Charismatic Churches*, Studies of Religion in Africa 38 (Leiden: Brill, 2010).

5. Brusco, *Reformation of Machismo*, 15.

6. Brusco, "Gender and Power," 77.

7. By way of analogy, the German term *evangelische* signifies "Protestant" despite its etymological relation to "Evangelical."

8. Brusco, "Gender and Power," 76.

9. Brusco outlines the causes and effects of "La Violencia" in *Reformation of Machismo*, 31–47, i.e., Chapter 3, "Religion and Politics."

10. Brusco, *Reformation of Machismo*, 130.

11. Brusco, *Reformation of Machismo*, 133–34.

12. Brusco, *Reformation of Machismo*, 6.

13. Brusco, *Reformation of Machismo*, 78.

14. Brusco, *Reformation of Machismo*, 84. Later, Brusco contrasts machismo with the male "breadwinner" role of the 1950s in the United States. According to this construction of masculinity, the ideal male provided financially for his family; because of the separation of the spheres within machismo, no such expectation that males would provide for their families exists (pp. 98–99).

15. Brusco, *Reformation of Machismo*, 137.

16. Brusco, *Reformation of Machismo*, 123.

17. Brusco, *Reformation of Machismo*, 138–39.

18. Frahm-Arp, *Professional Women*, 12, 122.

19. Frahm-Arp, *Professional Women*, 1; in South Africa, "shebeens" are taverns or pubs.
20. Frahm-Arp, *Professional Women*, 218.
21. Frahm-Arp, *Professional Women*, 218.
22. Frahm-Arp, *Professional Women*, 67.
23. Frahm-Arp, *Professional Women*, 12.
24. Frahm-Arp, *Professional Women*, 215.
25. Frahm-Arp, *Professional Women*, 216.
26. Frahm-Arp, *Professional Women*, 122.
27. Frahm-Arp, *Professional Women*, 123.
28. The geographic relationship of housing to jobs speaks to the realities of black South African life, particularly the effects of apartheid policies under which black people worked in, but could not live in, urban centers (Leonard M. Thompson, *A History of South Africa*, 2nd ed. [New Haven: Yale University Press, 1995], 193–94). When married couples live apart from one another, it creates additional stress and differs significantly from the families in Brusco's study, according to which husbands and wives lived together permanently in the same home.
29. Martin, "Pentecostal Gender Paradox," 56.
30. Descriptors such as alcohol abuse and marital infidelity overlap with Colombian machismo as described by Brusco.
31. My participants' complementarian view of marriage parallels Frahm-Arp's findings regarding male and female roles within marriage.
32. The concept of divorce hardly figures into the work of Brusco and Frahm-Arp.
33. The scenario of wives abusing or cheating on their husbands did not appear in my fieldwork.
34. Given the silence that shrouds domestic violence, it is likely that more of my participants had similar experiences. In the second congregation I studied, women were more reticent to discuss adultery and domestic violence. One factor might have been that my research assistant for that congregation was younger and unmarried, whereas in the first congregation my research assistant was older and married; that is, married women may have been more likely to confide in other married women.
35. Given that my participants described South African men as unwilling to use condoms, prohibiting women from divorcing adulterous husbands renders women exceedingly vulnerable to contracting HIV. Although South Africa does not have the highest infection rate, according to the 2010 UNAIDS report, South Africa does have more people living with HIV than any other country: 5.6 million (UNAIDS, *Global Report: UNAIDS Report on the Global AIDS Epidemic* [New York: UNAIDS, 2010], 28.]).
36. My fieldwork was approved by Vanderbilt University's Institutional Review Board; in accordance with IRB protocols, I have changed participants' names to ensure anonymity.
37. Brusco, *Reformation of Machismo*, 138–39.
38. Andrea Hollingsworth and Melissa D. Browning also highlight complex aspects of Pentecostalism (e.g., whether it is liberating and/or limiting) in their article, "Your Daughters Shall Prophesy (As Long as They Submit)," in *A Liberating Spirit: Pentecostals and Social Action*, ed. Michael Wilkinson and Steven M. Studebaker (Eugene, Ore.: Pickwick, 2010), 161–84.
39. I understand "flourishing" broadly to include women's spiritual, emotional, physical, and material well-being. I consider agency and freedom as the individual's capability to make choices when she encounters competing goods. In these regards, I draw on the capabilities approach as articulated by Martha Nussbaum, *Women and Human Development: The Capabilities Approach* (Cambridge: Cambridge University Press, 2000) and Amartya Sen, *Development as Freedom* (New York: Knopf, 1999); I also work from feminist notions of freedom as described by Nancy J. Hirschmann, *The Subject of Liberty: Toward a Feminist Theory of Freedom* (Princeton, N.J.: Princeton University Press, 2003).
40. Regarding the concept of constrained choices, Nancy Hirschmann describes freedom as essentially about choice, and choice involves the complicated interaction among

internal and external factors; Hirschmann highlights what people prefer when given the choice, whether people are given the choice, and whether they are then able to make it (Hirschmann, *Subject of Liberty*, ix). Enhancing freedom thus requires removing barriers—real and imagined—so that new possibilities can be created.

41. R. Marie Griffith, *God's Daughters: Evangelical Women and the Power of Submission* (Berkeley: University of California Press, 1997), 11. Griffith conducted an ethnographic study of the Women's Aglow Fellowship, the world's largest interdenominational women's organization. Her analysis of this charismatic women's group focused on the ways women understood, reinterpreted, communicated, and challenged "the traditionally Christian doctrine of female submission to male authority" (p. 14).

42. Griffith, *God's Daughters*, 211.

43. A *desideratum* would be an updated study to determine the prevalence of Colombian Pentecostals meeting in private homes rather than in public, free-standing churches.

44. Martin, "Pentecostal Gender Paradox," 56.

45. Brusco, "Gender and Power," 90.

46. For Pentecostalism, the primary source and norm of behavioral regulations is the Bible. Sociologically, one observes nearly absolute prohibitions that are grounded in Scripture with varying firmness. All three case studies have shown prohibitions on drinking alcohol to be characteristic of global Pentecostal teaching, and yet Jesus and the disciples drink wine in the gospels (e.g., at the Last Supper). My fieldwork revealed prohibitions of divorce, which did not exactly match biblical teaching, for just as God condemns divorce in Malachi 2:16, the same verse condemns violence; also, Jesus first condemns divorce and then presupposes divorce when prohibiting remarriage (Mark 10:2–12), and Paul lays down conditions for allowing divorce including adultery and an unbeliever who will not tolerate the Christian spouse's faith (1 Cor. 7:10–15). Theological studies and sociological ones can converge when inquiring into the Bible's meanings and communities' control of those meanings. For example, Sarojini Nadar has analyzed South African Pentecostal biblical interpretation, and she works out ways in which "life affirming rather than life denying interpretations of Scripture can be encouraged and practiced" ("'The Bible Says!' Feminism, Hermeneutics, and Neo-Pentecostal Challenges," *Journal for Theology of Southern Africa* 134 [2009]: 131–46, here 131).

47. My thanks to James Barker for his insights and encouragement throughout my research and writing processes.

SPIRIT/POWER

As several of the preceding chapters suggest, personal religious experience is a core feature of Pentecostalism. In this the individual has what is understood as a direct encounter with the Spirit of God, in which they are, in the parlance of Pentecostal theology, "baptized" or immersed in the essence of the Spirit. This experience in turn has effects in both the life of the individual and often beyond, to include family, community, and a larger engagement with society. In the following two chapters, the authors are particularly focused on the relationship between religious experience—of direct encounter with the Divine—and the growth of Pentecostalism.

Drawing on over a quarter century of studying Pentecostalism, William Kay first provides a reflection on the different emphases he has seen and studied within Pentecostalism, focusing on how experience is a part of each of these different aspects. Next, Kay builds on these reflections to demonstrate how religious experience is related to Pentecostal growth, based on his investigation of large Pentecostal churches in Southeast Asia, one of the regions where Pentecostal Christianity is growing most rapidly.

As Kay sets out his initial reflections, he makes an important observation about Pentecostal experience: that it is both a social and an individual spiritual experience, each flowing from the other. For Kay the welcoming community of Pentecostal Christians is a result of their feeling of community and natural caring for others that flows from Pentecostal experience. Further, he shows that while on the one hand Pentecostal spiritual experience is individualistic, on the other, it is dependent on the community—the social dimension— first as the community of believers needed for the individual to interpret the experience, and second, because these experiences generally are the result of a common religious experience shared with other believers. Ultimately, Kay shows that the rapid growth of Pentecostalism in Southeast Asia is related to the Pentecostal experience of the Spirit, which leads to the desire to spread the "good news" and to reach out in "hospitality" and caring to help others.

While the stereotype of Pentecostal experience is that of the individual engaging in glossolalia, or "speaking in tongues," Margaret Poloma and Matthew T. Lee investigate the role of "prophecy" and "prophetic prayer" in global Pentecostalism. Prophecy and prophetic prayer, Poloma and Lee tell us, are key experiences within Pentecostalism, and have been a central component in the growth of Pentecostalism since its earliest Azusa Street days to the present. While prophecy is the experience of the individual hearing the Spirit "speak" to them—whether directly or through another believer—prophetic prayer is the ongoing interactive dialogue with the Spirit through which prophecy occurs. Poloma and Lee argue that these key experiences are linked to what they frame as *godly love*; as the individual believer interacts with the Divine, and thus express love for God, the desire to serve others is increased. Similar to William Kay's point that evangelism and reaching out and caring for others go hand in hand, Poloma and Lee argue that godly love is at the heart of the biblical "great commandment" (to love God above all others, and to love others as oneself), and has worked in tandem with evangelism in facilitating global Pentecostal growth.

Overall, "experience" as a key component within Pentecostalism cannot be underestimated. The very notion that an individual can have a direct experience of the Divine—that one can be "filled" by the Spirit—is a powerful motivator not only to pursue a righteous life, but to act on what the Spirit is instructing one to do. This in turn has implications for the growth and spread of Pentecostalism, and as noted in many of the other chapters in this book, in areas as diverse as the ways that Pentecostals seek to engage their families, communities, and society, and how they may have an impact in larger political and economic structures.

13

Gifts of the Spirit

Reflections on Pentecostalism and Its Growth in Asia

WILLIAM K. KAY

Social and spiritual experience is at the heart of Pentecostalism. These two kinds of experience are interconnected. Survey data show Pentecostal ministers appreciate sensing the beauty of God in nature *and* singing Gospel hymns, the first being a personal and usually solitary activity and the second being congregational.[1] Indeed any spiritual experience with mystical overtones centering on feelings of unity with God will allow those feelings to ripple out to the rest of the universe, both material and human. Congregational activity—where many people do the same things all at once—is naturally conducive to social solidarity, and this is intensified when similar spiritual experiences underlie their common behavior.

In this chapter I will begin by outlining some of the broad contours of the history and current expression of Pentecostalism. Then, taking a closer look at several Pentecostal congregations in Southeast Asia, I will illuminate how Pentecostalism is taking shape in a region of the world where that movement—and Christianity in general—is growing most rapidly.

Experience

"Experience" is a slippery word that, while it may refer primarily to direct sensory impact on consciousness, also includes memory and interpretation of that consciousness. We might experience a dream or we might revisit an experience in memory for the purpose of analysis. Most Pentecostals are likely to believe that religious experience stands in the same relation to spiritual reality as sense experience stands in relation to material reality.

For this reason spiritual experience appears to come directly, as far as Pentecostals are concerned, from the Holy Spirit although, if pressed to explain where the Holy Spirit is, they are usually reduced to metaphor. The Spirit is like the wind that cannot be seen but whose presence can be felt. Traditionally, Pentecostals have spoken of a powerful encounter with the Holy Spirit that is a baptism—that is, an immersion in the Spirit that lasts for a relatively short period of time and is analogous to what happened to Jesus' disciples in Acts 2. Early Pentecostals were willing to give a description. After attending a prayer meeting for three months in 1913, Donald Gee, a British Pentecostal, wrote that he

> found it becoming increasingly difficult to adequately voice all the glory in my soul. This went on for about two weeks, and then one night, when praying all alone by my bedside before retiring, and when once again finding no English adequate to express the overflowing fullness of my soul, I found myself beginning to utter words in a new tongue. I was in a condition of spiritual ecstasy and wholly taken up with the Lord. (Ross 1974: 11)

Or, to take an example from Howard Carter, another Englishman of the same generation, speaking of what happened to him in 1915:

> To describe a spiritual experience is as impossible as to define the sweetness of an apple or the beauty of a flower. I may simply state that the spiritual blessing received that day met the great yearning of my soul, and satisfied me that the experience, which I had sought so long was now actually real. The Lord granted me the Gift of the Holy Spirit and the manifestation as on the Day of Pentecost, a definite experience of boundless love and joy filled me. (Carter 1971:28)

Both these men, on the strength of their religious convictions, were conscientious objectors during the Great War of 1914–18 (Kay 2007a). In both cases their religious experiences bolstered their religious beliefs and strengthened their resistance to jingoistic social pressures.[2]

My own reflection on the religious experience of the early Pentecostals is colored by an understanding of the 19th-century Romantic Movement with its revolutionary aspirations and its prioritization of individual apprehensions of the glories of nature. Especially in the work of Wordsworth, Keats, and Coleridge, but also in Goethe and the music of Beethoven, there is a nature mysticism colored by pantheism. These were men for whom the natural world spoke about beauty and sublimity. They were prone to hike in the mountains, gasp at waterfalls, and gaze up with awe at the starry sky. Subjective experience was valuable because it could be transformed into art, much as Pentecostals were later to transform subjective experience into theology. Or, to put this another way, the "subjective turn" of 20th-century philosophy was in line with the primacy Pentecostals gave to experience (Taylor 2007; Kay 2011).

As the 20th century unfolded, the means by which human experience could be amplified, captured, recorded, played back, and enriched increased. It was not simply the appearance of film or even of recording equipment to preserve forever the voices of Caruso or Lenin, but the equipment to amplify voices so as to enable huge crowds to hear a single speaker in a great concourse. Loud secular music could fill the largest arena and, in the churches, such sound systems could, if well used, enhance the corporate spiritual experience of worshippers.

While the technological means for enhancing experience grew, experience itself diversified. The sexual mysticism of D. H. Lawrence found a resting place in literature alongside the advocacy of drug use in the books of Aldous Huxley.[3] These two sources of experience—sex and drugs—were later to be formative of popular culture in the second part of the 20th century. It makes sense to see religious experience as an antidote as well as an alternative to these other sources of experience. So it is no surprise to discover David Wilkinson in the bestselling 1960s paperback, *The Cross and the Switchblade,* bringing young men and women from drug dependency through to a new way of life via an experience of the baptism in the Holy Spirit.

Wilkinson, a third-generation Pentecostal preacher, felt led by the Holy Spirit to New York and the knife-carrying gangs engaged in vicious turf war. He would offer the young men an escape from their fearful lives and the perpetual craving for another heroine-induced "high." His remedy was to pray for their conversion and then for their Spirit baptism (Wilkerson 1964). Today Teen Challenge, founded by Wilkerson in 1958, runs rehabilitation centers in 82 countries. It still prefers spiritual assistance to other means to combat withdrawal symptoms.

Discussion of the baptism of Holy Spirit has radiated in numerous directions. Theologically it has been challenged by dispensationalists who wish to confine miraculous events to the time of the early church (Ruthven 1993). Equally it has been challenged by evangelicals who wish to argue that religious experience of the kind claimed by Pentecostals belongs within the package of events that make up Christian initiation, specifically conversion (Dunn 1970). Arising from this discussion, the purpose of Spirit baptism has been variously proposed, some interpreters emphasizing mission and Christian service and others ecclesiological adjustments to the inner life of the church. Psychologically baptism in the Spirit has been examined in the context of speaking with other tongues, and there is now a long literature that at least shows that Pentecostals cannot credibly be accused of being mentally unstable or maladjusted (Kay 2006).

Some of these investigations, valuable though they are, appear to miss the central feature of many descriptions of the experience. Gee and Carter both draw attention to "the Lord" in their own Spirit baptism. The phenomenological contours of their experience had the effect of making Christ real to them, which, given the biblical claim that Christ is the one who baptizes in the Spirit, should not be surprising. In short, the experience claimed by Pentecostal Christians is felt to be identical to that enjoyed by earlier generations and, most of all, by the first generation of Christians. In this respect, baptism in the Spirit functions like the Roman Catholic doctrine of apostolic succession in that it appears to provide a continuous line from the beginning of the church until the present day. Whereas the Catholic doctrine seeks to establish spiritual descent from Peter, Pentecostal doctrine seeks to establish experiential descent from Acts.

Collective Experience in Meetings

Liturgical services follow a logical order intended to make a congregation ready for the main purpose of the gathering. A communion service, through readings from scripture and confession, will lead people to the taking of bread and wine; a marriage service, with suitable scripture readings, prayers and music, will lead up to the exchange of vows; and so on. The components of the service follow a sequence intended to bring everyone to a prescribed emotional and intellectual state.

Visiting a church in Birmingham in the United Kingdom one Sunday morning, I witnessed a time of exuberant worship. Then, when the congregation fell silent, someone began to sing an impromptu prophetic utterance. After a few moments another person added to the utterance seamlessly and then, like the bursting of fireworks in the night sky, a third person did the same. Each of these contributions blended uncannily with the rest and demonstrated the sense of congregational coordination that a good Pentecostal church can manifest. Here different people appeared to follow the biblical permission "For you can all prophesy in turn so that everyone may be instructed and encouraged" (1 Corinthians 14:32) in a way that was made more astonishing by the musical continuity.

People sometimes forget that where Pentecostal worship is at its best, it is also beautiful and, in some respects, picks up characteristics of ancient and elaborate liturgies. As far as Pentecostals who think about these things are concerned, this is because the worship of the church in earlier ages would have included spiritual gifts with the result that musical scores reflect this spirituality. Plainsong chant in the Orthodox worship sounds like singing in other tongues, so it is possible to understand the 20th-century outpouring of the Spirit as revealing the layers of shared experience underneath the ancient liturgies.

A powerful way of harnessing spiritual gifts occurs in the two days of prayer and fasting that the Newfrontiers congregation arranges for its leaders every quarter.[4] During the first day, intercessory prayer occurs in big or small groups, but by the second day, prophetic utterances and visions begin to abound. These become increasingly elaborate and will make an impact when more than one vocal contribution builds on what has been said or sung previously.

The sessions are all recorded, and the senior leaders will later go through the content of what has been said and assess it in what is seen as a biblical weighing process (1 Corinthians 14:29). When one subtracts the charismatic theology from this set of practices it is possible to see that the senior leadership of the movement is open to the voices of all the other several hundred people present. The vocal charismatic utterances are the means by which Pentecostal leaders hear from their constituents. Without the formal process of consultative committees there is a transfer of information backward and forward within the movement: preaching from the leaders to the flock sends information in one direction, and charismatic gifts within the flock allows information to flow back in the other.

The most dramatic demonstrations of spiritual power involve healing. Reinhard Bonnke, the German Pentecostal evangelist, has been preaching in Africa for decades.[5] These meetings are attended by open-air crowds that would match those drawn by the pope. When he came over to England to speak in Birmingham (which has a large African British population), Bonnke attracted about 15,000 people and filled the National Exhibition Centre. He came on to the stage and his first words were "God is here." This was met with respectful silence, so he shouted it again "God is *here*" and murmurs of assent were heard. He shouted louder, "*God* is here," and provoked cries of "amen," "yes" and so on. He went on to preach a forgettable message but, at the end, came the moment everyone was waiting for. He began to pray for people who had been brought to the front of the huge hall. Among them was a woman in a wheelchair he might have chosen to avoid, but he did not shirk the challenge. After he prayed for her with thousands watching, she began to run around the room to shouts of joy and collective exclamations of delight.

The Bonnke meeting generated emotions based on the religious significance attributed to the healing event. Many Pentecostals would understand the entire meeting as a spiritual experience, one at which God had "showed up" and confirmed the validity of the biblical message about miracles being available in this day and age. By contrast the Toronto Blessing, which attracted media coverage in the 1990s for its outward manifestations of laughing, crying, and falling over, was really concerned with inner healing (Hilborn 2001).

Trends and Fashions

Over the course of more than 40 years I have seen many Pentecostal trends and fashions come and go. Of these five are linked with experience:

Music: As the charismatic movement spread across the mainline churches and into Pentecostalism, music styles also changed. Musical technology assisted the changeover. The piano was replaced by the guitar and electric organ, and then accompanied by drums and other instruments. Music making was part of the creativity of Pentecostalism and, for a brief period, there was a transition as hymns were displaced by choruses. The old, ordered structure of the Pentecostal service with separate hymns and prayers metamorphosed into "a time of worship" that was put in the hands of a (young) "worship leader." He or she led the congregation in a continuous musical experience, effortlessly segueing from one tempo to the next.

The most thoughtful Pentecostal-Charismatic musicians, like John Wimber, appreciated the need to match church music to the tastes of contemporary young people and wrote songs accordingly. There was an attempt in the 1970s to theologize music either using the Tabernacle of David as a template for Christian worship and emphasizing dance (cf. Acts 15:16) or by interpreting worship as a dualistic battleground between satanic forces and divine proclamation. There was talk of prophetic trumpet playing or of the high praises of God to enact spiritual warfare against the dark cloud of "principalities and powers" described in Ephesians 6.

At its worst, Pentecostal music—too heavily influenced by youth culture—lost all sense of reverence, and the words of songs were swallowed up in the sounds of musical extravaganza that appeared to have no emotional content and little spiritual relevance. At their best, though, the musicians fade into the background while lifting the congregation into another realm: the words and sounds blend effortlessly with the focus of spiritual attention and add reality to what is intangible.

Eschatology: Eschatological Pentecostalism drew on the Adventism circulating through American nonconformist culture at the end of the 19th century. Much of this dated back to the dispensationalism of J. N. Darby and was incorporated into the Scofield Reference Bible. Although the major Pentecostal denominations feature the pre-millennial Second Coming of Christ within their fundamental doctrinal statements, an examination of Pentecostal publications in the early 20th century reveals a nuanced and varied set of beliefs about end times (McQueen 2011).

Eschatology points to the end of history, and usually for Christians, to the return of Christ, which is a source of hope. In psychological terms eschatology appears to function as a method of containing generalized anxiety. If an eschatological scheme points to social and natural disasters prior to the return of Christ, then each disaster at least has the benefit of indicating the eschatological scheme is unfolding according to plan. If an eschatological scheme is entirely optimistic and foresees only a gradual diffusion of Christian faith through the expanding kingdom of God, then each disaster is only temporary and minor and can be surmounted by a confidence in the good things that are on the horizon (Murray 1971).

During the 1930s European Pentecostals applied their eschatology to the frightening rise of militarism. There was a fear that the Antichrist had appeared, and attempts were made to fit the standard Pentecostal eschatological scheme onto major world events.[6] In the 1970s, particularly after the Yom Kippur War of 1973, when Israel once again gained control of the entire city of Jerusalem, Pentecostal preachers were to be heard speaking of the fact that Jerusalem was no longer trodden down by the Gentiles and that anti-Christian tribulation was bound to occur. Some preachers identified the European Union, which then had ten countries, with the ten toes of the statue in the book of Daniel. Others saw the invention of barcodes and credit cards as an indication that the entire financial system could be seized by malign power. Many of these eschatological worries found their way into such books as *The Late Great Planet Earth* (1970) and continue today on conspiracy-minded websites.

It would be too much to claim that eschatology is always directly linked with religious experience, but there may be evidence that eschatology heightens awareness and stimulates people for spiritual quest. Within a few days of the start of the Azusa Street revival in Los Angeles in 1906 an earthquake destroyed parts of San Francisco farther up the coast, and preachers like Frank Bartleman in a widely circulated tract interpreted these events as a divine judgment. He wrote, "I found the earthquake had opened many hearts."[7]

Prosperity: Many of the early Pentecostals had grown up in poverty. The earliest American Pentecostals were almost invariably without a college education and belonged to lower socioeconomic strata. The healing evangelists of the 1940s and '50s in the United States like Oral Roberts and T. L. Osborn had grown up in the Dust Bowl years of the Great Depression (Harrell 1975; 1985).[8] They naturally responded to this time of crisis by a seizing on biblical verses supporting divinely purposed prosperity.[9] Their teachings became part and parcel of Pentecostal teaching in the second half of the 20th century without ever being placed into denominational doctrinal statements.

Prosperity teaching had the effect of lifting the eyes of Pentecostals to the possibility of a better material future and, in this way, counteracted the old pessimistic eschatology that had motivated early missions. Prosperity teaching made the enjoyment of wealth acceptable, drew a whole cohort of business people into the orbit of Pentecostalism, and enabled them to see the ups and downs of their commercial activities as falling within the circle of God's care. For some business people, God speaks to them as clearly through the balance sheet as through the Bible, and if finances are bad they get down on their knees to pray. In this way material circumstances trigger spiritual activity.

Authority: Pentecostals have been wary of authority from the beginning. The first attempts to organize Pentecostals into denominations immediately ran into heavy criticism from those who believed any form of organization would restrict the freedom of the Spirit. Yet organization came. Pentecostals who formed their denominations following American Methodism took an Episcopal ecclesiology. The rest tended towards modified Congregationalism. Both ecclesiologies made use of annual or biannual ministerial conferences to make collective decisions binding on their own group. These conferences were occasions for preaching and fellowship but also became occasions for detailed constitutional wrangling that required preachers to develop quasi-legal acuteness, and Pentecostalism began to lose its early flexibility and adaptability.

The 1948–52 Latter Rain revival movement, originating in Canada, was one of a number of early signs that Pentecostal preachers were refusing to be bottled up by regulatory demands. By the 1970s, when the Charismatic movement was running strongly, British Pentecostals began to grow restless, and preachers started to circulate teaching about the necessity for 20th-century apostles and prophets. Apostles and prophets were never going to be subservient to constitutional arrangements because they themselves were the source of authority and direction. Most of these groupings—which might be called apostolic networks or "third wave"—held beliefs that were similar to those of the classical Pentecostals (Kay 2007b).[10]

Once apostolic authority replaced conference authority, a different dynamic ensued.[11] All apostles undoubtedly carried authority and, when this authority was being transferred to a successor or delegate, the apostle might take off his jacket and place it on the shoulders of the recipient of "the anointing."[12]

The doctrine of "anointing" derived from Hebrew Bible practice when kings and priests were marked out by oil symbolic of the Holy Spirit. When these ideas were transferred to today's church, they led to a way of thinking about charismatic gifting. This gifting could now be understood as a flow of divine power, a weight of glory, that encircled the apostolic or healing minister. Benny Hinn (b. 1952) made such teaching explicit and applied it to himself. Most traditional Pentecostals viewed these claims with suspicion: they knew of sick people who had remained unhealed after prayer, or they might have reservations about Hinn's stage *persona* or aspects of his theology. In this way Pentecostalism, even within a single denomination, might divide into a tabloid stream following healing evangelists through cable TV and a broadsheet stream preferring traditional spirituality open to charismatic gifts.

Deliverance: Baptism in the Spirit immediately gave to individuals a belief in the reality of the spirit world. The universe is no longer made of matter interspersed by vast vacant spaces between atoms or planets but rather populated by invisible angels, spiritual beings, and mysterious forces. Pentecostals saw an enchanted universe as well as demon-possessed individuals. Deliverance ministry, especially in African contexts, thrived and might become a routine part of church life. Depressed, schizophrenic, or fearful individuals might be helped by authoritative commands given by pastors to the spiritual forces by which these individuals felt themselves to be possessed.[13]

Exorcism is an obvious demonstration of spiritual power and becomes an ongoing aspect of conversion. I heard two Chinese women from Buddhist or animist backgrounds telling their house group leader of their fear of ghosts at night. The house group leader ran through a list of possible sources for such hauntings and then promised to do a "house cleansing" visit to decontaminate the property. What might seem odd to Western minds was that the house group leader was trained as an engineer, yet treated exorcism as matter-of-factly as he might have discussed the unblocking of drains. The interpenetration between modernity and ancient spiritual forces appears to occur among Pentecostals without any jarring disjunction. The authority of Jesus as Lord of the spiritual realm rings true in a culture that otherwise wards off spirits with incense, gifts to idols, or charms.

How are the historical and thematic lineaments outlined thus far playing out in the contemporary global context? To understand the current vitality of Pentecostalism, we can look at congregations in Southeast Asia, one of the regions where Charismatic Christianity is now growing.

Southeast Asia[14]

Global demographic trends indicate Asia is on the rise. While Europe's share of the world population will be "cut in half from 12.0 to 5.9 per cent" in the years from 2000 to 2100, in absolute terms its numbers will fall from 728 million to 538 million.[15] In the same period the whole of Asia's share of the world population will fall slightly from 60.6 to 55.4 percent, but its number of people will rise from 3.6 billion to 5 billion. Within Asia, the Southeast is a region where the attractions of political stability and openness to world markets have brought rapid population growth. From a population of 178 million in 1950 it is projected to reach 767 million by 2050.[16] Coupled with Southeast Asia's rising population is its economic prosperity: both Hong Kong and Singapore are placed in the top ten regions for per capita income by the World Bank and the CIA World Factbook. Malaysia is placed in the top third of the table, but its GDP places it still higher. These countries have a lifestyle and prosperity to which other countries in the region aspire, and their gleaming cities and iconic skylines beckon the future.

The transmission of Christianity to this part of the world has a long and complex history, but now approximately 10 percent of Hong Kong's population and 15 percent or more of Singapore's population is Christian. Many of these churches are Pentecostal in style. In Malaysia about 9 percent would be classified as Christian and, again, in the major cities there are thriving congregations. Because of their geographical location, demographic trajectory, and economic strength, churches in these areas can be seen as crucial to the shape of world Christianity as the 21st century progresses.

Anyone familiar with the history of Korea knows of its lengthy subservience to Japanese imperialism and then of its traumatic civil war (1950–53). In the post-war ruins David Yonggi Cho (b. 1936) began his ministry in what became the prosperous capital city of the south, Seoul. Using an old tent purchased from the U.S. Marines, he started to preach to Koreans. His message was one of healing because he himself had been healed of tuberculosis after prayer.[17] Aided at first by Pentecostal missionaries, he gradually established a substantial congregation. As he meditated on scripture he came to see the Gospel as inclusive of material improvement and even national hope. This belief that the Gospel is a "gospel of blessing" is now taken by many Korean Pentecostals to be foundational. Cho's church, built on the edge of the city, eventually became the largest in the world, situated symbolically on what became real estate of immense value.

Korean Pentecostals see the Gospel as transformative, as an answer to social and national distress. It can break the cycle of deprivation and lift a country—any country—from economic dependency and exploitation. For the post-war generation of Koreans, the message that was preached to them has been proved true. South Koreans with their world-class electronics and competitive car industry look over the militarized border at the poverty of their northern cousins and draw an obvious conclusion about Christianity and capitalism.

This is not to say that Korean Pentecostals only think of their faith in terms of their nation. On the contrary they are very clear that the Holy Spirit will bring personal blessing (Lee 2004). Cho's books have focused upon the threefold blessings available to Christians (spiritual, physical, and circumstantial) and, in this sense, his mindset is holistic and typically Asian. There have been

suggestions that Cho should be seen as a shaman, a holy man playing a traditional role in Asian culture (Hollenweger 1972: 474–77) but, not surprisingly,
this interpretation has been rejected by Pentecostals. The spiritual power of
Cho, Pentecostals argue, contrasts with shamanism and stands against it and
cannot be conflated with it (Ma 2004).

While Korea was never governed by the West, British involvement in
Southeast Asia included the colonization of Malaya, Hong Kong, and Singapore.
Christians had arrived in 1511 through Portuguese Roman Catholics. The
British opened the way for 19th-century Protestant missions and, in the 20th
century, transported Chinese workers into Malaya for the tin mines and
Tamil-speaking Indians for the rubber plantations. These two ethnic groups
increased in size while retaining their identities. The Chinese for the most part
were animist and the Indians Hindu. When Malaya became independent in
1957, the country's constitution was drawn up to perpetuate Islamic majority
rule. The numerous Malays were designated as Sunni Muslim, and it became
illegal for them to convert. The result of this was that the church only grew
among the Chinese and Indians.[18]

The Tamil community in Malaysia remains poor. One pastor told me that
many of the Tamils were marginalized, that their young people were prone to
drunkenness and educational levels were low. He also believed many members of the Hindu community were demon-possessed, and he prayed almost
routinely for the deliverance of any converts. This approach has since been
countered by Hindu emissaries from India who have arrived to warn their
community angrily against proselytizing Christians. More worrying for
Indian Christians has been the burning of their churches by Islamic radicals.
The debate over the right to use the word "Allah" inflamed inter-ethnic pas-
sions, and one pastor told me how arsonists had attacked his church and scattered his congregation.[19] The Malaysian government acted swiftly to dampen
this violence, and the pastor concerned moved to another town and started to
build a new congregation from scratch, believing that miracles and spiritual
warfare were the key to his success.

During the 1960s and '70s, when the Charismatic movement was in full
swing, significant numbers of young Chinese in Malaysia converted to
Christianity.[20] They spoke in tongues and believed in miracles and rejected the
religious tradition of their parents. This tradition, which demanded respect and
care for older people, accepted the reality of a spiritual dimension. Incense was
offered to statues or idols, propitious days had to be discovered by consulting
horoscopes, and provision made by burning money for the well-being of dead
ancestors. Firecrackers were set off at Chinese New Year to scare away demons.
Conversion to Pentecostal Christianity led to the rejection of these practices.
However, one of the most telling obstacles to conversion concerned family

ties to non-Christian Chinese parents. In my interviews with Pentecostal Chinese, they were clear that their biblical duty to honor their parents was far more meaningful than residual Confucian respect. Elderly parents found their Christian children offered them more practical help than non-Christian siblings. As a result conversions among elderly Chinese occurred some 20 years later. Pastors in Kuala Lumpur and Hong Kong told me stories of grandparents being baptized or making provision in their wills for a Christian rather than a Buddhist funeral.

Insofar as one can generalize about Chinese culture, it is pragmatic and family-based. The family base no doubt stems from centuries of Confucian teaching, but it is also a consequence of the Chinese diaspora. In common with many migratory people who have made the risky crossing from one country to another, the family network is the primary source of support. Strength in the family domain leads very neatly into the cell-group structure found in major Pentecostal churches, and this is facilitated by population density in high-rise buildings. All the large churches in Hong Kong, Singapore, and Kuala Lumpur appear to use cell groups as an essential building block.

This has a further consequence. In Chinese culture, so Chinese pastors told me, the woman is boss in the domestic sphere while the man is boss in the business sphere. Home groups are therefore the natural province of women. In Korea, famously, Cho ordained a large number of female deacons who became house-group leaders, and it was they who contributed to the accelerated growth of his church. The same is true in many other Pentecostal churches in thriving Asian cities, although it is also common to find a husband-and-wife team in charge of a home group with a husband as the musician and the wife as the teacher.

Pentecostal Christianity is starting to make a difference to Chinese commercial activities in the promotion of business ethics and in a rejection of the fickle power of luck. Chinese pastors told me of big hotels in Kuala Lumpur that, in their basements, have altars dedicated to Chinese gods. Others showed me how a set of buildings in Singapore is constructed in the shape of the Buddha's palm with a shorter building representing the thumb and taller buildings representing the fingers. Pentecostalism, to pragmatic Chinese, is a progressive religion—quite the opposite of the way it might be seen in the West. Pentecostalism liberates by removing the necessity to tread carefully around the taboos and superstitions of animistic culture. On the contrary, success is guaranteed by hard work and the grace of God and, in one Men's Meeting I attended, Pentecostal businesses were encouraged to treat their employees fairly.

Although many of the Pentecostal churches work with the grain of Chinese culture, at least one congregation has grown to several thousand in Hong Kong by developing what might be called a "Holy Spirit culture." This church is characterized by daily prayer, belief in apostolic ministry, healing campaigns, supernatural guidance and cell groups. It was one of the few churches that continued holding meetings during the SARS epidemic of 2003, believing that God would protect those who attended from harm. The pastor is believed to be an apostolic figure endowed with spiritual gifts, and the church includes a "school for prophets" that attempts to provide ongoing spiritual guidance for individuals and the church as a whole.

This church belongs to a group that is based in Taiwan and rooted in a Pentecostal culture that is at the same time deeply Chinese, probably deriving from 1930s missionary work by Brethren preachers who were later Pentecostalized. Its growth can be attributed to an enormous commitment of time and resources that is fired by Pentecostal zeal. No decision appears to be taken without looking for the guidance of the Spirit, and the whole congregation believes that every step of their journey is miraculously superintended by God. One of their pastors told me a long and complicated story of how money was given at the right moment, how a building became suddenly available, and how their founding pastor or apostle was led by a combination of spiritual gifts and miraculous coincidences. The extraordinarily rapid growth of this congregation from zero to 4,000 people in ten years is testimony to the current vitality of Pentecostalism.

Although I had expected that the animistic presuppositions embedded in Chinese tradition would assist the propagation of Pentecostal Christianity, the situation turns out to be more subtle than that. The supernaturalistic elements of Pentecostal Christianity do indeed dovetail with a default Chinese worldview, but *in addition* there are ordinary natural elements within Chinese culture on which Pentecostal churches have built. The family, the place of women, respect for authority, business acumen, adaptability, and the valuing of education are all consonant with Pentecostal churches of the 21st century. The process of Westernization, especially in Hong Kong and Singapore, dates back to the mid-19th century and British colonialism. Many of the best schools were founded by the churches and provided an excellent education as well as offering access to the English language and therefore the global culture that emerged after 1945. The prominence of women in Hong Kong and Singapore within the public sector contrasts with that of many other parts of the Asia, and the churches must be given some credit for this.[21] Pentecostalism, with its belief in an outpouring of the Spirit on men *and* women, contributed to this cultural flow.

One facet of Pentecostal Christianity has surprising affinities with the health preoccupations of Chinese medicine. Chinese culture has traditionally emphasized harmony between yin and yang, between opposites, and this notion fits in well with the notion of *shalom* or peace or a balance between the spiritual and the physical. There is some evidence that the Pentecostal doctrine of healing may be broadened to include reconciliation.[22] By this means healing is not only a miraculous intervention by the Holy Spirit in the life of a sick person but results from numerous acts of forgiveness and reparation, first in the family and then in the community. So the concept of healing expands out from bodily healing, although this is included, and through the operation of the Holy Spirit, adds a social dimension and makes an amalgam of spiritual and social experience.

Such a broadening of the interpretation of healing is also in line with the tendency of Chinese hermeneutics (Yieh 2009). Respect for sacred texts dates back to Confucian times and the focus of concern will often be moral. Along with its spiritual message, the Bible is treated a moral authority and one that should be interpreted for its benefit to the community as well as to the individual.[23]

The civil war in China that was won by Mao and his followers turned mainland China into a one-party Communist state after 1949. This had a ripple effect on many Chinese, spurring them to escape across the border to Hong Kong or Singapore.[24] A further migrant wave fled the cultural revolution of 1966–76. Independently of each other three Christians told me the story of their refugee fathers or grandfathers who had entered Hong Kong semi-illegally and had been fed, clothed, and educated by the churches and who, as a result, had a deep gratitude to Christian institutions even if, later in life, their own beliefs had drifted. Pentecostal churches, along with others, benefit from this pro-religious attitude.

The Chinese church finds itself poised between the influence of China itself and direct Western influence mediated through all the digital platforms by which the world speaks to itself.[25] Hollywood films open in Hong Kong and Singapore at practically the same time as they open in London. American preachers have access to the megachurches of Asia because the common language of English is available to both. The steadying voices of older missionaries and classical Pentecostals are now competing with the newer voices of apostolic networks bringing their neo-Pentecostal messages and insights. This polarity expresses the contrast between two kinds of spiritual experiences. There were people whose spiritual life was nourished by personal Bible reading and solitary devotion. Against this more introverted spirituality is the communal Pentecostal spirituality of speaking in tongues and exercising charismatic gifts within a collective setting.

Concluding Reflection

Despite the restrictive legal frameworks under which Pentecostal and charismatic churches operate in parts of Southeast Asia, they are growing within the Chinese, and to a lesser degree, the Indian diaspora.[26] These frameworks, although they are intended to reduce evangelism or proselytization, also affect the charitable work of Pentecostal churches. Where charitable work is in danger of infringing legal or cultural constraints, Pentecostals have to be careful to ensure that what they do is acceptable. In Malaysia one of the large Charismatic churches in Kuala Lumpur is building a hugely expensive youth center and dialysis unit. This is clearly a project that will benefit everyone regardless of religious affiliation. In Hong Kong and Singapore some of the larger international churches that worship primarily in English have mixed Chinese and Indian membership, and many run smaller subsidiary congregations for Filipinos and some will extend the list to Indonesian, Nepali, Cantonese, Mandarin, Sinhalese, Tamil, Thai, or Portuguese (Brazilian) speakers. The main congregation will subsidize the smaller congregations by, for instance, paying for pastoral staff drawn from the relevant ethnic or linguistic group. This is because the smaller congregations do not generate enough income to support their own pastors. In this sense the main congregation, inspired by a communal spirituality, is acting charitably toward migrant workers and the countries they represent.

In Hong Kong, where Christian charitable work from the 19th century was expressed by the building of schools and hospitals, there appears to be less sensitivity to humanitarian outreach with a religious dimension. One large international congregation runs a feeding program for poor Chinese, especially those who have come across the border and failed to gain employment. These people may be engaged in the street markets and, because they speak Mandarin rather than Cantonese, be unable to secure jobs in shops and businesses. By contrast, the most Pentecostal of the Pentecostal churches expresses its humanitarian instincts by sending money abroad, especially to the Joseph Storehouse, an interreligious aid center in Israel.[27]

Simple acts of kindness are fostered by home groups. Such groups appear to be universal and may be the basis for organizational patterns within the big congregations. For instance, one large Hong Kong church arranged its home groups into 11 or 12 "families" (or perhaps "tribes" is a better translation), each with their own pastor and Chinese symbol and banner. This large church, though the pastor speaks English, wishes to subsume his congregation's identity into Chinese-ness. Other pastors value their international identity knowing that familiarity with the English language opens Pentecostal churches to Western influence either through their connections with classical Pentecostal denominations or through a host of neo-Pentecostal, post-1970 networks. In all cases, these Southeast Asian congregations feel the pull of family ties across continents, for example between Koreans and Korean-Americans and between Chinese and American-born Chinese.

This means that trends mentioned earlier in the fields of music, eschatology, prosperity, authority, and deliverance may all be relevant to Asian churches. For the most part, the pastors who are successful have struck the right balance here and have avoided extremes. In megachurches the presentation of Christianity will often take place through drama and polished musical productions that are "seeker friendly."[28] Where churches do not have the resources to mount spectacular presentations, they will probably rely on house meetings (which have the advantage of being legally inoffensive in countries where proselytization is forbidden), by praying for those who are ill, by preaching a positive biblical message, and, as was said earlier, by building on elements in Chinese culture. Among the megachurches, apart from the exceptional Hong Kong congregation mentioned above, Pentecostal practices are almost invisible in the big Sunday meetings. Speaking in tongues may occur during the general volubility of collective prayer or song, and the laying on of hands will often be offered at the end of the service for those who need this sort of personal ministry. But in the open atmosphere of these churches at which newcomers are often present, the dramatic Pentecostal manifestations of prophecy are largely absent. The pastors are concerned to "do things decently and in order," and it is only in the house meetings or through the regular induction programs that new members would discover the Pentecostal-Charismatic nature of the congregation they have joined.

One final aspect of these growing churches is seen in their missionary impetus and generosity. Having received missionaries from the West (especially the United States and Canada), these churches are willing to send missionaries to the poorer countries of Southeast Asia—to Myanmar, the Philippines, and even as far Nepal and Thailand. Having known poverty, many of these Christians have been lifted by Asia's economic boom and are ready to give to those who have not. This combination of purposive activity and charity is potent, and its appeal to new and old church members has a communal aspect as well as a spiritual dimension.

NOTES

1. Data collected from 930 Pentecostal ministers in Britain from Assemblies of God, Elim, The Church of God, and the Apostolic Church found that, within a ten-item mysticism scale, the items "Sensing God in the beauty of nature" and "Singing Gospel hymns" both had item–rest of test correlations above 0.48. The scale was a mixture of nature items and church items and had an alpha coefficient of 0.7717 (Kay 2000: ch 8).

2. Assemblies of God in the USA had a pacifist component in the period between the two World Wars. British Assemblies of God included reference to pacifism in its constitutional documents in 1924.

3. Thomas de Quincey's *Confessions of an English Opium-eater* were published in 1822 but can hardly have been said to have been relevant to the drug culture of the period after 1960. Huxley (1954) is more relevant. Russell (1956) provides a brief first-hand account of Lawrence's sexual mysticism.

4. New Frontiers International Trust Limited (Registered UK Charity 1060001), "Newfrontiers, a worldwide family of churches together on a mission," http://newfrontierstogether.org/. The site displays an interactive map of the world that shows associated congregations on six continents and in many countries.

5. Christ for All Nations, "CfAN, Christ for All Nations, the ministry of Reinhard Bonnke," http://www.cfan.org/. The site is the gateway of the Reinhard Bonnke website and shows what his organization, Christ for All Nations, has been doing in different parts of the world. There are sections in seven languages in addition to English.

6. A regular series entitled "Watchman, What of the Night?" was published during the 1930s in *Redemption Tidings*, the British Assemblies of God denominational magazine. It made a point of reading international events through the spectacles of pre-millennial eschatology.

7. "The Old Landmark: Celebrating Our Apostolic Heritage," http://oldlandmark.wordpress.com/2009/02/12/earthquake-evangelism-the-san-francisco-quake-the-azusa-revival/ [accessed 23 April 2012]. The blog contains commentary on Bartleman's activities and quotations from his writings. See also Robeck (2006).

8. I spoke with Osborn in about 2006 and he told me of his early years playing a concertina in open-air meetings when he could hardly afford the price of a pair of shoes.

9. The verse originally favored was 3 John 1:2, "Beloved, I wish above all things that thou mayest prosper and be in health, even as thy soul prospereth" (King James Version). The word "prosper" was picked up and became a part of the standard teaching of Oral Roberts.

10. A panel (Michael McClymond, Margaret Poloma, Michael Wilkinson, John Bialecki, and myself) was assembled to discuss apostolic networks or the New Apostolic Reformation at the Society for Pentecostal Studies in Norfolk, Virginia, in 2012. Academic interest in the changing sociological shape of Pentecostalism has been slow to catch on.

11. Such claims were notable in Australian Assemblies of God and then later in British Assemblies of God. For a discussion of Pentecostal ecclesiology with an Australian slant see Clifton (2009).

12. I know of two occasions when this happened.

13. For further discussion see Kay and Parry (2011).

14. The information in this section is based on six formal interviews with Hong Kong pastors, nine formal interviews with Malaysian pastors, and one formal and four informal interviews with Singaporean pastors. In addition I lived in Hong Kong for three months at the start of 2012 and had numerous informal meetings with pastors and church members at this time as well as attending several kinds of church meetings. Information about Singapore and Kuala Lumpur was supplemented by visits to both these locations during the two years that the PCRI project lasted. In Kuala Lumpur and Hong Kong I organized data collecting ministerial conferences that required me to meet with groups of pastors and church workers. The protocols that govern research at the university which employs me, Glyndwr University in Wales, lead me to anonymize the sources of information where this is gained from interview.

15. United Nations, Department of Economic and Social Affairs, Population Division, "World Population to 2300," (2004), pdf downloaded from http://www.un.org/esa/population/publications/longrange2/WorldPop2300final.pdf (page 1) [accessed 23 April 2012]. The 254-page booklet contains population statistics, various scenarios, and expert interpretive essays.

16. Ibid.

17. This information is widely available though it was made real to me by a visit to Seoul in 2008.

18. General information about Malaysian Christianity, including Pentecostal Christianity, is given by Hunt, Hing, and Roxborough (1992).

19. See the following lengthy and detailed assessment of religious freedom that cites court cases and legal judgments to build up a picture of religious conditions in Malaysia: US Department of State: diplomacy in action, "Malaysia. Bureau of democracy, human

rights and labor," July-December, 2010 International Religious Freedom Report, http://
www.state.gov/j/drl/rls/irf/2010_5/168363.htm [accessed 18 Mar 2012], from which
the following quotation is taken: "On December 31, 2009, the High Court of Kuala
Lumpur held that the government's prohibition on the *Catholic Herald*'s use of the word
'Allah' was unconstitutional, ruling in the Catholic Church's favor. The decision fueled
opposition among the Malay majority, resulting in attacks on several places of worship.
The government immediately filed an appeal and a stay of the court's decision, and on
January 4 the trial court issued the requested stay pending a review of the decision by
the Court of Appeals."

20. Malaya became the Federation of Malaya in 1948 and then with the addition of Sabah,
    Sarawak, and Singapore became Malaysia in 1963. Singapore left in 1965 to become
    an independent country. The charismatic movement in Malaysia appears was trans-
    mitted through Scripture Union as well as the mainline churches (Hunt, Hing, and
    Roxborough 1992).

21. Information about Assemblies of God in Singapore is given in an illustrated authorized
    compilation edited by A. S. Abisheganaden (1992).

22. This information comes from discussion with at least one doctoral student from
    Korea.

23. Dr G. Wright Doyle, "Chinese Biblical Studies: Issues in Understanding and
    Interpretation" (notes on a colloquium on Chinese biblical studies sponsored by the
    Center for the Study of Christianity in China, King's College, London, held January
    17–21, 2009), posted on China Global Centre website http://www.globalchinacenter.
    org/analysis/christianity-in-china/chinese-biblical-studies-issues-in-understanding-a
    nd-interpretation.php.

24. I met one woman whose aunt, a Christian, had swum for 10 days to escape Mao's China.
    She had set out with about 200 people of whom only around 40 reached the safety of
    Hong Kong. The rest drowned.

25. Almost without exception the Chinese Pentecostal pastors I spoke to in Singapore and
    Hong Kong felt a desire to minister in the churches of mainland China and to support
    them either by offering training or financially.

26. The Maintenance of Religious Harmony Act of 1992 in Singapore discourages conver-
    sion from one religion to another (particularly Islam to Christianity) although its osten-
    sible provisions are to prevent interreligious ill-will and anti-government subversion.
    The Malaysian Constitution of 1957 guarantees religious freedom. However the effect
    of rulings by religious courts is to prevent the conversion of Muslims to Christianity,
    and a person's religious affiliation is given on their biometric identity card. The pastors
    I spoke to were not aware of religious oppression although some expressed the view
    that a great number of Malays would have become Christian if they had been allowed
    to do so. In Hong Kong the Basic Law provides for religious freedom and prohibits reli-
    gious discrimination, and religious societies are not required to register with the gov-
    ernment. The pastors I spoke to did not feel in any way hampered or threatened by this
    legislation.

27. See a news paragraph about "a humanitarian aid centre in the hills of Jerusalem,"
    "Standing with Israel: the Joseph Storehouse," *Charisma Magazine*, http://www.
    charismamag.com/index.php/newsletters/standing-with-israel/29421-the-joseph-
    storehouse.

28. Drama presentations were given by ICA in Hong Kong and by City Harvest and Trinity
    Christian Centre in Singapore.

14

Prophecy, Empowerment, and Godly Love

The Spirit Factor in the Growth of Pentecostalism

MARGARET M. POLOMA AND MATTHEW T. LEE

Introduction

"Do you want the nation of Mozambique?" This was the prophetic question Randy Clark spoke to Heidi Baker at a neopentecostal church service in Toronto in the mid-1990s.[1] At the time, Heidi was a burned-out missionary to Mozambique, overcome by feelings of powerlessness in the midst of widespread poverty and suffering brought on in part by a long civil war. According to Heidi, she and Randy did not know each other when he posed his prophetic question.[2] But he followed his question by prophetically proclaiming to Heidi, "The blind will see. The crippled will walk. The deaf will hear. The dead will be raised, and the poor will hear the good news."[3] Upon hearing these words Heidi perceived "the power of God pulsating through me," which left her "wholly undone, totally wrecked" by the "heavy, weighty glory of God."[4] She describes being unable to walk for several days in the aftermath of this powerful, prophetic experience involving two-way interactions with a prophet (Randy) and the Holy Spirit. For Heidi, the heart of this experience is divine love—a love that validates and empowers her and heals those to whom she ministers. God heals because God loves. This love is powerfully attractive to those who have joined Heidi in her ministry and to those who have converted to Christianity as a result of their work.

In the wake of her encounter with Randy, Heidi returned to Mozambique empowered to expect life-changing miracles. Instead, she encountered hostility (thugs with machine guns seized 55 of her ministry's buildings, including homes for orphans), disease (her husband and daughter contracted malaria, and she was diagnosed with multiple sclerosis), and disappointment (the blind did not see when she prayed for them). But she was not discouraged because she had learned to see past the immediate, material circumstances to a spiritual vision of a world transformed by God's all-powerful love. She writes, "But I knew I had a word—a promise—from God."[5] This divine promise—or prophetic word—when backed up by miraculous events, is central to the growth of pentecostalism in the world.[6] Heidi persisted in praying for every blind person she encountered for a year before she saw the first healing. The rest of the prophecy would gradually unfold with countless accounts of healing and miracles giving rise to thousands of churches. Heidi would be soon joined by a native Mozambican, a poor African who like Heidi relied more on the spiritual promptings of the Holy Spirit than carefully crafted programs for missionary outreach.

"Born into a long line of witch doctors, Surprise ('Surpresa') Sithole was destined for a life of fear, oppression, and poverty in the jungles of Africa. But at the age of fifteen, he was awakened in the middle of the night by an unfamiliar voice. Urgent, but not harsh, it told him to get up and leave his family immediately."[7] Thus begins the description of Surprise's autobiography, *Voice in the Night*. God's "voice in the night" led him on a journey rife with prophecy, miracles, and apparently starting thousands of churches while still a teenager. Reportedly he would speak in languages that he had never studied as he went on to pursue formal schooling and ongoing evangelistic outreach. Although he did not initially recognize the voice that instructed him, "Get out of the house. If you do not, you will die," it was a voice he now attributes to God.[8] As he followed the directions to leave his village and head into the jungle, he would soon encounter a man who had received instructions from God to go to a designated place and wait. This man would introduce Surprise to Christianity and light an evangelistic fervor in the 15-year-old boy that has burned intensely for over 25 years.

At first, Surprise had no Bible, much less any blueprint for planting churches. He recounts those early years of evangelizing as ones much like the descriptions of church planting in the biblical book of Acts:

> I stayed on a few days to teach the people what I knew about the Bible, which did not take very long. Nor did I know very much about structuring this new church. I knew that every church had a pastor and that Sunday was a special day because it was on that day that Jesus rose from the dead. I did not yet own a Bible, so we did not have the New Testament to guide us.
>
> We did, however, have the Holy Spirit to instruct us, and He did. In more than 25 years since then, as I have traveled and spoken

in churches all over the world, I have been amazed at how closely those first churches I planted in Africa followed the pattern set forth in the New Testament. As soon as I felt confident that the fledgling church was going to spread its wings and fly, I headed back out on the road.

Surprise first encountered Heidi in 1997 when she spoke at a church in South Africa where he was then attending Bible college during a respite from evangelism in Mozambique. He was impressed with Heidi and her husband Rolland and their organization Iris Ministries, but he assumed that this meeting would be the last he would see of them. A few weeks later, however, he had a prophetic dream involving Heidi:

> I saw her standing on a small hill and calling to me, 'Come over here. We need you!' A few nights later I had a similar dream. This time Heidi stood on the top of a tall building, again calling for me to come and help. Both dreams were so vivid that I knew God was talking to me, and so I immediately made plans to travel to Chihango, a community about twenty miles from the Mozambican capital of Maputo. Rolland and Heidi ran a children's home in Chihango where they cared for more than three hundred boys and girls.[9]

Surprise arrived in Chihango just as the children's home was being shut down by the government. Surprise even heard there was a reward offered to anyone who would kill Heidi. When the Bakers were forced to leave Chihango, however, the children followed them 20 miles to Maputo. There they could be seen moving in the supernatural gifts (prophesying, speaking in tongues, healing) as they had learned from the Bakers. Surprise had become convinced that he was being called to work with Iris Ministries when he was staying with another Iris volunteer. He reported falling out of bed three times trying to answer a phone that was not actually there—there was no phone service where they were staying. Surprise writes: "Yet I had heard the phone so clearly. That is when it occurred to me that God was trying to get my attention—He was making it clear that He wanted me to do something I had not yet done; make a full-time commitment to Iris Ministries. I got down on my knees and silently told Him that I would do as He asked."[10] Reflecting on the unexpected turn that his life has taken over the past 25 years—leaving his poor village steeped in witchcraft and becoming a well-known Christian evangelist—Surprise says, "I have learned about love beyond discrimination, and I have learned courage and a life of giving." This lesson of love, he claims, he has learned from Heidi.[11]

Prophecy, the Spirit Factor, and Godly Love

As evidenced from the wide array of scholarly articles in this volume, social scientific research on pentecostalism has blossomed within the past decade. Its significance as a global religion has moved beyond an occasional expository book or journal article to include ground-breaking, systematic empirical investigation. The academic community has at last come to recognize pentecostalism's phenomenal growth, a growth that has been commonly attributed to its being a "movement organization"—a reticulate organization, linked together by a variety of personal, structural, and ideological ties, which can be likened to a cellular organism. Its message reportedly travels along preexisting social relationships such as family, friendship, community, and shared migration.[12] Although polycephalous organizational fluidity is undoubtedly important to the rapid spread of pentecostalism, we contend that observation about organization may be but a reflection of a dynamic interactive process between Spirit and humans found at the heart of the pentecostal worldview that emphasizes religious experience.[13] Miller and Yamamori have referred to such subjective experiences in their insightful work on global Pentecostalism and social engagement as the S-factor or the Holy Spirit whom Pentecostals claim to experience as leading, guiding, and empowering them.[14]

An often-overlooked key to spiritual empowerment is prophecy, a gift of the Holy Spirit through which believers experience the usually inaudible "voice" of God speaking directly to them and/or through the prophetic words of others that lead them and guide their actions. The empowerment that Heidi Baker felt after receiving a prophetic word from Randy Clark (with the accompanying bodily sensation of the power of God), briefly described in the introduction, sustained her through the discouraging year that she spent in Mozambique praying for miracles to occur. But evidence of the Spirit factor, to which Heidi attributes the healing of the blind, is ultimately required to give credence to the prophecies. The growth of pentecostalism is fundamentally tied to the diverse ways in which the prophetic becomes manifest in the lives of real people, through some kind of transformation of life circumstances, such as healing of a physical illness, emotional problem, or estranged relationship. It can bring ministries together, as illustrated by Surprise's call to join Iris Ministries where, as we have seen, he reports Heidi taught him to love as God loves.

Using anecdotal narratives and a national survey, this chapter seeks to further understand prophecy through the lenses of godly love, a model that embodies the interaction ritual chains between Spirit and humans lying behind pentecostalism's reticulate organization. Godly love has been defined as *the dynamic interaction between divine and human love that enlivens and expands benevolence.*[15] In other words godly love is at the heart of the Great Commandment to love God above all things and to love others as oneself. In pentecostalism the Great Commandment, it can be argued, has worked in tandem with the biblical Great Commission of evangelism in facilitating global pentecostal growth. Furthermore, existing research on godly love suggests that prophecy, a particular experience of the S-factor in divine leading, guidance, and empowerment, can play a significant role in compassionate service. This is reflected in the explosive growth of Iris Ministries, one of many pentecostal and neopentecostal networks in which the Holy Spirit is believed to be the guiding force.[16] By responding to prophetic guidance, its founders model the marriage between benevolence and evangelism that is a hallmark of Christian growth generally throughout the world. Prophetic interactions tap deeply into the supernatural sources of empowerment in ways that are distinctive to pentecostalism and perhaps distinctively effective in fostering pentecostal growth.

Although most of our empirical research on godly love has been done in the American context, we believe it holds a key for understanding the growth of worldwide pentecostalism.[17] After questioning the adequacy of existing organizational and social psychological theses, Assemblies of God theologian Gary Tyra recently made the case that prophecy plays an important but often-overlooked role in accounting for pentecostalism's growth. As Tyra has stated, "...another reason why pentecostalism is growing so rapidly around the world is that more than a few rank-and-file Pentecostal believers have been willing to follow the personal leading of the Spirit of mission to speak and act prophetically into the lives of lost and hurting people living in their communities."[18] Tyra uses earlier observations and statistical research by Poloma and Green on the American Assemblies of God to provide empirical support for his thesis that explores "the relationship between prophetic speech and action, and the missional faithfulness of evangelical Christians."[19]

The dynamic relationship between prophetic spiritual experiences and mission activities is a specific case of godly love that describes how humans' cooperating with a loving God empowers benevolent service to others.[20] Before we continue to explore the relationship between prophecy and mission illustrated in the introductory account, it is important to discuss briefly what is meant by prophecy and consider the role it plays in the lives of many Christians—both Pentecostals and pentecostals—who claim to hear the voice of the Spirit and respond to it.

Prophecy in Pentecostal Perspective

Although prophecy is commonly understood as a prediction of future events, most pentecostals would agree with Gerald Shepherd who contends that "prophecy does not typically predict the future, but gives assurance, confirmation, warning, or spiritual encouragement."[21] Prophecy is better described as a *forth-telling* of God's word than as the *foretelling* of future events. At times predictions for the future are embedded in the forth-telling, but in more common use and understanding they are not. With the exception of a few men and women who claim to hold the "office of prophet" and who do claim to predict future events, prophecy is most often regarded as simply hearing a word from God and then acting on the divine directives. When Randy Clark asked Heidi Baker, "Do you want the nation of Mozambique?" and told her that the blind would see, as discussed at the beginning of this chapter, this was not akin to simply seeing in a crystal ball future events that were guaranteed to occur. Hence the question, "Do you want the nation of Mozambique?" Heidi had to say "yes" to this and then partner with God and other people (especially her husband Rolland, and others like Surprise Sithole) in interactions we have labeled "godly love" in order to translate the prophetic words into lived reality. She could have declined. She could have given up before the discouraging year was over. But she believed that a truth of God had been spoken and this knowledge was confirmed for her by the powerful bodily experience that accompanied the prophetic message given to her by Randy Clark.

The pentecostal practice of prophecy exemplified by the opening story about Heidi, Randy, and Surprise is a heritage from Judaism and is rooted in earliest Christian history. On the first Christian Pentecost (itself regarded as a fulfillment of Jesus's prophecy to send the Spirit to his early followers), the apostle Peter would quote the Jewish prophet Joel to explain the paranormal occurrences that had mystified onlookers: "In the last days, God says, I will pour out my Spirit on all people. Your sons and daughters will prophesy, your young men will see visions, your old men will dream dreams. Even on my servants, both men and women, I will pour out my Spirit in those days, and they will prophesy" (Acts 2:12–17, NIV). Judging from the Acts of the Apostles and the Pauline epistles, the early Christian church presented prophecy as a charism or spiritual gift to be sought by all believers. The practice of prophecy was no longer for only the few gifted Jewish men and women heralded as prophets. In writing on the "spiritual gifts," especially speaking in tongues (glossolalia) and prophecy, the Apostle Paul admonishes, "Follow the way of love and eagerly desire spiritual gifts, especially the gift of prophecy. For anyone who speaks in tongues does not speak to men but to God .... He who speaks in a tongue edifies himself, but he who prophesies edifies the church. I would like every one of you to speak in tongues, but I would rather have you prophesy" (1 Corinthians 14: 1–5, NIV). While speaking in tongues has often been regarded the hallmark of Pentecostal practices by scholars, prophecy unfortunately has commonly been overlooked.[22]

Clearly nuances in the definitions of prophecy and its practice in Christianity have shifted over time. The history of Christianity suggests further that prophecy has been understandably controlled, if not generally discouraged and even condemned, by religious institutions during most eras.[23] Prophecy, like many religious experiences, can threaten established doctrines and practices of existing institutions. Although various sects (including Catholic religious orders) and denominations have had prophetic origins, prophecy (even when acknowledged as part of Christian history) has rarely been encouraged for the masses. With the increasing institutionalization of Christian sects, prophecy, if accepted at all, has been identified with a church office or relegated to a rare experience for noted saints. Anchored in the biblical account of the first Christian Pentecost, examples of prophecy found in the book of Acts, and the writings about prophecy by the Apostle Paul, early Pentecostals would declare that the Spirit has been poured out on all believers and all can prophesy. What we are suggesting in this chapter is a plausible thesis that one of the reasons that pentecostalism has spread so dramatically is that, unlike most other Catholic and Protestant Christian traditions, it permits and even encourages the experience and practice of prophecy. Individuals and congregations find this freedom to prophesy to be empowering in sustaining personal spiritual vitality that may foster institutional growth.

Certain general definitional points can be noted about prophecy as it is found in the three major waves of the American pentecostal movement, all of which continue to have an impact on global pentecostalism. The first wave, generated by the Azusa Street Revival in Los Angeles in 1906–9, spawned Pentecostal denominations, including the Assemblies of God, the International Church of the Foursquare Gospel (Foursquare Church), the Church of God in Christ, and the Church of God (Cleveland, TN); the second wave is marked by the infiltration of the Pentecostal worldview into mainline denominations, Protestant, Catholic, and Orthodox, during the 1960s and '70s; and the third wave of neopentecostalism, which began in the 1980s and increased in strength through the revivals of the 1990s, deemphasized glossolalia as it placed more emphasis on healing and prophecy for successful evangelism. Prophecy as understood by pentecostals (and as taught even by the "prophets" reportedly holding "the office of prophet") is commonly expressed as a charisma or gift of divine grace available (at least in some degree) to all believers, enabling them to speak or act out messages from God that edify, encourage, and bless others.

Prophecy as forth-telling, suggests a recent national survey (Godly Love National Survey or GLNS; see Lee, Poloma, and Post 2013) that identified prophetic prayer as one of three major types of prayer, is familiar to many Christians in the United States. Moreover, prophetic prayer, in tandem with devotional or more ritualized prayer activities and mystical prayer experiences, helps us to better understand what lies behind experiences of divine love.[24] Experiencing God's love in turn is a significant variable in accounting for different measures of benevolent service to others. In other words, prayer (including prophetic prayer)[25] can be regarded metaphorically as the breath that draws in experiences of God's love—divine love that empowers benevolent service. Taking a closer look at the fluid relationship between prophetic prayer and an experiential love relationship with the divine that empowers benevolence can cast informative light on the thesis driving this chapter, namely that prophecy has played a significant role in the enactment of missionary work that fuels pentecostal growth.[26]

Prophetic Prayer and Godly Love

In his theoretical model of interpersonal Christian prayer (ICP), communication theorist E. James Baesler conceptualizes prayer as communication with God.[27] As prayer moves from active human monologue toward greater receptivity to the divine, it assumes the form of what Baesler describes as "radically divine communication" and is accompanied by feelings of "loving and being loved by God."[28] The metaphor of prayer as "radically divine communication" imbued with a sense of divine love finds support in Poloma and Lee's use of the GLNS to test statistical relationships between three major types of prayer and experiencing divine love.[29] Prayer—devotional, prophetic, and mystical—as already noted, accounted for nearly 80 percent of the variance in the divine love scale, a five-item measure that tapped reported experiences of God's love. Devotional prayer was measured and described in terms of human activities, including petition, thanksgiving, adoration, repentance, et cetera that are often experienced as processes in which the pray-er (after "disposing oneself to God") talks or listens to God.[30] Prophetic prayer, best described as Baesler's "dialogue with God," reflects collaboration between divinity and humanity as expressed through a request for divine guidance and then "hearing" a response from the divine. This response may come in the form of divine instruction to perform a specific act, which may be confirmed as the process unfolds through "prophetic words" from other human actors. The third prayer form, mystical prayer, represents a union of the soul and God, a communion with God. Baesler describes mysticism as "the peak of contemplation [that] is characterized by union, ecstasy, and/or rapture."[31]

Prophetic prayer is generally not a single act or event. It blends active and receptive prayer in an elongated dialogue and/or union with the divine that is fed by impressions, dreams, visions, and/or trances. The process of receiving a message believed to be from God and responding to it, therefore, cannot be adequately tapped with measures that are limited to asking about human activities, including how often or how long the pray-er prays. Prophetic prayer is an ongoing dialogue with God that is marked by receptivity, and it appears to play a significant role in lived religion. Furthermore, communication in prophetic prayer often includes human partners who give and receive words to stir up, to encourage, and to confirm prophetic directions intuited by the pray-er. Thus prophetic prayer involves relationships, both those formed with God as well as those that occur with other collaborators. Prophetic pray-ers may receive a word from God through another person, and/or they may give a message to another in response to divine prompting.[32] Our GLNS findings suggest that all three types of prayer—devotional, prophetic, and mystical—are commonly reported by Americans. Furthermore, as Baesler's model of prayer as communication has hypothesized, "loving and being loved by God" is generally an integral part of the prayer journey. Those respondents to our national survey whose high scores on the divine love scale reflected an enduring and intense love relationship with God frequently engaged in all three types of prayer. As demonstrated by the statistics and illuminated by the narratives, it is safe to say that all three types of prayer can blend together in a single song with divine love providing the background music. Commonly used measures of prayer fail to capture the richness and diversity to be found when prayer is conceptualized as communication with the divine and energized by love.

Figure 14.1 captures the interactive relationships through which prophetic prayer energizes "prophets" and their collaborators to engage in evangelism and missions, in turn fostering the growth of pentecostalism.[33] The prophetic pray-er dialogues with God, both praying to and loving God and receiving words (and love) from God. There are, at least potentially, two-way interactions between God and co-worker (who may or may not be prophetically oriented) and between the pray-er and co-worker. The arrows to and from God to "Evangelism, Missions, and Pentecostal Growth" indicate that prophetic prayer is not the only possible influence on these three outcomes. Other forms of prayer and interactions with God are also important. But this model highlights the potential contributions of a prophetic pray-er immersed in a social network involving dynamic interactions with God and others.

Of the three major prayer forms—devotional, prophetic, and mystical—prophetic prayer best reflects the model shown below as "hearing from God" leads to action (evangelism and missionary work). God and the pray-er are engaged in communication, a prophetic message is heard by the pray-er may (or may not) be confirmed by a potential collaborator, and the pray-er is empowered (through love energy experienced in prayer) to act based on the message that he or she believes God has spoken. The collaborator(s) who encourage, edify, and often work with the primary pray-er to accomplish divine directives

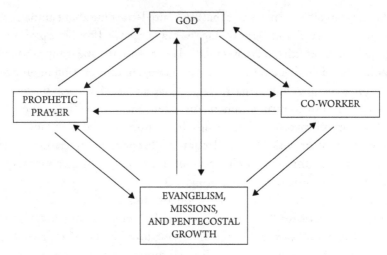

Figure 14.1 "Prophetic Prayer and Godly Love"

may also be engaged in interaction with God in prayer. Prophetic prayer, arguably, is the metaphorical breath that flows through pentecostal evangelism and
mission, as can be seen in our ongoing account of Iris Ministries

Iris Ministries

Founded by Rolland Baker, the grandson of a noted American missionary to
China, and his California-born wife Heidi, Iris Ministries was revitalized and
catapulted into fame during third-wave American Pentecostalism, specifically
through the revival that took place at the Toronto Airport Christian Fellowship
(now "Catch the Fire") at the close of the millennium.[34] Iris Ministries had
always been rooted in the pentecostal perspective where miracles and myster-
ies were common, but the Toronto Blessing marked a new beginning for their
mission, now located in Mozambique. Rolland Baker writes the following on
the Iris website about the spiritual foundation that has been central to Iris's
mission and ministry:

> It is impossible to be devoted to Jesus and not share Him, pure and sim-
> ple. We cannot see Him now, but God has ordained that we love Him by
> loving each other, whom we can see. He is love, and so we cannot sepa-
> rate the first commandment from the second. There are many callings,
> but none higher than to give water to the thirsty and food to the hungry.

The intercessors at home and the troops in the trenches are equals in the Kingdom. We learn to love just as we are gifted and called by God.

   Missions is [sic] our joy, the simple, logical outcome of knowing Jesus. We have life and hope; others don't. We have reason to rejoice; others don't. We have love in our hearts; others don't. We have food and clothes; others don't. We have health; others don't. We have family; others don't. We have no reason to be anxious; others are weighed down with cares. It is obvious that the calling of every believer in Jesus is to have a part in correcting these imbalances.

   That may take us across the street or around the world. It is also obvious that we should be utterly available to God to go anywhere and do anything, at any time. He can and will make a way as He leads us. That is the testimony of Iris Ministries, for thirty years.[35]

Supported by over 1,500 short- and long-term volunteers each year, Iris Ministries began with a divine call to serve Mozambique in a ministry that continues to grow and expand. The mission and ministry are further described as follows:

On the national level, we are committed to working with indigenous leaders, with the aim of facilitating a strong, empowered citizen leadership that can ultimately take the reigns [sic] of Iris's main in-country activities. In our home nation of Mozambique these include the building of schools, children centers, homes and churches; extensive feeding programs; evangelism and healing; well-drilling; medical care; training programs for local and international ministers; conference hosting and local pastoral care. In Mozambique, without exception, we are also committed to offering a home to every child we find who does not have a family. As our organizational capacity has grown we have been privileged to extend many of these activities to other nations, a growing list which currently includes Brazil, India, Indonesia, Israel, Kenya, Madagascar, Malawi, Nepal, Sierra Leone, South Africa, South Korea, Sudan and Tanzania.[36]

Personal Prophetic Direction

Heidi and Rolland Baker both believe that God is the Divine Choreographer who directs their lives. Each tells the account of how God spoke to them individually that they were to marry. (Heidi reported that God had told her in prayer that she would "marry Rolland Baker" before she ever met him—even providing his last name so she would not be confused.) Born to an affluent American family in Laguna Beach, California, in 1960, Heidi had her first dramatic encounter with God at age 16 in response to an altar call by an evangelist while serving on an Indian Reservation. After over 30 years in missionary work, she continues to report prophetic guidance and confirmation in directions she perceives to be coming from God. Heidi has become a much-sought revival speaker in the United States as thousands have heard her speak, watched YouTube videos of her talks, and have made long- and short-term mission trips to Mozambique. Heidi and Rolland have planted a reported 11,000 churches to date as they have modeled and taught countless others about the power of divine love working through human instruments to change the world.

In a forward to one of Heidi's books, Rolland confessed to needing "a real-life example of Jesus living in someone to such an extent that I would be inspired and motivated to consider living the Sermon (on the Mount) as not only realistic but also the only viable way to approach life and ministry in the Lord."[37] He shared how this "need" has been met by Heidi. Rolland writes the following descriptive and moving tribute about his wife:

> I know that our Lord has many such monuments of His grace among His people who are often hidden in the far corners of the world, but for me that encouragement came during the late 1970s when I met Heidi in a small charismatic church in Dana Point, California. She had a privileged upbringing, living on a private beach, and lacked for nothing in education, comforts, and opportunity. But even as a small girl growing up, she pulsed and radiated with a consuming hunger for God. Radically influenced by her sixth-grade teacher who had been a missionary, Heidi's heart turned toward the poor and suffering of other cultures. That teacher turned out to be my mother, and so our families became interlinked. When I met her, she was a pure, idealistic flower child in the Spirit, a teenager who at sixteen had already been mystically taken to heaven and commissioned by Jesus to be a missionary and a minister to Asia, England, and Africa.... Here was someone who could take no thought for tomorrow, seek first His Kingdom and His righteousness under any circumstance anywhere in the world, and in the most childlike simplicity pursue heaven on earth—in spite of all opposition and discouragement.[38]

When asked by Margaret in a private interview to identify a few of the factors or events that have shaped who she is today, Heidi Baker responded without hesitation:

> Ok, I can absolutely identify that—March 13, 1976. I was living on an
> Indian Reservation as an American field service student and someone
> called to me, "Come to a revival." I did not know what that meant.
> I was killing roaches in the dormitory, and I said "I don't care what
> a revival is." I just wanted to get away from the roaches, so I went.
> Seriously that's the only reason I went. I wanted to get away from the
> bugs.

Little did she know that the revival service—where she was but one of perhaps three white faces among 500 American Indians in attendance—would change her young life. The Navaho preacher in full Indian dress "was screaming how he always hated white people, just hated them," bringing great discomfort to the petite, white, blond 16-year-old from affluent Laguna Beach, California. But then the preacher began to share how Jesus came into his life and showed him love for all people—and that he had stopped hating white people! Heidi laughed as she jovially added, "I was very relieved because I was there really sticking out. No blending for me." She was drawn by the preacher's account of "how he met a Man who taught him to see people from the inside, and how to love ….He talked about our sin and our need for forgiveness and faith in Jesus." When the Indian preacher gave an altar call, not one person respond-ed—except for Heidi.[39] She described this experience in our interview with her as follows:

> I felt like God himself just took hold of my shirt and pulled me; I was
> the only one that night. I went forward just sobbing and crying. I was
> saying, "God, save me; get rid of my sin. I was powerfully transformed
> that day. I was 16 years old, and I have never looked back. That is the
> most important, defining moment of my life.

The next night Heidi was taken to a Holiness Pentecostal church by the pia-nist from the previous evening's revival service, who said to her: "I am so glad you are saved, but now you need the Holy Ghost."[40] Heidi told us through a simple statement what happened next during an experience commonly known at "being baptized in the Holy Spirit (Ghost)": "I fell to the floor, prayed in tongues, rolled down—I was a holy roller! I was fully initiated in this church that was just wild Pentecostal fire. I gave myself to Him (God). I just said, just take my life. I was transformed."

The third most important event that Heidi shared happened just two months (May, 1976) after Heidi was born-again and baptized in the spirit, an event that seemingly sealed the first two experiences with an intense mysti-cal experience and a call to ministry: "I was fasting and praying because these people told me that you must fast and pray and love Jesus and read the word (the Bible). I was so hungry for God." She continued:

> And on that day in May, I felt God—really all I can tell you is that He just stepped into the room. I was in this little loud church—a little tiny loud church—and suddenly I could not hear the preacher. I could not hear the piano playing on two sides. I was taken up, either I was taken up or He came down. And I heard, the only time in my entire life, the external, audible voice of God.
>
> I was surrounded in white light. He said, "You are called to be a minister and a missionary, to go to Africa, Asia and England." I have never looked back and I have never doubted that day. He transformed me. He said, "You are to be married to me." Oil ran down my arm. I came out three hours later and they told me I was frozen there for three hours. I had my hands lifted, and I did not twitch, and I did not move, and I did not hear a single sound in church.
>
> When I came out of this vision, I started laughing hysterically. I didn't know what was going on. I was just so full of joy that God could choose little me—that he would call me to Himself and that I could be chosen to preach. I had never seen a woman preacher. I'd never heard of one—never knew they were allowed to preach. In my background there were no women in ministry. But I heard God. I would never deny it. The next day—as a 16-year-old—I stepped out and started preaching on the streets. I have been preaching now for 33 years. I am in love; I'm really, really in love.

These three events—a salvation experience, being baptized into a baptism of love, and receiving a prophetic call to minister and preach—remain intimately intertwined in Heidi's mind as she proceeded to share the unfolding of her adult life and ministry in her interview with us. Heidi's story provides an exemplary illustration of a primary spiritual transformation in which intimacy with God brought empowerment for service and a strong sense of divine destiny at a very young age. It is a Divine Collaborator who has continued to prophetically lead and empower her for mission, a path that is followed by many who volunteer their services and their resources to Iris Ministries. The experience of ministry burnout in the early 1990s became another major marker in Heidi's missionary adventure. During the first few months of her transformative spiritual encounter as a California teenager, as we have seen, Heidi heard a prophetic calling to serve in "Asia, England, and Africa." Describing how the prophecy was fulfilled for each location would require several long stories. Suffice to say that Heidi and Rolland had spent 14 years as missionaries to Hong Kong and the Philippines, followed by a ministry to the homeless in London while they worked on their Ph.D.s in theology at Kings College. They moved to Pemba, Mozambique, in 1995, where they soon both experienced an incredible burn-out as they sought to begin a ministry in a country that was just emerging from a civil war. Both Heidi and Rolland would soon be revitalized through the "Toronto Blessing," a revival that went on for over a decade at the then–Toronto Airport Christian Fellowship (now "Catch the Fire—Toronto"). They write: "We had come to that meeting having lost everything and wanted to quit missionary work. Instead, we were tremendously empowered for service."[41]

Heidi has had many divine encounters that she has shared in books and through sermons/lectures (many of which can be found on YouTube). A particularly significant one for her mission and ministry involved Randy Clark, the American pastor who helped to launch the so-called "Toronto Blessing" revival. It occurred during the pastor's conference in Toronto in January 1998; as Randy was preaching on "dying to self and the holy fire of God," Heidi reportedly jumped from her seat, ran forward, and knelt beneath the stage. Of this event she would later write:

> The fire of God hit me, and I felt like I was literally going to burn up and die. I began to cry out, "I'm dying; I'm dying." I heard the Lord say, "Good, I want you dead!" Not knowing who I was, Randy grabbed my hand and told me there was an apostolic anointing on my life. He declared that I would see the blind healed and many miraculous healings. He asked me, "Do you want the nation? God's giving you a nation." I cried out, "Yes" and for hours the power of God flowed through my body like an electric current.
>
> Then I heard the Lord say, "You'll have hundreds of churches!" I began slapping the floor and laughing. It was the funniest thing I had ever heard! It had taken us 18 years to plant four churches. How could it ever be hundreds? But I knew I heard the Lord.[42]

Religious studies scholar Candy Gunther Brown reports that Iris Ministries "grew from two churches and a children's home to 7,000 churches and homes for 10,000 orphaned children—as miraculous healings, the supernatural multiplication of food, and resurrections of the dead fueled church growth in predominantly Muslim areas of one of the poorest countries in the world."[43] The spread of pentecostalism among the people of Mozambique have resulted in thousands of village churches, pastored by simple indigenous men and women, mentored by Iris Ministries, who have become pentecostal Christians. It would take a year of praying for "every blind person I would meet" ("we have many blind people in Mozambique," Heidi comments) before she would witness another part of Randy's prophecy come to pass. First one blind woman's sight was restored, then another, finally a third; now the blind receiving the gift of sight is a reported commonplace experience for the poor to whom Heidi and her co-workers minister.[44] For Heidi and for those trained at the Iris Harvest School of Missions in Pemba, Mozambique, for "Spirit-directed Kingdom ministry," prophecy is an integral part of missionary work.

Conclusion

As discussed and developed by other chapters in this edited collection, Pentecostalism, with origins commonly traced back to the Azusa Street Revival of 1906–9, has been one of (if not the) fastest growing religious movement of the 20th century—a movement found in every country of the world. Allan Anderson has attributed this growth to Pentecostalism's "emphasis on mission and evangelism" and to its "strong pneumatology."[45] William K. Kay similarly reports a strong relationship between charismatic and evangelical activities. For example, Kay argues that, after experiencing the Holy Spirit, when "people feel empowered to serve others, they do so and, in a virtuous circle, an entire congregation begins to grow." He concludes that, "churches which are compassionate towards people in need grow."[46] Both of these influences on church growth are clearly implicated in our discussion of prophetically motivated godly love. Anderson provides additional context for the disproportionate growth of churches in touch with the S-factor:

> Pentecostals place primary emphasis on being "sent by the Spirit" and depend more on what is described as the "Spirit's leading them" than on formal structures. People called "missionaries" are doing that job because the Spirit directed them to do it, often through some spiritual revelation like prophecy, a dream or a vision and even through an audible voice perceived to be that of God. In comparison to the "Missio Dei" of older Catholic and Protestant missions and the "obedience to the Great Commission" of evangelical missions, Pentecostal mission is first and foremost in the conviction that the Spirit is the motivating power behind this activity.[47]

It is Spirit empowerment—especially through "Spirit revelation," commonly referred to as prophecy—that has been the focus of this chapter. The missiology of pentecostals, as Anderson observes, differs from other Western Christians, both Catholic and Protestant, and Iris Ministries is not immune from critique from Western program-focused models. The nonacademic African native whom we introduced earlier in the article as a collaborator with Iris Ministries, Surprise Sithole, provides a description of his personal experience of church planting that supports Anderson's astute observation:[48]

> Later that year (1997), in September and November, I made more trips from White River to Beira. Each time, I spent a week at one of the new churches, sharing and teaching the people God's Word. Then I sent them out to share what I had taught them with people in other communities. They always did as I asked with great exuberance and joy. Churches were being planted and nurtured by people who had been followers of Christ for only a few weeks! They did not have a lot of Bible knowledge or any degrees in theology, but they had passion for lost souls and a willingness to do whatever God told them to do, and the results were truly amazing. Years later I had an opportunity to visit many of those churches in Sofala Province, and I was delighted to discoverer they were still going strong and still faithful to Jesus.

Although the observation about Spirit empowerment has been made at times by other theologians, religious historians, and missiologists, social scientists have been slow to take religious experience seriously.[49] Miller and Yamamori have taken an important step in proposing the S-factor and acknowledging that "there may be more to Pentecostal experience than most social science interpretations allow."[50] We go a step further suggesting that the interactive model of godly love may provide an avenue for examining pentecostal growth that supplements commonly identified social factors used to explain this global phenomenon. This model accepts the pentecostal premise that missionaries are co-workers with a God who walks and talks with them and that this is empowering, although we make no pretense that social science can prove or disprove that premise. Rather we assume that missionaries claiming to experience the divine through prophetic words and actions can have real effects that are amenable to scientific study. In accord with the well-known "Thomas Theorem"—if people believe something to be true, it can have real effects—we have suggested that the belief in and practice of prophecy plausibly does have a significant effect on pentecostal growth.

Although we have focused on one contemporary neopentecostal ministry whose founders have made their experiences of the prophetic widely known, our formal and informal interviews with other missionaries and the results of the GLNS indicate that prophetic experiences are both commonplace and enormously appealing in our largely disenchanted world of bureaucracy and mundane routines. It is not unreasonable to hypothesize that pentecostal missionary ventures are staffed with countless short- and long-term volunteers who believe they have had personal experiences of Spirit-empowered prophetic direction. These experiences have impacted not only their personal lives but also the people they serve. They have been an often-overlooked factor in the phenomenal growth of the global pentecostal movement.

NOTES

1. Baker, Heidi (with Shara Pradham). *Compelled by Love: How to Change the World through the Simple Power of Love in Action*. St. Mary, FL: Charisma House, 2008: 2.
2. Ibid., 1.
3. Ibid., 2.
4. Ibid., 2.
5. Ibid., 3.
6. We use a small "p" to designate global pentecostalism with its indigenous, often independent (non-denominational), evangelical/mainline Protestant, Catholic as well as denominational Pentecostal streams. "Pentecostalism" (with a capital P) best describes denominations that can be traced to revivals that gave birth to Pentecostal denominations, including the Church of God in Christ, Church of God (Cleveland, TN) and the Assemblies of God.
7. Sithole, Surprise (with David Wimbish). *Voice in the Night: The True Story of a Man and the Miracles that Are Changing Africa*. Bloomington, MN: Chosen, 2012.
8. Ibid., 15.
9. Ibid., 133.
10. Ibid., 134.
11. Ibid., acknowledgements.
12. Gerlach, L. P., and V. H. Hine. "Five Factors Crucial to the Growth and Spread of a Modern Religious Movement." *Journal for the Scientific Study of Religion* 7 (1968): 23–40. Gerlach, L. P. and V. H. Hine. *People, Power, Change: Movements of Social Transformation*. Indianapolis: Bobbs-Merrill, 1970. Gerloff, Roswith. "Pentecostals in the African Diaspora." In *Pentecostals after a Century*, edited by A. H. Anderson and W. J. Hollenweger. Sheffield: Sheffield Academic Press, 1999. Gerloff, Roswith. *A Plea for British Black Theologies: The Black Church Movement in Britain in Its Transatlantic Cultural and Theological Interaction*. (2 vols.) Frankfurt: Peter Lang, 1992. Poloma, Margaret M., "The Spirit Bade Me Go: Pentecostalism and Global Religion." Hartford Institute for Religious Research, accessed February 21, 2012, http://hirr.hartsem.edu/research/pentecostalism_polomaart1.html.
13. For a discussion of the pentecostal worldview that transcends denominational affiliations, see Lee, Matthew T., Margaret M. Poloma and Stephen G. Post (2013). *The Heart of Religion: Spiritual Empowerment, Benevolence, and the Experience of God's Love*. New York: Oxford University Press.
14. Miller, Donald E. and Tetsunao Yamamori. *Global Pentecostalism: The New Face of Christian Social Engagement*. Berkeley: University of California Press, 2007.
15. See also Poloma, Margaret M. and Ralph W. Hood, Jr. *Blood and Fire: Godly Love in a Pentecostal Emerging Church*. New York: New York University Press, 2008: 4; Lee, Matthew T. and Margaret M. Poloma. *A Sociological Study of the Great Commandment in Pentecostalism: The Practice of Godly Love as Benevolent Service*. Lewiston, NY: The Mellen Press, 2009: 7.
16. Originally we proposed a comparison between Iris Ministries and Youth With a Mission (YWAM), but space limitations led us to drop the comparative feature. YWAM is an international volunteer movement of pentecostal Christians founded in the 1960s that is networked around the globe, operating in more than 1,000 locations in over 180

countries, with over 18,000 staff and volunteers worldwide. For further discussion see Poloma, Margaret M., *The Assemblies of God at the Crossroads*. Knoxville: University of Tennessee Press 1989 and Poloma, Margaret M. and John C. Green. *The Assemblies of God: Godly Love and the Revitalization of American Pentecostalism*. New York: New York University Press, 2010.

17. See Poloma, Margaret M. and Brian F. Pendleton. "Religious Experiences and Institutional Growth Within the Assemblies of God." *Journal for the Scientific Study of Religion*, 24 (1989): 415–431. For data on the Assemblies of God (AG) that relates charismatic experiences to AG growth, see Poloma, Margaret M. and John C. Green, *Assemblies of God*.

18. Tyra, Gary. *The Holy Spirit in Mission*. Downers Grove, IL: IVP Academic, 2011: 118.

19. Ibid., p. 188. Poloma and Green, *Assemblies of God*.

20. Poloma and Hood, *Blood and Fire*; Lee and Poloma, *Sociological Study*; Poloma and Green, *Assemblies of God*; Lee, Poloma, and Post, *Heart of Religion*.

21. Shepherd, Gerald T. "Prophecy from Ancient Israel to Pentecostals at the End of the Modern Age." *The Spirit and the Church* 3 (2002): 47–70.

22. For an excellent historical discussion of the role visions, prophecy, and politics played in early Christianity, see Elaine Pagels, *Revelations*. Viking: New York, 2012.

23. Robeck, Cecil M., Jr., 2002. "The Gift of Prophecy." In Stanley M. Burgess and Eduard M. Van Der Maas (eds.), *The New International Dictionary of Pentecostal Charismatic Movements*, pp. 999–1012. Grand Rapids, MI: Zondervan. Poloma, Margaret M. and Matthew T. Lee. "The New Apostolic Reformation: Main Street Mystics and Everyday Prophets." In *Prophecy in the New Millennium: When Prophecies Persist*, edited by Sarah Harvey and Suzanne Newcombe, Surrey, UK: Ashgate, in press.

24. All three of the prayer scales proved to be statistically significant in a multiple regression analysis, explaining nearly 80 percent of the variance in experiencing God's love (adjusted R square =0.79). Those who scored high on experiencing God's love also scored high on prayer activity (beta=0.42), mysticism (beta =0.39) and prophetic prayer (beta=0.17). For further discussion see Poloma, Margaret M. and Matthew T. Lee. "The Flow from Prayer Activities to Receptive Prayer: Godly Love and the Knowledge that Surpasses Understanding." *Journal of Psychology and Theology* 39 (2011): 143–54; Lee, Poloma, and Post, *Heart of Religion*.

25. The five questions included in the GLNS prophecy scale and the percent of Americans who had each prophetic experience are as follows: "I have sensed a divine call to perform a specific act" (66%); "God has provided direction for me to do something through another person" (65%); "I have given a word from God to another person" (59%); "I have received a revelation directly from God" (41%); and "I have seen future events in dreams or visions before they happen" (41%). For further details, see Poloma and Lee, "Flow from Prayer Activities."

26. A reliable scale comprised of multiple items to measure a single phenomenon, when available, is more robust and provides a better measure than use of a single item. The four questions used to comprise the scale to measure *experiences of God's love* include the following: feeling God's love directly; feeling God's love through others; feeling God's love as the greatest power in the universe; and feeling God's love increasing your compassion for others. The alpha or reliability co-efficient is .93. For more information, see Lee, Poloma, and Post, *Heart of Religion*.

27. Baesler, E. James. *Theoretical Explorations and Empirical Investigations of Communication and Prayer*. Lewiston, NY: The Edwin Mellen Press, 2003.

28. Baesler, E. James. "A Model of Interpersonal Christian Prayer." *Journal of Communication and Religion* 22 (1999): 40–64, p. 51.

29. Poloma and Lee, "Flow from Prayer Activities."

30. Baesler, *Theoretical Explorations*, 10.

31. Ibid., 11.

32. Experiences of three-way and even corporate dialogue with the divine are reflected in two of the five questions that were part of the prophetic prayer scale. Sixty-five (65%) percent of respondents reported that "God had provided direction to do something

through another person," and 59 percent acknowledged that they had "given a word from God to another person."

33. This figure is a modified version of the diamond model of Godly Love discussed in Lee and Poloma, *Sociological Study*.

34. Poloma, Margaret M. (2003) *Main Street Mystics: The Toronto Blessing and Reviving Pentecostalism*. Walnut Creek, CA: AltaMira Press. See also the cover story by Tim Stafford in the May 2012 issue of *Christianity Today*, "Miracles in Mozambique," pp. 18–26.

35. Rolland and Heidi Baker's Iris Ministries website, http://www.irismin.org/news/newsletters/view/revival-as-missions-pure-and-simple, accessed December 9, 2011.

36. http://www.irismin.org/about/mission, accessed December 9, 2011.

37. Baker, Rolland "Foreword." In Heidi Baker (with Shara Pradham), *Compelled by Love*, p. x. St. Mary, FL: Charisma House.

38. Ibid., x–xi.

39. Baker, Rolland and Heidi Baker. *Always Enough: God's Miraculous Provision among the Poorest Children on Earth*. Grand Rapids, MI: Chosen Books, 2003: 24.

40. Baker and Baker, *Always Enough*, 25.

41. Baker, Rolland and Heidi Baker. "There is Always Enough." In *Experience the Blessing: Testimonies from Toronto*, edited by John Arnott, 47–61. Ventura, CA: Renew, 2000: 57.

42. Ibid., 59.

43. Brown, Candy Gunther. "Global Awakening: Divine Healing Networks and Global Community in North America, Brazil, Mozambique, and Beyond." In *Global Pentecostal and Charismatic Healing*, edited by Candy Gunther Brown, 351–69. New York: Oxford University Press, 2011: 353. A personal email from Heidi Baker's personal assistant (March 21, 2012) reported "some 10,000 in children's villages and in church based orphan care, while servicing as an umbrella organization for over 10,000 churches in Mozambique."

44. Baker, *Compelled by Love*; Brown, *Global Pentecostal and Charismatic Healing*; Brown, Candy Gunther, Stephen C. Mory, Rebecca Williams, and Michael J. McClymond. "Study of Therapeutic Effects of Proximal Intercessory Prayer on Auditory and Visual Impairments in Rural Mozambique." *Southern Medical Journal* 103 (2010): 864–69.

45. Anderson, Allan. *An Introduction to Pentecostalism*. Cambridge: Cambridge University Press, 2004: 206.

46. William K. Kay (2012) "Empirical and Historical Perspectives on the Growth of Pentecostal-Style Churches in Malaysia, Singapore and Hong Kong." Paper made available at the International Society of Empirical Research in Theology, Nijmegen, 19–21 April 2012.

47. Anderson, *An Introduction to Pentecostalism*, 206–7.

48. Sithole, *Voice in the Night*, 132.

49. For example, see Gary B. McGee (2010) *Miracles, Missions, & American Pentecostalism*. Maryknoll, NY: Orbis Books.

50. Miller and Yamamori, *Global Pentecostalism*, 220.

Conclusion

Pentecostalism in Global Perspective

RICHARD FLORY AND KIMON H. SARGEANT

Although Pentecostalism has roots that extend back almost 2,000 years, it was not until the turn of the 20th century that it became a distinct movement within Christianity and eventually a global phenomenon. Certainly there were what could be called "Spirit-led" religious movements in the United States, such as the Great Awakenings in the 18th and 19th centuries, that had significant effects on American society and particularly in the Methodist, Baptist, and other denominations. But the magnitude and spread of Pentecostalism following the Azusa Street Revival in Los Angeles, the Mukti Revival in India, and other similar renewalist movements around the world is of an unprecedented scale and scope. It was only relatively recently that scholars became more interested in understanding Pentecostalism, which has allowed this movement to develop "under the radar" of social scientists, historians, and other scholars. Indeed, the initial global explosion of Pentecostalism occurred after the so-called "founding theorists" in the social sciences laid the groundwork for understanding religion as something that ultimately would disappear from modern society. Yet, as the chapters in this volume show, Pentecostalism is vibrant, growing, and adapting to different social and cultural environments across the globe.

According to data from the Pew Forum on Religion and Public Life, there are now more than half a billion "renewalists"—which includes members of Pentecostal denominations such as the Assemblies of God, independent charismatic churches, and Catholic charismatics—across the globe, with the majority in the Global South. This represents more than a quarter (27.5%) of the world's Christian population and more than 8 percent (8.5%) of the world's population.[1] All signs suggest the continued growth of Pentecostalism, particularly in sub-Saharan Africa and the Americas, where about eight in ten of the world's Pentecostals reside. For example, in sub-Saharan Africa, renewalists comprise 21.3% of the population and 26.7% of the population in the Americas.[2] By contrast the highly rational/word-based fundamentalist movement seems to be losing momentum in the United States and elsewhere.[3]

While the incredible growth of renewalist Christianity is one of the most important global developments in religion in the modern world, this is by no means a uniform story of one religious movement gaining increasing market share over time. This movement is better understood as a stream of parallel or sister networks with some common areas of emphasis but also broad diversity in practice. In some countries Pentecostals have been elected to positions of political power, while in others, they have created political parties vying for power, which as Paul Freston notes (chapter 5), number more than 20 throughout just the Spanish-speaking republics. The growing political interest of some Pentecostals may be a sign of the movement's maturity, but political engagement remains a relatively smaller emphasis within Pentecostal circles. As this book shows, there are Pentecostal leaders who, while sharing some of the same Pentecostal beliefs as their more politically oriented fellow believers, are known for making great sacrifices to live with the poorest and most vulnerable, whether in their own or in completely foreign societies. These two examples are just a brief indication of the remarkable breadth and complexity of the global varieties of Pentecostal experiences and practices.

The expansion of the Pentecostal and charismatic movement over slightly more than 100 years raises interesting and important questions not only about such issues as how and why Pentecostalism has been so successful, but also about its appeal in an otherwise "rational" and scientific age and what lessons we might glean about the continuing appeal of religion and its role in societies around the globe. Three questions in particular are of key importance. First, how are we to make sense of the varieties of Pentecostal experience and expression in the modern world? Second, what is fueling this diverse movement's growth? And third, what are the implications of its growth not only for sociological theories about religion and its continued role in societies around the world, but also for understanding the role that Pentecostalism, and religion in general, may be playing in the life of modernizing secular societies?

In this conclusion, we use the empirical chapters in this volume to begin to make sense of these questions and also to raise new questions about the future of Pentecostalism, the role of religion in a "globalized" world, and the theoretical frameworks scholars and others use to understand these developments. In what follows, we will start with the distinctiveness of Pentecostal *experience*, and then broaden the focus to the social, cultural, and political contexts in which Pentecostals and charismatics operate with particular attention to the movement's *empowering* and *entrepreneurial* nature. Next we expand further to examine Pentecostals' *engagement* with their societies, taking into consideration the examples across the globe of an appealing outreach to the poor, the dispossessed, and the needy. Finally, we will conclude with some broader observations about what the global growth of Pentecostalism might tell us about the place of religion in the world today.

Pentecostal Experience

While many people might think of a particular set of beliefs that one must adhere to as the defining characteristic of a religion, there is much more to religion than simply understanding and assenting to specific truth claims. Indeed, the gathering together of groups of co-believers is a form of community that provides a sense of belonging and reinforces basic shared beliefs, and as important, helps to develop an emotional bond between believers, and between believers and the Divine. Sociologist Christian Smith has argued that to understand why Christianity "works" one must include an emotion-centered account of religious experiences, as well as doctrinal and institutional factors. Smith elaborates by noting that while Christianity's basic teachings stress such tenets as that one's life is significant, that there is forgiveness for mistakes, and that the universe is not a cold and empty place, these teachings create the context for meeting basic human emotional needs for significance, purpose, community, love, and care.[4] Similarly Joel Robbins, drawing on Randall Collins's theory of "interaction ritual chains," argues that such Pentecostal experiences as worshippers lifting their arms in praise, speaking in tongues, and the laying on of hands for healing, should be understood as ritual acts that create what Collins calls "emotional energy" that involves both a common focus and coordinated and embodied actions. In turn, these ritual acts serve to create an identity and sense of belonging, and bonds Pentecostal believers with their brethren at home and around the world. Collins argues that humans are in fact seekers of emotional energy, spending their time "trying to participate in as many successful interaction rituals they can" (Robbins 2009, 60). As applied here, this suggests that the emotional energy that Christianity, and specifically Pentecostalism, provides through these ritualized interactions is one key to understanding the appeal and success of Pentecostalism. That is, the certainty that particular stores of emotional energy can be filled whether through the ritual actions of two people praying together or through a large and lively worship service.

The practices that people are most likely to think of as distinctively Pentecostal—assuming they have any understanding of it—are dramatic religious experiences such as speaking in tongues, hearing God speak directly to them, and miraculous healings. The majority of Pentecostals around the world—for example 67 percent of Pentecostals in Brazil, 72 percent in Chile, 71 percent in Kenya, 65 percent in South Africa, and 51 percent in the United States—report that their worship services frequently include "signs of the Spirit" such as speaking in tongues or praying for miraculous healings.[5] For Pentecostals, these "signs" themselves are a result of prior experiences. As Allan Anderson points out earlier in this volume, two defining features of Pentecostalism are both types of religious experience—a personal encounter with the Spirit and a "born again" or conversion experience.[6]

Pentecostalism is not unique in having religious experience as a central feature of the movement. At the most fundamental level, all forms of religious belief, ritual, and affiliation, including conversions or other religious changes, involve some form of experience. For example, one might "feel" God's presence in worship or "hear" his voice while praying. This is particularly true for Pentecostalism in that the individual's direct experience with God begins with being "born again," and continues throughout one's life in the form of glossolalia, healing, prayer, and the like.

The possibility, even necessity, of a personal encounter with the Divine is the common thread that connects Pentecostal movements across time and place. Cecil M. Robeck, for example (chapter 2), examines the beginnings of Pentecostalism and finds that those in attendance at the revival meetings at Azusa Street were "intent on encountering the Spirit of God" and believed they did so through their dramatic experiences. Similarly, Timothy Wadkins (chapter 7) introduced us to "Pedro," who, after his conversion and baptism in the Holy Spirit, began to focus his attention and energy on his new church community, becoming a deacon within eight months, a supervisor of the small group ministry within two years, and ultimately becoming a pastor in the church. A final example is represented in the distinctive case of Heidi Baker, as reported by Margaret Poloma and Matthew Lee (chapter 14), who grew up as a well-to-do teenager in California. After having a dramatic personal encounter with God at age sixteen, she eventually became a Pentecostal missionary, caring for the "poorest of the poor" in Mozambique and, along with her husband Rolland, reports having planted 11,000 churches around the world. In each of these examples, and countless others, an individual's life-changing religious experience prompts him or her to convert to a Pentecostal form of Christianity, which in turn has had wide-ranging implications. Many of these dramatic experiences helped spark the worldwide movement of Pentecostalism, while other experiences spurred people to pursue noble, even heroic, work within their own societies or in others, to fulfill what they believe the Spirit is calling them to do.

While some of the specific experiences of Pentecostals may be unique to this movement, the human needs that they address are not. Pentecostalism provides a coherent story about the nature of the world and the significance of each person's life. The experiences, services, and practices of Pentecostalism help its followers develop a sense of purpose and personal meaning, community connection, and transcendent significance. All religious movements and many secular organizations try to provide such answers to the perennial human search for meaning. Where Pentecostals have excelled is in not limiting these answers to primarily philosophical or theological responses, but embedding the answers they offer in the lived and dynamic experiences of a religious community within a story that transcends one person's immediate circumstances—and that can also help transform them.

For Pentecostals, the engine of personal transformation is the variety of experiences that the movement cultivates. Often an individual does not fully understand what they have experienced and needs the social experience of other Pentecostal believers to provide a sense of a community of meaning, support, and an interpretation of their particular experiences. It is also within the context of the community that the religious experience often occurs. For example, receiving a word of prophecy from God would make little or no sense unless there was a community of fellow believers who can provide not only the audience for the prophecy, but the essential interpretation for the individual in terms of what they have experienced, and how it might be interpreted for themselves and perhaps for others in their church. It is thus in the context of the church community that Pentecostal believers come to understand not only how to understand what they have experienced, but also learn how to experience God,[7] and ultimately to understand their identity as Pentecostal Christians.

Key Elements of Pentecostal and Charismatic Experience

As noted above, the kinds of experience usually associated with Pentecostalism have to do with what are generally categorized as "spiritual gifts" such as speaking in tongues, healing, and prophesying. In this, it is understood that the Spirit indwells believers, and then they receive the gifts of the Spirit, which enables them to have further encounters with the Divine. This in itself is a powerful message to Pentecostal believers, that the Spirit of God directly inhabits their life, and then works through them to achieve God's purposes in the world, such as healing and redemption of the "lost." But the everyday experiences of Pentecostal life also involve more common practices such as music, community, and hospitality that also create a powerful sense of solidarity and mission among Pentecostals.

Lively worship, and more specifically music, is a key component of Pentecostal practice. The music in Pentecostal worship services is generally very energetic and takes a contemporary form in a way that is often indistinguishable from secular pop music, although of course the lyrics contain a distinctly Christian message. Hillsong Church in Australia, for example, has created a music business (Hillsong Music) that has produced 25 or more live albums—most of which have reached "gold" status sales in Australia—at least half a dozen children's music albums, and has influenced the musical styles and worship services of countless churches around the world. Music in Pentecostal churches is intended to create the emotional energy that can help people become open to "the leading of the Spirit."

Music is also a social experience.[8] It is in the communal experience of singing together that Pentecostals experience both a closeness to God and to each other, whether that is through a rousing song or a song that encourages an introspective moment. But music may also provide a spiritual experience for participants, sometimes creating a context in which the individual transcends her- or himself in direct communication with God, or perhaps for exhibiting spiritual gifts like speaking in tongues. To experience the music in Pentecostal worship is to experience both great exuberance and quiet introspection at different points in the service, all intended to bring believers closer to the kinds of spiritual experiences that they desire and are key to Pentecostalism.

Music, however, is only one part of the Pentecostal "formula" for success. Another important aspect of the Pentecostal experience is the intense and often warm church community. As several of the chapters in this volume have argued, Pentecostalism has been particularly successful among newly urbanized populations, providing a caring home for them that included both the spiritual and the social dimension. Pentecostal churches can be especially welcoming to those who have left their homes, either looking for work in a major city or leaving for another country, often providing for material needs and helping with finding employment and the like. Beyond the provision of basic needs, whether shelter or food, Pentecostal church community also serves to provide a particular personal identity for believers. That is, it is within the community of believers that individuals come to know who they are in a particular ecology of meaning and learn how to act according to that identity through interaction with other believers and through Pentecostal religious experiences.

This sense of community is an appealing aspect of Pentecostalism, at least as evidenced by the studies included in this volume. Pentecostals, whether through individuals or through churches, as William Kay suggests, extend hospitality, welcoming visitors to their community as a matter of course. As Andrew Chesnut has suggested, much of this hospitality is "natural" in that new believers are brought in through extended friendship and kin networks, which in turn enhances the feeling of close community and caring for immediate physical, as well as spiritual, needs.

The cumulative result of these experiences, as evidenced in part by the many stories provided in this volume, is that Pentecostalism can provide a form of personal cleansing and a chance for a new start in life. But not only are individuals "born again" through a dramatic encounter with the Divine—they are also welcomed into a new community of believers, which in turn helps them to create a new identity as Pentecostal Christians and also provides social, psychological, spiritual, and often material support. This transformation and commitment to a new community extends to many parts of their lives in that not only are they personally renewed, but they also now approach life with a new confidence, optimism, and vigor to do the work that they believe God would have them to do. Pentecostal religion is thus not an opiate, as Karl Marx argued, or some authoritative bureaucratic system that requires them to seek God through an arcane institutional system, or a backward-looking fundamentalist movement. It is instead an empowering and relatively open and democratic movement, open to the leadership skills of those with charismatic gifts. Freed from the institutional constraints of more traditional religious forms, Pentecostals can gain a new sense of personal agency, what in biblical terms might be called the "priesthood of all believers," in which each individual is imbued with spiritual power and authority to pursue God's work.

One of Pentecostalism's strengths is that it can empower different groups that have been marginalized in society or the church. One of the primary roots of the modern Pentecostal movement was the preaching and prayer services in 1906 Los Angeles, led by an African American man, that included a multiethnic conglomeration of people who were swept up into the movement. As Allan Anderson and Cecil M. Robeck have documented, many of those early missionary ministers were women and people of color who were empowered to go around the world to spread their message. This form of Spirit empowerment continues to this day, although the extent of empowerment of everyone who becomes a Pentecostal Christian must be tempered by other variables. For example, fairly early in the development of Pentecostalism, racial divisions developed as denominations formed around racial and ethnic lines. In this volume, Estrelda Alexander argues (chapter 11) that although women started many of the early efforts within Pentecostalism, their efforts were taken over by men as the movement became more institutionalized. Similarly Katherine Attanasi shows (chapter 12) that for women in patriarchal societies, Pentecostalism *can* be empowering to women, although it is not always. Yet, the overall life perspective of Pentecostal believers tends to be one of future-minded optimism, not only that their lives will improve, but that through their actions in the world, they will in turn improve their families, communities, and nations.

Agency, Empowerment, and Entrepreneurship

Pentecostals have become effective competitors in the global religious economy, in large part because they promote and thrive on the ability of individuals to make a religious choice—to choose to be Catholic or Pentecostal, or
maybe even something else. Viewing religion in this way, as a set of preferences from among market choices, has some valuable explanatory power. As
R. Andrew Chesnut (chapter 3) has argued, "Since it is the tastes and pref-
erences of religious consumers that largely determine the fate of any given
religious enterprise in a competitive economy, consideration of the large class
of popular religious consumers who have purchased the Pentecostal product
is imperative." In Chesnut's framing, he gives us some memorable categories
through which to investigate Pentecostalism. For example, his "army of amateurs," who spread the message of Pentecostalism, and his observation that
most converts in Latin America convert to Pentecostalism through relational
ties that they already have. These are important observations and provide one
lens through which to understand the success of Pentecostalism in the religious marketplace.

The particular strengths of the market model are evident in how it provides
a parsimonious explanation to what is otherwise a complex movement with
many expressions around the world. For example, Pentecostals are indeed
entrepreneurial in their approach to establishing new organizations, modify-
ing old ones, and attracting converts. They have been able to gain a competitive advantage in the religious marketplace through their innovative methods,
particularly their ability to enculturate their message to local societies, ethnic groups, and social strata. In comparison to established and more organizationally complex competitors like the Catholic Church, Pentecostals have
relatively low start-up costs. Except in those instances where a Pentecostal
church is part of a larger denomination, there is often no need to go through
the organizational bureaucracy to start a new ministry, plant a new church, or
otherwise pursue what they believe is their Divine mission.

Similarly, there are low barriers to entering ministry for Pentecostals. Owing
to the generally less hierarchical organizing schema within Pentecostalism, formal theological training is not necessarily required for pastoral or leadership
roles. Many Pentecostal churches use an "apprenticeship" model, where the
next generation of pastors are identified and trained in the churches, rather than
in professional seminaries. Some Pentecostal believers receive a "direct calling" from God to enter the ministry, and they thus start out on their own. The
absence of required training for ministers allows both individuals and churches
to expand the ranks of Pentecostal ministry outside of any central authority,
thus expanding the potential reach of the Pentecostal message.

Just as Pentecostalism has proven to be entrepreneurial and innovative in start-ups, it also allows for Pentecostals to be entrepreneurial in forming break-off groups. In market terms, if an individual or group of individuals sees an opportunity in the religious marketplace that is not being exploited by either their own church or any other group, they can start up a new church. There is no need to go through a bureaucracy or find a seminary-trained minister; instead, they simply find a place to meet, create a new identity, and start off on their own. In David Martin's terms, Pentecostalism is a "fissiparous movement" that is simply good at starting new congregations or denominations—as the Spirit leads. This tendency, in many ways, leads to a stronger Pentecostal movement overall. That is, the tension inherent in the potential for new groups to form out of older organizations serves not only to offer new expressions of Pentecostalism, but ultimately forces more mainstream Pentecostal groups to be more creative and innovative in their ministry efforts in order to compete with newer groups that are forming.

The source of this low start-up/low barrier-to-entry approach is how Pentecostalism puts an emphasis on the "priesthood of all believers"—or an army of amateurs, per Chesnut—into action. As Juan Martínez shows (chapter 10), Latino Pentecostal immigrants continue that model, breaking the mold of how to do Protestant mission work, by simply deciding to create new mission activities, often outside of any denominational affiliations that they may have. As Martínez notes, they do mission work "off the books," because they never "got the memo" about needing large resources, or perhaps even permission, to establish the types of mission activities that they have created. This of course is not to suggest that established Protestant missions will adopt this model; rather, they will most certainly continue on as they traditionally have, owing in part to the vast amount of resources (following the market model again) that most denominations have invested in those efforts. However, what Martínez shows us is that in many ways, one of the most cost-effective ways to pursue mission activity—which of course should remind readers of the original Azusa Street mission activities that Robeck has described—will likely come from the kinds of informal missionaries that Martínez describes, thereby leading to further growth of Pentecostalism.

Pentecostals have also proven adept at capitalizing on their ability to put different media forms to innovative use in promoting and publicizing their endeavors. While there are certainly examples of Pentecostal groups that are utilizing newer forms of digital media such as email blasts, texting, websites, or Facebook, often the most effective way to reach the masses with their message is through media that is much more pervasive in the areas of the world where Pentecostalism is seeing the most growth: television, radio, or even printing pamphlets to hand out en masse. All of these media forms come into play when Pentecostal groups organize massive rallies such as March for Jesus in São Paulo, or the annual Holy Ghost Congress in Nigeria that includes literally millions of Pentecostal believers.

Pentecostal groups primarily use these different forms of media as a way to reinforce beliefs and practices with fellow Pentecostals, to organize and communicate with their members, and to create networks of cooperation between diverse Pentecostal groups. In this way, Pentecostals have exploited particular media and market niches as a way to communicate their message to fellow Pentecostal believers, but also to "normalize" their brand of religion in the larger religious marketplace.

Thus in many ways, different forms of mass media, combined with the Pentecostal emphasis on the Spirit and the individual, creates and promotes the democratization of the sacred; it is available to all without the need of it being mediated through a priest, a ritual structure, or a religious hierarchy. This in itself gives Pentecostalism a competitive advantage over the more traditional forms of its Christian (and other) competitors.

While the market model of religion has significant explanatory insight to make sense of the establishment and growth of Pentecostalism at the societal and community level, there are nevertheless limits to what the market model can explain about Pentecostalism and its role in the world. The explanatory power of economic models seems to work best at the organizational level, but is not as convincing when explaining individual religious experience. Personal conversion and religious switching, for example, are not the same as, say, changing brands of toothpaste or soda—it is not always about "utility maximization" or even deferring rewards to some eternal by-and-by. Pentecostalism provides the possibility of powerful and life-changing encounters with the Divine, which are generally witnessed by others, whether in a small group or in the presence of thousands, and are difficult to account for in purely market-choice terms. As well, religious affiliation brings with it a strong mix of cultural identity, community boundaries, relational ties, and a sense of where one "fits" into the world. That is, religion is as much about who one is, as it is about what choices one makes or what one believes.

Thus, religious experience does, sometimes, trump personal taste or preference. If we think about how ephemeral our choices are for consumer products—how loyal are we really to Coke, Nike, or Toyota?—it is hard to imagine a global religious movement that has grown at the rate and distribution that Pentecostalism has, that is based solely on market preference. To exclude the non-rational religious experiences that are a core part of Pentecostalism as important explanatory variables leaves us with an incomplete theoretical toolkit with which to think about religious movements like Pentecostalism. Indeed, many of the conversion narratives we have heard include the idea that people were not prepared for what happened to them as they encountered the Divine, and they certainly did not imagine some sort of Pentecostal experience that would, literally, change their lives. In particular, such rational choice models fall short in explaining the motivations and the kind of work that people like Mama Maggie in Cairo, Heidi Baker in Mozambique, and Pedro in El Salvador have pursued as a result of their religious experiences.

Finally, it is important to note that Pentecostalism has tended to thrive primarily in countries that already have relatively open market conditions. Thus to argue for a "free religious market approach" assumes that certain market conditions are already in existence, and that Pentecostalism is able to operate within that free religious marketplace. As Henri Gooren has shown (chapter 4), the particular mix of political alignments between dominant religious groups (the Catholic Church in Paraguay) and key government officials, economic conditions, relative rates and levels of urbanization, and other elements of internal national history, is crucial to whether Pentecostalism will take root and expand in any particular society. We can see this a different way in Timothy Wadkins's (chapter 7) description of how El Salvador has moved from a society with a land-based economy dominated by a few families, who in cooperation with the ruling religious and political elites, dominated all aspects of life in El Salvador for hundreds of years. It was only with the breakdown of that socioeconomic and political system, and not coincidentally when El Salvador began to enter the global marketplace and become an increasingly urban society, that the larger environment allowed for the growth of Pentecostalism. Thus the free religious marketplace requires a certain level of religious freedom either from state-sponsored limitations or religious monopolies, such as with Orthodoxy in Russia and Armenia, and until relatively recently with the Catholic Church in many Latin American countries.

Enculturation and Social Engagement

As Pentecostalism has grown and expanded into many different societies around the world, it has also become more of a public presence, whether through extensive social-outreach ministries, joint efforts with public officials to improve different segments of their societies, or in the political realm. Recall the examples given throughout this book, ranging from the Pentecostal political presences in Latin America, large-scale marches through Rio, to the multimillion-person rallies that take place annually in Lagos, Nigeria. Taken together, what then can we conclude about Pentecostalism's impact on the societies and cultures in which it is thriving? As different authors have noted throughout this book, Pentecostalism has demonstrated the ability to adapt to different sociocultural contexts.[9] But how does this happen?

Culture

Perhaps most significantly, Pentecostal leaders tend to come from the societies, classes, and ethnic groups that each congregation is trying to reach. That is, church leaders are pretty much the same as their congregants, receiving the "call" from the Spirit to become a minister or lay leader, and reinforcing not only that any Pentecostal believer can be a leader or otherwise used by God to do his work, but effectively flattening the distinctions between leaders and congregants. Thus, as Andrew Chesnut has argued among Latin American Pentecostals, both leaders and congregants tend to be poor, while elsewhere, such as in Nigeria and El Salvador, there are also middle-class Pentecostal churches, in each case made up of people from similar backgrounds, all seeking a common religious experience, and personal and cultural goals. This in turn encourages a less top-down, more democratic approach to religious organization. Many pastors and lay leaders have little or no theological training, instead having been educated in business or science, which can lead to a different emphasis than we might find in religious settings that are more hierarchical and require formal training.

While Pentecostalism adapts to the indigenous culture is which it located, it has also managed to create its own culture of sorts. Thus in societies where one's life chances are oriented more around survival, Pentecostalism presents another option that is anti-fatalistic about life (Freston, chapter 5). More than that, it is optimistic and forward-looking: you can change yourself, your family, community, and maybe even the world. This "culture of optimism" is regularly renewed through the many opportunities for religious experience in worship and other perhaps less formal settings that are at the heart of Pentecostalism. Pentecostal believers constantly reinforce their beliefs in the power of the Spirit through, as Joel Robbins has identified them, ritualistic experiences that can be performed by anyone, seemingly at any time.[10]

Beyond the organizations and culture that Pentecostals have created, Pentecostalism has a modernizing effect in that it challenges the magic and animism in traditional religions, replacing multiple spirits with *the* Spirit. Exorcism then has an effect beyond the individual salvation that results from the casting out of demons: it also replaces worldviews informed by magic and animism with a more "rational" monotheistic religious perspective, while preserving the "otherworldliness" of the immanence of the Spirit. This, coupled with its emphasis on the individual and the empowerment and personal agency that comes from being "filled" with the Spirit, allows Pentecostalism to flourish within modernity by encouraging a worldview that is more compatible with a rapidly modernizing and capitalist society yet that remains an oasis of ecstatic experience and community.

At the same time, it is important to remember that the effects of Pentecostalism are not always positive. Just as individuals can be empowered to do good in the world, so can they be empowered for self-aggrandizement and enrichment, and the more unscrupulous can take advantage of those who are looking for deliverance from lifetimes of misery and suffering. This can be manifested in many different ways, whether through the "health and wealth" preachers who encourage people to keep giving their money to them or false healers who take advantage of the physically and emotionally distressed.

Overall however, we must acknowledge the importance of the ability of Pentecostalism to empower individuals and organizations to pursue their (Spirit-motivated) goals as well as the uncanny ability of Pentecostalism to adapt to particular social and cultural settings through "indigenizing" itself by way of local converts, whether they are political leaders or more common folk looking to improve their own lives and the lives of their families and communities. This is in part what Danny McCain (chapter 8) has in mind when he argues that Pentecostal believers in Nigeria are seeking to put the values of the "kingdom of God" into practice in society. The principles they have in mind are loving and caring for others, promoting individual responsibility, and promoting a more just society.

Outreach

Beyond indigenizing or enculturating to its host cultures, "progressive Pentecostals" have in recent years spawned many impressive social outreach programs and communities oriented to caring for those in need (Miller and Yamamori 2007). The examples provided in this volume of such efforts all have a common underlying theme: that the individuals or churches that create and operate these social outreach programs, regardless of their particular emphasis, are all rooted in Pentecostal religious experiences that lead them to create these programs. Margaret Poloma and Matthew Lee describe the experiences and healing ministries of Heidi Baker, framing the experiences in the Pentecostal understanding of "prophecy," meaning that God was directing—or better, telling—her that he wanted her to care for the poor and the orphans.

While Heidi Baker did launch a ministry of compassion, other examples of social outreach show different approaches and emphases amongst Pentecostals. Danny McCain has shown us how in Nigeria, Pentecostal church leaders are working at reforming important sectors of Nigerian society, such as education, health care, and civil rights and responsibilities. These leaders do not have formal seminary training, but are college educated and often with experience and success in the secular business world. Thus their education and business success, coupled with their religious experiences and how they understand the Bible (owing to their literal reading of scripture, they do believe that they are required to care for the poor), has not only heightened their awareness of problems in Nigerian society, but has allowed them to devise new ways that Pentecostal groups can work with government agencies to bring about reform.

Similarly, although at a significantly different level of social power than what McCain described, Juan Martínez has shown us how "poor to poor" mission activities have also included a significant social outreach component. For example, in Ensenada one church from the Los Angeles area has established a home-building mission, emulating the Habit for Humanity model to build affordable and sustainable housing.

Accounting for Pentecostal Success and Growth

So what does account for the remarkable success of Pentecostalism across the globe in the last century? The authors in this volume have identified many important factors, although they have not agreed on one simple formula for success. But there is clearly an important balance between social-contextual factors and internal factors that contribute to this movement's growth. In the former category, one of the most important is the displacement that urbanization causes in many countries, which provides an opportunity for Pentecostal congregations to reach out to these displaced urban populations and help them plant new community and religious roots. At a more practical level, Pentecostals engage in activities that lead to civic and social transformation, which is another source of their appeal. Pentecostals have shown themselves adepts at providing particular services that meet the needs of individuals and families, and thus serve to draw people into their churches and ministries.

Further, as noted previously, Pentecostalism has primarily thrived in contexts that already have a certain amount of religious freedom, whether that is a result of the state allowing religious freedom, or, where there is no such freedom, at least a weakened religious monopoly. In addition, the social and economic context must also allow for Pentecostalism to be established and grow. Taken together, the chapters in this volume would suggest that a combination of greater religious freedom and some form of a market economy that encourages individualism work together to created the social, political and economic contexts in which Pentecostalism thrives.

In addition to these contextual factors, Pentecostalism also provides a religious worldview that simultaneously replaces a spiritual realm that is animated with many spirits with one in which its Spirit is the most powerful. That is, while promoting an anti-animistic, monotheistic focus, it also maintains a place for the supernatural, in which miracles can, and often do, happen. Further, Pentecostalism is structured and organized in a way that frequently enables it to outperform the market competition. Many Pentecostal leaders are not only charismatic in the "gifts of the Spirit," but they are also gifted as leaders and entrepreneurs. While there are some large churches and organizations within Pentecostalism with a top-down organizational authority structure, there still is a very significant focus on entrepreneurship and risk-taking, often motivated by the "promptings of the Spirit," that contribute to a democratic spirit and general lack of formal bureaucracy across the movement. Pentecostals can create warm, close-knit communities, often with a prominent role for women. And their strict yet joyful, passionate yet purposeful forms of strict moral boundaries can serve to redirect energies toward family, church, and community.

Concluding Comments: Pentecostalism in Global Perspective

Social scientific theories of religion have long predicted the inevitable demise of religion in the modern world, in general positing that as society becomes ever more rational and modern, religions, like all other premodern myths, will simply lose their social utility and fall to the wayside. Although this "secularization" approach has come on hard times in some quarters, it is still a theoretical position maintained not only by many social scientists, but has recently enjoyed a more popular resurgence among the so-called "new atheists,"[11] and maintains a hold both in academic studies and in more popular treatments.

While it is certainly true that processes of secularization have taken place,[12] particularly in Western societies, to leave it at that would be an incomplete claim about religion and its current and future place in societies around the globe. That is, such a claim leaves us with the uncomfortable reality that the majority of the world is still religious, and more specific to our interests here, would require some significant work to explain the emergence, growth and spread of the modern global Pentecostal movement. Thus while social differentiation and the mostly privatized forms of religion that are prevalent in most modern societies indicate that religion is no longer (if it ever was) the dominant social institution, modernization does not necessarily lead to the "inevitable" decline of religion, as evidenced by the exponential growth of Pentecostalism over the last century.

Yet, this does not necessarily mean that religion, and particularly Pentecostalism, is content to be relegated to the private sphere of personal belief. As several chapters in this volume have argued, there are many different roles that Pentecostalism plays in the public sphere of its host societies, ranging from political parties and candidates, to the establishment of expansive social ministries, to efforts to reform larger social structures. Pentecostalism may not be challenging the privatization of religion per se, but neither is it necessarily relegated to a realm of purely personal belief. The dynamics of these historical processes are contingent, multifaceted, and move in more than one overarching direction.

In the end, it seems difficult to justify on evidentiary grounds that secularization is, or will, necessarily take place across all the different sectors of society and in the lives of individuals and communities. Pentecostalism is still growing at a phenomenal rate and, while it is certainly an individualistic belief system, it is not sidelined from taking on important social roles from its unique religious perspective. What is puzzling then is why some secularization theorists persist in arguing that religion will inevitably disappear as modern, rational, scientific approaches to life take its place, instead of theorizing about religion as they would any other social institution. That is, just as social scientists expect other social institutions, like for example the family, to change and adapt to meet the needs and demands of individuals and societies over time, why should we not expect that religion would adapt and survive in a similar manner?

What is perhaps a better approach to understanding the current and future role of religion in general, and Pentecostalism more specifically, is that it will continually adapt to whatever environment in which it finds itself. This changes the task from explaining how secularization may be making incursions into different religious systems to one of explaining how religion manages to change and adjust to new circumstances. Thus if we conceptualize religion as we do any other institutional sphere, we should expect it to change and adapt over time as it seeks to survive and thrive in the midst of new social, cultural, political, and economic developments. Of course some religions may have an easier time adapting than others. From what we have seen in the chapters included in this volume, those religions that have more hierarchy, bureaucracy, and formal authority are doing less well than Pentecostalism, which overall has fewer of those characteristics. To the extent that Pentecostalism develops those characteristics and becomes like its competitors, the less likely it will be to survive in that form over the longer term.

Further, as we argued earlier in this chapter, Pentecostalism is not a singular movement; rather, it is best thought of as a stream of parallel networks that have common areas of emphasis while maintaining a broad diversity in practice. Thus one way that Pentecostalism adapts—and other religions, too—is by offering a "product" that differentiates it from other religious products available in the religious marketplace. Indeed the "free religious market" models such as utilized by Andrew Chesnut (chapter 3) would argue that it is precisely through the competition that the religious economy engenders that new religious groups emerge and gain market share and others can become revitalized through being forced to compete with these upstart groups. That is, competition can lead to more groups emerging and adapting to offer their product to potential believers, whether a variety of Pentecostal groups or other, non-Pentecostal religious groups.[13] Where we would part company with this perspective is in its reduction of religious experience, belief, and identity to individual "religious taste." As we stated previously, there is more to religious belief and identity than "taste," and following that metaphor, food requires substance for it to be worthwhile eating. Thus while competition may make religious groups more innovative in producing religious offerings that better fit the needs and desires of more people, the substance of Pentecostalism emanates from the core experiences of the Divine and the empowerment and individual purpose that results.

Another feature of Pentecostalism that argues against the decline narrative is that it has flourished in societies even as they modernize and become more integrated into the world capitalist system and create better economic opportunities for their citizens. The inclusion of nation-states in the global capitalist system, and in the process modernizing their societies, should predict that Pentecostalism (and religion more generally) would decline as the rational processes of the market take dominance in all areas of life. However, quite the opposite is happening. Pentecostalism is taking root and expanding in precisely those regions where, in part as a result of their relatively recent inclusion in the global capitalist system, and accompanied by rapid modernization and urbanization, there is fertile ground for it to take root and expand throughout the population. Further, Pentecostalism is exploiting opportunities in a more open social field that the secular state has abandoned, whether because of increased religious freedom or through filling gaps in providing services to the poor. Pentecostalism thus becomes a legitimate option because of the successes its adherents can point to—changed lives, improved family relations, better personal opportunities through living a more ordered life—changes that not only improve individual lives, but whole communities.

One further observation should be made here. Not only is Pentecostalism thriving in these regions, but it is also being exported through international flows of labor, as workers move around the world seeking work. This process can be seen in Nigerian Pentecostal churches that Afe Adogame describes (chapter 9) in Dallas and Houston, Texas. While these American versions of

Nigerian Pentecostal churches have established themselves beyond a strictly Nigerian membership, they also serve the large Nigerian population that has emigrated to the United States in search of jobs. In a different way, this process can also be seen in the "poor to poor" mission activities of the Latino Pentecostals that Juan Martínez describes, who are on the one hand following the international labor possibilities, while on the other are engaging in Pentecostal mission work even as they are migrating, looking for better economic opportunities. Other examples can be found around the world. It should be only slightly surprising that there are communities of Pentecostal believers in different countries in the Middle East, all of whom are in some way connected to jobs and economic opportunities in the region.

It may certainly be true that, as some observers have noted, Pentecostalism exhibits some of the same personal and social outcomes described by Max Weber in *The Protestant Ethic and the Spirit of Capitalism*, namely personal industriousness and a rational outlook on life, and beyond the individual, laying the groundwork for a successfully capitalist society.[14] However, Pentecostalism has also proven to be opportunistic, utilizing the different openings available in a globalized world—such as ease of global travel and "modern" (and now digital) communication—to spread its message around the world, since the very beginning of the movement. Further, rather than a strictly, per Weber, "this-worldly asceticism" that encourages sober, rational work and eschews sensory pleasures, Pentecostalism at its very core resists the extreme rationalizing tendencies inherent in capitalism. As Jean Comaroff has pointed out, Pentecostalism "takes untempered affect as a sign of the power of the true faith, and harnesses the pursuit of worldly desire to the advent of God's kingdom in the here and now" (2008, 13). That is, even as Pentecostal believers become more fit to a rational, global capitalist system, this always exists in tension with the experiential; the potential that the Spirit may enter one's life and provide the individual (or church or community) with a new voice, or vision, for their lives. This persistent expectation of the direct experience of the Divine works to keep Weberian rationalism in check, maintaining an "enchanted" world despite the pressures toward rationalization.

The "Spirit Factor"

Finally, we must ask what role, if any, does the "S factor," as Miller and Yamamori (2007) have framed it, have in explaining the phenomenal success of Pentecostalism in its global expansion. Miller and Yamamori argue that any account of Pentecostalism must take seriously what Pentecostals themselves believe—or perhaps more accurately experience—namely, the role of the

Spirit. In this they maintain that there is no need to argue for the ontological reality of the Holy Spirit, but rather only to acknowledge that the Spirit seems to have an actual effect in the lives and community of Pentecostals, and that to reduce it to a false consciousness or to merely a collective effervescence that functions to make people feel as one does not help further our understanding of the Pentecostal phenomenon.

We would agree with this assessment and would not want to reduce Pentecostalism, or any religion, to its social functions or the socioeconomic correlates that help us to understand its different forms. Rather, we acknowledge that Pentecostalism offers particular beliefs, and as important, religious experiences that both individuals and communities of believers take to heart and upon which they act. That is, Pentecostals really believe that God cares for them and that they can work to help fulfill his plans on earth; that they can have direct contact with and experience of the Divine; and that these beliefs and experiences compel them to act in different ways—whether just transforming their own lives or through serving others as an act of obedience to what they believe and have experienced.

Further, we would argue that the immanence of the Divine, through which the individual can at any time have direct communication with God, is likely more palpable and persuasive as compared to the distant transcendent Christian God that can be a feature of Catholic theology and practice, and perhaps other forms of Protestant Christianity, where access to God is still mediated through the often arcane theological interpretations of church specialists. This experience of the Divine also helps to make Pentecostalism a more formidable competitor to other spirits as well—the proof, for Pentecostal believers, is in the results. Individual experience with the Spirit provides the believer with a special feeling of purpose that in turn empowers their individual agency and imparts confidence that they can defeat the "demons" that beset them. Once changed, they are freed to pursue courses of action in their lives that they often could not have conceived of previously. Thus understanding the multifaceted role of the Spirit in the Pentecostal experience is crucial to understanding how Pentecostalism "works."

Finally, the ongoing dynamic between routinization and charisma—between institutionalizing experience into large-scale bureaucratic structures and the dynamism of individual believers filled with the Spirit—is itself built into Pentecostalism. If a particular church becomes too complex and depersonalized, Pentecostal believers can always find a new church, or even start a new ministry effort or otherwise embark out on their own, depending on how the Spirit may lead them. After all, once unleashed from bureaucratic and ecclesial controls, the Spirit does what it will and makes itself available to everyone.

NOTES

1. Pew Forum, *Global Christianity*, p. 67. Also, see the Appendix in this volume, "By the Numbers: The Global Expansion of Pentecostalism" for two articles that provide a broader statistical portrait of global Pentecostalism. Todd Johnson provides a demographic analysis of the growth and spread of Pentecostalism since 1906, and John Green analyzes the Pew Forum survey of Pentecostalism in ten countries.

2. Pew Forum, *Global Christianity*, p. 68.

3. For one explanation of the difference between fundamentalist and Pentecostal growth, see Joel Robbins, "Pentecostal Networks and the Spirit of Globalization," p. 63.

4. Christian Smith, "Why Christianity Works," 165–178.

5. Pew Forum, *Spirit and Power*, p. 16.

6. Anderson stresses three distinct elements of Pentecostalism: (1) the central emphasis on the experience of the Spirit; (2) the "born again" or conversion experience that accompanies acceptance into a Pentecostal community; and (3) the dualistic worldview that distinguishes between the "world" and the "church," between the "devil" and the "divine," between "sickness" and "health" (citing Droogers).

7. On learning how to experience God in a Pentecostal context, see Luhrmann, *When God Talks Back*.

8. On music as a social experience in church worship settings, see Marti, *Worship Across the Racial Divide*.

9. David Martin has described this as Pentecostalism's "amazing capacity to become indigenous." David Martin, *Future of Christianity*, p. 69.

10. Robbins, "Pentecostal Networks and the Spirit of Globalization," 55–66.

11. See, for example, Richard Dawkins, *The God Delusion*; Christopher Hitchens, *God Is Not Great*; Sam Harris, *Letter to a Christian Nation*.

12. See Casanova, *Public Religions in the Modern World*, p. 211 for a delineation of these processes.

13. For an example of this approach see Rodney Stark and Buster G. Smith, "Pluralism and the Churching of Latin America."

14. See Max Weber, *The Protestant Ethic and the Spirit of Capitalism*. On Pentecostalism and the Weber argument, see Berger, "Max Weber Is Alive and Well, and Is Living in Guatemala.

Appendix

BY THE NUMBERS: THE GLOBAL
EXPANSION OF PENTECOSTALISM

Throughout this volume, several authors have made the claim that Pentecostalism has grown at a remarkable rate from its very beginning, expanding into a global phenomenon within a hundred years of its emergence. Indeed as Allan Anderson pointed out in chapter 1, by 1916—only ten years after the Azusa Street Revival—Pentecostal missionaries could be found in forty-two countries outside of North America and Europe. Todd Johnson gives us an idea of what that growth looks like over the last hundred years, showing how the demographic center of Christianity shifted from the West (the United States and Europe) to the Global South, both in the growth of individual Pentecostal believers and in the proliferation of Pentecostal denominations. Johnson charts this growth from the early twentieth century and into the second decade of the twenty-first century.

Johnson's chapter is also an excellent place to begin to understand the wide variety of strands of Pentecostalism around the world. His taxonomy allows readers to understand that Pentecostalism isn't a monolithic religious group, but rather that the larger movement contains many different groups that tend toward certain beliefs and practices, whether within Pentecostal denominations, indigenous (i.e., non-white and non-missionary-planted) denominations, and those who remain in non-Pentecostal denominations, but who, nonetheless, exhibit characteristics that can identify them as Pentecostals. Overall, Johnson's chapter shows where Pentecostal groups are growing and those countries where growth is decreasing or leveling out. These findings suggest promising new avenues of investigation of the reasons why Pentecostal Christianity is growing at different rates in different countries and regions around the world.

Moving beyond the historical growth rates and typology of Pentecostal development that Johnson provides, John Green presents an overview of current Pentecostal and charismatic Christianity, using the Pew Forum's ten-nation public opinion survey to describe its salient characteristics and attitudes.[1] Although not a global portrait of all Pentecostal religious communities, Green's discussion puts more flesh on the demographic bones that Johnson outlines. Green's analysis shows that, on the one hand, Pentecostals tend to be distinctive from other Christians with regard to engaging in the gifts of the Spirit and holding traditional Christian beliefs, while, on the other hand, they are more similar when it comes to social, civic, and political attitudes, and often resemble their fellow citizens on these dimensions of public life.

Green's analysis may cause the careful reader to ask how his findings fit with claims made in other chapters in this volume that suggest different conclusions. In this it is important to keep in mind the unit of analysis that the author is using, in this case, a more macro look at the characteristics of Pentecostals in ten different countries rather than a specific country or region, which may show somewhat different results. For example, Andrew Chesnut focuses on Latin America, and argues that the typical Pentecostal is poor and female, which while true for that region, is not the global (i.e., ten-country survey) norm reported by Green. This in turn highlights the importance of both the macro analysis, which gives a general orientation to what Pentecostalism looks like around the world, and studies that focus on one country or a somewhat larger region. That is, explaining the variation in the relative growth rates of Pentecostalism in different regions and how it is understood and expressed in different parts of the world allows for a better understanding of its apparent ability to adapt (or not) to different social, political, and cultural settings.

NOTE

1. The Pew Forum, *Spirit and Power*.

Appendix 1

GLOBAL PENTECOSTAL DEMOGRAPHICS

TODD M. JOHNSON

One of the most remarkable aspects of Christianity at the beginning of the twenty-first century is how different the demographic profile of the contemporary movement is from the Christianity of a hundred years ago. In 1910, over 80 percent of all Christians were European or North American. Today, adherents in those regions account for less than 40 percent of the total Christian population.[1] This demographic shift to the Global South has thus informed most major analyses of world Christianity over the past four decades,[2] including, most recently, the work of Philip Jenkins.[3]

The expansion of Christianity in the Global South has produced thousands of new denominations and networks, a proliferation of movements nowhere more apparent than in Africa.[4] In 1910 there were approximately 5,000 Christian denominations worldwide. This number increased to 20,000 by 1970 and has now more than doubled to 41,000. The vast majority of these groups are Protestant and Independent.[5]

These geographic and demographic changes have come about in tandem with a flourishing of Renewalist enthusiasm in virtually all traditions within Christianity. Alternately called Pentecostal or Charismatic, Renewalist movements grew from just over one million adherents in 1900 to nearly 600 million by 2010.

The Global Demographics of the Pentecostal/ Charismatic Renewal

Following the research outlined above, population figures were compiled country by country for all denominations. The results are presented here in a series of tables with commentary. Table A1.1 is a summary of the global

Renewalist context extending from 1910 to projected populations 2025. The table reveals at least six interesting trends:

1. Over the period 1910–2010 Renewalist movements grew at nearly four times the growth rate of both Christianity and the world's population. From 2010–25, it is expected to grow twice as fast as both.
2. In 2010 Renewalists made up over one-quarter of all Christians. By 2025 these groups are expected to account for more than 30 percent of all Christians.
3. While Charismatics (Type 2) were the fastest growing of the types from 1910–2010, Pentecostals (Type 1) are expected to grow faster than the other two types from 2010–25.
4. In 2010 the largest of the three types were Independent Charismatics (Type 3) at 259 million, but Charismatics (Type 2) were not far behind at 234 million.
5. Renewalists were most numerous in Latin America in 2010, but Africa will likely surpass Latin America before 2025.
6. Renewalists grew fastest in Asia over the period 1910–2010. This will likely be the case from 2010–25 as well.

In 1910 the three largest Renewalist populations were in South Africa, Nigeria, and the United States (see Table A1.2 below). South Africa contained a much higher concentration of Pentecostal Christians than any other country (16.4 percent, see Table A1.3 below) due to the growing presence of indigenous African movements with Pentecostal characteristics in the early twentieth century. In 2010, the countries with the most Renewalists were Brazil, the United States, China, and Nigeria. Wherever Christianity reached during the twentieth century, to a large extent Renewalists did as well.

Countries where large populations adhered to animistic and spiritist traditions generally embraced Pentecostalism due to its emphasis on signs, wonders, and miracles—phenomena that are often compatible with beliefs in tribal religions. One example of this trend is found in sub-Saharan Africa, where dominant ethnoreligions gave way to Christianity over the past century. Today, countries with the highest percentages of Renewalists are found in the Global South, with a preponderance of countries in southern Africa (Table A1.3).

Renewalist movements are currently growing fastest in countries in which Christianity is relatively new, such as Afghanistan and Cambodia (Table A1.4). The fastest growth rates over the entire century (1910–2010) reveal those countries that now have some of the largest Renewalist populations, such as Brazil, the Philippines, and DR Congo. Many regions saw up to 15–17 percent annual growth rates where both Christians and nonbelievers embraced this form of Christianity. This huge influx of adherents comes from a variety of ethnicities and Christian backgrounds.

Table A1.1 **Renewalists in Global Context, 1910–2025**

Category	1910	100-year trend, %pa	2010	15-year trend, %pa	2025
GLOBAL POPULATION	1,758,412,000	1.4	6,895,889,000	1.0	8,002,979,000
GLOBAL CHRISTIANITY	611,810,000	1.3	2,269,200,000	1.2	2,727,153,000
GLOBAL RENEWALISTS	1,203,300	6.4	584,490,000	2.4	828,427,000
as percentage of global Christianity	0.2%	5.0	25.8%	1.1	30.4%
Pentecostals (Type 1)	25,000	8.6	91,560,000	2.6	134,500,000
Classical Pentecostals	25,000	8.5	88,868,000	2.6	131,000,000
Oneness Pentecostals	0	10.7	2,692,000	1.8	3,500,000
Charismatics (Type 2)	14,000	10.2	234,237,000	2.2	324,827,000
Anglican Charismatics	1,000	10.3	18,647,000	2.0	25,000,000
Catholic Charismatics	12,000	10.1	176,553,000	2.3	250,000,000
Protestant Charismatics	1,000	11.0	34,827,000	1.7	45,000,000
Orthodox Charismatics	0	11.2	4,190,000	0.9	4,800,000
Marginal Charismatics	0	5.4	20,000	2.0	27,000
Independent Charismatics (Type 3)	1,164,300	5.6	258,693,000	2.4	369,100,000
(a) 100% Charismatic networks					
Oneness	30,000	6.2	11,841,000	1.7	15,200,000

(Continued)

Table A1.1 **Continued**

Category	1910	100-year trend, %pa	2010	15-year trend, %pa	2025
Pentecostal (former Type 1)	1,060,000	4.4	75,853,000	1.8	99,000,000
Apostolic	30,000	7.3	32,896,000	2.1	45,000,000
Charismatic (former Type 2)	15,000	8.3	44,237,000	3.2	71,000,000
Deliverance	0	8.9	515,000	3.0	800,000
Full Gospel	14,000	6.4	6,714,000	2.7	10,000,000
Media	0	9.7	1,052,000	2.4	1,500,000
Non-traditional, house, cell	5,000	7.4	6,314,000	3.1	10,000,000
Word of Faith	0	10.9	3,067,000	2.6	4,500,000
Zion	9,500	7.0	8,282,000	1.3	10,000,000
Hidden Muslim, Hindu, or Buddhist believers	700	6.6	425,000	2.3	600,000
(b) individuals in non-Charismatic networks	100	14.4	67,497,000	2.8	101,500,000
RENEWAL MEMBERS ON 6 CONTINENTS					
Renewal members in Africa	1,101,000	5.2	175,816,000	2.8	265,057,000
Renewal members in Asia	5,800	10.5	129,590,000	3.3	210,881,000
Renewal members in Europe	26,300	7.1	24,418,000	1.7	31,546,000
Renewal members in Latin America	15,300	9.8	181,645,000	1.5	226,082,000
Renewal members in Northern America	54,400	7.4	68,969,000	1.7	89,020,000
Renewal members in Oceania	500	9.4	4,052,000	2.5	5,841,000

Source: World Christian Database, Brill, June 2011. %pa means average annual growth rate, per cent per year, between dates specified.

Table A1.2 **Countries with the most Renewalists, 1910 and 2010**

Country	Renewalists 1910	Country	Renewalists 2010
South Africa	989,000	Brazil	105,223,000
Nigeria	111,000	United States	65,884,000
United States	53,400	China	52,611,000
Germany	22,000	Nigeria	48,322,000
Trinidad & Tobago	11,800	Philippines	30,931,000
China	2,100	South Africa	23,786,000
India	2,000	DR Congo	20,686,000
France	1,000	India	19,643,000
Canada	1,000	Mexico	14,304,000
North Korea	1,000	Colombia	14,028,000

Source: World Christian Database, Brill, June 2011.

Table A1.3 **Countries with the highest percentage of Renewalists, 1910 and 2010**

Country	% 1910	Country	% 2010
South Africa	16.4	Marshall Islands	56.3
Trinidad & Tobago	3.6	Brazil	54.0
Nigeria	0.6	Guatemala	51.0
Bahamas	0.2	Swaziland	50.7
Guyana	0.2	Zimbabwe	50.0
Liberia	0.1	South Africa	47.5
Jamaica	0.1	Botswana	43.4
United States	0.1	Saint Vincent	39.6
Costa Rica	0.1	Chile	38.3
Germany	0.0	Ghana	36.2

Source: World Christian Database, Brill, June 2011.

Table A1.4 **Countries with the fastest growth rates of Renewalists, 1910–2010 and 2000–2010**

Country	1910–2010*	Country	2000–2010*
Brazil	17.6	Afghanistan	14.3
Philippines	16.1	Cambodia	9.6
DR Congo	15.7	Burkina Faso	7.2
Mexico	15.2	Qatar	7.1
Colombia	15.2	Singapore	5.3
Kenya	15.0	Laos	5.2
Ethiopia	14.7	United Arab Emirates	5.2
Ghana	14.7	Mali	5.1
Guatemala	14.5	Papua New Guinea	5.0
Uganda	14.4	Niger	5.0

* annual average growth rate, per cent per year, between dates specified.

Source: *World Christian Database*, Brill, June 2011.

As outlined above, the demographics of Renewalists are best understood by its constituent parts, namely, the three types: Pentecostals, Charismatics, and Independent Charismatics. Tables A1.5–7 show, for each of these types, the countries with the highest populations of Renewalists, the highest percentages of Renewalists in the overall population, and the highest percentages of Renewalists among all Christians. These figures show that while all Renewalists are numerous in China, Brazil, and the United States (see Table A1.2), Brazil has by far the most Pentecostals (Table A1.5) and Charismatics (Table A1.6), with the latter composing the largest bloc of Renewalists in the country. In contrast, Independent Charismatics are most numerous in China and the United States (Table A1.7), both in absolute terms and as percentages of Renewalists in those countries.

Pentecostals (Type 1)

Countries with the largest numbers of Pentecostals are Brazil, Nigeria, and the United States (Table A1.5). Pentecostals in the Marshall Islands (population 54,000) constitute both the highest percentage of all Christians (46.5 percent) and of the population of the country (44.4 percent). Pentecostal

Table A1.5 **Pentecostals (Type 1) in 2010**

Highest population		Highest percentage of country		Highest percentage of Christians	
Country	Adherents	Country	% of country	Country	% of Christians
Brazil	25,586,000	Marshall Islands	44.4	Marshall Islands	46.5
Nigeria	7,646,000	Vanuatu	26.5	Cambodia	38.0
United States	6,191,000	Dominica	22.3	Burkina Faso	37.4
Indonesia	4,170,000	Jamaica	14.8	Vanuatu	28.3
Ghana	3,504,000	Montserrat	14.7	Dominica	23.6
Kenya	2,998,000	Ghana	14.4	Ghana	23.5
South Korea	2,988,000	Barbados	14.2	Mauritius	22.5
South Africa	2,393,000	American Samoa	13.9	Jamaica	17.5
Angola	2,100,000	Papua New Guinea	13.4	Guyana	16.8
India	1,851,000	Saint Vincent	13.3	Montserrat	15.7

Source: World Christian Database, Brill, June 2011.

denominations depend mainly on foreign missions and church planting as means of growth. Interestingly, Pentecostals make up a high percentage of all Christians in Cambodia, where Christianity as a whole has grown recently.

Charismatics (Type 2)

Countries with the largest numbers of Charismatics include Brazil, the United States, and the Philippines (Table A1.6). Guatemala is the country with the highest percentage of Charismatics in the total population, while Mauritius has the highest percentage in the Christian population. Charismatics typically grow by recruiting new members from within existing denominations. Roman Catholics in some countries have stagnant or declining numbers of Charismatics (United States), while others continue to grow rapidly (Brazil, Philippines).

Table A1.6 **Charismatics (Type 2) in 2010**

Highest population		Highest percentage of country		Highest percentage of Christians	
Country	Adherents	Country	% of country	Country	% of Christians
Brazil	60,666,000	Guatemala	35.3	Mauritius	47.6
United States	23,481,000	Brazil	31.1	Guatemala	36.2
Philippines	22,200,000	Colombia	27.1	Brazil	34.2
Nigeria	13,569,000	Philippines	23.8	Colombia	28.3
Colombia	12,554,000	Mauritius	15.6	Philippines	26.5
Mexico	10,134,000	Uganda	15.6	Nigeria	18.8
Ethiopia	6,477,000	Puerto Rico	15.4	Uganda	18.2
DR Congo	5,858,000	Chile	14.7	Chile	16.8
Argentina	5,478,000	Saint Helena	14.3	Puerto Rico	16.1
Uganda	5,197,000	Argentina	13.6	Saint Helena	15.0

Source: World Christian Database, Brill, June 2011.

Independent Charismatics (Type 3)

While found in many of the same countries as Pentecostals and Charismatics, Independent Charismatic populations are largest in China, the United States, and Nigeria (Table A1.7). Independent Charismatics experience growth by planting new churches and by schisms from traditional denominations. Of the three types, Independent Charismatics are most strongly concentrated in regions of the Global South where new forms of Christianity have grown most dramatically in the past hundred years.

Pentecostal, Charismatic, and Independent Charismatic congregations continue to grow in Africa, Asia, and Latin America while slowing in Northern America and Europe. Exceptions to this trend can be found among Independents in the United States (still growing) and Charismatics in Europe (some growth among Roman Catholics). Another significant trend is the migration of Renewalists from the Global South to the Global North. Thus, some of the largest congregations in Europe are African Independent

Table A1.7 **Independent Charismatics (Type 3) in 2010**

Highest population		Highest percentage of country		Highest percentage of Christians	
Country	Adherents	Country	% of country	Country	% of Christians
China	49,357,000	Swaziland	46.3	North Korea	86.5
United States	36,213,000	Zimbabwe	42.2	Nepal	69.1
Nigeria	27,107,000	Botswana	39.6	Botswana	60.9
Brazil	18,971,000	South Africa	36.5	Zimbabwe	59.0
South Africa	18,294,000	Chile	23.2	Swaziland	52.8
DR Congo	14,706,000	DR Congo	22.3	China	45.8
India	13,541,000	Saint Vincent	21.2	South Africa	44.7
Philippines	7,492,000	Nigeria	17.1	Bhutan	43.7
Zimbabwe	5,303,000	Ghana	16.2	Nigeria	37.6
Kenya	4,494,000	El Salvador	14.2	Niger	29.9

Source: World Christian Database, Brill, June 2011.

Charismatic in origin. In the United States, many recent Hispanic arrivals, both legal and illegal, are either Catholic Charismatics or Pentecostals.[6]

Conclusion

A demographic overview of Renewalists (all types) illustrates the complexities of both the global spread of the movement and the striking diversity of the congregations themselves. While current ways of understanding Pentecostals, Charismatics, and Independent Charismatics reveal a religious phenomenon of immense proportions, strategies for classifying, counting, and assessing these movements are likely to continue to evolve for years to come. In the meantime, hundreds of millions of Christians across all traditions will continue to experience some form of renewal—bringing vitality in some denominations and schism in others. They will also promote social transformation in some communities and engender isolation in others. What is certain is that, for the foreseeable future, Christianity as a whole will continue to experience growth pains on a global scale.

NOTES

1. Todd M. Johnson and Kenneth R. Ross, eds., *Atlas of Global Christianity, 1910–2010* (Edinburgh: Edinburgh University Press, 2009), 8.
2. See Walbert Bülhmann, *The Coming of the Third Church* (Maryknoll, NY: Orbis Books, 1976); David Barrett, "AD 2000: 350 million Christians in Africa," *International Review of Mission* 59, no. 233 (January 1970): 39–54; and the writings of Andrew Walls (especially *The Missionary Movement in Christian History: Studies in the Transmission of the Faith*, Maryknoll, NY: Orbis Books, 1996), and Lamin Sanneh, (especially *Whose Religion Is Christianity? The Gospel Beyond the West*, Grand Rapids, MI: Eerdmans, 2003).
3. Especially *The Next Christendom: The Coming of Global Christianity* (Oxford: Oxford University Press, 2002); followed by *New Faces of Global Christianity: Believing the Bible in the Global South* (Oxford: Oxford University Press, 2007).
4. See David B. Barrett, *Schism and Renewal in Africa: An Analysis of Six Thousand Contemporary Religious Movements* (Oxford: Oxford University Press, 1968).
5. A table showing the breakdown of these is found in David B. Barrett, George Thomas Kurian, and Todd M. Johnson, eds., *World Christian Encyclopedia*, 2nd ed. (New York: Oxford University Press, 2001), 16–18.
6. Pew Hispanic Center, *Changing Faiths: Latinos and the Transformation of American Religion* (Washington, D.C.: Pew Research Center, 2007), 27.

Appendix 2

PENTECOSTAL GROWTH AND IMPACT IN LATIN AMERICA, AFRICA, AND ASIA

Findings from a Ten-Country Survey

JOHN C. GREEN

Pentecostalism broadly defined is one of the fastest growing segments of global Christianity. For example, the *World Christian Database* estimates that at least one-quarter of the world's two billion Christians belong to faith communities that stress the gifts of the Holy Spirit, such as speaking in tongues and divine healing. These communities are, however, diverse in religious terms. The *World Christian Database* uses the broader term "renewalist" to capture the diversity of these communities, including classic Pentecostals and charismatics. Classic Pentecostals are often seen as central to the growth of this segment of global Christianity, while charismatics reflect the impact of this growth on other Christian communities. The size and diversity of these communities raise two closely related questions: what characteristics of renewalists contribute to their growth and what impact might the growing numbers of renewalists have on societies around the globe?

This chapter offers evidence relevant to these questions drawn from a ten-country public opinion survey conducted at the 100th anniversary of the 1906 Azusa Street Revival, generally regarded as the origin of the contemporary renewalist movements. Although not a comprehensive global portrait of renewalists, this evidence includes basic information about their characteristics and attitudes, and how they differ from their fellow citizens.

We find the spiritual descendants Azusa Street Revival located in diverse and dynamic communities around the globe, distinctive in some religious practices but in other respects not outside of the mainstream of the societies in which they live. This general assessment is based on four main survey findings.

First, renewalists are distinctive with respect to religious experiences associated with the Holy Spirit, but also in their commitment to traditional Christian practices and beliefs, including a strong emphasis on sharing their faith with non-believers.

Second, renewalists are not always distinctive in demographic terms. For example, they are not necessarily drawn disproportionately from the lower socioeconomic sectors of society and do not come disproportionately from women.

Third, renewalists tend to hold distinctive attitudes on social issues, especially sexuality. On these matters, they tend to be very traditional, but with a degree of complexity in their views. The renewalists tend not to be distinctive on other kinds of issues, including views on social welfare, where renewalists often hold progressive views. Renewalists tend to be at least as supportive of a prominent political role for religion as are other religious groups within each country.

Fourth, renewalists are quite diverse within and across the countries surveyed, often making up a large part of the Christian and Protestant populations, with charismatics typically outnumbering Pentecostals. The proportion of converts within renewalist communities varies considerably, ranging from large minorities to small minorities in number. National context is often important in accounting for these religions variations as well as differences in issue attitudes.

This evidence has implications for understanding the growth and impact of the renewalists around the globe. The faith-based distinctiveness of renewalists suggests that they can offer clear religious alternatives to potential converts, while their lack of demographic distinctiveness suggests that such offers may be widely accessible to the population at large. At the same time, renewalists' emphasis on traditional sexual morality may contribute to growth by natural increase. For these reasons and others, the impact of renewalists on their societies is likely to vary by topic, with the strongest impact occurring among issues directly tied to their distinctive faith.

Data and Definitions

This essay summarizes the results of a ten-nation survey undertaken by the Pew Research Center's Forum on Religion & Public Life in 2006 with generous support from the Templeton Foundation.[1] The ten nations surveyed included the United States; Brazil, Chile, and Guatemala in Latin America; Kenya, Nigeria, and South Africa in Africa; and in Asia, the Philippines, South Korea, and parts of India. These countries were chosen to provide a sense of the range of renewalist Christianity around the world.

The surveys were conducted under the direction of Princeton Survey Research Associates International and the methodology varied with local conditions and practical considerations. For example, the survey in the United States was a telephone survey of a national probability sample, while in India it involved face-to-face interviews in disproportionately Christian districts of three states where Christians are numerous. Each of these surveys had an over-sample of renewalists. (Additional details about survey methodology are located below.)

Here the term "renewalist" is used to describe both Pentecostals and charismatics. A "Pentecostal" is defined as a respondent who belongs to a Pentecostal denomination (either a church founded shortly after the Azusa Street Revival, such as the Assemblies of God or the Church of God in Christ, or a church founded more recently, such as the Brazil-based Universal Church of the Kingdom of God). A "charismatic" is defined as a Christian respondent who *does not* belong to a Pentecostal denomination, *but who* nevertheless identifies themselves as a "charismatic Christian" or "Pentecostal Christian" apart from denominational affiliation, *or* who reports speaking in tongues at least several times a year.

Size of the Renewalist Populations

These surveys provide an independent and systematic estimate of the size and composition of the renewalist populations in each locale surveyed (see Table A2.1). There is substantial variation in the number of renewalists from country to country, ranging from a low of 5% in the regions of India surveyed to a high of 60% in Guatemala. In every nation surveyed except India, renewalists make up at least 10% of the adult population, and in three countries (Brazil, Guatemala, and Kenya) renewalists approach or exceed 50%.

In terms of the composition of the renewalist population, Pentecostals outnumber charismatics in just two countries (Kenya and Nigeria), while in all the other countries, charismatics outnumber Pentecostals by at least two to one. Pentecostals are more concentrated in Latin America and Africa (ranging from 9% of the population in Chile to 33% in Kenya) than they are in the United States or Asia (ranging from 1% of the population in the regions of India surveyed to 5% in the United States). The largest charismatic populations are in Brazil (34%), Guatemala (40%), and the Philippines (40%). In several other countries, including the United States, Chile, Kenya, and South Africa, approximately one in five people are charismatic.[2]

In six of the ten countries surveyed, renewalists account for a majority of the overall Protestant population (see Table A2.2); in five nations (Brazil, Chile, Guatemala, Kenya, and the Philippines), more than two-thirds of all

Table A2.1 **Estimated Size of Renewalist Populations**

	Pentecostals	Charismatics	Total (Renewalists)
United States	5%	18%	=23%
Latin America			
Brazil	15	34	=49
Chile	9	21	=30
Guatemala	20	40	=60
Africa			
Kenya	33	23	=56
Nigeria	18	8	=26
South Africa	10	24	=34
Asia			
India (localities)	1	4	=5
Philippines	4	40	=44
South Korea	2	9	=11

Protestants are Pentecostal or charismatic. In Nigeria, renewalists account for six in ten Protestants. These patterns confirm that renewalists are an important part of Christianity in many places in the world.[3]

Religious Characteristics

Renewalists, especially Pentecostals, differ from other Christians in certain important respects, perhaps most notably in their experiences with the gifts of the Holy Spirit. In addition, renewalists stand out because of their extensive engagement in traditional Christian practices and intense commitment to traditional Christian beliefs. In these regards, renewalists are highly distinctive in religious terms within the countries surveyed. However, renewalists are quite diverse in terms of religious affiliation and this diversity tends to reflect the characteristics of Christianity in their countries.

A good place to begin looking at the religious characteristics of renewalists is with religious affiliation (see Table A2.3). Pentecostals are defined by membership in specific denominations, but the exact denominations vary by country. In Chile and South Korea, large majorities of Pentecostals belong to older Pentecostal denominations. For example, nearly all Pentecostals

Table A2.2 **Renewalists and Protestantism**

	% of Protestants who are ...			
	Pentecostals	Charismatics	Non-renewalists	Total Protestant/ AIC†
United States	10	18	72	=100 (n = 388)
Latin America				
Brazil	72	6	22	=100 (n = 148)
Chile	59	19	22	=100 (n = 87)
Guatemala	58	27	15	=100 (n = 341)
Africa				
Kenya	50	23	27	=100 (n = 436)
Nigeria	48	12	40	=100 (n = 289)
South Africa	14	29	57	=100 (n = 533)
Asia				
India (localities)*	–	–	–	–
Philippines	37	30	33	=100 (n = 89)
South Korea	9	29	62	=100 (n = 150)

†African Independent Church

*Results for India are not reported here because the general population survey in that country included only a small number of Protestants.

in South Korea are members of the Assemblies of God. In three nations (Guatemala, Nigeria, and the Philippines), Pentecostals are drawn primarily from newer Pentecostal denominations. For instance, in Nigeria more than 80% of Pentecostals belong to newer churches, such as the Church of God Mission International or the Redeemed Christian Church of God. In the five other nations, Pentecostals are more evenly divided between older and newer denominations. In South Africa, for example, four in ten Pentecostals belong to newer denominations while the remaining six in ten belong to older ones.

Interestingly, the surveys find that for the most part, Pentecostals are more likely to have changed affiliation than other Christians, and in two countries, Brazil and the Philippines, majorities of Pentecostals report having experienced a change in religious affiliation. However, in other countries half or more of Pentecostals say that they have been lifelong members of their current denomination.

Table A2.3 **Renewalists and Changes in Religious Affiliation**

	% saying they have not always belonged to their current religion			
	All	*Pentecostals*	*Charismatics*	*Other Christians*
United States	29%	43%	29%	27%
Latin America				
Brazil	26	62	10	13
Chile	18	39	14	9
Guatemala	26	49	19	14
Africa				
Kenya	26	42	21	13
Nigeria	9	36	–	8
South Africa	16	18	13	11
Asia				
India (localities)	3	10	6	1
Philippines	12	74	10	8
South Korea	21	13	16	16

Question wording: Have you always been (insert religion)?

The religious affiliation of charismatics tends to reflect the religious composition of the general population in each country. In countries with large Catholic populations large majorities of charismatics are Roman Catholics, such as Brazil (95%), Philippines (85%), Chile (76%), and Guatemala (65%). But in countries where Catholics are outnumbered by Protestants, other Christians, or non-Christians, charismatics tend to contain fewer Catholics, such as the United States (38%), Kenya (35%), India (33%), South Africa (16%), and South Korea (13%).

The proportion of converts among the renewalists surveys varies considerably, measured as a change from childhood affiliation. In two countries, Brazil (62%) and the Philippines (74%), a large majority of Pentecostals are converts. And in five countries, Guatemala (49%), Unites States (43%), Nigeria (42%), Kenya (42%) and Chile (39%), large minorities are converts. However, converts make up only small minorities in South Africa (18%), South Korea (13%), and India (10%).

Charismatics tended to report lower rates of conversion (reflecting in part the fact that the definition used here does not involve religious affiliation). The largest number of converts among charismatics is in the United States (29%),

Kenya (21%), Guatemala (19%), South Korea (16%), Chile (14%), South Africa (13%), Brazil (10%), the Philippines (10%), and India (6%).

In all countries, conversions are most common among young adults or children. Taken together, these figures suggest that at least in some part of the world, the growth has been due to natural increase within renewalist communities.

Gifts of the Holy Spirit

What about the distinctive religious practices of renewalists? In all ten countries surveyed, overwhelming majorities of Pentecostal church attendees say that their religious services include people practicing the gifts of the Holy Spirit, such as speaking in tongues or praying for divine healing, on at least an occasional basis (see Figure A2.1). Such reports are particularly common in Latin America and Africa, where pluralities of Pentecostals in most countries report that their services include these activities either always (Brazil, Guatemala, South Africa) or frequently (Chile, Kenya). Reports of such services are less common in Asia, where pluralities in the regions of India surveyed, the Philippines, and South Korea report that such phenomena occur only occasionally. Reports of signs of the spirit are also common among charismatics, although less so than among Pentecostals.

In all the countries surveyed, majorities of Pentecostals say they have experienced or witnessed a divine healing of an illness or injury (see Table A2.4). In every country except the United States (where 62% of Pentecostals report having experienced or witnessed divine healing) and South Korea (where 56% of Pentecostals are personally familiar with divine healing), more than seven in ten Pentecostals report having experienced or witnessed a miraculous cure. Such experiences are also fairly common among charismatics. In South Korea, for instance, charismatics are just as likely to report having experienced divine healing as Pentecostals. And in three other locales (Guatemala, Kenya, and the Indian states surveyed) majorities of charismatics say they are familiar with divine healings.

Although many renewalists report attending religious services where speaking in tongues is common, fewer report that they themselves regularly speak or pray in tongues (see Table A2.5). In fact, in six of the ten countries, more than four in ten Pentecostals say they *never* speak or pray in tongues. Indeed, the only country in which a majority of Pentecostals say they speak or pray in tongues on a weekly basis is Guatemala.

Compared to renewalists, reports of having experienced the gifts of the Holy Spirit are rarer among non-renewalist Christians in the countries surveyed. With the exceptions of Nigeria and the Indian states, majorities of

% saying services frequently include signs of the spirit*

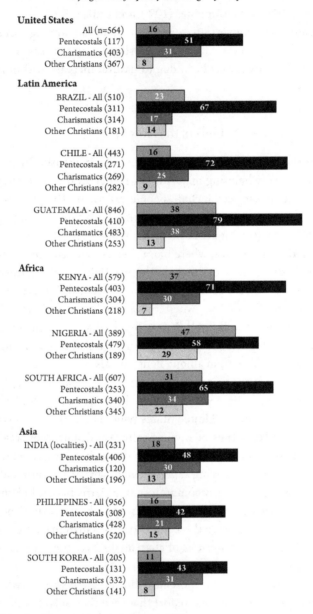

United States
All (n=564)
Pentecostals (117)
Charismatics (403)
Other Christians (367)

Latin America
BRAZIL - All (510)
Pentecostals (311)
Charismatics (314)
Other Christians (181)

CHILE - All (443)
Pentecostals (271)
Charismatics (269)
Other Christians (282)

GUATEMALA - All (846)
Pentecostals (410)
Charismatics (483)
Other Christians (253)

Africa
KENYA - All (579)
Pentecostals (403)
Charismatics (304)
Other Christians (218)

NIGERIA - All (389)
Pentecostals (479)
Other Christians (189)

SOUTH AFRICA - All (607)
Pentecostals (253)
Charismatics (340)
Other Christians (345)

Asia
INDIA (localities) - All (231)
Pentecostals (406)
Charismatics (120)
Other Christians (196)

PHILIPPINES - All (956)
Pentecostals (308)
Charismatics (428)
Other Christians (520)

SOUTH KOREA - All (205)
Pentecostals (131)
Charismatics (332)
Other Christians (141)

**Based on Christians who attend religious services.*

Question wording: When you attend religious services, how often do they include people speaking in tongues, prophesying, praying for miraculous or divine healings, or displaying physical signs of the spirit such as laughing and shaking? Would you say always, frequently, occasionally, or never?

Figure A2.1. Signs of the Spirit in Religious Services

Table A2.4 **Divine Healings**

	% saying they have witnessed or experienced a divine healing			
	All	*Pentecostals*	*Charismatics*	*Other Christians*
United States	29%	62%	46%	28%
Latin America				
Brazil	38	77	31	32
Chile	26	77	37	24
Guatemala	56	79	63	47
Africa				
Kenya	71	87	78	47
Nigeria	62	79	–	75
South Africa	38	73	47	32
Asia				
India (localities)	44	74	61	55
Philippines	38	72	44	30
South Korea	10	56	61	20

Question wording: Have you ever (insert item)?
a. experienced or witnessed a divine healing of an illness or injury?

non-renewalist Christian church attendees (ranging from 52% in South Korea to 79% in the United States) say their church services never feature behaviors such as speaking in tongues or prophesying. And compared to renewalists, other Christians have generally had less experience with divine healing, though in Nigeria and in the Indian states surveyed majorities also report experiencing or witnessing miraculous cures. Other religious experiences that tend to be more common among renewalists than among other Christians include exorcisms and giving and interpreting prophecy.

Traditional Christian Practices and Beliefs

In addition to practicing the gifts of the Holy Spirit, renewalists tend to engage in traditional Christian practices at somewhat higher rates than non-renewalists

Appendix 2

Table A2.5 **Speaking in Tongues**

	% saying they speak or pray in tongues ...*	
	Weekly or more	*Never*
United States—All (n = 619)	14%	74%
Pentecostals	33	49
Charismatics	50	32
Latin America		
Brazil—All (n = 643)	8	85
Pentecostals	29	50
Charismatics	8	84
Chile—All (n = 510)	8	84
Pentecostals	25	45
Charismatics	30	38
Guatemala—All (n = 854)	37	55
Pentecostals	53	35
Charismatics	53	39
Africa		
Kenya—All (n = 642)	19	61
Pentecostals	38	27
Charismatics	23	53
Nigeria—All (n = 649)	9	76
Pentecostals	37	32
South Africa—All (n = 720)	11	76
Pentecostals	38	41
Charismatics	26	57
Asia		
India (localities)—All (n = 725)	8	75
Pentecostals	41	54
Charismatics	51	34
Philippines—All (n = 995)	10	77
Pentecostals	34	45
Charismatics	18	65

Table A2.5 **Continued**

	% saying they speak or pray in tongues ... *	
	Weekly or more	Never
South Korea—All (n = 346)	4	67
Pentecostals	45	18
Charismatics	31	12

*Based on those who identified themselves as belonging to a particular religion.

Question wording: How often do you speak or pray in tongues? Would you say every day, more than once a week, once a week, at least once a month, several times a year, less often or never?

(see Table A2.6). For example, the vast majority of Pentecostals report attending religious services at least once a week. In the United States and the regions of India surveyed, at least six in ten report weekly attendance, and in the other countries, this figure increases to at least three in four. Majorities of charismatics in every country except Brazil and Chile also say they attend church at least once a week.

In most of the countries surveyed, majorities of the general population say they pray to God every day. Despite the generally high level of private prayer among all groups, Pentecostals, and, to a lesser extent, charismatics, report a higher level of private devotion. In nearly every country, at least two-thirds of Pentecostals pray every day, and majorities of charismatics also report praying every day. The only exception is South Korea, where only a minority of Pentecostals and charismatics pray daily.

Renewalists hold many of the same traditional beliefs as other Christians, but tend to hold them more intensely. Views of the Bible provide a good example of this pattern (see Table A2.7). In all the countries surveyed, many Christians believe that the Bible is the word of God and is to be taken literally. But in nearly every country, the number of Pentecostals who are biblical literalists is higher. (The lone exception is the Philippines, where Pentecostals and other Christians are about equally likely to express this point of view.) Similarly, in seven of the ten countries, charismatics are at least slightly more likely than non-renewalist Christians to view the Bible as literally true.

Belief in the intervention of supernatural forces in everyday life is common among renewalists around the world.

For example, majorities of Pentecostals say that miracles still occur today just as they did in ancient times (see Figure A2.2). In every country, more than four-fifths of Pentecostals hold this belief. This finding is perhaps not surprising given that most Pentecostals claim to have experienced or witnessed

Table A2.6 **Church Attendance**

	% saying they attend church at least once a week			
	All	*Pentecostals*	*Charismatics*	*Other Christians*
United States	44%	65%	63%	50%
Latin America				
Brazil	38	86	32	32
Chile	29	79	43	28
Guatemala	64	87	77	67
Africa				
Kenya	80	92	89	64
Nigeria	76	83	–	89
South Africa	55	75	71	55
Asia				
India (localities)	36	60	52	51
Philippines	62	90	65	58
South Korea	28	79	78	75

Question wording: Aside from weddings and funerals how often do you attend religious services … more than once a week, once a week, once or twice a month, a few times a year, seldom, or never?

Muslims were asked: On average, how often do you attend the mosque for salah and Jum'ah Prayer? More than once a week, once a week for Jum'ah, once or twice a month, a few times a year, seldom, or never?

divine healings, exorcisms, or direct revelations from God. However, belief in miracles is by no means unique to Pentecostals. In every country, majorities of both charismatics and non-renewalist Christians also say that miracles still happen, but hold these views with less intensity than Pentecostals.

Sharing Faith with Non-believers

Pentecostals around the world report making a concerted effort to share their faith with non-believers (see Figure A2.3). In eight of the ten countries, majorities say they share their faith with non-believers *at least once a week*. And relatively few Pentecostals (ranging from a low of 3% in South Korea to a high of 33% in the Indian states surveyed) say they *never* share their faith with non-believers.

Table A2.7 **Views of Scripture**

	% saying Bible is ...		
	Word of God to be taken literally	Word of God NOT to be taken literally	Written by men, not word of God
United States—All	35%	41%	19%
Pentecostals	76	16	5
Charismatics	48	41	5
Other Christians	37	48	12
Latin America			
Brazil—All	53	30	12
Pentecostals	81	14	2
Charismatics	49	37	7
Other Christians	65	21	12
Chile—All	39	37	17
Pentecostals	83	15	1
Charismatics	54	30	9
Other Christians	37	45	12
Guatemala—All	77	14	5
Pentecostals	89	6	2
Charismatics	81	12	4
Other Christians	72	21	2
Africa			
Kenya—All	80	18	*
Pentecostals	91	9	0
Charismatics	84	15	0
Other Christians	73	26	0
Nigeria—All	88	10	*
Pentecostals	94	4	1
Other Christians	82	17	0
South Africa—All	59	26	7
Pentecostals	72	24	2
Charismatics	72	22	2
Other Christians	63	27	5

(Continued)

Table A2.7 **Continued**

	% saying Bible is ...		
	Word of God to be taken literally	Word of God NOT to be taken literally	Written by men, not word of God
Asia			
India (localities)—All	50	18	29
Pentecostals	90	6	5
Charismatics	82	9	10
Other Christians	66	16	16
Philippines—All	53	40	5
Pentecostals	55	44	1
Charismatics	49	45	6
Other Christians	54	39	4
South Korea—All	33	20	27
Pentecostals	88	8	2
Charismatics	82	13	3
Other Christians	58	24	9

Question wording: Which one of these statements comes closest to describing your feelings about [INSERT "THE BIBLE" FOR CHRISTIANS; "THE KORAN" FOR MUSLIMS; "SACRED SCRIPTURES" FOR ALL OTHERS]? The [Bible is/the Koran is/sacred scriptures are] the actual word of God and [is/are] to be taken literally, word for word OR [the Bible is/the Koran is/sacred scriptures are] the word of God, but not everything in [it/them] should be taken literally, word for word OR [the Bible is a book/the Koran is a book/sacred scriptures were] written by men and [is/are] not the word of God.

Except in Kenya and the parts of India surveyed, charismatics report sharing their faith less frequently than Pentecostals. Only in Guatemala, Kenya, and South Korea do majorities of charismatics report sharing their faith with others on a weekly basis. In contrast, other Christians are generally less likely than renewalists to frequently share their faith with others. In fact, in most countries, pluralities or even majorities (in Brazil and the Philippines) of other Christians say they never engage in such activities.

In sum, renewalists are distinctive in religious terms within their countries, both regarding the special gifts of the spirit and traditional Christian beliefs and practices. But this religious distinctiveness occurs within the context of diverse religious affiliations.

% completely agreeing miracles still occur

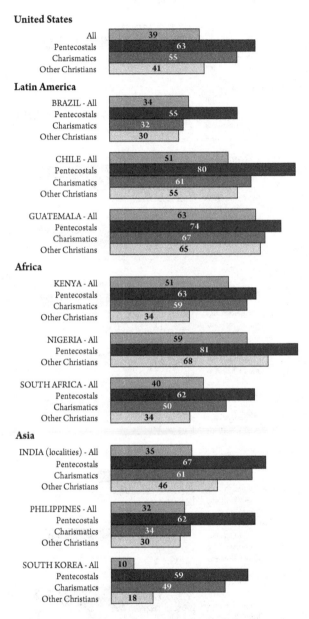

United States
- All — 39
- Pentecostals — 63
- Charismatics — 55
- Other Christians — 41

Latin America

BRAZIL - All — 34
- Pentecostals — 55
- Charismatics — 32
- Other Christians — 30

CHILE - All — 51
- Pentecostals — 80
- Charismatics — 61
- Other Christians — 55

GUATEMALA - All — 63
- Pentecostals — 74
- Charismatics — 67
- Other Christians — 65

Africa

KENYA - All — 51
- Pentecostals — 63
- Charismatics — 59
- Other Christians — 34

NIGERIA - All — 59
- Pentecostals — 81
- Other Christians — 68

SOUTH AFRICA - All — 40
- Pentecostals — 62
- Charismatics — 50
- Other Christians — 34

Asia

INDIA (localities) - All — 35
- Pentecostals — 67
- Charismatics — 61
- Other Christians — 46

PHILIPPINES - All — 32
- Pentecostals — 62
- Charismatics — 34
- Other Christians — 30

SOUTH KOREA - All — 10
- Pentecostals — 59
- Charismatics — 49
- Other Christians — 18

*Question wording: Now I am going to read you a series of statements on some different topics. For each one, please tell me if you completely agree with it, mostly agree with it, mostly disagree with it, or completely disagree with it. The first/next one is: **miracles still occur today as in ancient times.** Do you completely agree, mostly agree, mostly disagree, or completely disagree?*

Figure A2.2. Miracles

% saying share faith at least weekly

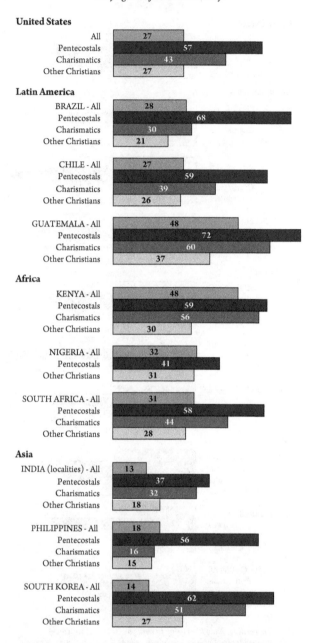

United States
All — 27
Pentecostals — 57
Charismatics — 43
Other Christians — 27

Latin America
BRAZIL - All — 28
Pentecostals — 68
Charismatics — 30
Other Christians — 21

CHILE - All — 27
Pentecostals — 59
Charismatics — 39
Other Christians — 26

GUATEMALA - All — 48
Pentecostals — 72
Charismatics — 60
Other Christians — 37

Africa
KENYA - All — 48
Pentecostals — 59
Charismatics — 56
Other Christians — 30

NIGERIA - All — 32
Pentecostals — 41
Other Christians — 31

SOUTH AFRICA - All — 31
Pentecostals — 58
Charismatics — 44
Other Christians — 28

Asia
INDIA (localities) - All — 13
Pentecostals — 37
Charismatics — 32
Other Christians — 18

PHILIPPINES - All — 18
Pentecostals — 56
Charismatics — 16
Other Christians — 15

SOUTH KOREA - All — 14
Pentecostals — 62
Charismatics — 51
Other Christians — 27

Question wording: How often do you share your faith with non-believers?
Would you say every day, more than once a week, once a week, at least
once a month, several times a year, less often or never?

Figure A2.3. Sharing Faith with Non-believers

Demographic Characteristics

Contrary to what might have been expected, the surveys found that renewalist Christianity is not always distinctive in demographic terms. One case in point is income: renewalists do not draw disproportionately from the lower socioeconomic sectors of society. Whether Pentecostals and charismatics have higher or lower income levels than the general population very much depends on the country in question (see Table A2.8).

In the United States, for instance, Pentecostals do tend to be poorer than other religious groups; 58% of Pentecostals have a household income that places them in the bottom two income categories, compared with 41% for the population overall. The differences between Pentecostals and the general population are smaller but still notable in Chile (44% vs. 35%) and Guatemala (48% vs. 40%). However, in most of the countries surveyed, those with lower incomes are not more prevalent among renewalists. For example, in Brazil, Kenya, Nigeria, South Africa, the regions of India surveyed, the Philippines and South Korea, renewalist populations do not include a disproportionately high number of lower-income people. South Korea and the regions of India surveyed have a notably *larger* percentage of higher-income people among Pentecostals than in the general population. In South Korea, for example, 63% of Pentecostals are in the upper two income categories, compared with only 49% of the general population.

Similarly, in the regions of India surveyed, 59% of Pentecostals fall into the two higher-income groups, compared with only 39% of the general population. And in South Africa, there is a higher percentage of Pentecostals (29%) in the highest income bracket than among the general population (20%). Pentecostals have somewhat lower income levels than charismatics in the United States, but they have higher income levels in the Indian states surveyed. In the other countries, differences in the income levels of Pentecostals and charismatics tend to be less pronounced.

These surveys also revealed that renewalists are not disproportionately women. Although roughly half or more of the renewalist populations in all the countries surveyed are female, the percentage of renewalists who are female tends to resemble the proportion of women in each country as a whole. In addition, the number of children born to renewalists closely resembles the numbers among the general populations surveyed, with the exception of Nigeria, where Pentecostals have significantly fewer children than the general population. Finally, the average age of renewalists does not differ significantly from that of the general population in any of the countries surveyed.[4]

Table A2.8 **Income**

	% of Religious Group in Income Category†			
	1-Low	*2*	*3*	*4-High*
United States—All	21%	20%	23%	21%
Pentecostals	29	29	23	10
Charismatics	24	20	22	16
Other Christians	18	19	23	24
Latin America				
Brazil—All	21	20	30	17
Pentecostals	20	20	28	13
Charismatics	16	22	32	19
Other Christians	26	20	32	14
Chile—All	16	19	18	36
Pentecostals	17	27	23	21
Charismatics	17	20	21	30
Other Christians	13	19	18	40
Guatemala—All	16	24	18	22
Pentecostals	19	29	19	18
Charismatics	20	25	16	21
Other Christians	13	18	20	24
Africa				
Kenya—All	69	16	5	1
Pentecostals	66	20	7	*
Charismatics	61	19	5	1
Other Christians	71	15	5	1
Nigeria—All	27	14	8	13
Pentecostals	33	15	8	8
Other Christians	21	12	7	17
South Africa—All	17	21	18	20
Pentecostals	12	22	17	29
Charismatics	12	23	16	22
Other Christians	18	20	19	21

Table A2.8 **Continued**

	% of Religious Group in Income Category†			
	1-Low	*2*	*3*	*4-High*
Asia				
India (localities)—All	19	38	15	24
Pentecostals	7	26	25	34
Charismatics	13	36	24	22
Other Christians	19	37	13	26
Philippines—All	21	30	15	15
Pentecostals	12	35	23	10
Charismatics	19	35	13	15
Other Christians	21	25	17	16
South Korea—All	14	27	31	18
Pentecostals	11	24	36	27
Charismatics	10	22	31	34
Other Christians	8	23	35	20

†Specific response options vary from country to country. Income categories have been designed, as nearly as possible, to resemble quartiles. Thus, figures should be used only to compare groups within countries and not to make cross-national comparisons. Figures do not sum to 100 because DK/Ref responses are not shown.

Taken together, these demographic findings suggest that renewalists are not always distinctive in demographic terms within their countries. However, a few caveats are in order. This survey is limited to ten countries and it is possible that a stronger relationship between renewalism and demography may hold in other places. Indeed, the survey results reveal considerable diversity by country. It is also possible that there are important variations among renewalists, with, for example, some particular Pentecostal groups having lower economic status. Finally, there may be variations in the links between renewalism and demography by religious commitment and time of conversion.

Social, Civic, and Political Attitudes

What are the attitudes of renewalists on social, civic, and political questions? Renewalists all around the world tend to hold very traditional views on sexual matters, sometimes standing out even in countries where the general population is quite conservative. In this regard, renewalists tend to be distinctive within their countries. However, there is a good deal of nuance in the political application of these views on issues such as the AIDS epidemic and abortion. Most renewalists say that women should be allowed to serve in religious leadership roles, but women are not viewed as the equal of men in all social circumstances. On other kinds of issues, renewalists are less distinctive within their countries. For instance, on social welfare issues, renewalists often hold progressive views. Interestingly, the surveys also found that renewalists are just as willing as non-renewalists to endorse a role for religion in the political life of their nations.

Social Issues

In most of the countries surveyed, majorities of the general population hold traditional views on sexuality (see Table A2.9). In eight of the ten countries, for instance, at least half of the general population says that homosexuality can never be justified. In Kenya and Nigeria, there is virtual unanimity on this question: 98% of the public in these two countries says homosexuality can never be justified. But even in these conservative contexts, Pentecostals stand out for their moral traditionalism. In five of the seven countries outside of Africa, Pentecostals are substantially more opposed to homosexuality than are non-renewalist Christians. A similar pattern emerges on other sexual issues, including prostitution, extramarital sex, and polygamy.

Although renewalists tend to subscribe to strict sexual mores, many reject the idea that AIDS is God's punishment for immoral sexual behavior (see Table A2.10). Majorities of Pentecostals in five countries (Brazil, Chile, the Philippines, the United States, and South Africa) reject the idea that those with AIDS have incurred God's wrath, as do at least half of charismatics in most countries. There are, however, exceptions to this pattern; in Guatemala, Kenya, and South Korea, majorities of Pentecostals say that AIDS is divine retribution for sexual immorality, as do majorities of charismatics in Kenya and South Korea. And in seven countries, Pentecostals are more likely than non-renewalist Christians to say that AIDS is a punishment from God.

A similarly complex pattern emerged with regard to attitudes on abortion. Large numbers of people in most of the countries surveyed are opposed to abortion—with the United States being the only country where less than half say abortion is never justified (see Table A2.11). Most Pentecostals (ranging from 64% in the United States to 97% in the Philippines) and charismatics (ranging from 57% in the United States to 96% in the Philippines) share the view that abortion can never be justified.

But while populations in most countries are morally opposed to abortion, they are more closely divided on the question of whether governments should prevent women from obtaining abortions. In Brazil, for instance, 48% of the

Table A2.9 **Sexual Morality**

	% saying behavior is never justified			
	Homo-sexuality	*Prostitution*	*Extra-marital sex*	*Polygamy*
United States—All	50%	67%	37%	71%
Pentecostals	80	81	64	71
Charismatics	59	78	47	74
Other Christians	54	73	37	77
Latin America				
Brazil—All	49	61	29	83
Pentecostals	76	81	63	94
Charismatics	46	57	26	85
Other Christians	46	64	21	85
Chile—All	32	49	22	81
Pentecostals	64	70	44	90
Charismatics	39	56	29	84
Other Christians	30	49	20	82
Guatemala—All	63	63	67	86
Pentecostals	73	71	77	89
Charismatics	61	63	66	86
Other Christians	61	65	68	90
Africa				
Kenya—All	98	93	79	60
Pentecostals	99	96	91	77
Charismatics	98	94	86	73
Other Christians	98	91	61	46
Nigeria—All	98	94	91	54
Pentecostals	97	92	91	88
Other Christians	98	94	86	84
South Africa—All	70	80	51	66
Pentecostals	79	83	68	81
Charismatics	70	81	54	68
Other Christians	72	81	47	67

(Continued)

Table A2.9 **Continued**

	% saying behavior is never justified			
	Homo-sexuality	Prostitution	Extra-marital sex	Polygamy
Asia				
India (localities)—All	72	72	78	78
Pentecostals	87	86	84	90
Charismatics	86	87	90	92
Other Christians	85	81	86	88
Philippines—All	56	86	77	92
Pentecostals	86	95	95	97
Charismatics	59	87	86	95
Other Christians	52	86	69	94
South Korea—All	78	87	78	95
Pentecostals	90	97	92	95
Charismatics	90	96	95	95
Other Christians	86	88	85	95

Question wording: Please tell me, for each of the following statements, whether you think it can always be justified, sometimes be justified, or never be justified. a. homosexuality ... b. prostitution ... g. sex between people who are not married to each other ... i. polygamy.

public agrees with the statement that the government should not interfere with a woman's ability to have an abortion, while 49% disagree. Chile, South Africa, and the regions of India surveyed are also similarly divided. A comparable pattern holds among Pentecostals and charismatics.

Gender Issues

Historically, women have played a prominent role in helping to shape renewalist Christianity. It might be expected, therefore, to find that Pentecostals have a more egalitarian outlook on gender roles compared with non-renewalists, and this expectation is born out in views of the appropriateness of having female clergy. In five countries (Guatemala, Kenya, Nigeria, the Philippines, and South Korea), Pentecostals are more willing to allow women to serve as pastors or church leaders compared with other Christians (see Figure A2.4).

Table A2.10 **AIDS as God's Punishment**

	% agreeing AIDS is God's punishment			
	All*	Pentecostals	Charismatics	Other Christians
United States	20%	34%	30%	15%
Latin America				
Brazil	27	37	23	26
Chile	21	42	29	19
Guatemala	44	51	44	39
Africa				
Kenya	59	62	69	53
Nigeria	43	45	–	34
South Africa	46	37	44	46
Asia				
India (localities)	38	42	44	39
Philippines	42	48	39	41
South Korea	45	77	72	55

*Based on those who identified themselves as belonging to a particular religion or believing in God. U.S. n = 681; Brazil n = 690; Chile n = 569; Guatemala n = 1000; Kenya n = 653; Nigeria n = 650; S. Africa n = 788; India localities n = 726; Philippines n = 1000; S. Korea n = 420.

Question wording: Now I am going to read you a series of statements on some different topics. For each one, please tell me if you completely agree with it, mostly agree with it, mostly disagree with it, or completely disagree with it. The first one is (insert item). Do you completely agree, mostly agree, mostly disagree, or completely disagree? i.e., AIDS is God's punishment for immoral sexual behavior.

Table A2.11 **Abortion**

	% saying abortion is never justified			
	All	Pentecostals	Charismatics	Other Christians
United States	45%	64%	57%	45%
Latin America				
Brazil	79	91	76	82
Chile	71	88	76	72
Guatemala	85	90	85	86

(Continued)

Table A2.11 **Continued**

	% saying abortion is never justified			
	All	*Pentecostals*	*Charismatics*	*Other Christians*
Africa				
Kenya	88	88	89	81
Nigeria	94	95	-	96
South Africa	73	78	69	74
Asia				
India (localities)	68	78	88	77
Philippines	97	97	96	97
South Korea	54	77	70	65
	% saying government should not interfere with obtaining an abortion			
	All	*Pentecostals*	*Charismatics*	*Other Christians*
United States	64%	41%	53%	62%
Latin America				
Brazil	48	41	51	51
Chile	46	28	43	45
Guatemala	58	61	58	54
Africa				
Kenya	18	19	18	16
Nigeria	30	37	–	32
South Africa	46	47	47	46
Asia				
India (localities)	46	53	47	43
Philippines	25	21	21	29
South Korea	62	41	52	55

Question wording: Please tell me, for each of the following statements, whether you think it can always be justified, sometimes be justified, or never be justified: h. abortion
Question wording: Please tell me whether you completely agree, mostly agree, mostly disagree or completely disagree with the following statements: c. The government should not interfere with a woman's ability to have an abortion

% agreeing women should be allowed to serve as pastors/priests

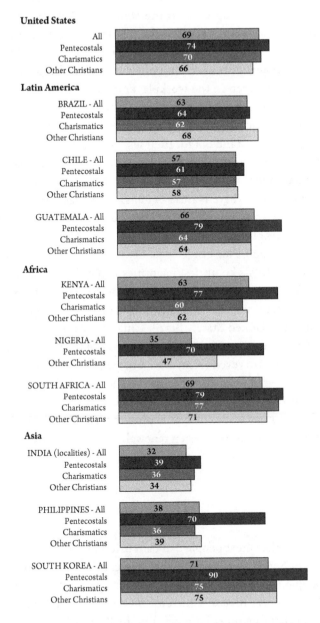

United States
- All — 69
- Pentecostals — 74
- Charismatics — 70
- Other Christians — 66

Latin America

BRAZIL - All — 63
- Pentecostals — 64
- Charismatics — 62
- Other Christians — 68

CHILE - All — 57
- Pentecostals — 61
- Charismatics — 57
- Other Christians — 58

GUATEMALA - All — 66
- Pentecostals — 79
- Charismatics — 64
- Other Christians — 64

Africa

KENYA - All — 63
- Pentecostals — 77
- Charismatics — 60
- Other Christians — 62

NIGERIA - All — 35
- Pentecostals — 70
- Other Christians — 47

SOUTH AFRICA - All — 69
- Pentecostals — 79
- Charismatics — 77
- Other Christians — 71

Asia

INDIA (localities) - All — 32
- Pentecostals — 39
- Charismatics — 36
- Other Christians — 34

PHILIPPINES - All — 38
- Pentecostals — 70
- Charismatics — 36
- Other Christians — 39

SOUTH KOREA - All — 71
- Pentecostals — 90
- Charismatics — 75
- Other Christians — 75

Question wording: Now I am going to read you another series of statements on some different topics. For each statement, please tell me if you completely agree with it, mostly agree with it, mostly disagree with it or completely disagree with it. The first/next one is: women should be allowed to serve as pastors or priests.

Figure A2.4. Female Clergy

Pentecostals in the ten countries surveyed also express generally egalitarian views when it comes to other aspects of gender roles (see Table A2.12). For instance, majorities agree with the statement that a working mother can establish just as warm and secure a relationship with her children as a mother who does not work outside the home. There is also widespread support among renewalists and non-renewalists alike for egalitarian views when it comes to women in the workplace; in six of the ten countries surveyed, majorities of the public disagree with the statement that when jobs are scarce, men should have more right to a job than women. Publics in Asia and Nigeria, however, stand out for their less egalitarian views on this question; in these countries, at least six in ten agree that when jobs are scarce, men should have more right to a job than women. And unlike the question about women pastors, there is little evidence to suggest that Pentecostals are more egalitarian than others in their views of working mothers and women in the workplace.

Furthermore, support for gender equality in the countries surveyed is far from unqualified. In six countries, majorities agree that a wife must always obey her husband. Only in the United States, Brazil, Chile, and South Korea do majorities disagree with that statement. And on this question, Pentecostals in six nations (the United States, Brazil, Chile, Guatemala, the Philippines, and South Korea) are somewhat less egalitarian than the public as a whole. In five of the countries surveyed (Kenya, Nigeria, and all three Asian nations) at least half of the overall population agrees that, on the whole, men make better political leaders than women. In the United States and all three Latin American countries, however, majorities take the opposite view. There are relatively few differences within countries between renewalists and non-renewalists on this question.

Social Trust

When asked whether most people can be trusted or not, majorities in every country except South Korea say no, that one cannot be too careful in dealing with people (see Figure A2.5). This view is particularly widespread in Latin America, where 85% of Chileans, 88% of Guatemalans, and 95% of Brazilians say that one must be careful in dealing with people, and in the Philippines, where 95% are generally distrustful. Social trust is most common in the parts of India surveyed (where 41% say that most people can be trusted) and the United States (where 35% share this point of view). There are few differences between renewalists and others when it comes to general trust in others.

Table A2.12 **Gender Issues**

	% agreeing that ...			
	Men have greater right to jobs than women	Working mothers can establish just as warm relationships	Men make better political leaders	A wife must always obey her husband
United States—All	14%	75%	26%	24%
Pentecostals	29	70	37	46
Charismatics	20	71	32	37
Other Christians	12	75	25	20
Latin America				
Brazil—All	25	67	30	38
Pentecostals	29	69	36	61
Charismatics	26	65	29	34
Other Christians	30	72	36	42
Chile—All	36	72	32	31
Pentecostals	41	61	40	52
Charismatics	40	72	31	35
Other Christians	36	73	31	29
Guatemala—All	39	64	38	65
Pentecostals	40	59	40	73
Charismatics	32	59	33	58
Other Christians	44	70	40	66
Africa				
Kenya—All	35	76	51	90
Pentecostals	25	81	43	89
Charismatics	34	80	48	88
Other Christians	42	74	65	85
Nigeria—All	66	69	78	98
Pentecostals	59	72	67	97
Other Christians	59	78	77	97
South Africa—All	40	77	49	71
Pentecostals	36	79	43	76

(Continued)

Table A2.12 **Continued**

	% agreeing that ...			
	Men have greater right to jobs than women	Working mothers can establish just as warm relationships	Men make better political leaders	A wife must always obey her husband
Charismatics	36	81	51	74
Other Christians	39	77	48	69
Asia				
India (localities)—All	69	66	67	86
Pentecostals	74	79	73	85
Charismatics	70	74	72	94
Other Christians	64	69	64	85
Philippines—All	76	75	65	57
Pentecostals	69	77	62	68
Charismatics	73	76	61	55
Other Christians	77	74	67	58
South Korea—All	60	59	51	23
Pentecostals	65	59	50	40
Charismatics	70	64	55	42
Other Christians	60	58	47	26

Question wording: Now I am going to read you another series of statements on some different topics. For each statement, please tell me if you completely agree with it, mostly agree with it, mostly disagree with it or completely disagree with it. The first one is (insert item). How about (insert next item)?

a. when jobs are scarce, men should have more right to a job than women.

b. on the whole, men make better political leaders than women do.

c. a wife must always obey her husband.

d. a working mother can establish just as warm and secure a relationship with her children as a mother who does not work.

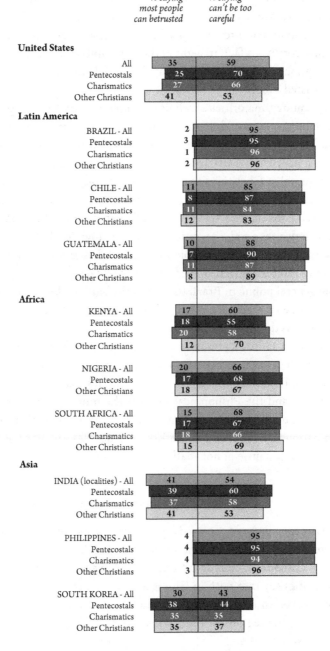

	% saying most people can be trusted	% saying can't be too careful

United States

- All — 35 / 59
- Pentecostals — 25 / 70
- Charismatics — 27 / 66
- Other Christians — 41 / 53

Latin America

BRAZIL - All — 2 / 95
- Pentecostals — 3 / 95
- Charismatics — 1 / 96
- Other Christians — 2 / 96

CHILE - All — 11 / 85
- Pentecostals — 8 / 87
- Charismatics — 11 / 84
- Other Christians — 12 / 83

GUATEMALA - All — 10 / 88
- Pentecostals — 7 / 90
- Charismatics — 11 / 87
- Other Christians — 8 / 89

Africa

KENYA - All — 17 / 60
- Pentecostals — 18 / 55
- Charismatics — 20 / 58
- Other Christians — 12 / 70

NIGERIA - All — 20 / 66
- Pentecostals — 17 / 68
- Other Christians — 18 / 67

SOUTH AFRICA - All — 15 / 68
- Pentecostals — 17 / 67
- Charismatics — 18 / 66
- Other Christians — 15 / 69

Asia

INDIA (localities) - All — 41 / 54
- Pentecostals — 39 / 60
- Charismatics — 37 / 58
- Other Christians — 41 / 53

PHILIPPINES - All — 4 / 95
- Pentecostals — 4 / 95
- Charismatics — 4 / 94
- Other Christians — 3 / 96

SOUTH KOREA - All — 30 / 43
- Pentecostals — 38 / 44
- Charismatics — 35 / 35
- Other Christians — 35 / 37

*Question wording: Generally speaking, would you say that most people can
be trusted or that you can't be too careful in dealing with people?*

Figure A2.5. Trust in Others

But while the publics surveyed are generally distrustful, some groups and organizations are deemed more trustworthy than others (see Table A2.13). Both renewalists and non-renewalists, for instance, say that their family members are trustworthy. In fact, in eight of the ten countries (Kenya and Nigeria are the exceptions), overall majorities say that people in their immediate family can be trusted a lot.

In every country, majorities of religious people also say that people at their own church or place of worship can be trusted at least to some extent (though only in the United States does an overall majority say that their fellow church members can be trusted *a lot*). In six countries, Pentecostals were more likely than non-renewalist Christians to say that church members can be trusted a lot. Renewalists and non-renewalists alike generally are less trusting of people from other religions than they are of people from their own churches.

Neighbors also tend to be accorded a relatively high level of trust. In eight countries, majorities say that people in their neighborhoods can be trusted at least some. Interestingly, however, relatively few people, ranging from 2% among the general public in Brazil to 29% in the United States, say that their neighbors can be trusted a lot. Renewalists express similar levels of trust in their neighbors as do their fellow citizens.

While trust in family members, fellow church members, and neighbors is relatively high, trust in other organizations is relatively low. For instance, majorities in only four countries (the United States, Kenya, the regions of India surveyed, and the Philippines) say that the military can be trusted at least to some extent. By contrast, in five countries, including all three Latin American nations, Nigeria, and South Korea, majorities say that the military can be trusted only a little or not at all.

Keys to Personal Economic Success

Majorities in every country surveyed report that a variety of factors are important to determining personal economic success or failure (see Table A2.14). One of the paramount factors is faith in God: in every country except South Korea, majorities say that faith in God is a very important factor in people's economic success. In most countries, including Brazil, Guatemala, all three African nations, the regions of India surveyed, and the Philippines, support for this view exceeds 70%.

In five countries, this view is more common among Pentecostals than among non-renewalist Christians. In the United States, for instance, more than 80% of Pentecostals see faith in God as very important to economic success, compared with only 56% among other Christians. In all ten countries,

Table A2.13 **Trust in Other People**

	% saying can trust a lot			
	Family	*Neighbors*	*Fellow church members**	*People of other faiths*
United States—All	70%	29%	51%	23%
Pentecostals	66	20	57	22
Charismatics	64	24	44	22
Other Christians	72	32	51	24
Latin America				
Brazil—All	52	2	13	3
Pentecostals	50	2	23	3
Charismatics	49	1	7	2
Other Christians	58	2	12	4
Chile—All	75	14	32	10
Pentecostals	75	11	54	11
Charismatics	76	15	42	10
Other Christians	79	16	25	11
Guatemala—All	73	15	40	12
Pentecostals	76	12	48	11
Charismatics	74	17	41	13
Other Christians	75	17	38	13
Africa				
Kenya—All	46	9	36	8
Pentecostals	50	10	36	9
Charismatics	47	8	37	10
Other Christians	48	7	33	7
Nigeria—All	42	4	23	4
Pentecostals	43	5	26	7
Other Christians	33	1	14	2
South Africa—All	62	13	41	16
Pentecostals	55	14	46	19
Charismatics	65	15	47	20
Other Christians	64	11	38	17

(Continued)

Table A2.13 **Continued**

	% saying can trust a lot			
	Family	Neighbors	Fellow church members*	People of other faiths
Asia				
India (localities)—All	74	25	34	26
Pentecostals	74	24	60	17
Charismatics	72	16	49	19
Other Christians	71	28	38	24
Philippines—All	85	15	35	13
Pentecostals	86	18	51	15
Charismatics	83	11	34	16
Other Christians	86	15	34	12
South Korea—All	73	5	16	1
Pentecostals	76	6	31	3
Charismatics	77	10	32	4
Other Christians	75	6	22	2

* "All" row based on those who identified themselves as belonging to a particular religion.
U.S. n = 518; Brazil n = 643; Chile n = 510; Guatemala n = 854; Kenya n = 642;
Nigeria n = 649; S. Africa n = 720; India n = 725; Phil. n = 995; S. Korea n = 346

Question wording: I'm going to read a list of institutions and people. For each one, please
tell me whether you feel that you can trust them a lot, some, only a little, or not at all.
First, how about (insert item), do you feel you can trust them a lot, trust them some, trust
them only a little, or not trust them at all? How about (insert next item), would you say
you can trust them a lot, some, only a little, or not at all?
a. people in your immediate family
b. people in your neighborhood
g. people from other religions
h. people at your church or place of worship

Table A2.14 **Keys to Success**

	% saying very important factor in economic success						
	Faith in God	Hard work	Education	Fate	Govt. policies	Personal contacts	Parents' economic situation
United States—All	56%	84%	84%	34%	36%	50%	36%
Pentecostals	81	88	90	53	47	54	53
Charismatics	76	86	83	45	38	49	42
Other Christians	56	86	83	32	35	51	31
Latin America							
Brazil—All	93	57	93	55	29	67	67
Pentecostals	99	57	96	48	24	66	63
Charismatics	95	58	93	57	30	66	68
Other Christians	94	61	95	57	29	69	72
Chile—All	57	58	85	28	28	55	49
Pentecostals	85	50	82	22	21	41	41
Charismatics	69	59	84	32	28	50	50
Other Christians	63	61	86	28	29	58	50
Guatemala—All	87	86	92	51	35	62	66
Pentecostals	87	86	92	50	40	65	63
Charismatics	88	85	92	55	41	61	68
Other Christians	89	87	92	50	33	66	64
Africa							
Kenya—All	88	94	74	19	45	48	47
Pentecostals	92	95	78	17	47	45	49
Charismatics	95	94	78	18	47	48	52
Other Christians	83	89	78	21	43	52	47
Nigeria—All	95	84	81	55	41	57	58
Pentecostals	94	86	88	49	43	59	55
Other Christians	91	85	85	50	42	55	53

(Continued)

Table A2.14 **Continued**

	% saying very important factor in economic success						
	Faith in God	Hard work	Education	Fate	Govt. policies	Personal contacts	Parents' economic situation
South Africa—All	74	87	86	35	30	42	40
Pentecostals	89	89	91	44	33	48	42
Charismatics	82	86	87	40	33	48	44
Other Christians	76	88	85	36	29	38	38
Asia							
India (localities)—All	75	94	95	30	33	56	56
Pentecostals	88	97	94	55	30	54	41
Charismatics	95	94	97	30	27	52	52
Other Christians	82	96	96	29	34	53	49
Philippines—All	94	92	95	34	42	48	61
Pentecostals	98	93	94	26	45	40	63
Charismatics	96	92	97	32	41	48	65
Other Christians	93	93	94	34	40	45	57
South Korea—All	16	77	50	18	27	53	21
Pentecostals	64	73	47	8	25	56	13
Charismatics	59	76	49	12	21	49	15
Other Christians	35	78	48	12	31	54	22

Question wording: As I read from a list, please tell me how important each factor is in people's economic success. Is (insert item) a very important, somewhat important, not too important, or not at all important factor(s) in people's economic success?
a. hard work
b. fate
c. people's parents' economic situation
d. faith in God
e. government policies
f. personal connections and contacts
g. education

two other factors deemed very important to success are hard work and education, and in this regard, renewalists and non-renewalists express similar views.

While there is a strong consensus across countries that hard work, education, and faith in God are important determinants of economic success or failure, most respondents also recognize that these attributes alone are not sufficient to guarantee economic prosperity. In every country, majorities (including both renewalists and non-renewalists) say that personal connections and contacts and people's parents' economic situation are each at least somewhat important in determining economic success. And in nine countries (with the lone exception of Kenya), majorities say that economic success or failure is, at least in part, determined by government policies and fate.

Free Market, Government Guarantees, and Globalization

In all ten countries surveyed, there is strong support for a free market economy (see Table A2.15). In every nation, majorities agree that most people are better off in a free market economy, even though some people are rich and some are poor. On this question, the opinions of Pentecostals and charismatics tend to resemble those of non-renewalists.

But support for a free market economy is not associated with opposition to government efforts to provide for a basic standard of living. In all the countries surveyed, majorities also agree that government should guarantee every citizen enough to eat and a place to sleep. Here again, the opinions of Pentecostals and charismatics tend, for the most part, to be roughly similar to those of non-renewalists.

In every country, substantial majorities say that their country benefits at least to some extent from increased influence of international business practices, trade, ideas, communication, and products from other countries, such as food and TV programs. Renewalists and non-renewalists alike view such increased international ties as beneficial for their countries.

Religion and Politics

Traditionally, renewalist Christianity has been associated with a reluctance to intermingle religion with politics. These surveys find, however, that renewalists tend to be at least as supportive of a prominent political role for religion as are other groups. For instance, in eight out of the ten countries surveyed, large majorities of Pentecostals say that religious groups should express their views on day-to-day social and political questions, a view held also by at least

Table A2.15 **The Free Market and Government Aid**

	% agreeing that ...	
	Most are better off in free market	Govt. should aid citizens
United States—All	75%	70%
Pentecostals	60	77
Charismatics	67	79
Other Christians	79	66
Latin America		
Brazil—All	72	93
Pentecostals	78	95
Charismatics	73	93
Other Christians	75	93
Chile—All	52	87
Pentecostals	47	90
Charismatics	46	86
Other Christians	56	85
Guatemala—All	72	92
Pentecostals	74	92
Charismatics	73	90
Other Christians	71	92
Africa		
Kenya—All	87	83
Pentecostals	83	80
Charismatics	87	86
Other Christians	85	87
Nigeria—All	88	94
Pentecostals	89	96
Other Christians	86	88
South Africa—All	74	85
Pentecostals	74	88
Charismatics	84	89
Other Christians	73	83

Table A2.15 **Continued**

	% agreeing that ...	
	Most are better off in free market	Govt. should aid citizens
Asia		
India (localities)—All	79	85
Pentecostals	72	78
Charismatics	88	92
Other Christians	77	86
Philippines—All	86	94
Pentecostals	83	97
Charismatics	85	93
Other Christians	85	95
South Korea—All	86	77
Pentecostals	88	87
Charismatics	86	79
Other Christians	90	83

Question wording: Please tell me whether you completely agree, mostly agree, mostly disagree or completely disagree with the following statements. (Read list)
a. Most people are better off in a free market economy, even though some people are rich and some are poor
b. The government should guarantee every citizen enough to eat and a place to sleep

seven in ten charismatics in seven countries. In most cases, renewalists and non-renewalist Christians all share this conviction (see Table A2.16).

However, the regions of India surveyed and South Korea are exceptions to this pattern. In these two places, majorities of the population (54% in the regions of India surveyed and 58% in South Korea) say that religious groups should keep out of political matters. Renewalists in these countries are also less supportive of religious groups speaking out about politics compared with renewalists in other countries.

Even though most renewalists believe that God is active in the world and support religious involvement in politics, they are divided on whether God fulfills his purposes through politics (see Figure A2.6). In three countries

Table A2.16 **Religious Groups and Politics**

	% saying that religious groups should ...	
	keep out of political matters	*express views on political questions*
United States—All	35%	61%
Pentecostals	14	79
Charismatics	23	71
Other Christians	36	61
Latin America		
Brazil—All	39	57
Pentecostals	33	65
Charismatics	35	61
Other Christians	44	53
Chile—All	37	59
Pentecostals	30	65
Charismatics	34	61
Other Christians	34	61
Guatemala—All	27	70
Pentecostals	25	72
Charismatics	24	73
Other Christians	28	69
Africa		
Kenya—All	16	83
Pentecostals	15	84
Charismatics	13	87
Other Christians	14	85
Nigeria—All	22	75
Pentecostals	16	79
Other Christians	26	69
South Africa—All	31	63
Pentecostals	25	70
Charismatics	26	70
Other Christians	34	60

Table A2.16 **Continued**

	% saying that religious groups should ...	
	keep out of political matters	express views on political questions
Asia		
India (localities)—All	54	42
Pentecostals	46	48
Charismatics	42	52
Other Christians	53	42
Philippines—All	38	61
Pentecostals	36	63
Charismatics	37	63
Other Christians	39	60
South Korea—All	58	36
Pentecostals	43	50
Charismatics	38	56
Other Christians	42	51

Question wording: In your opinion, should religious groups keep out of political matters—or should they express their views on day-to-day social and political questions?

(Guatemala, Nigeria, and South Korea), majorities of Pentecostals say that God fulfills his purposes through politics and elections, and they are joined by a majority of charismatics in South Korea. By contrast, in four other countries (Brazil, Chile, Kenya, and the Philippines), majorities of both Pentecostals and charismatics take the opposite view, disagreeing that God fulfills his purposes through politics.

Given that many renewalists reject the notion that God fulfills his purposes through politics and elections, it is perhaps not surprising that most renewalists *do not* express a desire for a government that is explicitly Christian. Indeed, in seven countries, majorities or pluralities of Pentecostals say that there should be a separation between church and state, and they are joined by majorities or pluralities of charismatics in eight countries (see Figure A2.7). Only in Nigeria did a clear majority of Pentecostals say that the government should take special steps to "make our country a Christian country"; in the United States and Kenya, however, roughly half of Pentecostals also express this view.

% saying God fulfills his purposes through politics

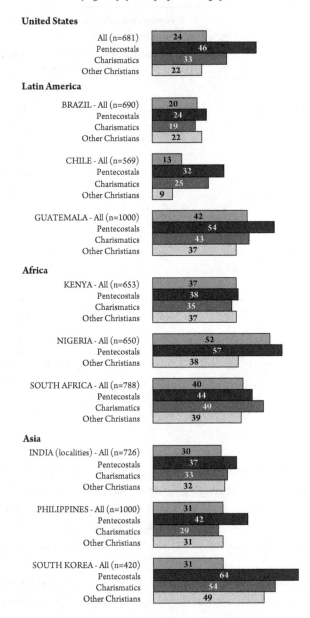

*Based on those who identified themselves as belonging to a particular religion or believing in God.

Question wording: Now I am going to read you a series of statements on some different topics. For each one, please tell me if you completely agree with it, mostly agree with it, mostly disagree with it, or completely disagree with it. The first/next one is God fulfills his purposes through politics and elections. Do you completely agree, mostly agree, mostly disagree, or completely disagree?

Figure A2.6. God and Politics

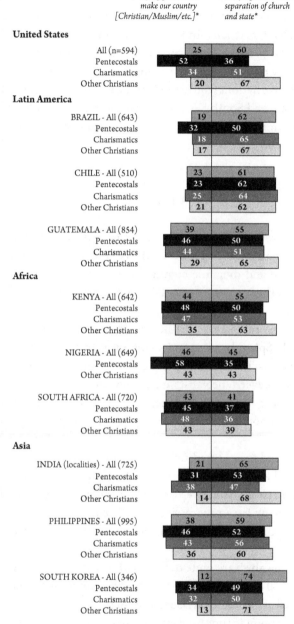

	% saying govt should make our country [Christian/Muslim/etc.]*	% saying should have separation of church and state*
United States		
All (n=594)	25	60
Pentecostals	52	36
Charismatics	34	51
Other Christians	20	67
Latin America		
BRAZIL - All (643)	19	62
Pentecostals	32	50
Charismatics	18	65
Other Christians	17	67
CHILE - All (510)	23	61
Pentecostals	23	62
Charismatics	25	64
Other Christians	21	62
GUATEMALA - All (854)	39	55
Pentecostals	46	50
Charismatics	44	51
Other Christians	29	65
Africa		
KENYA - All (642)	44	55
Pentecostals	48	50
Charismatics	47	53
Other Christians	35	63
NIGERIA - All (649)	46	45
Pentecostals	58	35
Other Christians	43	43
SOUTH AFRICA - All (720)	43	41
Pentecostals	45	37
Charismatics	48	36
Other Christians	43	39
Asia		
INDIA (localities) - All (725)	21	65
Pentecostals	31	53
Charismatics	38	47
Other Christians	14	68
PHILIPPINES - All (995)	38	59
Pentecostals	46	52
Charismatics	43	56
Other Christians	36	60
SOUTH KOREA - All (346)	12	74
Pentecostals	34	49
Charismatics	32	50
Other Christians	13	71

*U.S.: Based on those who identified themselves as Christian. Other countries: based on those who identified themselves as belonging to a particular religion.

Question wording: Which comes closer to your view? The government should take special steps to make our country a [INSERT RELIGION FROM Q3 - CHRISTIAN/MUSLIM/ETC.] country, OR there should be a separation between [INSERT CHURCH/MOSQUE AS APPROPRIATE] and government?

Figure A2.7. Separation of Church and State

Nevertheless, Pentecostals in eight of the ten countries express *more* support for government action to make their countries Christian countries than do non-renewalist Christians. In fact, in four of these countries (the United States, Brazil, the parts of India surveyed, and South Korea), Pentecostals are approximately twice as likely as non-renewalist Christians to express this point of view. In five nations (the United States, Guatemala, Kenya, the regions of India surveyed, and South Korea), charismatics are also at least somewhat more willing than non-renewalist Christians to support making their countries Christian countries.

Summary

Based on the surveys of renewalist Christianity in ten countries at the 100th anniversary of the Azusa Street Revival, we find its spiritual descendants located in diverse and dynamic communities, distinctive in some religious practices but in other respects not outside of the mainstream of the societies in which they live.

Renewalists are religiously distinctive, especially regarding the experience of the Holy Spirit, but also in its commitment to traditional Christian practices and beliefs, including a strong emphasis on sharing their faith with non-believers. However, renewalists are not always distinctive in demographic terms. For example, they do not necessarily draw disproportionately from the lower socioeconomic sectors of society or come disproportionately from women.

Renewalists tend to hold traditional values on social issues, especially sexual matters, but there is some complexity in these views. In contrast, renewalists do not tend to have distinctive views on other kinds of issues, such as social welfare, where many have progressive views. Renewalists tend to be at least as supportive of a prominent political role for religion as are other religious groups.

However, renewalists are quite diverse within and across the ten countries surveyed. National context is often important in accounting for these religious variations as well as variation on issues attitudes.

Surveys at one point in time have limitations in addressing questions regarding the growth and impact of renewalist Christianity. Nevertheless, these findings have implications for these questions. Renewalists may have grown—and may continue to grow—because they can be effective competitors in the "religious marketplace." This feature is partly due to their religious distinctiveness, including commitment to sharing their faith with others, and partly because of their lack of demographic distinctiveness. Their emphasis on traditional sexual morality may be associated with natural increase as well. Under these circumstances, the impact of renewalists on their societies is likely to vary by topic, with the strongest impact occurring on issues directly tied to their distinctive faith.

Survey Methodology

In each country, surveys were conducted under the direction of Princeton Survey Research Associates International. The surveys in Guatemala, Nigeria, the Philippines, and the United States are based on national samples. The survey in Chile is based on a national sample but excludes non-continental and remote areas, and the survey in Kenya is based on a national sample but excludes the largely Muslim North Eastern Province. In Brazil, South Africa, and South Korea, the surveys are based on urban samples.

In India, the survey was conducted in three states believed to have among the highest percentage of Christians in India: Tamil Nadu, Kerala, and Meghalaya. Within the three selected states, districts with the highest proportion of Christians were first selected, and then sampling points were randomly selected from these districts. The survey is NOT representative of the general population of India, nor is it representative of the population of the three Indian states in which it was conducted.

In each country, interviews were conducted among the general public and among oversamples of renewalists. The information below details the number of interviews conducted among the general public in each country, as well as the total number of interviews conducted among Pentecostals and charismatics.

Brazil
Sample design:	Probability sample of urban cities
Mode:	Face-to-face with adults 18+
Language:	Portuguese
Fieldwork dates:	May 13–May 30, 2006
Sample size:	General public—700; Pentecostals—313; Charismatics—329
Margin of Error:	General public 4%; Pentecostals 6%; Charismatics 5%

Chile
Sample design:	National probability sample, excluding non-continental and remote areas
Mode:	Face-to-face with adults 18+

Language: Spanish
Fieldwork dates: May 12–May 28, 2006
Sample size: General public—600; Pentecostals—276;
                                    Charismatics—286
Margin of Error: General public 4%; Pentecostals 6%;
                                    Charismatics 6%

Guatemala
Sample design: National probability sample
Mode: Face-to-face with adults 18+
Language: Spanish
Fieldwork dates: May 5–May 31, 2006
Sample size: General public—1,005; Pentecostals—
                                    410; Charismatics—487
Margin of Error: General public 3%; Pentecostals 5%;
                                    Charismatics 4%

India
Sample design: Probability sample of disproportionately
                                    Christian districts of three states—Tamil
                                    Nadu, Kerala, and Meghalaya
Mode: Face to face with adults 18+
Languages: Hindi, Tamil, and Malayalam
Fieldwork dates: May 16–June 9, 2006
Sample size: General public—726; Pentecostals—409;
                                    Charismatics—125
Margin of Error: General public 4%; Pentecostals 5%;
                                    Charismatics 9%

Kenya
Sample design: National probability sample, excluding
                                    North Eastern Province
Mode: Face-to-face with adults 18+
Languages: English and Kiswahili
Fieldwork dates: May 17–May 26, 2006
Sample size: General public—655; Pentecostals—403;
                                    Charismatics—306
Margin of Error: General public 4%; Pentecostals 5%;
                                    Charismatics 6%

Nigeria
Sample design: National probability sample

Mode: Face-to-face with adults 18+
Languages: Yoruba, Igbo, Hausa, and English
Fieldwork dates: May 15–July 27, 2006
Sample size: General public—650; Pentecostals—483;
                         Charismatics—67
Margin of Error: General public 4%; Pentecostals 4%;
                         Charismatics N/A (Due to the small num-
                         ber of Nigerian charismatics surveyed,
                         results for Nigerian charismatics are not
                         presented here.)

Philippines
Sample design: National probability sample
Mode: Face-to-face with adults 18+
Languages: Tagalog, Cebuano, and Ilonggo
Fieldwork dates: May 6–May 29, 2006
Sample size: General public—1,000; Pentecostals—
                         309; Charismatics—433
Margin of Error: General public 3%; Pentecostals 6%;
                         Charismatics 5%

South Africa
Sample design: National probability sample of urban areas
Mode: Face-to-face with adults 18+
Languages: Afrikaans, Pedi, Sotho, Tswana, Xhosa,
                         Zulu, and English
Fieldwork dates: May 11–May 27, 2006
Sample size: General public—800; Pentecostals—259;
                         Charismatics—344
Margin of Error: General public 3%; Pentecostals 6%;
                         Charismatics 5%

South Korea
Sample design: National probability sample of urban cities
Mode: Face-to-face with adults 18+
Language: Korean
Fieldwork dates: May 8–May 26, 2006
Sample size: General public—600; Pentecostals—131;
                         Charismatics—333
Margin of Error: General public 4%; Pentecostals 9%;
                         Charismatics 5%

United States

Sample design:	National probability sample
Mode:	Telephone
Languages:	English and Spanish
Fieldwork dates:	July 20–September 7, 2006
Sample size:	General public—739; Pentecostals—119; Charismatics—421
Margin of Error:	General public 4%; Pentecostals 9%; Charismatics 5%

NOTES

1. This essay is an abridged and adapted version of the full report of the survey's findings. The full report can be read in its entirety at http://pewforum.org/surveys/pentecostal.
2. In the United States, 18% of charismatics are classified as such solely because they describe themselves as Charismatic Christians; 15% of charismatics qualify solely because they describe themselves as Pentecostal Christians but do not belong to explicitly Pentecostal denominations; 43% of charismatics are classified as such solely because they say they speak in tongues; and the remaining 24% of U.S. charismatics qualify as such by multiple measures.
3. For more information on the religious demography of the countries surveyed, see the original report, http://pewforum.org/surveys/pentecostal.
4. For a fuller description of the demography of renewalists, see the original study, http://pewforum.org/surveys/pentecostal.

BIBLIOGRAPHY

Aaron, Sushil J. 2009. "Emulating Azariah: Evangelicals and Social Change in the Dangs." In *Evangelical Christianity and Democracy in Asia,* ed. David H. Lumsdaine, 87–129. New York: Oxford University Press.

Adeboye, E. A. 1989. *How To Turn Your Austerity to Prosperity.* Lagos: The CRM.

Abisheganaden, A. S., ed. 1992. *A History of the Assemblies of God of Singapore.* Singapore: Abundant Press.

Abrams, Minnie. 1906. *The Baptism of the Holy Ghost and Fire.* Kedgaon, India: Mukti Mission Press.

Adelaja, Sunday. *Churchshift.* 2008. Lake Mary, FL: Charisma House.

———. *Spearheading a National Transformation.* 2008. Kiev: Fares Publishing House.

Adeyemi, Sam. *We Are the Government.* 2010. Lagos: Pneuma Publishing, Ltd.

Adogame, Afe. 2004a. "Contesting the Ambivalences of Modernity in a Global Context: The Redeemed Christian Church of God, North America." *Studies in World Christianity* 10(1): 25–48.

———. 2004b. "Engaging the Rhetoric of Spiritual Warfare: The Public Face of Aladura in Diaspora." *Journal of Religion in Africa* 34(4): 493–522.

———. 2005a. "To Be or Not To Be? Politics of Belonging and African Christian Communities in Germany." In *Religion in the Context of African Migration,* ed. A. Adogame and C. Weisskoppel, 95–112. C. Bayreuth: Bayreuth African Studies Series.

———. 2005b. "African Christian Communities in Diaspora." In *African Christianity: An African Story,* ed. O. U. Kalu, 494–514. Pretoria: Department of Church History, University of Pretoria.

Akande, Laolu. 2003. "Multi-million Dollar Redemption Camp Underway in U.S." *The Guardian,* April 8.

Alexander, Estrelda. 2006. *The Women of Azusa Street.* Cleveland, OH: Pilgrim Press.

Anderson, Allan H. 2001. *African Reformation: African Initiated Christianity in the 20th Century.* Trenton, NJ, and Asmara, Eritrea: Africa World Press.

———. 2004. *An Introduction to Pentecostalism: Global Charismatic Christianity.* Cambridge: Cambridge University Press.

———. 2006. "To All Points of the Compass: The Azusa Street Revival and Global Pentecostalism," *Enrichment: A Journal for Pentecostal Ministry,* 11(2): 164–172.

———. 2007. *Spreading Fires: The Missionary Nature of Early Pentecostalism.* London: SCM Press and Maryknoll, NY: Orbis.

_____. 2010. "Varieties, Taxonomies, and Definitions." In *Studying Global Pentecostalism: Theories and Methods,* eds. Allan Anderson, Michael Bergunder, Andre Droogers, and Cornelis van der Laan, 13–27. Berkeley: University of California Press.

_____. 2013 *To the Ends of the Earth: Pentecostalism and the Transformation of World Christianity.* New York: Oxford University Press.

Anheier, Helmut K. 1989. "Private Voluntary Organizations and Development in West Africa: Comparative Perspectives." In *The Nonprofit Sector in International Perspective,* ed. Estelle James, 337–57. New York: Oxford University Press.

_____. and Lester M. Salamon, eds. 1998. *The Nonprofit Sector in the Developing World.* Manchester, UK: Manchester University Press.

Annis, Sheldon. 1987. *God and Production in a Guatemalan Town.* Austin, TX: University of Texas Press.

Asamoah-Gyadu, K. 2005. *African Charismatics: Current Developments within Independent Indigenous Pentecostalism in Ghana.* Leiden: Brill.

Austin, Alvyn. 1980. *Aimee Semple McPherson.* Don Mills, ON: Fitzhenry and Whiteside.

Babatunde, Wale. *Awake! Great Britain.* 2005. Chichester, UK: Xpression Books.

_____. 2002. *Great Britain has Fallen.* Chichester, UK: New Wine Press.

Baesler, E. James. 1999. "A Model of Interpersonal Christian Prayer." *Journal of Communication and Religion* 22:40–64.

_____. 2003. *Theoretical Explorations and Empirical Investigations of Communication and Prayer.* Lewiston, NY: Edwin Mellen Press.

Bahr, Robert. 1979. *Least of All Saints: The Story of Aimee Semple McPherson.* Englewood Cliffs, NJ: Prentice-Hall.

Baker, Heidi, with Shara Pradham. 2008. *Compelled by Love: How to Change the World through the Simple Power of Love in Action.* St. Mary, FL: Charisma House.

Baker, Rolland, and Heidi Baker. 2000. "There Is Always Enough." In *Experience the Blessing: Testimonies from Toronto,* ed. John Arnott, 47–61. Ventura, CA: Renew.

_____. 2003. *Always Enough: God's Miraculous Provision among the Poorest Children on Earth.* Grand Rapids, MI: Chosen Books.

Barratt, T. B. 1906. "The Seal of My Pentecost," *Living Truths* 6:12, 736–738.

Barratt, Thomas Ball. 1927. *When the Fire Fell and an Outline of My Life.* Oslo, Norway: Alfons Hansen & Sønner.

Barrett, David B. 1968. *Schism and Renewal in Africa: An Analysis of Six Thousand Contemporary Religious Movements.* Oxford: Oxford University Press.

_____. 1970. "AD 2000: 350 Million Christians in Africa." *International Review of Mission* 59, no. 233 (January): 39–54.

_____, ed. 1982. *World Christian Encyclopedia.* Nairobi: Oxford University Press.

_____, Todd M. Johnson, and Peter F. Crossing. 2006a. "Missiometrics 2006: Goals, Resources, Doctrines of the 350 Christian World Communions." *International Bulletin of Missionary Research* 30(1): 27–30.

_____, Todd M. Johnson, and Peter F. Crossing. 2006b. "Global Table A. 50 Shared Goals: Status of Global Mission, AD 1900 to AD 2025." *International Bulletin of Missionary Research* 30(1): 28.

_____, George Thomas Kurian, and Todd M. Johnson, eds. 2001. *World Christian Encyclopedia,* 2nd ed. New York and Oxford: Oxford University Press.

Barro, Robert J. 1999. "Determinants of Democracy." *The Journal of Political Economy* 107(6, part 2): S158–83.

Bartleman, Frank. 1909. *My Story: "The Latter Rain."* Columbia, SC: John M. Pike.

_____. 1925. *How Pentecost Came to Los Angeles: As It Was in the Beginning.* Los Angeles: F. Bartleman.

_____. 1980 [1925]. *Azusa Street.* S. Plainfield, NJ: Bridge Publishing.

Bastian, Jean-Pierre. 1990. *Historia del Protestantismo en América Latina.* Mexico City: Casa Unida de Publicaciones.

Berger, Peter. 1969. *The Sacred Canopy*. Garden City, NY: Anchor Books.

_____. 2010. "Max Weber Is Alive and Well, and Is Living in Guatemala: The Protestant Ethic Today." *Review of Faith and International Affairs* 8(4): 3–9. Available at http://dx.doi.org/10.1080/15570274.2010.528964, accessed May 27, 2012.

Bergunder, Michael. 2008. *The South Indian Pentecostal Movement in the Twentieth Century*. Grand Rapids, MI: Eerdmans.

Berryman, Phillip. 1996. *Religion in the Megacity*. Maryknoll, NY: Orbis.

Beyerlein, Kraig. 2004. "Specifying the Impact of Conservative Protestantism on Educational Attainment." *Journal for the Scientific Study of Religion* 43(4): 505–18.

Blumhofer, Edith. 1993. *Aimee Semple McPherson: Everybody's Sister*. Grand Rapids, MI: William B. Eerdmans Publishing Company.

_____. 1994. "For Pentecostals, A Move toward Racial Reconciliation." *Christian Century* 111(14): 445.

_____. 2002. "William H. Durham: Years of Creativity, Years of Dissent." In *Portraits of a Generation: Early Pentecostal Leaders*, ed. James R. Goff, Jr., and Grant Wacker. Fayetteville: University of Arkansas Press.

_____. 2006. "Azusa Street Revival." *Christian Century* 123(5): 22.

Borlase, Craig. 2006. *William Seymour: A Biography*. Lake Mary, FL: Charisma House.

Bollen, Kenneth A. 1979. "Political Democracy and the Timing of Development." *American Sociological Review* 44:572–87.

_____. 2001. *Cross-National Indicators of Liberal Democracy, 1950–1990* [Computer file]. 2nd ICPSR version. Chapel Hill: University of North Carolina [producer], 1998. Ann Arbor, MI: Inter-University Consortium for Political and Social Research [distributor].

_____. and Robert W. Jackman. 1985a. "Economic and Noneconomic Determinants of Political Democracy in the 1960s." *Research in Political Sociology* 1:27–48.

_____. and Robert W. Jackman. 1985b. "Political Democracy and the Size Distribution of Income." *American Sociological Review* 50:438–457.

Bourgault, Jacques, and Stephane Dion. 1993. "Public Sector Ethics in Quebec: The Contrasting Society." In *Corruption, Character and Conduct*, ed. John W. Langford and Allan Tupper, 67–89. Toronto: Oxford University Press.

Brennan Kathleen, M. and Andrew S. London. 2001. "Are Religious People Nice People? Religiosity, Race, Interview Dynamics and Perceived Cooperativeness." *Sociological Inquiry* 71(2): 129–44.

Brettell Caroline B., and James F. Hollifield, eds. 2007. *Migration Theory: Talking Across Disciplines*. New York: Routledge.

Brouwer, Steve, Paul Gifford, and Susan Rose. 1996. *Exporting the American Gospel: Global Christian Fundamentalism*. New York and London: Routledge.

Brown, Candy Gunther. 2011. "Global Awakening: Divine Healing Networks and Global Community in North America, Brazil, Mozambique, and Beyond." In *Global Pentecostal and Charismatic Healing*, ed. Candy Gunther Brown, 351–69. New York: Oxford University Press.

_____. Stephen C. Mory, Rebecca Williams, and Michael J. McClymond. 2010. "Study of Therapeutic Effects of Proximal Intercessory Prayer on Auditory and Visual Impairments in Rural Mozambique." *Southern Medical Journal* 103:864–69.

Brumback, Carl. 1961. *Suddenly... From Heaven: A History of the Assemblies of God*. Springfield, MO: Gospel Publishing House.

Brusco, Elizabeth. 1993. "The Reformation of Machismo: Asceticism and Masculinity Among Columbian Evangelicals." In *Rethinking Protestantism in Latin America*, ed. Virginia Garrard-Burnett and David Stoll, 143–158. Philadelphia: Temple University Press.

_____. 1995. *The Reformation of Machismo: Evangelical Conversion and Gender in Colombia*. Austin: University of Texas Press.

_____. 2010. "Gender and Power." In *Studying Global Pentecostalism: Theories and Methods*, ed. Allan Anderson et al., 74–92. Berkeley: University of California Press.

Budijanto, Bambang. 2009. "Evangelicals and Politics in Indonesia: The Case of Surakarta." In *Evangelical Christianity and Democracy in Asia*, ed. David H. Lumsdaine, 155–83. New York: Oxford University Press.

Bülhmann, Walbert. 1976. *The Coming of the Third Church*. Maryknoll, NY: Orbis Books.

Bundy, David. 1992. "Spiritual Advice to a Seeker: Letters to T. B. Barratt from Azusa Street, 1906." *Pneuma: The Journal of the Society for Pentecostal Studies* 14(2): 159–70.

Burdick, John. 1999. "What is the Color of the Holy Spirit? Pentecostalism and Black Identity in Brazil." *Latin American Research Review* 34(2): 109–31.

_____. 2010. "Religion and Society in Contemporary Latin America." *Latin American Politics and Society* 52(2): 167–76.

Burgess, Stanley M., ed. 2002. *New International Dictionary of Pentecostal and Charismatic Movements*. Grand Rapids, MI: Zondervan.

Burkhart, Ross E. and Michael S. Lewis-Beck. 1994. "Comparative Democracy: The Economic Development Thesis." *American Political Science Review* 88(4): 903–910.

Butler, Anthea. 2006. "Constructing Different Memories: Recasting the Azusa Street Revival." In *The Azusa Street Revival and Its Legacy*, ed. Harold D. Hunter and Cecil M. Robeck, Jr., *193–201*. Cleveland, TN: Pathway Press.

Cadge, Wendy, and Robert Wuthnow. 2006. "Religion and the Non-Profit Sector." In *The Nonprofit Sector: A Research Handbook, 2nd* ed., ed. Walter Powell and Richard Steinberg, 485–505. New Haven, CT: Yale University Press.

Carothers, Thomas. 1998. "The Rule of Law Revival." *Foreign Affairs* 77(2): 95–106.

Carter, John. 1971. *Howard Carter: Man of the Spirit*. Nottingham: AoG Publishing House.

Carter, Miguel. 1990. "The Role of the Paraguayan Catholic Church in the Downfall of the Stroessner Regime." *Journal of Interamerican Studies and World Affairs* 32(4): 67–121.

_____. 1991. *El papel de la iglesia en la caída de Stroessner*. Asunción, Paraguay: RP Ediciones.

Casanova, Jose. 2001. "Religion, the New Millennium, and Globalization." *Sociology of Religion* 62:415–41.

_____. 2004. *Public Religions in the Modern World*. Chicago: University of Chicago Press.

Castles, S., and M. Miller. 2003. *The Age of Migration*. 3rd ed. New York: The Guilford Press.

Cavanaugh, William T. 2009. *The Myth of Religious Violence: Secular Ideology and the Roots of Modern Conflict*. New York: Oxford University Press.

Central Intelligence Agency (CIA). *The World Factbook: Paraguay* [online]. Retrieved from https://www.cia.gov/library/publications/the-world-factbook/geos/pa.html, February 25, 2011.

Cesar, Waldo. 2001. "From Babel to Pentecost: A Social-Historical-Theological study of the Growth of Pentecostalism." In *Between Babel and Pentecost: Transnational Pentecostalism in Africa and Latin America*, ed. Andre Corten and Ruth Marshall-Fratani, 22–40. Bloomington: University of Indiana Press.

Chan, Kim-Kwong. 2009. "The Christian Community in China: The Leaven Effect." In *Evangelical Christianity and Democracy in Asia*, ed. David H. Lumsdaine, 43–86. New York: Oxford University Press.

Chesnut, R. Andrew. 2003. *Competitive Spirits: Latin America's New Religious Economy*. New York: Oxford University Press.

_____. 1997. *Born Again in Brazil*. New Brunswick, NJ: Rutgers University Press.

Christian, Patricia, Michael Gent, and Timothy Wadkins. 2011. "The Advance of the Spirit in El Salvador: Twenty Years of Survey Evidence of Pentecostal Growth." Unpublished manuscript (under consideration by *Latin American Research Review*).

Clague, Christopher, Suzanne Gleason, and Stephen Knack. 2001. "Determinants of Lasting Democracy in Poor Countries: Culture, Development, and Institutions." *Annals of the American Academy of Political and Social Science* 573:16–41.

Clark, Terry Nichols. 1975. "The Irish Ethic and the Spirit of Patronage." *Ethnicity* 2:305–59.

Clawson, David L.. 2006. *Latin America and the Caribbean: Lands and Peoples*. 4th ed. Boston, MA: McGraw-Hill.

Cleary, Edward L. 2011. *The Rise of Charismatic Catholicism in Latin America.* Gainesville: University Press of Florida.

Clifton, Shane 2009. *Pentecostal Churches in Transition.* Leiden: Brill.

Coleman, Kenneth M., Edwin Eloy Aguilar, José Miguel Sandoval, and Timothy J. Steigenga. 1993. Protestantism in El Salvador: Conventional Wisdom versus the Survey Evidence." In Rethinking Protestantism in Latin America , ed. Virginia Garrard-Burne" and David Stoll. Philadelphia: Temple University Press.

Coleman, Simon. 2000. *The Globalisation of Charismatic Christianity: Spreading the Gospel of Prosperity.* Cambridge: Cambridge University Press.

Colletti, Joseph. 1990. "Ethnic Pentecostalism in Chicago: 1890–1950." Ph.D. diss., Birmingham, England: University of Birmingham.

Comaroff, Jean. 1985. *Body of Power, Spirit of Resistance: The Culture and History of a South African People.* Chicago: University of Chicago Press.

_____. 2008. "Uncool Passion: Nietzche Meets the Pentecostals." European University Institute, Max Weber Programme, Lecture delivered June 18, 2008. http://cadmus.eui. eu/bitstream/handle/1814/9928/MWL_2008_10.pdf?sequence=1. Accessed May 27, 2012.

Cook, Glenn A. "The Azusa Street Meeting." Los Angeles, CA: Glenn A. Cook, no date; pamphlet.

Cox, Harvey. 2006. "Spirits of Globalization: Pentecostalism and Experiential Spiritualities in a Global Era." In *The Spirits of Globalism,* ed. Sturla Stalsett, 11–21. London: SCM Press.

Creech, Joe. 1996. "Visions of Glory: The Place of the Azusa Street Revival in Pentecostal History." *Church History* 65(3): 405–24.

Crenshaw, Edward M. 1995. "Democracy and Demographic Inheritance: The Influence of Modernity and Proto-Modernity on Political and Civil Rights, 1965 to 1980." *American Sociological Review* 60: 702–718.

Dawkins, Richard. 2008. *The God Delusion.* New York: Mariner Books.

Dayton, Donald W. 1987. *Theological Roots of Pentecostalism.* Peabody, MA: Hendrickson Publishers.

Deng, Zhaoming. 2011. "Indigenous Chinese Pentecostal Denominations." In *Asian and Pentecostal: The Charismatic Face of Christianity in Asia,* ed. Allan Anderson and Edmond Tang, 369–93. Oxford: Regnum.

DeGenova, Nicholas. 2007. *Working the Boundaries: Race, Space and "Illegality" in Mexican Chicago.* Durham, NC: Duke University Press.

Dempster, Murray W., Byron D. Klaus, and Douglas Petersen, eds. 1999. *The Globalization of Pentecostalism. A Religion Made to Travel.* Oxford: Regnum.

Deseret News. 2008. *2009 Church Almanac.* Salt Lake City, UT: Deseret News.

Diamond, Larry. 1999. *Developing Democracy: Toward Consolidation.* Baltimore: Johns Hopkins University Press.

Donahue, Michael J., and Peter L. Benson. 1995. "Religion and the Well-Being of Adolescents." Journal of social Issues 51(2): 145–160.

Droogers, André. 2001. "Globalisation and Pentecostal Success." In *Between Babel and Pentecost: Transnational Pentecostalism in Africa and Latin America,* ed. A. Corten and R. Marshall-Fratani, 41–61. Bloomington: Indiana University Press.

Duarte P., Rogelio. 1994. *El desafío protestante en el Paraguay.* Asunción, Paraguay: Centro Cristiano de Comunicación Creativa.

Dunch, Ryan. 2001. *Fuzhou Protestants and the Making of Modern China, 1857–1927.* New Haven, CT: Yale University Press.

Dunn, James D. G. 1970. *Baptism in the Holy Spirit.* London: SCM Press.

Durkheim, Émile. 1966 [1897]. *Suicide: A Study in Sociology.* New York: Free Press.

Early, John D. 1973. "Education via Radio among Guatemalan Highland Maya." *Human Organization* 32: 221–29.

Englund, Harri. 2007. "Pentecostalism beyond Belief: Trust and Democracy in a Malawian Township." *Africa* 77:477–99.

Enquist, Per Olov. 2005. *Lewi's Journey*. New York, NY: Overlook Duckworth.

Espinosa, Gastón. 2004. "The Pentecostalization of Latin American and U.S. Latino Christianity." *Pneuma: The Journal of the Society for Pentecostal Studies* 26(2): 262–92.

Finke, Roger, and Rodney Stark. 1992. *The Churching of America, 1776–1990*. New Brunswick, NJ: Rutgers University Press.

Fitzgerald, Scott and Jennifer Glass. 2008. "Can Early Family Formation Explain the Lower Educational Attainment of U.S. Conservative Protestants?" *Sociological Spectrum* 28: 556–577.

Fitzgerald, Scott and Jennifer Glass. 2012. "Conservative Religion, Early Transitions to Adulthood and the Intergenerational Transmission of Class." *Research in the Sociology of Work* 23: 49–72.

Fortuny, Patricia, and Henri Gooren. (forthcoming). "Neither Catholics nor Protestants: Mormons, Jehovah's Witnesses, Adventists, and 'La Luz del Mundo.'" In *The Cambridge History of Religions in Latin America*, ed. Paul Freston and Virginia Garrard-Burnett. Cambridge: Cambridge University Press.

Frahm-Arp, Maria. 2010. *Professional Women in South African Pentecostal Charismatic Churches*. Studies of Religion in Africa 38. Leiden: Brill.

Frankiel, Sandra Sizer. 1988. *California's Spiritual Frontiers: Religious Alternatives in Anglo-Protestantism, 1850–1910*. Berkeley: University of California Press.

Freedom House. 2004. "Freedom in the World, 2004." New York: Freedom House. http://www.freedomhouse.org/report/freedom-world/freedom-world-2004

Freston, Paul. 2001. *Evangelicals and Politics in Asia, Africa and Latin America*. New York: Cambridge University Press.

_____. 2004. *Protestant Political Parties: A Global Survey*. Aldershot, UK: Ashgate.

_____. 2008. "Introduction: The Many Faces of Evangelical Politics in Latin America." In *Evangelical Christians and Democracy in Latin America*, ed. Paul Freston, 3–36. New York: Oxford University Press.

Garner, Robert C. 2000. "Religion as a Source of Social Change in the New South Africa." *Journal of Religion in Africa* 30(3): 310–43.

Garrard-Burnett, Virginia. 1998. *Living in the New Jerusalem: Protestantism in Guatemala*. Austin: University of Texas Press.

Gasiorowski, Mark J., and Timothy J. Power. 1998. "The Structural Determinants of Democratic Consolidation: Evidence from the Third World." *Comparative Political Studies* 31:740–71.

Geise, Ernst. 1965. *Jonathan Paul, Ein Knect Jesu Christi: Leben und Werk*. Altdorf, Germany: Missionsbuchhandlung und Verlag.

Gerlach, L. P., and V. H. Hine. 1968. "Five Factors Crucial to the Growth and Spread of a Modern Religious Movement." *Journal for the Scientific Study of Religion* 7:23–40.

_____. 1970. *People, Power, Change: Movements of Social Transformation*. Indianapolis: Bobbs-Merrill.

Gerloff, Roswith. 1999. "Pentecostals in the African Diaspora." In *Pentecostals after a Century*, ed. A. H. Anderson and W. J. Hollenweger, 67–86. Scheffield: Scheffield Academic Press.

_____. 1992. *A Plea for British Black Theologies: The Black Church Movement in Britain in Its Transatlantic Cultural and Theological Interaction*. 2 vols. Frankfurt am Main: Peter Lang.

Gifford, Paul. 1990. "Prosperity: A New and Foreign Element in African Christianity." *Religion* 20:373–88.

_____. 1998. *African Christianity: Its Public Role*. London: Hurst.

_____. 2001. "The Complex Provenance of Some Elements of African Pentecostal Theology." In *Between Babel and Pentecost: Transnational Pentecostalism in Africa and Latin America*, ed. A. Corten. and R. Marshall-Fratani, 62–79. Bloomington: Indiana University Press.

_____. 2004. *Ghana's New Christianity: Pentecostalism in a Globalizing African Economy.* Bloomington: Indiana University Press.

Gill, Anthony. 1998. *Rendering Unto Caesar: The Catholic Church and the State in Latin America.* Chicago: University of Chicago Press.

Glass, Jennifer and Jerry Jacobs. (2005) "Childhood Religious Conservatism and Adult Attainment among Black and White Women." Social Forces 84(1): 555–579.

Goff, Jr., James R. 1988. *Fields White Unto Harvest: Charles F. Parham and the Missionary Origins of Pentecostalism.* Fayetteville, AR: University of Arkansas Press.

Gombrich, Richard, and Gananath Obeyesekere. 1988. *Buddhism Transformed: Religious Change in Sri Lanka.* Princeton, NJ: Princeton University Press.

Gooren, Henri. 1999. *Rich among the Poor: Church, Firm, and Household among Small-Scale Entrepreneurs in Guatemala City.* Latin America Series 13. Amsterdam: Thela.

_____. 2001. "Reconsidering Protestant Growth in Guatemala, 1900–1995." In *Holy Saints and Fiery Preachers: The Anthropology of Protestantism in Mexico and Central America,* ed. James W. Dow and Alan R. Sandstrom, 169–203. Westport, CT: Praeger.

_____. 2003. "The Religious Market in Nicaragua: The Paradoxes of Catholicism and Protestantism." *Exchange* 32(4): 340–60.

_____. 2010a. *Religious Conversion and Disaffiliation: Tracing Patterns of Change in Faith Practices.* New York: Palgrave-Macmillan.

_____. 2010b. "The Pentecostalization of Religion and Society in Latin America: First Findings from Paraguay." Paper presented at the annual meeting of the Society for the Scientific Study of Religion (SSSR) in Baltimore, MD, October 28–30.

_____. 2012. "The Catholic Charismatic Renewal in Latin America." *Pneuma: The Journal of the Society for Pentecostal Studies* 34(2): 185–207.

Grady, L. 2002. "Nigeria's Miracle: How a Sweeping Christian Revival Is Transforming Africa's Most Populous Nation." *Charisma and Christian Life* 27, no. 10 (May): 38–41.

Grayson, James Huntley. 2002. *Korea: A Religious History.* New York: RoutledgeCurzon.

Grier, Robin. 1997. "The Effect of Religion on Economic Development: A Cross National Study of 63 Former Colonies." *Kyklos* 50:47–62.

Griffith, R. Marie. 1997. *God's Daughters: Evangelical Women and the Power of Submission.* Berkeley: University of California Press.

Grim, Brian J. 2009. "Pentecostalism's Growth in Religiously Restricted Environments." *Society* 46: 484–95.

_____. and Roger Finke. 2011. *The Price of Freedom Denied: Religious Persecution and Conflict in the 21st Century.* New York: Cambridge University Press.

Guiso, Luigi, Paola Sapienza, and Luigi Zingales. 2003. "People's Opium? Religion and Economic Attitudes." *Journal of Monetary Economics* 50:225–82.

Hackett, Conrad and D. Michael Lindsay. 2008. "Measuring Evangelicalism: Consequences of Different Operationalization Strategies." *Journal for the Scientific Study of Religion* 47(3): 499–514.

Hanciles, Jehu. 2008. *Beyond Christendom: Globalization, African Migration, and the Transformation of the West.* Maryknoll, NY: Orbis Books.

Hadenius, Axel. 1992. *Democracy and Development.* Cambridge: Cambridge University Press.

Hahm, Chaibong. 2004. "World Religions and Democracy: The Ironies of Confucianism." *Journal of Democracy* 15:93–107.

Hanratty, Dannin M., and Sandra W. Meditz, eds. 1988. *Paraguay: A Country Study* [online]. Washington, DC: GPO for the Library of Congress, 1988. Retrieved October 28, 2008 from http://countrystudies.us/paraguay/.

_____. eds. 2005. *Paraguay: A Country Profile* [online]. Washington, DC: Federal Research Division for the Library of Congress. Retrieved October 28, 2008 from http://lcweb2.loc.gov/frd/cs/profiles/Paraguay.pdf.

Harrell, D. E. 1975. *All Things are Possible.* Bloomington: Indiana University Press.

_____ 1985. *Oral Roberts: An American life.* Bloomington: Indiana University Press.

Harris, Sam. 2008. *Letter to a Christian Nation*. New York: Vintage Books.

Hastings, Adrian. 1994. *The Church in Africa, 1450–1950*. Oxford: Clarendon.

Heidenheimer, A. J. 1996. "The Topography of Corruption: Explorations in a Comparative Perspective." *International Social Science Journal* 158(3): 337–47.

Hilborn, D., ed. 2001. *'Toronto' in Perspective*. Carlisle, UK: Paternoster.

Hildebrandt, Jonathan. 1981. *History of the Church in Africa*. Achimota, Ghana: Africa Christian Press.

Hirschmann, Nancy J. 2003. *The Subject of Liberty: Toward a Feminist Theory of Freedom*. Princeton, NJ: Princeton University Press.

Hitchens, Christopher. 2009. *God Is Not Great: How Religion Poisons Everything*. New York: Twelve, Hachette Book Group, Inc.

Holland, Clifton L. 2006. "Paraguay." In *Worldmark Encyclopedia of Religious Practices: Volume 3, Countries M–Z*, ed. Andrew Riggs, 205–9. Detroit, MI: Thomson Gale.

Hollenweger, Walter J. 1972. *The Pentecostals*. London: SCM Press.

_____. 1997. *Pentecostalism: Origins and Developments Worldwide*. Peabody, MA: Hendrickson Publishers.

Hollingsworth, Andrea, and Melissa D. Browning. 2010. "Your Daughters Shall Prophesy (As Long as They Submit)." In *A Liberating Spirit: Pentecostals and Social Action*, ed. Michael Wilkinson and Steven M. Studebaker, 161–84. Eugene, OR: Pickwick.

Holmes, Pamela M. S. 2010. "Zelma Argue's Theological Contribution to Early Pentecostalism." In *Winds from the North: Canadian Contributions to the Pentecostal Movement*, ed. Michael Wilkinson and Peter Althouse, 129–150. Boston: Brill.

Hong, Joshua Young-gi. 2009. "Evangelicals and the Democratization of South Korea since 1987." In *Evangelical Christianity and Democracy in Asia*, ed. David H. Lumsdaine, 185–234. New York: Oxford University Press.

Howard Ecklund, Elaine and Jerry Z. Park. 2007. "Religious Diversity and Community Volunteerism Among Asian Americans: An Initial Portrait." *The Journal for the Scientific Study of Religion* 46(2): 233–244.

Howell, Beth Prim. 1960. *Lady on a Donkey*. New York: E. P. Dutton.

Hull, Brooks B. and Frederick Bold. 1995. "Preaching Matters: Replication and Extension." *Journal of Economic Behavior and Organization* 27: 143–149.

Hunt, R., L. K. Hing, and J. Roxborough, eds. 1992. *Christianity in Malaysia: A Denominational History* Petaling Jaya, Malaysia: Pelanduk Publications.

Hunt, S., and Nicola Lightly. 2001. "The British Black Pentecostal 'Revival': Identity and Belief in the 'New' Nigerian Churches." *Ethnic and Racial Studies* 24, no. 1 (January): 104–24.

Huxley, A. 1954. *The Doors of Perception*. New York: Harper & Row.

Instituto Superior de Estudos da Religião (ISER). 1996. *Novo Nascimento: Os Evangelicos em Casa, na Igreja e na Politica*. Rio de Janeiro: ISER.

Instituto de Opinion Publica. 2010. *Crece protestantismo en América Latina* [online]. Retrieved December 15, 2010 from http:/radiolaprimerisima.com/noticias/general/82918/crece-protestantismo-en-america-latina.htm (press release, August 16, 2010).

_____. 2011. *El Pentecostalismo y la Cultura en El Salvador Moderno*. San Salvador: Universidad Francisco Gavidia.

Jaffarian, Michael. 2004. "Are There More Non-western Missionaries than Western Missionaries?" *International Bulletin of Missionary Research* 28, no. 3 (July): 131–32.

Jenkins, Philip. 2002. *The Next Christendom: The Coming of Global Christianity*. New York and Oxford: Oxford University Press.

_____. 2007. *New Faces of Global Christianity: Believing the Bible in the Global South*. Oxford: Oxford University Press.

Jerryson, Michael K., and Mark Juergensmeyer. 2010. *Buddhist Warfare*. New York: Oxford University Press.

Johnson, Byron R., Spencer De Lie, David B. Larson, and Michael McCullough. 2000. "A Systematic Review of the Religiosity and Delinquency Literature: A Research Note." *Journal of Contemporary Criminal Justice* 16(1): 32–52.

Johnson, Todd M. 2007. *World Christian Database*. Leiden: Brill Online, www. worldchristiandatabase.org.

_____. 2009. "The Global Demographics of the Pentecostal and Charismatic Renewal." *Social Science and Modern Society* 46, no. 6 (November/December): 479–83.

_____. and Kenneth R. Ross, eds. 2009. *Atlas of Global Christianity, 1910–2010*. Edinburgh: Edinburgh University Press.

_____. David B. Barrett, and Peter F. Crossing. 2011. "Christianity 2011: Martyrs and the Resurgence of Religion." *International Bulletin of Missionary Research* 35(1): 28–29.

Johnstone, Patrick. 1995. *Operation World*. Carlisle, UK: OM Publishing.

_____. and Jason Mandryk. 2001. *Operation World*. Carlisle, UK: Paternoster Lifestyle.

Jones, E. Jeanette. 1941. "Delivered from the Jaws of Death." *Pentecostal Evangel* (Oct 18): 4–5.

Kalu, Ogbu. 2000. *Power, Poverty and Prayer: The Challenges of Poverty and Pluralism in African Christianity, 1960–1996*. Frankfurt am Main: Peter Lang.

_____. 2008. *African Pentecostalism: An Introduction*. 2008. Oxford: Oxford University Press.

_____. 2012. "West African Christianity: Padres, Pastors, Prophets and Pentecostals." In *Introducing World Christianity*, ed. Charles E. Farhadian, 36–50. Oxford: Wiley-Blackwell.

Kamens, David H. 1988. "Education and Democracy." *Sociology of Education* 61: 114–27.

_____. 2003. "Liberty's Advances in a Troubled World." *Journal of Democracy* 14:100–13.

Karatnycky, Adrian. 1999. "The 1998 Freedom House Survey: The Decline of Illiberal Democracy." *Journal of Democracy* 10: 112–125.

_____. 2003. "Liberty's Advances in a Troubled World." *Journal of Democracy* 14(1): 100–113.

Kay, William K. 2006. "The Mind, Behaviour and Glossolalia: A Psychological Perspective." In *Speaking in Tongues: Multi-disciplinary Perspectives*, ed. M. J. Cartledge, 174–205. Carlisle, UK: Paternoster.

_____. 2007a. "Donald Gee: An Important Voice of the Pentecostal Movement." *Journal of Pentecostal Theology* 16(1): 133–53.

_____. 2007b. *Apostolic Networks in Britain: New Ways of Being Church*. Milton Keynes: Paternoster.

_____. 2011. "Modernity and the Arrival of Pentecostalism in Britain." *PentecoStudies* 10(1): 50–71.

_____. 2012. "Empirical and Historical Perspectives on the Growth of Pentecostal-style Churches in Malaysia, Singapore and Hong Kong." Paper presented at the International Society of Empirical Research in Theology, Nijmegen, Netherlands, April 19–21.

_____. and R. Parry, eds. 2011. *Deliverance and Exorcism: Interdisciplinary Perspectives*. Milton Keynes: Koorong.

King, Paul L. 2006. *Genuine Gold: The Cautiously Charismatic Story of the Early Christian and Missionary Alliance*. Tulsa, OK: Word and Spirit Press.

Kosambi, Meera, ed. and trans. 2000. *Pandita Ramabai through Her Own Words: Selected Works*. New Delhi: Oxford University Press.

Kuo, Chengtian. 2002. "Democracy and Religion in Taiwan." Paper presented at the annual meeting of the American Political Science Association, Boston, MA, August 29–September 1.

Kurzman, Charles, and Erin Leahey. 2004. "Intellectuals and Democratization, 1905–1912 and 1989–1996." *American Journal of Sociology* 109(4): 937–986

La Porta, Rafael, Florencio Lopez-de-Silanes, Andrei Shleifer, and Robert W. Vishny. 1997. "Trust in Large Organizations." *American Economic Review* 87(2): 333–38.

_____. 1999. "The Quality of Government." *Journal of Law, Economics, and Organization* 15(1): 222–79.

Lalive d'Epinay, Christian. 1969. *Haven of the Masses*. London: Lutterworth.

Lam, Pui-Yan. 2002. "As the Flocks Gather: How Religion Affects Voluntary Association Participation." *Journal for the Scientific Study of Religion* 41(3): 405–22.

Lavin, Peter. 1986. *Alexander Boddy, Pastor and Prophet: Vicar of All Saints Sunderland, 1886–1922*. Monkwearmouth, Sunderland, UK: Wearside Historic Churches Group.

Leonard, Karen, Alex Stepick, Manuel Vásquez, and Jennifer Holdaway. 2005. *Immigrant Faiths Transforming Religious Life in America*. Lanham, MD: Altamira Press.

Lee, Matthew T., and Margaret M. Poloma. 2009. *A Sociological Study of the Great Commandment in Pentecostalism: The Practice of Godly Love as Benevolent Service.* Lewiston, NY: Edwin Mellen Press.

Lee, Matthew T., Margaret M. Poloma, and Stephen G. Post. 2012. *The Heart of Religion*. New York: Oxford University Press.

Lee, Young-hoon. 2004. "The Life and Ministry of David Yonggi Cho and the Yoido Full Gospel Church." *Asian Journal of Pentecostal Studies* 7(1): 3–20.

Levine, Daniel H. 2008. "Conclusion: Evangelicals and Democracy—the Experience of Latin America in Context." In *Evangelical Christians and Democracy in Latin America*, ed. Paul Freston, 207–23. New York: Oxford University Press.

Levitt, Peggy. 2007. *God Needs No Passport: Immigrants and the Changing Religious Landscape.* New York: The New Press.

Lewis, Paul H. 1980. *Paraguay under Stroessner*. Chapel Hill: University of North Carolina Press.

Lim, David S. 2009. "Consolidating Democracy: Filipino Evangelicals between People Power Events, 1986–2001." In *Evangelical Christianity and Democracy in Asia*, ed. David H. Lumsdaine, 235–84. New York: Oxford University Press.

Lipford, Jody, Robert E. McCormick and Robert D. Tollison. 1993. "Preaching Matters." *Journal of Economic Behavior and Organization* 21: 235–250

Lipset, Seymour Martin. 1994. "The Social Requisites of Democracy Revisited: 1993 Presidential Address." *American Sociological Review* 59:1–22.

_____. and Gabriel S. Lenz. 2000. "Corruption, Culture and Markets." In *Culture Matters: How Values Shape Human Progress*, ed. L. E. Harrison and S. P. Huntington, 112–24. New York: Basic Books.

Londregan, John Benedict and Keith T. Poole. 1996. "Does High Income Promote Democracy?" *World Politics* 49(1): 1–30.

López Rodríquez, Darío. 2008. "Evangelicals and Politics in Fujimori's Peru." In *Evangelical Christianity and Democracy in Latin America*, ed. Paul Freston, 131–61. New York: Oxford University Press.

Lovett, Leonard. 1973. "Perspective on the Black Origins of the Contemporary Pentecostal Movement." *Journal of the Interdenominational Theological Center* 1, no. 1 (Fall): 36–49.

_____. 1975. "Black Origins of the Pentecostal Movement." In *Aspects of Pentecostal-Charismatic Origins, ed.* Vinson Synan, 123–41. Plainfield, NJ: Logos International.

Luce, Alice E. 1950. *Pictures of Pentecost in the Old Testament*. Springfield, MO: Gospel Publishing House.

Luhrmann, T. M. 2012. *When God Talks Back: Understanding the American Evangelical Relationship with God*. New York: Alfred A. Knopf.

Lumsdaine, David H., ed. 2009. *Evangelical Christianity and Democracy in Asia*. New York: Oxford University Press.

Ma, Wonsuk. 2004. "Asian Pentecostalism: A Religion Whose Only Limit Is the Sky." *Journal of Beliefs and Values* 25(2): 191–204.

Macfarquhar, Larissa. 2003. "The Strongman." *The New Yorker*. 79(13): 50ff.

MacRobert, Iain. 1988. *The Black Roots and White Racism of Early Pentecostalism in the U.S.A.* London: Macmillan.

Manglos, Nicolette, and Alexander Weinreb. 2012. "Religion and Grassroots Interest in Politics in Sub-Saharan Africa." Unpublished manuscript.

Mariano, Ricardo. 1999. *NeoPentecostais: Sociologia do Novo Pentecostalismo no Brasil*. São Paulo: Edicoes Loyola.

Mariz, Cecília Loreto. 1994. *Coping with Poverty: Pentecostal Churches and Christian Base Communities in Brazil*. Philadelphia, PA: Temple University Press.

Marsh, Christopher, and Artyom Tonoyan. 2009. "The Civic, Economic, and Political Consequences of Pentecostalism in Russia and Ukraine." *Society* 46:510–16.

Marshall, Paul. 2000. *Religious Freedom in the World: A Global Report on Freedom and Persecution*. Nashville, TN: Broadman and Holman.

Marti, Gerardo. 2012. *Worship Across the Racial Divide: Religious Music and the Multiracial Congregation.* New York: Oxford University Press.

Martin, Bernice. 2001. "Pentecostal Gender Paradox: A Cautionary Tale for the Sociology of Religion." In *The Blackwell Companion to Sociology of Religion,* ed. Richard K. Fenn, 52–66. Malden: Blackwell.

Martin, David. 1990. *Tongues of Fire: The Explosion of Protestantism in Latin America.* Oxford, UK: Blackwell.

_____. 1994. "Evangelical and Charismatic Christianity in Latin America." In *Charismatic Christianity as a Global Culture,* ed. Karla Poewe. Charleston: University of South Carolina Press.

_____. 2002. *Pentecostalism: The World Their Parish.* Oxford, UK: Blackwell.

_____. 2011. *The Future of Christianity.* Surrey, England: Ashgate.

Martin, Larry. 1999. *The Life and Ministry of William J. Seymour and a History of the Azusa Street Revival.* The Complete Azusa Street Library CASL 1. Joplin, MO: Christian Life Books.

Maxwell, David. 2000. "'Catch the Cockerel before Dawn': Pentecostalism and Politics in Post-Colonial Zimbabwe." *Africa: Journal of the International African Institute* 70:249–77.

McGee, Gary B. 1991. "Pentecostal Strategies for Global Mission: A Historical Assessment," pp. 203–224 in Murray W. Dempster, Byron D. Klaus, Douglas Petersen, eds., *Called and Empowered: Global Mission in Pentecostal Perspective* (Peabody, MA: Hendrickson Publications.

_____. 2002. "The Story of Minnie F. Abrams: Another Context, Another Founder." In *Portraits of a Generation: Early Pentecostal Leaders,* ed. James R. Goff, Jr., and Grant A. Wacker, 100–4. Fayetteville: University of Arkansas Press.

McGee, Gary B. 1999. "'Latter Rain' Falling in the East: Early-Twentieth-Century Pentecostalism in India and the Debate over Speaking in Tongues." *Church History* 68(3): 648–65.

McLean, Sigrid. 1927. *Over Twenty Years in China.* Minneapolis, MN: Sigrid McLean.

McQueen, L. R. 2011. "Eschatological Variety in Early Wesleyan Pentecostal Periodicals." *Journal of the European Pentecostal Theological Association* 32(2): 5–12.

Meyer, Birgit. 2010. "Pentecostalism and Globalization." In *Studying Global Pentecostalism: Theories and Methods,* ed. Allan Anderson, et al., 113–130. Berkeley: University of California Press.

Midlarsky, Manus I. 1998. "Democracy and Islam: Implications for Civilizational Conflict and the Democratic Peace." *International Studies Journal* 42:485–511.

Miguez, Daniel. 1999. "Exploring the Argentinian Case: Religious Motives in the Growth of Latin American Pentecostalism." In *Latin American Religion in Motion,* ed. Christian Smith and Joshua Prokopy. New York: Routledge.

Miller, Donald E., and Tetsunao Yamamori. 2007. *Global Pentecostalism: The New Face of Christian Social Engagement.* Berkeley: University of California Press.

Moore, Barrington, Jr. 2000. *Moral Purity and Persecution in History.* Princeton, NJ: Princeton University Press.

Moorhead, Max Wood, ed. 1922. *Missionary Pioneering in Congo Forests: A Narrative of the Labours of William F. Burton and his Companions in the Native Villages of Luba-land.* Preston, UK: R. Seed & Sons.

Moreno, Pedro. 1999. "Evangelical Churches." In *Religious Freedom and Evangelization in Latin America,* ed. Paul Sigmund, 49–69. Maryknoll, NY: Orbis.

Murray, I. H. 1971. *The Puritan Hope.* Edinburgh: Banner of Truth.

Nadar, Sarojini. 2009. "'The Bible Says!' Feminism, Hermeneutics, and Neo-Pentecostal Challenges." *Journal for Theology of Southern Africa* 134:131–146.

Nelson, Douglas J. 1981. "For Such a Time as This: The Story of Bishop William J. Seymour and the Azusa Street Revival, A Search for Pentecostal/Charismatic Roots." Ph.D. diss., Birmingham, England: Faculty of Arts, Department of Theology, University of Birmingham.

Nelson, Douglas J. 1988. "The Black Face of Church Renewal: The Meaning of a Charismatic Explosion, 1901–1985," in Paul Elbert, ed. *Faces of Renewal: Studies in Honor of Stanley M. Horton* (Peabody, MA: Hendrickson, 1988), 172–191.

Nieuwbeerta, Paul, Gerrit B. De Geest, and Jacques J. Siegers. 2003. "Street-Level Corruption in Industrialized and Developing Countries." *European Societies* 5(2): 139–165.

Numbere, Nonyem E. *A Man and a Vision: A Biography of Apostle Geoffrey D. Numbere.* 2008. Diobu, Nigeria: Greater Evangelism Publications.

Nussbaum, Martha. 2000. *Women and Human Development: The Capabilities Approach.* Cambridge: Cambridge University Press.

Oddie, Geoffry A. 1978. *Social Protest in India: British Protestant Missionaries and Social Reforms, 1850–1900.* Columbia, MO: South Asia Books.

Ojo, Matthews A. 1996. "Charismatic Movements in Africa." In *Christianity in Africa in the 1990s*, ed. C. Fyfe and A. Walls, 92–110. Edinburgh: University of Edinburgh Centre of African Studies.

_____. 2006. *The End-Time Army: Charismatic Movements in Modern Nigeria.* Trenton, NJ: Africa World Press.

Ortiz, Olga Odgers, and Juan Carlos Ruiz Guadalajara. 2009. *Migración y Creencias Pensar en las Religiones en Tiempo de Movilidad.* Tijuana: El Colegio de la Frontera Norte and San Luis Potosí: El Colegio de San Luis.

Osterberg, Arthur. 1966. "I Was There," *Full Gospel Business Men's Fellowship International: Voice* (May 1966), 18.

Österlund, Markus. 2001. *Politics in the Midst of Terror.* Helsinki: Finnish Society of Sciences and Letters.

Owens, Robert R. 1998. *Speak to the Rock: The Azusa Street Revival: Its Roots and Its Message.* Lanham, MD: University Press of America.

Paldam, Martin. 2001. "Corruption and Religion: Adding to the Economic Model." *Kyklos* 54(2/3): 383–414.

Pearce, Lisa D. and Dana L. Haynie. 2004. "Intergenerational Religious Dynamics and Adolescent Delinquency." Social Forces 82(4): 1553–1572.

Pedrone-Colombani, Sylvie. 1998. *Le Pentecotisme au Guatemala: Conversion et Identite.* Paris: CNRS Editions.

Pew Forum on Religion and Public Life. 2006. *Spirit and Power: A 10-Country Survey of Pentecostals.* Washington, DC: Pew Research Center. (http://pewforum.org/surveys/pentecostal/).

_____. 2011. *Global Christianity: A Report on the Size and Distribution of the World's Christian Population.* Washington, DC: Pew Research Center.

_____. 2011. *Global Survey of Evangelical Protestant Leaders.* Washington, DC: Pew Research Center. (http://www.pewforum.org/christian/evangelical-protestant-churches/global-survey-of-evangelical-protestant-leaders.aspx).

Pew Hispanic Center. 2007. *Changing Faiths: Latinos and the Transformation of American Religion.* Washington, DC: Pew Research Center.

Pfeiffer, James. 2004. "Civil Society, NGOs, and the Holy Spirit in Mozambique." *Human Organizations* 63(3): 359–72.

Philpott, Daniel. 2004. "Christianity and Democracy: The Catholic Wave." *Journal of Democracy* 15:32–46.

Plett, Rodolfo. 1988. *El protestantismo en el Paraguay.* Asunción, Paraguay: FLET/IBA.

_____. 2000. *Crecimiento evangélico en el Paraguay: Estadística, evaluación, proyección hacía el futuro.* Asunción, Paraguay: FLET.

Polity IV Project. 2012. *Polity IV.* http://www.systemicpeace.org/polity/polity4.htm.

Potter, Joseph E., Ernesto F. L. Amaral, and Robert D. Woodberry. 2011. "The Growth of Protestantism in Brazil and Its Impact on Male Earnings, 1970–2000." Unpublished paper.

Poloma, Margaret M. 2000. "The Spirit Bade Me Go: Pentecostalism and Global Religion." Hartford Institute for Religious Research. Accessed February 21, 2012, http://hirr.hartsem.edu/research/pentecostalism_polomaart1.html.

_____. 2003. *Main Street Mystics: The Toronto Blessing and Reviving Pentecostalism.* Walnut Creek, CA: Alta Mira Press.

_____. and John C. Green. 2010. *The Assemblies of God: Godly Love and the Revitalization of American Pentecostalism.* New York: New York University Press.

_____. and Ralph W. Hood, Jr. 2008. *Blood and Fire: Godly Love in a Pentecostal Emerging Church.* New York: New York University Press.

_____. and Matthew T. Lee. 2013. "The New Apostolic Reformation: Main Street Mystics and Everyday Prophets." In *Prophecy in the New Millennium: When Prophecies Persist,* ed. Sarah Harvey and Suzanne Newcombe. Surrey, UK: Ashgate.

_____. and Matthew T. Lee. 2011. "The Flow from Prayer Activities to Receptive Prayer: Godly Love and the Knowledge that Surpasses Understanding." *Journal of Psychology and Theology* 39:143–54.

_____. and Brian F. Pendleton. 1989. "Religious Experiences and Institutional Growth Within the Assemblies of God." *Journal for the Scientific Study of Religion* 24:415–31.

Programa de Naciones Unidos para el Desarrollo (PNUD; English: United Nations Development Program). 2008. *Informe Nacional sobre Desarrollo Humano: Equidad para Desarrollo, Paraguay 2008.* Asunción, Paraguay: PNUD.

Putnam, Robert D. 1993. *Making Democracy Work: Civic Traditions in Modern Italy.* Princeton, NJ: Princeton University Press.

_____. 2000. *Bowling Alone.* New York: Touchstone.

Rambo, Lewis R. *Understanding Religious Conversion.* 1993. New Haven, CT: Yale University Press.

Red Evangélica de Comunicación (REDECOM). 2010. *686 mil evangélicos en Paraguay* [online]. Retrieved December 15, 2011 from http://www.redecom.org/index.php?option=com_content&view=article&id=57:686mil-evangelicos-en-paraguay&catid=1:latest-news (press release, June 26, 2010).

Redeemed Christian Church of God, The. 2001. *The Redeemed Christian Church of God North America, Inc.: General Information and Church Planting Manual* (Fall 2001 Edition). Greeneville, TX: RCCG North America.

Redeemed Christian Church of God, The. 2002. *Christian Character,* a publication of RCCGNA (June 2002). Greeneville, TX: RCCG North America.

Redeemed Christian Church of God, The. 2002/2003. *Sunday School Manual I.* Greeneville, TX: RCCG North America.

Redeemed Christian Church of God, The. 2003. *The Structure, Administration and Finance of the Redeemed Christian Church in North America.* Greeneville, TX: RCCG North America.

Regnerus, Mark D. 2003. "Moral Communities and Adolescent Delinquency: Religious Contexts and Community Social Control." *Sociological Quarterly* 44:523–54.

_____. and Glen H. Elder, Jr. 2003. "Religion and Vulnerability among Low-Risk Adolescents." *Social Science Research* 32:633–58.

_____. Christian S. Smith, and David Sikkink. 1998. "Who Gives to the Poor? The Influence of Religious Tradition and Political Location on the Personal Generosity of Americans toward the Poor." *Journal for the Scientific Study of Religion* 37(3): 481–93.

Robbins, Joel. 2004. "The Globalization of Pentecostal and Charismatic Christianity." *Annual Review of Anthropology* 33:117–43.

_____. 2009. "Pentecostal Networks and the Spirit of Globalization: On the Social Productivity of Ritual Forms." *Social Analysis* 53, no. 1 (Spring): 55–66.

_____. 2010. "Anthropology of Religion." In *Studying Global Pentecostalism: Theories and Methods,* ed. Allan Anderson et al., 156–178. Berkeley: University of California Press.

Robeck Jr., Cecil M. 1991. "William J. Seymour and the 'Bible Evidence'." In *Initial Evidence: Historical and Biblical Perspectives on the Pentecostal Doctrine of Spirit Baptism,* ed. Gary B. McGee, 72–95. Peabody, MA: Hendrickson Publishers.

_____. 2002. "The Gift of Prophecy." In *The New International Dictionary of Pentecostal Charismatic Movements,* ed. Stanley M. Burgess and Eduard M. Van Der Maas, 999–1012, Grand Rapids, MI: Zondervan.

_____. 2006. *The Azusa Street Mission and Revival: The Birth of the Global Pentecostal Movement.* Nashville, TN: Nelson Reference and Electronic.

_____. 2011. "The Azusa Street Mission and the Historic Black Churches: Two Worlds in Conflict in Los Angeles' African American Community." In *Afro-Pentecostalism: Black Pentecostal and Charismatic Christianity in History and Culture,* ed. Amos Yong and Estrelda Alexander, 21–42. New York: New York University Press.

Robert, Dana L. 2000. "Shifting Southward: Global Christianity Since 1945." *International Bulletin of Missionary Research* 24:50–58.

Roberts, Bryan R. 1968. "Protestant Groups and Coping with Urban Life in Guatemala." *American Journal of Sociology* 73(6): 753–67.

Robinson, Tracy. 2006. "Taxonomies of Conjugality," Global Law Working Paper, New York University School of Law, November, 2006.

Ross, I. R. 1974. "Donald Gee: In Search of a Church: Sectarian in Transition." PhD diss., Toronto University.

Russell, B. 1956. *Portraits from Memory and other Essays.* London: George Allen & Unwin.

Ruthven, J. M. 1993. *On the Cessation of the Charismata: The Protestant Polemic on Postbiblical Miracles.* Sheffield: Sheffield Academic Press.

Salamon, Lester M., and Helmut K. Anheier. 1996. "Social Origins of Civil Society: Explaining the Nonprofit Sector Cross-Nationally." Working Papers of the Johns Hopkins Comparative Nonprofit Sector Project, no. 22, ed. Lester M. Salamon and Helmut K. Anheier. Baltimore: The Johns Hopkins Institute for Policy Studies.

_____. 1997. "The Third World's Third Sector in Comparative Perspective." Working Papers of the Johns Hopkins Comparative Nonprofit Sector Project, no. 24, ed. Lester M. Salamon and Helmut K. Anheier. Baltimore: The Johns Hopkins Institute for Policy Studies.

Sanders, Rufus G. W. 2001. *William Joseph Seymour: Black Father of the 20th Century Pentecostal/Charismatic Movement.* Sandusky, OH: Alexandria Publications.

Sandholtz, Wayne, and William Koetzle. 2000. "Accounting for Corruption: Economic Structure, Democracy and Trade." *International Studies Quarterly* 44:31–50.

Schüssler Fiorenza, Elisabeth. 1995. *In Memory of Her: A Feminist Theological Reconstruction of Christian Origins.* London, UK: SCM Press.

Serbin, Kenneth P. 1999. "The Catholic Church, Religious Pluralism, and Democracy in Brazil." Kellogg Institute Working Paper #263.

Sexton, James D. 1978. "Protestantism and Modernization in Two Guatemalan Towns." *American Ethnologist* 5:280–301.

Sen, Amartya. *Development as Freedom.* 1999. New York: Knopf.

Seymour, W. J. 1915. *The Doctrines and Discipline of the Azusa Street Apostolic Faith Mission of Los Angeles, Cal. 1915 with Scripture Readings.* Los Angeles, CA: privately published.

Shepherd, Gerald T. 2002. "Prophecy from Ancient Israel to Pentecostals at the End of the Modern Age." *The Spirit and the Church* 3:47–70.

Sherman, Amy L. 1997. *The Soul of Development: Biblical Christianity and Economic Transformation in Guatemala.* New York: Oxford University Press.

Shew, Paul Tsuchido. 2003. "History of Early Pentecostal Movement in Japan: The Roots and Development of the Pre-War Pentecostal (1907–1945)." PhD dissertation. Pasadena, CA: Fuller Theological Seminary, School of Theology.

Sikkink, David, and Christian Smith. 1998. "Religion and Ethical Decision-Making and Conduct on the Job: Reconsidering the Influence of Religion in the Economic and Business Sphere." Paper presented at the annual meeting of the Society for the Scientific Study of Religion, Montreal, Quebec, Canada. October 8–10.

Sithole, Surprise, with David Wimbish. 2012. *Voice in the Night: The True Story of a Man and the Miracles that Are Changing Africa.* Bloomington, MN: Chosen.

Sloos, William. 2010. "The Story of James and Ellen Hebden: The First Family of Pentecost in Canada." *Pneuma* 32(2): 181–202.

Smidt, Corwin, ed. 2003. *Religion as Social Capital: Producing the Common Good.* Waco, TX: Baylor University Press.

_____. John C. Green, Lyman A. Kellstedt, and James L. Guth. 1998. "The Spirit-Filled Movements and American Politics." In *Religion and the Culture Wars: Dispatches from the Front*, ed. J. C. Green, J. L. Guth, C. E. Smidt, and L. A. Kellstedt, 219–39. Lanham, MD: Rowman & Littlefield.

Smilde, David. 2007. *Reason to Believe: Cultural Agency in Latin American Evangelicalism.* Berkeley: University of California Press.

Smith, Christian. 1991. *The Emergence of Liberation Theology: Radical Religion and Social Movement Theory.* Chicago: University of Chicago Press.

_____. 2007. "Why Christianity Works: An Emotions-Focused Phenomenological Account." *Sociology of Religion* 68(2): 165–78.

Smith, Christian S. and Robert D. Woodberry. 2001. "Sociology of Religion." In *The Blackwell Companion to Sociology*, ed. Judith Blau, 100–113. Cambridge: Blackwell.

Somaratna, G. P. V. 1996. *Origins of the Pentecostal Mission in Sri Lanka.* Marihana-Nugegoda: Margaya Fellowship of Sri Lanka.

Stafford, Tim. 2004. "India Undaunted: Escalating Repression Can't Seem to Dampen the Church's Growth." *Christianity Today* 48(5): 28–35.

Stalsett, Sturla J. 2006. "Offering On-Time Deliverance: The Pathos of Neo-Pentecostalism and the Spirits of Globalization." In *The Spirits of Globalism*, ed. Sturla Stalsett, 198–212. London: SCM Press.

_____. ed. 2006. *The Spirits of Globalization.* London: SCM Press.

Stanley, Brian. 2004. "Twentieth Century World Christianity: A Perspective from the History of Missions." In *Christianity Reborn: The Global Expansion of Evangelicalism in the Twentieth Century*, ed. Donald M. Lewis, 52–86. Grand Rapids, MI: Eerdmans.

Stark, Rodney. 2001. "Gods, Rituals, and the Moral Order." *Journal for the Scientific Study of Religion* 40(4): 619–36.

_____. and William Bainbridge. 1987. *A Theory of Religion.* New York: Peter Lang.

_____. and Roger Finke. 2000. *Acts of Faith: Explaining the Human Side of Religion.* Berkeley: University of California Press.

_____. and Buster G. Smith. 2012. "Pluralism and the Churching of Latin America." *Latin American Politics and Society* 54:35–50. doi: 10.1111/j.1548-2456.2012.00152.x. Accessed June 6, 2012.

Steigenga, Timothy J. 2001. *The Politics of the Spirit: The Political Implications of Pentecostal Religion in Costa Rica and Guatemala.* Lanham, MD: Lexington Books.

Stepan, Alfred. 2000. "Religion, Democracy and the 'Twin Tolerations'." *Journal of Democracy* 11:37–57.

Stulz, Rene M., and Rohan Williamson. 2003. "Culture, Openness, and Finance." *Journal of Financial Economics* 70(3): 313–49.

Tambiah, Stanley J. 1993. "Buddhism, Politics, and Violence in Sri Lanka." In *Fundamentalisms and the State*, ed. Martin E. Marty and R. Scott Appleby, 589–619. Chicago: University of Chicago Press.

Tasie, G. O. M. 1978. "The Church in the Niger Delta." In *The Nigerian Story*, ed. Ogbu Kalu, 323–332. Ibadan: Daystar Press.

Tax, Sol, and Robert Hinshaw. 1970. "Panajachel a Generation Later." In *The Social Anthropology of Latin America*, eds. W. Goldschmidt and H. Hoijer, 175–195. Los Angeles: Latin American Center of the University of California.

Taylor, Charles. 2007. *A Secular Age.* Cambridge, MA: The Belknap Press of Harvard University Press.

Tejirian, Eleanor H., and Reeva Spector Simon, eds. 2002. *Altruism and Imperialism: Western Cultural and Religious Mission in the Middle East.* New York: Middle East Institute, Columbia University.

Thompson, Leonard M. 1995. *A History of South Africa.* 2nd ed. New Haven, CT: Yale University Press.

Thompson, N. C. 2009. *Journey into Destiny.* Jos: TONAJO Publishing House.

Thrasher, Lillian. 1983. *Letters from Lillian.* Springfield, MO: Assemblies of God, Division of Foreign Missions.

Tocqueville, Alexis de. 1988. *Democracy in America.* New York: HarperCollins.

Treisman, Daniel. 2000. "The Causes of Corruption: A Cross-National Study." *Journal of Public Economics* 76:399–457.

Trejo, Guillermo. 2009. "Religious Competition and Ethnic Mobilization in Latin America: Why the Catholic Church Promotes Indigenous Movements in Mexico." *American Political Science Review* 103(3): 323–42.

———. 2012. *Popular Movements in Autocracies; Religion, Repression and Indigenous Collective Action in Mexico.* New York: Cambridge University Press.

Tyra, Gary. 2011. *The Holy Spirit in Mission.* Downers Grove, IL: IVP Academic.

UNAIDS. 2010. *Global Report: UNAIDS Report on the Global AIDS Epidemic.* New York: UNAIDS.

Urshan, Andrew D. 1910. "Pentecost among the Persians in Chicago," *The Bridegroom's Messenger* 3:69.

Urshan, Andrew D. 1918. *The Story of My Life.* St. Louis, MO: Gospel Publishing House.

Urshan, Andrew D. [1967] 1982. *The Life Story of Andrew Bar David Urshan: An Autobiography of the Author's First Forty Years.* Portland, OR: Apostolic Book Publishers.

Van der Laan, Cornelis. 2006. "What Good Can Come from Los Angeles: Changing Perceptions of the North American Pentecostal Origins in Early Western European Pentecostal Periodicals." In *The Azusa Street Revival and Its Legacy,* ed. Harold D. Hunter and Cecil M. Robeck, Jr., 141–160. Cleveland, TN: Pathway Press.

Van der Veer, Peter. 2001. *Imperial Encounters.* Princeton, NJ: Princeton University Press.

Van Dijk, R. 2000. *Christian Fundamentalism in Sub-Saharan Africa: The Case of Pentecostalism.* Occasional Paper. Copenhagen: Centre of African Studies, University of Copenhagen.

Vásquez, Manuel, and Marie Friedmann Marquardt. 2003. *Globalizing the Sacred: Religion across the Americas.* Piscataway, NJ: Rutgers University Press.

Verba, Sidney, Kay Lehman Schlozman, and Henry E. Brady. 1995. *Voice and Equality: Civic Voluntarism in American Politics.* Cambridge, MA: Harvard University Press.

Vingren, Ivar. 1994. *Det började I Pará: Svensk Pingstmission I Brasilien.* Ed. Gunilla Nyberg, Jan-Åke Alvarsson, and Jan-Endy Johannesson. Ekerö, Sweden: MissionsInstitutet-PMU.

Wadkins, Timothy. 2006. "Pentecostal Power: Conversions in El Salvador." *Christian Century* (November 14): 26–29.

———. 2008. "Getting Saved in El Salvador: The Preferential Option of the Poor." *International Review of Mission* 9(384/385): 31–49.

Wagner, Peter, and Joseph Thompson. 2003. *Out of Africa.* Ventura, CA: Regal Books.

Wakefield, Gavin. 2006. *Alexander Boddy: Pentecostal Anglican Pioneer.* Carlisle, England: Paternoster Press.

Walls, Andrew F. 2000. "Of Ivory Towers and Ashrams: Some Reflections on Theological Scholarship in Africa." *Journal of African Christian Thought* 3, no. 1 (June): 1–5.

Ware, Vicki-Ann, Anthony Ware, Matthew Clarke and Grant Buchanan. 2013. "Understanding Pentecostal Motivations for Undertaking Community Development in South East Asia: Evidence of an Expanded Understanding of Holistic Mission," in *Handbook of Research on Religion and Development,* ed. Matthew Clarke. Cheltenham, UK: Edward Elgar Publishing

Watt, Peter. 1992. *From Africa's Soil: The Story of the Assemblies of God in Southern Africa.* Cape Town, SA: Struik Christian Books.

Weber, Max. [1906] 1992. *The Protestant Ethic and the Spirit of Capitalism.* New York: Routledge.

White, David Gordon. 2009. *Sinister Yogis.* Chicago: University of Chicago Press.

Wiarda, Howard J. 2001. *The Soul of Latin America: The Cultural and Political Tradition*. New Haven, CT: Yale University Press.

Wilkerson, David. 1964. *The Cross and the Switchblade*. New York: Pyramid Books.

Wilkinson, Steven. 2004. *Votes and Violence: Electoral Competition and Ethnic Riots in India*. New York: Cambridge University Press.

Willems, Emilio. 1967. *Followers of the New Faith: Culture Change and the Rise of Protestantism in Brazil and Chile*. Nashville, TN: Vanderbilt University Press.

Wilson, Everett A. 1983. "Sanguine Saints: Pentecostalism in El Salvador." *Church History* 52 (June): 186–98.

Woodberry, Robert D. 1999. "Religion and Democratization: Explaining a Robust Empirical Relationship." Paper presented at the Annual Meeting of the Religious Research Association, Boston, MA.

_____. 2004. "The Shadow of Empire: Christian Missions, Colonial Policy and Democracy in Postcolonial Societies." PhD dissertation, Department of Sociology, University of North Carolina–Chapel Hill.

_____. 2006. "The Economic Consequences of Pentecostalism." *Society* 44:29–35.

_____. 2008. "Pentecostalism and Economic Development." In *Markets, Morals, and Religion*, ed. J. B. Imber, 157–77. New Brunswick, NJ: Transaction Publishers.

_____. (2012). "The Missionary Roots of Liberal Democracy." *American Political Science Review*. 106(2): 244–274.

_____. and Timothy Samuel Shah. 2004. "Christianity and Democracy: The Pioneering Protestants." *Journal of Democracy* 15:47–61.

_____., Jerry Park, and Lyman A. Kellstedt with Mark Regnerus and Brian Steensland. 2012. "The Measure of American Religious Traditions: Theoretical and Measurement Considerations." *Social Forces* 91(1): 65–73.

World Bank. 1997. *World Development Report*. New York: Oxford University Press.

Yieh, John. 2010. "The Bible in China: Interpretations and Consequences," in *Handbook of Christianity in China, Volume 2: 1800 to Present*, ed. R. Gary Tiedemann, 891–913. Leiden: Brill

You, Jong-Sung, and Sanjeev Khagram. 2005. "A Comparative Study of Inequality and Corruption." *American Sociological Review* 70(1): 136–57.

Young, Michael P. 2002. "Confessional Protest: The Religious Birth of U.S. National Social Movements." *American Sociological Review* 67(5): 660–88.

Yuasa, Key. 2001. "Louis Francescon: A Theological Biography 1866–1964." Th.D. diss., Genève, Switzerland: Faculté Autonome de Théologie Protestante de L'Université de Genève.

Zhai, Jiexia Elisa. 2006. "Religion and Gender Equality in Contemporary Taiwan." Dissertation proposal, Sociology, University of Texas at Austin.

_____. and Robert D. Woodberry. 2011. "Religion and Educational Ideals in Contemporary Taiwan." *Journal for the Scientific Study of Religion* 50(2): 307–27.

INDEX